LIBRARY OF NEW TESTAMENT STUDIES

667

Formerly the Journal for the Study of the New Testament Supplement series

Editor
Chris Keith

Editorial Board
Dale C. Allison, Lynn H. Cohick, R. Alan Culpepper,
Craig A. Evans, Jennifer Ey., Robert Fowler, Simon J. Gathercole,
Juan Hernández Jr., John S. Kloppenborg, Michael Labahn,
Matthew V. Novenson, Love L. Sechrest, Robert Wall,
Catrin H. Williams, Brittany E. Wilson

The Moral Life According to Mark

M. John-Patrick O'Connor

LONDON • NEW YORK • OXFORD • NEW DELHI • SYDNEY

T&T CLARK
Bloomsbury Publishing Plc
50 Bedford Square, London, WC1B 3DP, UK
1385 Broadway, New York, NY 10018, USA
29 Earlsfort Terrace, Dublin 2, Ireland

BLOOMSBURY, T&T CLARK and the T&T Clark logo are trademarks of
Bloomsbury Publishing Plc

First published in Great Britain 2022
Paperback edition published 2023

Copyright © M. John-Patrick O'Connor, 2022

M. John-Patrick O'Connor has asserted his right under the Copyright, Designs and Patents
Act, 1988, to be identified as Author of this work.

For legal purposes the Acknowledgments on p. ix constitute an extension
of this copyright page.

All rights reserved. No part of this publication may be reproduced or transmitted
in any form or by any means, electronic or mechanical, including photocopying,
recording, or any information storage or retrieval system, without prior permission in
writing from the publishers.

Bloomsbury Publishing Plc does not have any control over, or responsibility for,
any third-party websites referred to or in this book. All internet addresses given in this
book were correct at the time of going to press. The author and publisher regret any
inconvenience caused if addresses have changed or sites have ceased to exist,
but can accept no responsibility for any such changes.

A catalogue record for this book is available from the British Library.

Library of Congress Cataloging-in-Publication Data
Names: O'Connor, M. John-Patrick, author.
Title: The moral life according to Mark / M. John-Patrick O'Connor.
Description: London ; New York : T&T Clark, 2022. |
Series: The library of New Testament studies, 2513-8790 ; 667 |
Includes bibliographical references and index. |
Summary: "This volume argues that the Gospel of
Mark, as the first biography of Jesus, was instructive for the moral
life of early Christians"– Provided by publisher.
Identifiers: LCCN 2021052323 (print) | LCCN 2021052324 (ebook) |
ISBN 9780567705587 (hb) | ISBN 9780567705594 (epdf) | ISBN 9780567705617 (epub)
Subjects: LCSH: Ethics in the Bible. | Bible. Mark–Theology.
Classification: LCC BS2585.6.E8 O26 2022 (print) | LCC BS2585.6.E8 (ebook) |
DDC 226.3/06–dc23/eng/20211117
LC record available at https://lccn.loc.gov/2021052323
LC ebook record available at https://lccn.loc.gov/2021052324

ISBN: HB: 978-0-5677-0558-7
PB: 978-0-5677-0562-4
ePDF: 978-0-5677-0559-4
ePUB: 978-0-5677-0561-7

Series: Library of New Testament Studies, volume 667
ISSN 2513-8790

Typeset by Newgen KnowledgeWorks Pvt. Ltd., Chennai, India

To find out more about our authors and books visit www.bloomsbury.com
and sign up for our newsletters.

For Kristen, Copeland, and Mila

Contents

Acknowledgments		ix
List of Abbreviations		xi
1	**A Neglected Factor in Markan Studies**	**1**
	1.1 Introduction	1
	1.2 Christological Overshadowing in the Twentieth Century	3
	1.3 Conclusion	12
2	**The Moral Environment of Ancient Biographies**	**15**
	2.1 Introduction	15
	2.2 Mark and Biographies	17
	2.3 Biography and Morality	19
	2.4 A Survey of Select Primary Sources	22
	2.5 Conclusion: What Does All This Mean for Mark?	38
3	**Moral Accountability according to Mark**	**41**
	3.1 Introduction	41
	3.2 Moral Reasoning in Mark	42
	3.3 A World in Conflict: Moral Accountability in Mark's Prologue	45
	3.4 Moral Accountability in God's Family	58
	3.5 Moral Accountability to God's Authority	64
	3.6 Conclusion	69
4	**The Accountable Self according to Mark**	**71**
	4.1 Introduction	71
	4.2 Virtues in Mark	73
	4.3 Virtuous Practices	91
	4.4 Conclusion	107
5	**Evil in the Gospel of Mark**	**111**
	5.1 Introduction	111
	5.2 The Personification of Evil in Mark	113
	5.3 Human Responsibility in Mark: An Account of Vice	121

5.4	Punitive Consequences in Mark	135
5.5	Conclusion: Evil's Role in the Moral Landscape of Mark	139

Conclusion	141
Bibliography	145
Index of Ancient Sources	173
Index of Modern Authors	195

Acknowledgments

This book began after several casual conversations with C. Clifton Black. During his doctoral seminar on Mark in the fall of 2015, which he hosted at his dining room table, our cohort would discuss all things Mark, eventually reading Dan O. Via's *The Ethics of Mark's Gospel* (1985) together. As his student, I owe a great deal to his constant encouragement, diligent reading of previous drafts, and faithful commitment to my ideas. I am also indebted to the other members of my dissertation committee, Dale Allison and George Parsenios, for contributing a wealth of invaluable insights. I must also thank other faculty mentors at Princeton Seminary who offered encouragement and inspiration to me during my graduate studies, Jacqueline Lapsley, Dennis Olson, Lisa Bowens, Beverly Gaventa, and James Charlesworth. Further gratitude belongs to Ron Herms, Kari Brodin, Brad Embry, and Blaine Charrette who sparked an interest in me for research during my undergraduate years. I also owe appreciation to Joel Estes and Eric Barreto for their comments on an earlier draft of Chapter 3 during our New Testament Research Colloquium. To my colleagues in the New Testament department, Jolyon Pruszinski, Jim Neumann, Nate Johnson, Heelee Velez, and Devlin McGuire, for their good humor and company. To my friends, Brady Beard, Tyler Davis, and G. B. McClanahan, who listened to many ideas, however dull.

I would like to thank our world-class library staff, Kate Skrebutenas, Susan Britt, and Jeremy Wallace, for meeting each of my resource needs along the way. A special thanks is owed to the Louisville Institute and Edwin Aponte. The Louisville postdoctoral fellowship allowed for extra time and resources to complete this project in a timely manner. To *Catholic Biblical Quarterly* for granting permission to reprint a section of Chapter 3 published as "Moral Accountability according to Mark" (*CBQ* 83 [2021]: 599–618). The editorial team at Bloomsbury/T&T Clark deserves heartfelt appreciation: thank you to Chris Keith and Sarah Blake for their oversight, interest, and attention to detail. Thank you also to Jonathan Nash, Shyam, and all others involved in the editing process. I am indebted to the diligent work of a highly skilled team for this final result.

I wish to thank my parents to whom many of my first questions were directed. But most of all, I owe an unpayable debt of gratitude to Krista for her constant love and support. As graduate students, we made a life together in Princeton. Without your wit and adventure, I am lost. And to our children, Copeland and Mila, may you exorcise every form of evil from this world. This book is dedicated to them with gratitude.

Abbreviations

AARCC	American Academy of Religion Cultural Criticism Series
AB	Anchor Bible
ABD	*Anchor Bible Dictionary*. Edited by David N. Freedman. 6 vols. New York: Doubleday, 1992.
AGAJU	Arbeiten zur Geschichte des antiken Judentums und des Urchristentums
AJT	*American Journal of Theology*
ANRW	*Aufstieg und Niedergang der römischen Welt: Geschichte und Kultur Roms im Spiegel der neueren Forschung*. Edited by H. Temporini and W. Hasse. New York: de Gruyter, 1972–.
ANTC	Abingdon New Testament Commentaries
ATR	*Anglican Theological Review*
AYBRL	Anchor Yale Bible Reference Library
BDAG	Bauer, Walter, Frederick W. Danker, William F. Arndt, and F. Wilbur Gingrich. *Greek-English Lexicon of the New Testament and Other Early Christian Literature*. 3rd rev. ed. Chicago: University of Chicago Press, 1999.
BETL	Bibliotheca Ephemeridum Theologicarum Lovaniensium
BIS	Biblical Interpretation Series
BJS	Brown Judaic Studies
BLS	Bible and Literature Series
BMW	Bible in the Modern World
BNTC	Black's New Testament Commentaries
BO	Biblica et orientalia
BR	*Biblical Research*
BS	Biblical Seminar
BTB	*Biblical Theology Bulletin*
BWANT	Beiträge zur Wissenschaft vom Alten und Neuen Testament
BzA	Beiträge zur Altertumskunde
BZNW	Beihefte zur Zeitschrift für die neutestamentliche Wissenschaft
CBNTS	Coniectanea Biblica New Testament Series
CBQ	*Catholic Biblical Quarterly*
CBQMS	Catholic Biblical Quarterly Monograph Series
CBR	*Currents in Biblical Research*
CCSA	Corpus Christianorum Series Apocryphorum
CCSL	Corpus Christianorum Series Latina
CEASG	Collection d'études anciennes. Série grecque
CEB	Common English Bible

CEJL	Commentaries on Early Jewish Literature
CFTL	Clark's Foreign Theological Library
CGTC	Cambridge Greek Testament Commentary
CJA	Christianity and Judaism in Antiquity
CL	Collection Latomus
CSAP	Continuum Studies in Ancient Philosophy
DELG	Dictionnaire étymologique de la langue grecque
DJBA	*Dictionary of Jewish Babylonian Aramaic of the Talmudic and Geonic Periods*. Edited by Michael Sokoloff. Baltimore, MD: John Hopkins University Press, 2002.
DJD	Discoveries in the Judaean Desert
EBR	*Encyclopedia of the Bible and Its Reception*. Edited by Hans-Josef Klauck et al. Berlin: de Gruyter, 2009–.
EJL	Early Judaism and Its Literature
EKK	Evangelisch-Katholischer Kommentar
ES	Emerging Scholars
ET	English translation
FC	Fathers of the Church
FRLANT	Forschungen zur Religion und Literatur des Alten und Neuen Testaments
FTS	Frankfurter Theologische Studien
ExpTim	*Expository Times*
GCRM	Greek Culture in the Roman World
GCS	Die Griechischen Christlichen Schriftsteller
GR	*Greece and Rome*
HA	*History of Animals*
HAM	Histoire ancienne et médiévale
HBM	Hebrew Bible Monographs
HCS	Hellenistic Culture and Society
HibJ	*Hibbert Journal*
HTR	*Harvard Theological Review*
HU	Hallische universitätsreden
ICC	International Critical Commentary
JAAR	*Journal of the American Academy of Religion*
JAJSup	Journal of Ancient Judaism Supplements
JBL	*Journal of Biblical Literature*
JCPS	Jewish and Christian Perspectives Series
JQR	*Jewish Quarterly Review*
JR	*Journal of Religion*
JSHJ	*Journal for the Study of the Historical Jesus*
JSJ	*Journal for the Study of Judaism*
JSNT	*Journal for the Study of the New Testament*
JSNTSup	Journal for the Study of the New Testament Supplement Series
JSOT	*Journal for the Study of the Old Testament*
JSPSup	Journal for the Study of the Pseudepigrapha Supplement Series

JTS	*Journal of Theological Studies*
LAB	Liber Antiquitatum Biblicarum
LBT	Library of Biblical Theology
LCL	Loeb Classical Library
LNTS	Library of New Testament Studies
LQ	*Lutheran Quarterly*
LSCP	London Studies in Classical Philology
LSJ	Liddell, Henry George, Robert Scott, and Henry Stuart Jones. *A Greek-English Lexicon*. 9th ed. with revised supplements. Oxford: Clarendon, 1996.
LSTS	Library of Second Temple Studies
LXX	Septuagint
MS	Mnemosyne Supplements
MT	Masoretic Text
NA	Neutestamentliche Abhandlungen
NA^{28}	Nestle-Aland Novum Testamentum Graece 28
NASB	New American Standard Bible
NCBC	New Century Bible Commentary
Neot	*Neotestamentica*
NIGNTC	New International Greek New Testament Commentary
NIV	New International Version
NKJV	New King James Version
NovT	*Novum Testamentum*
NovTSup	Supplements to Novum Testamentum
NPNF	Nicene and Post-Nicene Fathers
NRSV	New Revised Standard Version
NTL	New Testament Library
NTS	*New Testament Studies*
NTTS	New Testament Tools and Studies
OPIAC	Occasional Paper Institute for Antiquity and Christianity
OTP	*Old Testament Pseudepigrapha*. Edited by James H. Charlesworth. 2 vols. Garden City, NY: Doubleday, 1983–5.
PC	Proclamation Commentaries
PG	Patrologia graeca [=Patrologiae cursus completus: Series graeca]. Edited by J.-P. Migne. 162 vols. Paris, 1857–86.
PGM	*Papyri Graecae Magicae: Die griechischen Zauberpapyri*. Edited by Karl Preisendanz. 2nd ed. Stuttgart: Hiersemann, 1950–.
PMLT	The Père Marquette Lecture in Theology
PMS	Patristic Monograph Series
PTSDSSP	Princeton Theological Seminary Dead Sea Scrolls Project
PVTG	Pseudepigrapha Veteris Testamenti Graece
QD	Quaestiones Disputatae
RGRW	Religions in the Graeco-Roman World
RP	Religious Perspectives
RSV	Revised Standard Version

SAM	Studies in Ancient Medicine
SANt	Studia Aarhusiana Neotestamentica
SB	Stuttgarter Bibelstudien
SBB	Stuttgarter biblische Beiträge
SBFA	Studium Biblicum Franciscanum Analecta
SBL	Society of Biblical Literature
SBLDS	Society of Biblical Literature Dissertation Series
SBLMS	Society of Biblical Literature Monograph Series
SBLRBS	Society of Biblical Literature Resources for Biblical Study
SBLSBS	Society of Biblical Literature Sources for Biblical Study
SBT	Studies in Biblical Theology
SC	Sources Chrétiennes
SCHNT	Studia ad Corpus Hellenisticum Novi Testamenti
SEC	*Studies in Christian Ethics*
SJ	Studies in Judaism
SJSJ	Supplements to the Journal for the Study of Judaism
SJT	*Scottish Journal of Theology*
SNTSMS	Society for New Testament Studies Monograph Series
SNTW	Studies of the New Testament and Its World
SPA	Studies in Philo of Alexandria
SPCK	Society for Promoting Christian Knowledge
SPS	Sacra Pagina Series
SS	Semeia Studies
STDJ	Studies on the Texts of the Desert of Judah
TANZ	Texte und Arbeiten zum neutestamentlichen Zeitalter
TCH	Transformation of the Classic Heritage
TCLA	Texts from Christian Late Antiquity
TDNT	*Theological Dictionary of the New Testament*. Edited by Gerhard Kittel and Gerhard Friedrich. Translated by Geoffrey W. Bromiley. 10 vols. Grand Rapids, MI: Eerdmans, 1964–76.
TTCBS	T&T Clark Biblical Studies
TTGRS	Texts and Translations: Graeco-Roman Religion Series
TUGAL	Texte und Untersuchungen zur Geschichte der altchristlichen Literatur
TynBul	*Tyndale Bulletin*
USQR	*Union Seminary Quarterly Review*
VC	*Vigiliae Christianae*
VCSup	Vigiliae Christianae Supplements
WBC	Word Biblical Commentary
WGRWSup	Writings from the Greco-Roman World Supplement Series
WUNT	Wissenschaftliche Untersuchungen zum Neuen Testament
ZAC	*Zeitschrift für antikes Christentum*
ZNW	*Zeitschrift für die Neutestamentliche Wissenschaft*
ZTK	*Zeitschrift für Theologie und Kirche*
ZGZB	Zürcher Grundrisse zur Bibel

1

A Neglected Factor in Markan Studies

1.1 Introduction

This book proposes that Mark's Gospel is moral in nature. At the outset, the various terms "moral," "morality," "moral life," "ethics," and/or "ethical," without proper definition, portend stumbling blocks for the reader. For this reason, this chapter hopes to clear the ground, evaluating how previous studies have implemented various, sometimes wildly different, definitions for these terms in order to produce an "ethic of Mark" and, in turn, to reveal the need in Markan studies for an "ethics" of a different kind.

First, I begin with a definition. My use of "moral" throughout this study invokes Leander Keck's definition of the "moral life":

> The moral life is both broader and deeper than morality (patterned behavior) or morals (actions deemed right by a community), for it has to do with the sort of person one is (the doer) as well as with the grounding of what is to be done or not done (the deed). To speak of the moral life is to draw attention to one's responsibility, however circumscribed, for the shape of one's life. ... [T]he moral life is more than decision making, for it has to do with what becomes habitual and so exposes one's character. It refers to life actually lived, whereas the word *morality*, being an abstracted noun, signals that the subject matter has been detached from life so that it can be analyzed as a self-consistent whole. To reflect on Jesus' role in the moral life, therefore, is to reflect on his impact on the way life is lived when it is open to his influence.[1]

As Chapter 2 will reveal, this study operates under the assumption that, generically, Mark's closest first-century analogy is a *bios*. As such, it teaches its readers how to live according to the life of its central character, Jesus. In writing, the evangelists constructed a Jesus from history, in the "perfect tense," just as Keck himself attempts to "say who Jesus was so that his significance can become clear at a later time."[2] Keck, as a historian of Jesus, participates in a task introduced by Mark, the author of the first

---

[1] Leander Keck, *Who Is Jesus? History in the Perfect Tense* (Minneapolis, MN: Fortress Press, 2001), 152. Keck is not the first to refer to the "moral life" when constructing an ethics of Jesus. See also George Matheson, *Landmarks of New Testament Morality* (London: James Nisbet, 1888), 238.

[2] Keck, *Who Is Jesus?*, 7. C. Clifton Black arrives at a similar conclusion for Mark and the New Testament historian ("Mark as Historian of God's Kingdom," *CBQ* 71 [2009]: 64–83).

life of Jesus.³ The very DNA of the Gospel of Mark, in other words, is moral (cf. Mark 1:14–15).⁴

Unfortunately, much of New Testament ethics has been consumer-driven. As Keck puts it, "the paramount concern has been to present what the New Testament says about matters of interest to current readers—marriage and divorce, war and peace, loyalty to the state and dissent or the role of women in the home and in public institutions."⁵ In this way, modern moral reflection, centered on how one should act, has displaced ancient moral reflection, centered on how one should live.⁶ And for Mark, how one should live is fundamentally a theological question.⁷

---

3   For this project, I assume Markan priority. For a concise overview of what appears to remain the consensus in the field, see Mark Goodacre, *The Case against Q: Studies in Markan Priority and the Synoptic Problem* (Harrisburg, PA: Trinity Press International, 2002), 19–45.
4   Wayne Meeks's definition of morality gravitates closer to the abstract, describing it as naming "a dimension of life, a pervasive and, often, only partly conscious set of value-laden dispositions, inclinations, attitudes and habits" (*Origins of Christian Morality: The First Two Centuries* [New Haven, CT: Yale University Press, 1993], 4).
5   Leander Keck, "Rethinking 'New Testament Ethics,'" *JBL* 115 (1996): 7. The same critique was leveled by Bruce C. Birch and Larry L. Rasmussen in the 1970s: "The treatment of those biblical stories, symbols, images, paradigms, and beliefs expressly at the point of their shaping of moral character has found little systematic reflection. Indeed, Christian ethics in America has given too little attention to these forms of communication in general, an omission no doubt due to its preoccupation with decision-making and action on specific moral issues" (*The Bible and Ethics in the Christian Life* [Minneapolis, MN: Augsburg Publishing House, 1976], 104–5). For similar sentiment, see also Lisa Sowle Cahill, "Christian Character, Biblical Community, and Human Values," in *Character and Scripture: Moral Formation, Community, and Biblical Interpretation*, ed. William P. Brown (Grand Rapids, MI: Eerdmans, 2002), 3–17.
    Relevant examples of consumer-driven ethics include the so-called Chicago School, whose pioneering works include Shailer Mathews's *The Social Teaching of Jesus: An Essay in Christian Sociology* (New York: Macmillan, 1897) and Shirley Jackson Case's *The Social Origins of Christianity* (Chicago: University of Chicago Press, 1923). These works aimed to understand the Gospels by placing modern social themes at their forefront (e.g., empire, social environment, class structure). For a helpful summary of sociological approaches, see Richard Horsley, *Sociology and the Jesus Movement* (New York: Crossroad, 1989), 1–12. One might also look to the more recent examples for consumer-driven biblical ethics: Donald Guthrie, *New Testament Theology* (Downers Grove, IL: InterVarsity Press, 1981), 940–52; Daniel J. Harrington and James F. Keenan, who offer a disjointed account of "biblical" and then "moral" perspectives on subjects germane to the New Testament but whose book is driven topically as a "heuristic probe" (*Jesus and Virtue Ethics: Building Bridges between New Testament Studies and Moral Theology* [Chicago: Sheed & Ward, 2002], xv); Robertson McQuilkin and Paul Copan, *An Introduction to Biblical Ethics: Walking in the Way of Wisdom*, 3rd ed. (Downers Grove, IL: InterVarsity Press Academic, 2014), offer "biblical" solutions for issues as wide-ranging as dating, romance, and racism.
6   This does not imply that ancient ethics were uniform. There are scholarly definitions for ancient ethics that seek to evaluate the ancient ethical system as distinct from a modern one. Julia Anna, for example, describes the difference as follows: "Ancient theories assume that the moral agent internalizes and applies the moral theory to produce the correct answers to hard cases; but the answers themselves are not part of the theory. Nor are they produced by the theory in the sense that applying the theory to a simple description of a hard case will automatically generate a correct answer" (*The Morality of Happiness* [New York: Oxford University Press, 1995], 6–7). The agent's internalization of the "good" is what leads to good decisions, often without a sustained "ethical" discussion of what good decisions may include. In the case of Plato, according to James Warren, the good life "is one in which the agent will possess and display various excellent traits of character—virtues—and so ethical inquiry must concentrate on the proper identification of those virtues and the recommendation of various recipes for their acquisition" ("Plato," in *The Cambridge History of Moral Philosophy*, ed. Sacha Golob and Jens Timmermann [New York: Cambridge University Press, 2017], 30–1). For Mark's Gospel, the moral agent is motivated by God's kingdom (1:14–15) and God's will (3:35), not on the specific moral actions required of the agent.
7   Consider Abraham Malherbe's comment, "The philosophers retained their stress on reason and reliance on the self in striving for virtue. Christians, on the other hand, stressed reliance on God, Christ, and the

1.2 Christological Overshadowing in the Twentieth Century

According to Dan O. Via, ' [Mark's] ethical import has been neglected, especially the complexity and problematics [that] it introduces into ethical reflection."[8] This book claims that Mark's "ethical import" has been shortchanged in twentieth-century scholarship due to the relative paucity of ethical teachings by Jesus in Mark (compared with the other Synoptic Gospels, e.g., Matt 5:2–7:27; 10:5–42; 23:2–39; 24:4–25:46; Luke 6:20–49; 10:2–37; 11:2–13, 29–52; 19:11–27). For this reason, Mark's "ethics"[9] are often shelved by biblical scholars and theologians alike in favor of Matthew's and Luke's.[10]

Holy Spirit, and considered the moral life a corollary to their knowledge of God and the divine will" (*Moral Exhortations: A Greco-Roman Sourcebook* [Philadelphia: Westminster Press, 1986], 15).

[8] Dan O. Via, *The Ethics of Mark's Gospel: In the Middle of Time* (Philadelphia: Fortress Press, 1985), 3.

[9] My use of the phrase "Mark's ethics" here and occasionally elsewhere, reflects the nomenclature of previous studies. Mark does not have an "ethics" in the sense of reflections on a set of abstract moral principles. This book, as stated above, prefers the moral life to describe Mark's ethical program.

[10] Mark 8:22–10:52 tends to get all the attention, if the matter is considered at all. Richard Burridge rightly calls this characterization a mistake, committed by those who seek in Mark "an ethical treatise like the Sermon on the Mount or at least a collection of pithy sayings" (*Imitating Jesus: An Inclusive Approach to New Testament Ethics* [Grand Rapids, MI: Eerdmans, 2007], 184). A few examples suffice. C. F. Schmid, on using Mark for New Testament theology, states, "Mark is distinguished by little else than his brevity" (*Biblical Theology of the New Testament*, trans. G. H. Venables, CFTL 27 [Edinburgh: T&T Clark, 1877], 17). D. Hermann Jacoby states, "Few words will suffice to determine the ethical nature of the Gospel of Mark" (*Neutestamentliche Ethik* [Königsberg: Thomas & Oppermann, 1899], 413). L. H. Marshall favors Matthew for ethics: "Scattered throughout the teaching of Jesus, and specifically frequent in the Sermon on the Mount, are numerous moral imperatives" (*The Challenge of New Testament Ethics* [London: Macmillan, 1946], 99). Guthrie's section on "personal ethics" glosses over Mark entirely in favor of Matthew's and Luke's beatitudes (*New Testament Theology*, 895–907). Raymond F. Collins implies the same when he says, "First, it appears that each of these evangelists sees the moral life as integral to the Christian life ... particularly Matthew and Luke" (*Christian Morality: Biblical Foundations* [Notre Dame, IN: University of Notre Dame Press, 1986], 32). John Donahue writes, "I will suggest that while Mark's discourse [4:1–20] serves his Christology and the summons to discipleship, Matthew stresses more the ethics of discipleship and the relation of ethics to eschatology" (*The Gospel in Parable: Metaphor, Narrative, and Theology in the Synoptic Gospels* [Philadelphia: Fortress Press, 1988], 64, italics original; see also his preference for Matthew and Luke's "ethics" in ibid., 194–216). J. Ian H. McDonald says, "Mark's Gospel ... contains relatively little moral teaching" (*The Crucible of Christian Morality* [New York: Routledge, 1998], 108). Peter W. Gosnell claims that the Gospels are morally instructive as *bioi* but expounds only on Matthew and Luke without a single reference to Mark (*The Ethical Vision of the Bible: Learning Good From Knowing God* [Downers Grove, IL: InterVarsity Press Academic, 2014], 408). For other examples of favoring Matthew and Luke over Mark in New Testament ethics, see also Matheson, *New Testament Morality*, 262; Lindsey Dewar, *An Outline of New Testament Ethics* (Philadelphia: Westminster Press, 1949), 41–8; R. Newton Flew, *Jesus and His Way: A Study of the Ethics of the New Testament* (London: Epworth Press, 1963), 32–59; George E. Ladd, *A Theology of the New Testament* (Grand Rapids, MI: Eerdmans, 1974), 120–34; Eduard Lohse, *Theological Ethics of the New Testament*, trans. Eugene Boring (Minneapolis, MN: Fortress Press, 1991), 74–80; David P. Gushee and Glen H. Stassen, *Kingdom Ethics: Following Jesus in Contemporary Context*, 2nd ed. (Grand Rapids, MI: Eerdmans, 2016), xvii–xviii, 1. John's Gospel has received similar neglect in regard to ethical content: for an overview, see Lindsey M. Trozzo, *Exploring Johannine Ethics: A Rhetorical Approach to Moral Efficacy in the Fourth Gospel Narrative*, WUNT 2.449 (Tübingen: Mohr Siebeck, 2017), 5–15 and Christopher W. Skinner, "Ethics and the Gospel of John: Toward an Emerging New Consensus?," *CBR* 18 (2020): 280–304.

To begin with, the history of scholarship on Mark, until recently, has neglected the more ethical tones of the second Gospel.[11] As Allen Verhey puts it, "the very assumption that Mark devotes very little of his Gospel to moral teaching needs to be challenged."[12] In part, the overwhelming interest in Markan Christology, especially in twentieth-century redaction criticism, has left Markan moral discourse on the sidelines. Summarizing a number of Markan studies before her, Suzanne Watts Henderson notes, "Markan scholarship has frequently viewed the evangelist's Christological agenda as a 'way in' to the gospel's portrait of discipleship"[13]—and not only as a "way in" to Mark's *discipleship* motif but also as a "way in" to the Gospel's entire theological meaning. Henderson correctly attributes this scholarly obsession with Markan Christology to the "Wredestrasse."[14] William Wrede's watershed *Das Messiasgeheimnis in den Evangelien* (1901)[15] set the table of Markan studies around a central dish: Christology.[16] Henderson's contention is that this scholarly predisposition toward Christology in Mark has produced, among other things, a set of false dichotomies: a disproportionate interest in the second half of Mark for "seeing clearly" Jesus's identity (the turning point at 8:27); a fixed gaze on Jesus's identity, often split between the "post-Easter" and "pre-Easter" presentations; and, finally, a frequent contrast between Jesus and his disciples.[17] This study adds yet another false dichotomy to Henderson's list. In scholarly studies of Mark, preoccupation with Christology often sidelines morality.[18] William Telford articulates this dichotomy with precision: "The primary thrust of the Gospel [of Mark] is Christological, as I have argued, and not ethical."[19] Telford's comment divorces two otherwise inseparable notions for Mark: what is in fact the central thrust of Mark's so-called ethics is Christology, and vice versa.

---

[11] See, once more, n. 10. This is not to say that biblical theologians have neglected Markan *theology*. Studies of this nature on Mark's theology often say little to nothing about Mark's perspective on the moral life; cf. Hans Conzelmann, *An Outline of the Theology of the New Testament*, trans. John Bowden (New York: Harper & Row, 1969), 140–4; Leon Morris, *New Testament Theology* (Grand Rapids, MI: Zondervan, 1986), 95–113; I. Howard Marshall, *New Testament Theology: Many Witnesses, One Gospel* (Downers Grove, IL: InterVarsity Press, 2004), 58–94.

[12] Allen Verhey, *The Great Reversal: Ethics and the New Testament* (Grand Rapids, MI: Eerdmans, 1984), 78; see also Via, *Ethics of Mark's Gospel*, 3; Burridge, *Imitating Jesus*, 159.

[13] Suzanne Watts Henderson, *Christology and Discipleship in the Gospel of Mark* (New York: Cambridge University Press, 2006), 245.

[14] Ibid., 6. T. W. Manson appears to have been the first to coin "Wredestrasse" in "The Life of Jesus: Some Tendencies in Present-Day Research," in *The Background of the New Testament and Its Eschatology: In Honour of C. H. Dodd*, ed. W. D. Davies and D. Daube (Cambridge: Cambridge University Press, 1956), 211–21; see also Norman Perrin, "The Wredestrasse Becomes the Hauptstrasse: Reflections on the Reprinting of the Dodd Festschrift," *JR* 46 (1966): 296–300.

[15] ET William Wrede, *The Messianic Secret*, trans. J. C. G. Greig (Cambridge: J. Clarke, 1971).

[16] Thus, Jack D. Kingsbury: "Wrede has had more influence on the way in which the Gospel according to Mark has been interpreted than perhaps any other scholar" (*The Christology of Mark's Gospel* [Philadelphia: Fortress Press, 1983], 1). For a full summary of Wrede's contribution and scholarly responses, see ibid., 1–23; C. Clifton Black, *The Disciples according to Mark: Markan Redaction in Current Debate*, 2nd ed. (Grand Rapids, MI: Eerdmans, 2012), 12–18.

[17] Henderson, *Christology and Discipleship*, 9–15.

[18] As I will argue below, this same dichotomy can exist in studies of Markan discipleship. Discipleship and the moral life are two sides of the same coin in Mark.

[19] William R. Telford, *The Theology of the Gospel of Mark* (New York: Cambridge University Press, 1999), 221.

For more evidence of the Wredestrasse, one might also consider the legacies of Rudolf Bultmann and Martin Dibelius. Dibelius, for instance, finds that "Mark evidently valued a tradition which contained words of Jesus but which did not offer a narrative giving the context."[20] So, too, Bultmann, who declares that "Mark is not sufficiently master of his material to be able to venture on a systematic construction himself."[21] In the hands of the form critics, Mark becomes a virtually mindless conduit of tradition. Wrede's tendency to "minimize Mark's impact on tradition" would open the door for later redaction criticism and its lingering preoccupation with discovering Mark's Christology.[22]

The Impact of Redaction Criticism

The next stage of development in Markan studies is *Redaktionsgeschichte*, or redaction criticism, which facilitated an interest in Mark's theological personality as an author of a distinct text. The progenitor of modern redaction criticism is Willi Marxsen, who, quite unlike Wrede, finds in Mark a "thoroughly unique theologian."[23] This stage of research was the heyday of Christological explorations into Mark's meaning. In C. Clifton Black's assessment, "there seems to have been almost as many different interpretations of Mark's Christology as the number of exegetes proposing them."[24] Eduard Schweizer's short survey of various Christological theories for Mark—from divine-man and anti-Palestinian types to anti-resurrection polemics and a suffering Son of Man Christology—adequately portrays the vastly diverse landscape.[25] A predominant theme within these studies was the use of Christological titles for the exclusive purpose of determining Mark's authorial intentions, proposing a speculative *Sitz im Leben* for solving the "Christological problem." Among its more positive contributions, redaction criticism offered confidence in Mark as a creative author with distinct theological interests. At the same time, redaction criticism also brought with it several "liabilities."[26] For the purpose of this section, I will limit myself to two of these so-called liabilities.

First, Markan redaction criticism often privileged "thematic concerns as strictly theological in character."[27] The theme of Christology, for example, became a central focus for redaction-critical studies of Mark. This, of course, was not a prerequisite

---

[20] Martin Dibelius, *From Tradition to Gospel*, trans. Bertram L. Woolf (London: James Clarke, 1971), 236.
[21] Rudolf Bultmann, *The History of the Synoptic Tradition*, trans. J. Marsh (New York: Harper & Row, 1963), 350. One should keep in mind that Dibelius and Bultmann reached different conclusions about Mark and oral tradition. While Dibelius emphasized Mark as a collector of traditions, Bultmann occasionally spoke of theological motives for Matthew, Mark, and Luke. For a brief summary, see Norman Perrin, *What Is Redaction Criticism?* (Philadelphia: Fortress Press, 1969), 13–21.
[22] Perrin, *What Is Redaction Criticism?*, 12.
[23] Willi Marxsen, *Mark the Evangelist: Studies on the Redaction History of the Gospel*, trans. James Boyce (Nashville, TN: Abingdon Press, 1969), 216.
[24] Black, *Disciples*, 30.
[25] Eduard Schweizer, "Towards a Christology of Mark?," in *God's Christ and His People: Studies in Honour of Nils Alstrup Dahl*, ed. Jacob Jervell and Wayne A. Meeks (Oslo: Universitetsforlaget, 1977), 29–42.
[26] See Black's valuable list of "assets" and "liabilities" of redaction criticism in *Disciples*, 267–76.
[27] Ibid., 273.

of redaction criticism; rather, it was a trend in mid-to-late twentieth-century scholarship. More specifically, titles for Christ became the exclusive means by which Mark's theological meaning was abstracted.[28] Norman Perrin, an ardent advocate of redaction criticism, states that "a major purpose in the writing of the Marcan Gospel is Christological."[29] While this statement is prima facie defensible, Perrin does little to establish any other major purposes for Mark, or the implications for such a purpose. According to Perrin, a title-focused analysis of Mark's Christology reveals the thrust of the second Gospel: "Mark sets out to correct the false Christology of his own day."[30] Perrin's view aligns with Theodore Weeden's, who also understood "the source of conflict between the Markan disciples and the Markan Jesus [to be] clearly christological."[31] Paul J. Achtemeier follows: "Mark from a wide variety of perspectives has pointed unmistakably to the fact that a major reason—if not *the* major reason—for the writing of Mark centers around the christological problem."[32] Studies of this kind flatten out Christology in Mark to a historical problem to be solved by studying various titles attributed to Jesus. It is my own contention that Mark's Christology is moral in nature. Jesus's status as God's son (1:1) is the principal *telos* for his moral activity. Said another way, to ignore the moral intentions for Mark's Christology is to misunderstand Mark's Christology altogether. The two must not be separated.

John Donahue's published dissertation under Perrin serves as yet another example of this first liability. An exercise in redaction criticism, Donahue analyzes the passion narrative of Mark with a keen eye toward Mark's use of Christological traditions.[33] In the end, it is Mark's Christology Donahue is after, full stop. Donahue's conclusion that "the trial narrative becomes the culmination of Mark's Christology" serves the exclusive end of revealing Mark's *Sitz im Leben*.[34] In this sense, "Son of Man Christology" reveals "a community which itself is undergoing trials."[35] A summary of this tendency by

---

[28] A trend modeled, for example, by the litany of "Son of Man" studies during this era. In many cases, Mark's use of the Son of Man tradition becomes a stepping stone for historical Jesus research, as in Oscar Cullmann, *The Christology of the New Testament*, trans. Shirley C. Guthrie and Charles A. M. Hall, rev. ed. (Philadelphia: Westminster Press, 1963); and A. J. B. Higgins, *Jesus and the Son of Man* (London: Lutterworth Press, 1964), 26–75. Other studies focused on Mark's use of the Son of Man tradition to obtain Mark's theological "pattern" or meaning, as in Morna D. Hooker, *The Son of Man in Mark: A Study of the Background of the Term "Son of Man" and Its Use in St. Mark's Gospel* (Montreal: McGill University Press, 1967); and Douglas R. A. Hare, *The Son of Man Tradition* (Minneapolis, MN: Fortress Press, 1990), 183–211.

[29] Norman Perrin, "The Creative Use of the Son of Man Traditions by Mark," *USQR* 23 (1968): 357–65, here 357.

[30] Norman Perrin, "Towards an Interpretation of the Gospel of Mark," in *Christology and a Modern Pilgrimage: A Discussion with Norman Perrin*, ed. Hans Dieter Betz (Claremont, CA: New Testament Colloquium, 1971), 21.

[31] Theodore J. Weeden, *Mark: Traditions in Conflict* (Philadelphia: Fortress Press, 1971), 52. For Weeden, the title most often uttered by Jesus, that is, the suffering Son of Man, became the key to understanding Mark's corrective Christology.

[32] Paul J. Achtemeier, *Mark*, PC (Philadelphia: Fortress Press, 1975), 41.

[33] While John Donahue's study reaches beyond Christology, this is the major focus of his investigation, frequently referring to the layer of "Christological material" of which Mark supposedly makes use (*Are You the Christ? The Trial Narrative in the Gospel of Mark*, SBLDS 10 [Missoula, MT: Society of Biblical Literature, 1973], 50, 139–88, 237–40).

[34] Ibid., 238.

[35] Ibid.

Donahue and others is epitomized in the following quote by Maria Horstmann: "To acquire the image of Christ in the second Gospel is to ask for the theological intention of the redactor."[36] Many more studies might be included here.[37] As Howard Clark Kee would later warn, "an approach to Mark which begins with almost exclusive concern for the Christological problem is not asking the right questions."[38]

The theme of discipleship also typifies this first liability.[39] If one considers discipleship to be a morally loaded concept, then it is especially strange that few studies of this nature offer sustained *moral reflection* on this theme. Ernest Best, for example, claims that "Mark used the historical tradition about Jesus ... with a theological purpose in mind."[40] However, Best seems to place a false dichotomy between "moral rules" and "rules as conditions of discipleship" from the outset of his investigation.[41] Once more, the two should not be separated. Furthermore, Best's definition for discipleship, to follow Christ without ever becoming Christ,[42] lacks serious moral reflection. Best's theological conclusion for Markan discipleship flattens out larger moral questions (e.g., for what purpose? To do *what exactly?*). Prior to Best, Robert P. Meye offered an evaluation of the role of the disciples in Mark that focused on the didactic aspects of Jesus's ministry (what Meye calls the "Messianic *didache*").[43] Such an endeavor would offer, one might think, a consideration of the moral dimensions of Jesus's teaching. Disappointingly, discipleship for Meye amounts to "messianic revelation" or "a message of hope."[44] In yet another example, Francis J. Moloney's comments on Mark 1:16-20

---

[36] Maria Horstmann, *Studien zur markinischen Christologie. Mk 8,27 – 9,13 als Zugang zum Christusbild des zweiten Evangeliums*, NA 6 (Münster: Verlag Aschendorff, 1969), 1.

[37] The reduction of Mark's Gospel to Christology and nothing more is captured well in the statement by Sherman E. Johnson: "The theology of Mark is essentially a Christology" (*A Commentary on the Gospel According to St. Mark*, 2nd ed., BNTC [London: A & C Black, 1972], 9). Representative of redaction-critical studies interested in Markan Christology are Johannes Schreiber, "Die Christologie des Markusevangeliums–Beobachtungen zur Theologie und Komposition des zweiten Evangeliums," *ZTK* 58 (1961): 154-83; Philipp Vielhauer, "Erwägungen zur Christologie des Markusevangeliums," in *Zeit und Geschichte: Dankesgabe an Rudolf Bultmann zum 80. Geburtstag*, ed. Erich Dinkler (Tübingen: Mohr, 1964), 155-69; Heinz-Dieter Knigge, "The Meaning of Mark: The Exegesis of the Second Gospel," *Interpretation* 22 (1968): 53-70; Horstmann, *Studien zur Markinischen Christologie*; and Paul J. Achtemeier, "'He Taught Them Many Things': Reflections on Marcan Christology," *CBQ* 42 (1980): 465-81; see also Eduard Schweizer, who claims that "Mark's objective is to proclaim Jesus as the Son of God. It is not his purpose to produce a description of the life of Jesus" (*The Good News According to Mark*, trans. Donald H. Madvig [Richmond: John Knox Press, 1970], 12).

[38] Howard Clark Kee, *Community of the New Age: Studies in Mark's Gospel* (Philadelphia: Westminster Press, 1977), 1.

[39] That discipleship occupies a "true storm center" in redactional studies of Mark, see Black, *Disciples*, 45-64.

[40] Ernest Best, *Following Jesus: Discipleship in the Gospel of Mark*, JSNTSup 4 (Sheffield: JSOT Press, 1981), 10.

[41] Ibid., 14. Best comes close in places, but often turns to Christology ("the way of the cross") as Mark's ethic for discipleship. I will argue below that Jesus's way of the cross is a consequence of his moral obligation to do God's will (3:35; 14:36).

[42] Ernest Best, "Discipleship in Mark: Mark 8.22-10.52," *SJT* 23 (1970): 334-5. Best repeatedly claims in this piece that he does not want to invoke an *imitatio Christi* ethic; that he does exactly this, see Black, *Disciples*, 136.

[43] Robert P. Meye, *Jesus and the Twelve: Discipleship and Revelation in Mark's Gospel* (Grand Rapids, MI: Eerdmans, 1968), 136.

[44] Ibid., 224. Unfortunately, Meye circumvents morality and turns to Christology to underscore the nature of discipleship in Mark. For a critical response to Meye's position, see Black, *Disciples*, 103-6.

are ripe for moral reflection but receive little.⁴⁵ Moloney observes that Jesus's request at the outset of Mark amounts to taking one's own life: "For a first-century Galilean fisherman it would have been suicidal to leave the tools of trade."⁴⁶ Surely leaving one's family and trade would have both moral impetus and implications, but the passage receives little reflection to that end.

The second liability produced by redaction critics was to shift attention to the middle section (8:22–10:52) as central for understanding Markan theology.⁴⁷ As had been previously acknowledged by some form critics, this section of Mark contains a relatively stable literary unit, composed mainly of Jesus's teaching.⁴⁸ Horstmann, for example, refers to this section as "the theological center of the book."⁴⁹ While it is true that redaction criticism drew attention to "the Evangelists as authors of literary products,"⁵⁰ Mark's literary showstoppers continued to be the center of the Gospel (8:22–10:52) alongside Mark 13 and the concluding passion narrative (Mark 14–16).⁵¹ Once more, Perrin serves as a useful foil. Since he can determine with confidence that Mark 8:27–10:45 is a "very carefully composed section of the Gospel," this justifies his treating the three passion predictions within it as "reflecting the Marcan theology."⁵² While determining the extent of Mark's editorial activity yields varying degrees of certainty among redaction-critical scholars, many zero in on this central section.⁵³

---

⁴⁵ The closest Francis J. Moloney comes is "radical dependence on Jesus" ("The Vocation of the Disciples in the Gospel of Mark," *Salesianum* 43 [1981]: 487–516, here 515). As Chapter 3 will outline, leaving one's family in a first-century context would be considered an immoral action in many cases.

⁴⁶ Ibid., 515.

⁴⁷ See Black, *Disciples*, 273.

⁴⁸ See Wrede, *Messianic Secret*, 122–3.

⁴⁹ Horstmann, *Studien zur Markinischen Christologie*, 2.

⁵⁰ Black, *Disciples*, 267.

⁵¹ For Mark 13, consider the paramount study by Rudolf Pesch, *Naherwartungen: Tradition und Redaktion in Mk 13* (Düsseldorf: Patmos-Verlag, 1968). Similarly, Martin Kähler's description of Mark and the Synoptics as "passion narratives with extended introductions" remained influential ("Etwas herausfordernd könnte man sie Passionsgeschichten mit ausführlicher Einleitung nennen": *Der sogenannte historische Jesus und der geschichtliche, biblische Christus* [Leipzig: Deichert, 1892; repr. Berlin: Berlin University Press, 2013], 65 n. 25).

⁵² Perrin, "Son of Man Traditions," 363–4; Perrin, "Interpretation of the Gospel of Mark," 1–13. For a similar case, see Joachim Gnilka, *Das Evangelium nach Markus*, EKK 2 (Zürich: Benziger, 1978), 1.31. Robert H. Stein agrees with Perrin: "The Proper Methodology for Ascertaining a Markan Redaction History," *NovT* 13 (1971): 181–98.

⁵³ Richard Edwards remarks, "The central section of the Gospel (8:27-10:52) is the most important for Mark" ("A New Approach to the Gospel of Mark," *LQ* 22 [1970]: 333–4). Ulrich B. Müller refers to Mark 8:22–10:52 as "the main section [*Hauptabschnitt*]" intended to unveil Jesus as the "suffering Son of Man" ("Die christologische Absicht des Markusevangeliums und die Verklärungsgeschichte," *ZNW* 64 [1973]: 159–93). Gregg S. Morrison calls this section "a turning point in the Gospel," exclusively related to "Markan Christology" (*The Turning Point in the Gospel of Mark: A Study in Markan Christology* [Eugene, OR: Pickwick, 2014]1), but Morrison's observation is nothing new: cf. Gnilka, *Markus*, 1:30; Johnson, *St. Mark*, 146. Via considers Mark 10 as "a relatively self-contained unit" that "contains a concentration of ethical and other related materials which make it a microcosm of the Gospel" (*Ethics of Mark's Gospel*, 78); see also Dennis E. Nineham, *The Gospel of Saint Mark* (Philadelphia: Westminster Press, 1963), 37–8; Quentin Quesnell, *The Mind of Mark: Interpretation and Method through the Exegesis of Mark 6,52*, Analecta biblica 38 (Rome: Pontifical Biblical Institute, 1969), 126–9; Schweizer, *The Good News According to Mark*, 165–225, 384–5; William L. Lane, *The Gospel According to Mark: The English Text with Introduction, Exposition and Notes* (Grand Rapids,

The consistent irony within these studies is that a section robust with ethical content is eclipsed by concerns for Christology. The passion predictions especially (Mark 8:31; 9:30–32; 10:32–34) distract from an otherwise ethically rich portion of Mark. Furthermore, when ethical studies in Mark do appear, the impact of redactional studies and their parochial focus on Mark 8:22–10:52 remains. The so-called theological meaning of Mark, supposedly on display in this central section, is transformed into Mark's separate treatise on "ethics" equivalent to Matthew's Sermon on the Mount.

The Move to Literary Criticism

Responding in part to the authorial focus of redaction criticism, a litany of studies surfaced attempting to reclaim Mark's story: a shift away from the author to the text. Thus, Perrin, while still very much wielding its tools, declares that Markan redaction criticism "needs to be supplemented by other critical methods."[54] Perrin prescribes a "blend" of redaction criticism, general literary criticism, and literary-form criticism.[55] Perrin's rallying cry around literary-critical studies of Markan Christology continues to attract followers.[56] In this regard, Jack D. Kingsbury's study is in many ways characteristic. Taking his cues as well as his major points of departure from Wrede, Kingsbury attempts a literary-critical reading of Mark to retrieve Jesus's identity. Kingsbury hopes to push beyond the needless bifurcation of "corrective" Christology in studies before him: the divide between divine "Son of God" and human "Son of Man" titles installed by Wrede and typified by Weeden. Instead, Kingsbury proposes an investigation of Mark's titles for Jesus sensitive to "the medium of the story Mark tells."[57] One consequence of Kingsbury's study, and studies of this kind, is that while Mark's story is given full attention, it is still trapped within the narrow interest of titular Christology, void of any consideration for what Christology might entail for moral living.[58] Edwin K. Broadhead builds upon Kingsbury by analyzing titles for Jesus within Mark as "a narrative presentation or performance."[59] He offers equal weight to titles as they appear in Mark's narrative (e.g., prophet, priest, teacher, shepherd). Although

---

MI: Eerdmans, 1974), 288; Siegfried Schulz, *Neutestamentliche Ethik*, ZGZ 3 (Zürich: Theologischer Verlag, 1987), 441–6.

[54] Norman Perrin, "The Christology of Mark: A Study in Methodology," *JR* 51 (1971): 173–87, here 174.

[55] Ibid., 174–6. It should be noted that by the end of his career, Perrin had left redaction criticism behind for literary criticism; see Norman Perrin, *Jesus and the Language of the Kingdom: Symbol and Metaphor in New Testament Interpretation* (Philadelphia: Fortress Press, 1976), 7–12.

[56] See David Rhoads, Joanna Dewey, and Donald Michie, *Mark as Story: An Introduction to the Narrative of a Gospel*, 3rd ed. (Philadelphia: Fortress Press, 2012); Ole Davidsen, *The Narrative Jesus: A Semiotic Reading of Mark's Gospel* (Aarhus: Aarhus University Press, 1993); Jacob Chacko Nalupurayil, *The Identity of Jesus in Mark: An Essay on Narrative Christology*, SBFA 49 (Jerusalem: Franciscan Printing Press, 2000); Paul L. Danove, *The Rhetoric of the Characterization of God, Jesus, and Jesus' Disciples in the Gospel of Mark*, JSNTSup 290 (New York: T&T Clark, 2005); Elizabeth Struthers Malbon, *Mark's Jesus: Characterization as Narrative Christology* (Waco, TX: Baylor University Press, 2009).

[57] Kingsbury, *The Christology of Mark's Gospel*, xi.

[58] In Kingsbury's case, the conclusion of redaction critics before him (e.g., Weeden, Perrin, Achtemeier, and Petersen) is simply reversed: Mark prefers the Son of God title to the Son of Man.

[59] Erwin K. Broadhead, *Naming Jesus: Titular Christology in the Gospel of Mark*, JSNTSup 175 (Sheffield: Sheffield Academic Press, 1999), 29.

Mark is assigned "a larger, more complex strategy of characterization," virtually no consideration is given to its implications for the moral life.[60]

A more recent iteration of Kingsbury's ambitions may be found in Elizabeth Struthers Malbon's *Mark's Jesus* (2009). Malbon asks, "How does the Gospel of Mark characterize Jesus?"[61] Though she claims to avoid theological questions (i.e., the "how" of Markan Christology), Malbon's literary investigation is still motivated by a long-standing Christological agenda in Markan studies: the Wredestrasse. Her observations on, for example, "exemplary characters" in Mark as evidence of "reflected christology" invite moral reflection, but, once more, little is given.[62]

Christology, in sum, has long captured the spotlight of Markan studies, often to the neglect of the Gospel's moral interests. Likewise, the popular theme of discipleship, while ripe for sustained moral reflection, often receives little. To be clear, this study does not attempt to surgically remove the dominant themes of Christology or discipleship from Mark's conception of the moral life—an absurd notion. Rather, it intends to shift the lens through which Mark's story has been interpreted toward a more ethically attentive reading. Discipleship and Christology are two features of Mark's broader theological and moral program.

From Christology to Ethics

As stated previously, Henderson's criticism of studies of discipleship in Mark may also apply to studies of ethics in Mark: scholarly interest in Jesus's identity has overlooked the "nature of Jesus' messiahship," specifically the nature of how a follower of Jesus ought to live.[63] The net result of this Christology frenzy has yielded a dearth of ethically motivated studies in Mark. Furthermore, the shadow cast by Christology studies, as I have shown, extends over discipleship studies as well. One sees this legacy especially in scholarship that claims to investigate the moral or ethical tones of the Gospels. Here, I will cite a few examples. Victor Paul Furnish suggests that Mark is more concerned with Christology than morality: "Nor does Mark stress Jesus' healing ministry as a model for the love, compassion, and active goodwill which might properly characterize the Christian life."[64] J. L. Houlden follows: "For [Mark], as for John, it appears that facing and settling moral problems, in the everyday sense, was not a primary concern."[65] Likewise, Georg Strecker opines, "The Gospel of Mark does not explicitly raise the question of the significance of Jesus for the faith of the community."[66] Finally,

---

[60] Broadhead's final words in his conclusion come close: "The titular Christology constructed in this Gospel prescribes both hearing and discipleship" (ibid., 174).
[61] Malbon, *Mark's Jesus*, 13.
[62] Malbon's section on exemplary characters as mirrors for "how Jesus relates to God and thus to others" is embedded with commentary applicable to Mark's moral life (ibid., 230).
[63] Henderson, *Christology and Discipleship*, 12.
[64] Victor Paul Furnish, *The Love Command in the New Testament* (Nashville, TN: Abingdon Press, 1972), 74. For an additional list of studies, see also n. 10 above.
[65] J. L. Houlden, *Ethics and the New Testament* (Harmondsworth: Penguin, 1973), 45.
[66] Georg Strecker, *Theology of the New Testament*, trans. M. Eugene Boring (Louisville, KY: Westminster John Knox Press, 2000), 362. Mark is directly contrasted to Matthew, who, according to Strecker, thoroughly "ethicizes" the tradition (ibid., 378). There are some notable exceptions, such as Ralph P.

Jack T. Sanders concludes dismissively: "Regarding how the Christian was expected to relate to his fellow Christian, Mark has almost nothing to say."[67] When studies of Markan ethics do appear they do so under the stubborn guise of Christology. Willi Marxsen, in his work, *New Testament Foundations for Christian Ethics*, offers Christology as the wheel on which Christian ethics turns: "Hence Christology turns out to be not only indispensable—this could be a postulate—but unavoidable if we proceed in a methodologically deliberate manner."[68] Ethics, for Marxsen, are found in the individual Christologies of the New Testament, or in his words, an "ethics oriented toward Jesus" because "the historical Jesus cannot be found."[69] Marxsen's instincts are correct, insofar as, for the Gospel of Mark, the character of Jesus is one unavoidable aspect of Mark's moral life; however, Mark's moral warrants for the pressing reality of God's kingdom, modeled, in part, by the words and actions of Jesus,[70] derive first and foremost from God.[71] In this sense, Christology ought to be considered a subset of Markan theology. Marxsen's study on ethics comes close to the subject of theology but remains focused on Christology.

A secondary issue is that the history of scholarship on Markan ethics has largely favored Jesus's teaching over his actions, condensing the Gospel's story into smaller, extractable sections. This appears to be a remnant attitude of *Formgeschichte* in historical Jesus research, interested primarily in Jesus's words,[72] and the redaction-critical interest in the center section of Mark's Gospel, which houses the bulk of Jesus's teaching (8:22–10:52). Udo Schnelle's *Theology of the New Testament* models this trend in two ways. First, Schnelle focuses on Jesus's teaching in Mark (e.g.. "The way of faith is for Mark the way of discipleship, in which Jesus's teaching is the norm for living and acting"[73]); second, Schnelle extracts "ethical" content mainly from chs. 8 through

---

Martin, who claimed that "Mark has an intensely practical interest" (*Mark: Evangelist and Theologian* [Exeter: Paternoster Press, 1972], 161).

[67] Jack T. Sanders, *Ethics in the New Testament: Change and Development* (Philadelphia: Fortress Press, 1975), 33.

[68] Willi Marxsen, *New Testament Foundations for Christian Ethics*, trans. O. C. Dean Jr. (Minneapolis, MN: Fortress Press, 1993), 28.

[69] Ibid., 37.

[70] Keck defines a warrant as that which "anchors the action in reality and so intends to persuade the mind by exposing the inherent, necessary, substantive connection between a specified reality and the deed" ("Rethinking," 11).

[71] As John Donahue has demonstrated, interest in Christology has also led to a neglect of the study of God in Mark: "Mark constantly relates proper instruction on discipleship not only to proper understanding of the necessity of suffering but to a proper understanding of the relation of Jesus to God" ("A Neglected Factor in the Theology of Mark," *JBL* 101 [1982]: 590); see also M. Eugene Boring, "Markan Christology: God Language for Jesus?" *NTS* 45 (1999): 451–71; James S. Hanson, *The Endangered Promises: Conflict in Mark*, SBLDS 171 (Atlanta, GA: Society of Biblical Literature, 2000), 1–4; Danove, *Characterization of God*, 28–55; Larry Hurtado, *God in New Testament Theology*, LBT (Nashville, TN: Abingdon Press, 2010), 18–20; Matthew S. Rindge, "Reconfiguring the Akedah and Recasting God: Lament and Divine Abandonment in Mark," *JBL* 131 (2012): 755–74.

[72] Gerd Theissen and Annette Merz, *The Historical Jesus: A Comprehensive Guide*, trans. John Bowden (Minneapolis, MN: Fortress Press, 1998), 2–8.

[73] Udo Schnelle, *Theology of the New Testament*, trans. M. Eugene Boring (Grand Rapids, MI: Eerdmans, 2009), 423.

10 of Mark.[74] In another example, Whitney Taylor Shiner's otherwise excellent study of the rhetoric of discipleship in Mark restricts Jesus's moral demands mostly to "the teaching of chapters eight through ten."[75] These occasional nods to ethics in Mark tend to neglect the larger narrative in content, chiefly as a story, as well as in form, as a type of ancient biography.

1.3 Conclusion

After a survey of recent studies on ethics and Mark, it would seem that Ernst Käsemann's verdict on a New Testament "ethic" is no longer true, at least as it pertains to the second evangelist.[76] In the last thirty-five years, a growing number of scholars have acknowledged the narrative world of Mark, highlighting the words and actions of Jesus when describing Mark's moral program. This would indicate a turning of the tide regarding ethical interest in Mark. While interpretive methods differ in aim, methodology, and conclusion, it seems fair to conclude that the disparaging judgment of such scholars as Houlden, Sanders, and Telford—that Mark is wanting in ethical content—is categorically untrue. The once ubiquitous neglect, or underestimation, of Mark's Gospel in studies of New Testament ethics is turning a corner.[77]

Even so, this chapter has highlighted several needs that remain in describing the moral world of Mark's Gospel. First and foremost, the genre of Mark has often been neglected. As Chapter 2 will demonstrate, ancient biographies have a moral fiber built into their framework. To understand the ethical character of the Gospel, one must begin with an adequate assessment of what, exactly, a Gospel entails. Second, the Wredestrasse has proven long-standing, especially with regard to Christological interest in Mark. While Christology is certainly one facet of Mark's moral life, it is my contention that this is only one coefficient of Mark's presentation of God and the cosmic powers in contention with God. Third, the eruption of literary and narrative-critical readings of Mark, with varying degrees of effectiveness, has produced a preference for modern literary techniques over historical-critical analysis. Analogous historical evidence proves more effective in discerning the nature and character of the

---

[74] Ibid., 423–5.

[75] Whitney T. Shiner, *Follow Me! Disciples in Markan Rhetoric*, SBLDS 145 (Atlanta, GA: Scholars Press, 1995), 198. Consider Hugh Anderson:

> The materials of 8:27–10:52 have for the most part come from the tradition, while a solid historical substratum no doubt underlies many of the sayings and incidents, the preaching and catechetical interest of the Church as well as the editorial purpose of the Evangelist appear to have played their part in the formulation of the section. ... [T]he Evangelist thought of the section first and foremost less as a faithful account of the past than as a word in season, or indeed a sermon, to the Church of his day. (*The Gospel of Mark*, NCBC [London: Marshall, Morgan & Scott, 1976], 208)

[76] Ernst Käsemann: "The 'ethic' of the New Testament puts forward without any hesitation single injunctions in almost casuistic fashion" (*New Testament Questions of Today*, trans. W. J. Montague [London: SCM Press, 1969], 197).

[77] For an in-depth analysis of relevant studies that contribute to this turn in Markan studies, see M. John-Patrick O'Connor, "Void of Ethics No More," *CBR* (forthcoming).

moral life described within Mark's Gospel. Fourth, the problem remains that, other than Via's monograph, very few studies dedicated to Mark's moral life have appeared. The range of attempts outlined above usually appear as chapters in larger studies on New Testament ethics or morals, which, by nature of limited space or outright neglect, tend to shortchange the complexities of Mark's moral world.

Finally, the studies listed above tend to overlook one consistently bizarre piece of Mark's moral life. In Mark, Jesus tells parables *in order to* (ἵνα; confuse (cf. ὅτι in Matt 13:13), a characteristic that leaves insiders ousted and brings outsiders in. His actions do not welcome simple "imitation," as some have suggested, because they are occasionally destructive (5:1-20; 11:20-25) or downright offensive (7:24-30); this Jesus may tear families apart (1:16-20; 3:31-35) and locate the power of God's kingdom in the unlikeliest of places (10:14). His disciples, a first-century teacher's curriculum vitae, fail to understand him at almost every turn. Why would Mark, if writing to announce the "good news of Jesus Christ the Son of God" (1:1), not offer an easier, more inviting way? Why does this teacher speak in such dense parables? If Mark has an ethic at all, the opaque, often confusing moral directives for his reader conclude not in heroism but in fear and silence (16:8). Via picks up on this near absurdity of Mark's moral program:

> If Mark is to be considered as one authoritative source for constructive Christian ethics, not only must the Markan norms be taken into account but also the paradoxical, ironical, presentation of ethical enablement must be an element in the Christian understanding of existence with its moral project.[78]

It is precisely this "paradoxical, ironical presentation" with which this study hopes to reckon: a glaring feature of the Markan story that previous studies have ignored. In order to do so, I now turn to historical analogies from Mark's period. If Mark writes something akin to a biography of Jesus, how might this inform his presentation of the moral life?

---

[78] Via, *Ethics of Mark's Gospel*, 191.

2

The Moral Environment of Ancient Biographies

2.1 Introduction

To say that scholarly probes into the genre of Mark are many is a vast understatement: "They are as the sand of the sea" (Gen 22:17).[1] This chapter's contribution to a moral reading of Mark's Gospel, nonetheless, must not be underestimated. Studies on Markan ethics tend to dodge questions related to genre for modern narrative analysis.[2] Within the historical context of the first century, ancients were not concerned primarily with the casuistry or deontology of modern philosophers; they concerned themselves with the moral formation of the self.[3] One medium that expressed this ancient moral matrix was biography, or so this chapter claims.

A starting place for our discussion begins with Friedrich Leo, who placed the genre of Hellenistic biography firmly within the Aristotelian school.[4] While Leo's conclusions have fallen out of vogue his research raised provocative questions about the relationship between history, historiography, and biography in antiquity. One line of questioning raised by Leo, which has been rigorously debated since, is the relationship, if any, between the genre of biography and ethics. While the degree to

---

[1] For a helpful survey, see Cilliers Breytenbach, "Current Research on the Gospel according to Mark: A Report on Monographs Published from 2000–2009," in *Mark and Matthew I, Comparative Readings: Understanding the Earliest Gospels in their First-Century Settings*, ed. Eve-Marie Becker and Anders Runesson, WUNT 271 (Tübingen: Mohr Siebeck, 2011), 21–3.

[2] See, once more, O'Connor, "Void of Ethics No More."

[3] See, once more, Julia Annas sketch of the differences between ancient and modern ethics (*The Morality of Happiness*, 4–10). This type of moral formation of the self, found in antiquity, is not restricted to only ancient literary works. A similar phenomenon occurs in artistic depictions, see Margaret R. Miles, "Achieving the Christian Body: Visual Incentives to Imitations of Christ in the Christian West," in *Interpreting Christian Art: Reflections on Christian Art*, ed. Heidi J. Hornik and Mikeal C. Parsons (Macon, GA: Mercer University Press, 2004), 1–23.

[4] Friedrich Leo, *Die griechisch-römische Biographie nach ihrer literarischen Form* (Leipzig: Teubner, 1901); for a full evaluation and critique of Leo's position, see Andrew Momigliano's *The Development of Greek Biography* (Cambridge, MA: Harvard University Press, 1971) and *The Development of Greek Biography*, exp. ed. (Cambridge, MA: Harvard University Press, 1993), 105–22. See also William W. Fortenbaugh, "Biography and the Aristotelian Peripatos," in *Die griechische Biographie in hellenistischer Zeit: Akten des internationalen Kongresses vom 26.–29. Juli 2006 Würzburg*, ed. Michael Erler and Stefan Schorn, BzA 245 (New York: Walter de Gruyter), 45–76.

which biographies are a direct by-product of Aristotle's school remains uncertain,[5] Leo's thesis launches the present chapter's discussion: Greco-Roman conceptions of morality regularly find their way into Hellenistic biographies. Even among Greek historians, biographical vignettes were told for moral formation.[6] Polybius, when describing the life of Philopoemen of Megalopolis, suddenly breaks script (*Hist.* 10.21.2–8). Instead of outlining the chronological details of the life of Philopoemen, as was the custom of an ancient historian, he writes,

> It is indeed a strange thing that authors should narrate circumstantially the foundation of cities, telling us when, how, and by whom they were founded ... while they pass over in silence the previous training and the objects of the men who directed the whole matter. For inasmuch as it is more possible to emulate [ζηλῶσαι] and to imitate [μιμήσασθαι] living men than lifeless buildings, so much more important for the improvement of a reader [ἐπανόρθωσιν τῶν ἀκουόντων] is it to learn about the former.[7]

As this excerpt from Polybius discloses, historians could write about living men and women for the "improvement of a reader,"[8] even if they did not understand themselves to be writing within a particular subgenre of encomium, for example (e.g., *Hist.* 10.21.8). For this reason, Maël Goarzin refers to "biographical discourse" instead of "biography" in order to "explain common features found in different texts from the

---

[5] Momigliano and Fortenbaugh claim more forcefully, for example, that Aristoxenus, and his *Lives of Socrates and Plato*, was the "first Peripatetic biographer" (Momigliano, *Greek Biography*, exp. ed., 76–7; Fortenbaugh, "Biography and the Aristotelian Peripatos," 76).

[6] E.g., Diodorus, *Bibl.* 11.46.1; 15.1.1; Lucian, *De Hist. Cons.*, 59–63. A claim made by both Leo, *Biographie*, 109; and Charles W. Fornara, *The Nature of History in Ancient Greece and Rome* (Berkeley: University of California Press, 1983), 35; cf. Adela Yarbro Collins, *Mark: A Commentary*, Hermeneia (Minneapolis, MN: Fortress Press, 2007), 37. Note also Simon Swain's comment that biographical material may be found in small vignettes: "[Biographical texts] may be complete, from birth to death, or sectional and partial" ("Biography and Biographic in the Literature of the Roman Empire," in *Portraits: Biographical Representation in the Greek and Latin Literature of the Roman Empire*, ed. Mark J. Edwards and Simon Swain [New York: Oxford University Press, 1997], 1–2) . Furthermore, Arthur P. Urbano has demonstrated that biographies in late antiquity derive from their philosophical and intellectual ancestors, and, as such, are teaming with "philosophical competition" (*The Philosophical Life: Biography and the Crafting of Intellectual Identity in Late Antiquity*, PMS 21 [Washington, DC: Catholic University of America Press, 2013], 1–31).

[7] Quotation taken from Thomas Hägg, *The Art of Biography in Antiquity* (New York: Cambridge University Press, 2012), 96, with Greek inserted by author. Polybius is a good example, especially considering the scholarly debate over his "moral" or "practical" interpretation of history. Friedrich Nietzsche calls Polybius the "great teacher who, by reminding us of the sudden misfortunes of others, exhorts us steadfastly to bear the reverses of fortune" (*On the Advantage and Disadvantage of History for Life*, trans. Peter Preuss [Cambridge: Hackett, 1980], 15). Consider also the statement by Arthur M. Eckstein: "Indeed, among the ancient historical writers now extant, no one more frequently breaks his narrative in order to comment in moralizing terms on human character and the lessons of life" (*Moral Vision in the Histories of Polybius*, HCS 6 [Berkeley: University of California Press, 1995], 17); for a similar assessment, see also Dirk Frickenschmidt, *Evangelium als Biographie: Die vier Evangelien im Rahmen antiker Erzählkunst*, TANZ 22 (Tübingen: Francke, 1997), 142–3.

[8] For a full discussion of this passage, see Hägg, *Art of Biography*, 95–8.

same period of time."[9] The moral formation of the self, which is found in biographical discourse, is at the center of the present chapter's investigation.

2.2 Mark and Biographies

Greco-Roman biographies provide one historical analogy for understanding Mark's moral world.[10] They are, by no means, the only historical analogy for understanding Mark.[11] As David Aune notes, this is one of the pitfalls of scholars who argue Mark is *not* a biography: they define the Greco-Roman biography genre too narrowly.[12] I claim, instead, that Greco-Roman *bioi* and *vitae* offer us a close analogy to Mark in its final, written form and that Mark, in places, "intentionally transgressed" this macro-genre of biography.[13] Put another way, quoting Aune once more, "Mark in particular is a type of Greco-Roman biography in the special sense that it is a parody of that genre."[14] This "special sense" is important in that Mark's Gospel, when pressed, undoubtedly transgresses traditional biography criteria.[15] In part, this is because the

---

[9] Moël Goarzin, "Presenting a Practical Way of Life through Biographical Discourse: The Examples of Gregory of Nyssa and Marinus," in *Tradition and Transformation: Dissent and Consent in the Mediterranean: Proceedings of the 3rd CEMS International Graduate Conference* (Kiel: Solivagus-Verlag, 2016), 115–29.

[10] Throughout, my use of "Mark" refers to the Gospel not the author.

[11] I hope to avoid pigeonholing my project by placing Mark within a rigidly defined genre or subgenre. An example of this can be found in the work of Moses Hadas and Mortor Smith (*Heroes and Gods: Spiritual Biographies in Antiquity*, RP 13 [New York: Harper & Row, 1965]) in their attempt to fit the Gospel of Luke into the specific biographical type of aretalogy. See the critique of Howard Clark Kee, "Aretalogy and Gospel," *JBL* 92 (1972): 402–22.

[12] David E. Aune, "Genre Theory and the Genre-Function of Mark and Matthew," in *Mark and Matthew I: Comparative Readings: Understanding the Earliest Gospels in their First-Century Settings*, ed. Eve-Marie Becker and Anders Runesson, WUNT 271 (Tübingen: Mohr Siebeck, 2011), 145–75.

[13] Ibid., 174–5. Final written form appeases those who understand Mark as a set of unfinished "memoires." For an overview of the arguments, see Vernon K. Robbins, *Jesus the Teacher: A Socio-Rhetorical Interpretation of Mark* (Minneapolis, MN: Fortress Press, 1992), 60–9; James A. Kelhoffer, "'How Soon a Book' Revisited: EUANGELION as a Reference to 'Gospel' Materials in the First Half of the Second Century," *ZNW* 95 (2004): 1–34; and Matthew D. C. Larsen, "Accidental Publication, Unfinished Texts and the Traditional Goals of New Testament Textual Criticism," *JSNT* 39 (2017): 362–87. It is also worth considering Eve-Marie Becker's argument that the macro-genre of historiography ought to include biography. For Becker, Mark is a type of "person-centered historiographical narrative" and not properly a biography, which is to say that many features of historiography and biography overlap (*The Birth of Christian History: Memory and Time from Mark to Luke–Acts*, AYBRL [New Haven, CT: Yale University Press, 2017], 71–85).

[14] Aune, "Genre Theory," 147. For language of parody, see also Norman Petersen, "Can One Speak of a Gospel Genre?" *Neot* 28 (1994): 137–58. Petersen, unfortunately, concludes negatively that Mark "makes for a rather strange biography; which is why it is not one" (ibid., 148). To the contrary, Mark's strangeness is better understood in light of the ancient biographical genre.

[15] Matthew and Luke appear to fit the genre category better than Mark (cf. David E. Aune, *The New Testament in its Literary Environment* [Philadelphia: Westminster Press, 1987], 63–76; and David E. Aune, "Greco-Roman Biography," in *Greco-Roman Literature and the New Testament: Selected Forms and Genres*, ed. David E. Aune, SBLSBS 21 [Atlanta, GA: Scholars Press, 1988], 121–5). Two rebuttals of Mark as a type of Greco-Roman biography come from M. Eugene Boring, *Mark: A Commentary*, NTL (Louisville, KY: WJKP, 2007), 7–8; and Michael E. Vines, *The Problem of Markan Genre: The Gospel of Mark and the Jewish Novel*, Academia Biblica 3 (Atlanta, GA: Society of Biblical Literature, 2002), 15–31 Vines's objections may be so summarized: (1) Any biographical features in Mark are restricted to "its focus on the life and activities of a single individual in a rough

genre of biography has proven to be a more broad and complex category than previous scholarship assumed,[16] so much so that some have speculated discarding the term "genre" altogether.[17] Nonetheless, a growing list of scholars have insisted on placing the Gospels within the broad family of ancient biographies.[18] In so doing, one may respect

---

chronological framework"; (2) Mark's syntax and style reflect "popular literature"; and (3) biography does not make adequate sense of Mark's "apocalyptic understanding of history" (*Problem of Markan Genre*, 22). Vines, along with Mary Ann Tolbert on whom he depends (*Sowing the Gospel: Mark's World in Literary-Historical Perspective* [Minneapolis, MN: Fortress Press, 1989]), seem to pass along the *Hoch/Kleinliteratur* hangover from form criticism. Vines's narrow description of Greco-Roman biography overlooks the possibility that Mark was creatively transformed for distinct purposes (Aune, "Genre Theory," 167). Boring overplays Mark's Christology, listing five reasons for Mark's differences from biographies: (1) The depiction of Jesus's as "truly human and truly divine" by way of the messianic secret; (2) the apocalyptic dimension of Mark's understanding of history; (3) Mark's "two-level drama," in which Jesus speaks to "past history" *and* the present community; (4) "The narrative is episodic but not anecdotal"; and (5) Jesus's use of parables (*Mark*, 7–8). Boring's concerns about Mark's genre are accurate and recall Rudolf Bultmann's concerns (*Die Geschichte der synoptischen Tradition*, 10th ed., FRLANT 29 [Gottingen: Vandenhoeck & Ruprecht, 1995], 398). I contend that Mark's Christological differences showcase the ways in which the second Gospel was shaped to suit a distinct theological agenda.

[16] See Patricia Cox, *Biography in Late Antiquity: A Quest for the Holy Man*, TCH 5 (Berkeley: University of California Press, 1983), 1–65; Hägg, *Art of Biography*, 10–98.

[17] See discussion in Hägg, *Art of Biography*, 2–3, 148–86.

[18] Scholars who understand the Gospels as biographies within the last thirty-five years include (among others) the following: Hubert Cancik, "Die Gattung Evangelium. Markus im Rahmen der antiken Historiographie," in *Markus-Philologie: Historische, literargeschichtliche und stilistische Untersuchungen zum zweiten Evangelium*, ed. H. Cancik, WUNT 33 (Tübingen, J. C. B. Mohr, 1984), 85–113; Martin Hengel, *Studies in the Gospel of Mark* (Philadelphia: Fortress Press, 1985), 32 and 139–40 n. 8; Meeks, *Origins of Christian Morality*, 197–9; N. T. Wright, *The New Testament and the People of God* (London: SPCK, 1992), 381; F. G. Downing, "A Genre for Q and Socio-Cultural Context for Q: Comparing Sets of Similarities with Sets of Differences," *JSNT* 55 (1994): 3–26; Frickenschmidt, *Evangelium als Biographie*; Lawrence Wills, *The Quest of the Historical Gospels: Mark, John, and the Origins of the Gospel Genre* (New York: Routledge, 1997), 18; Richard Bauckham, "For Whom Were the Gospels Written?," in *The Gospels for All Christians: Rethinking the Gospel Audiences*, ed. Richard Bauckham (Grand Rapids, MI: Eerdmans, 1998), 28; James Dunn, *Jesus Remembered: Christianity in the Making* (Grand Rapids, MI: Eerdmans, 2003), 185; Dale C. Allison, "Structure, Biographical Impulse, and the *Imitatio Christi*," in *Studies in Matthew: Interpretation Past and Present* (Grand Rapids, MI: Baker Academic, 2005), 135–55; Seán Freyne, "Early Christian Imagination and the Gospels," in *The Earliest Gospels: The Origins and Transmission of the Earliest Christian Gospels, the Contributions of the Chester Beatty Gospel Codex P45*, ed. Charles Horton, JSNTSup 258 (New York: T&T Clark, 2004), 2–12 ; Seán Freyne, "Mark's Gospel and Ancient Biography," in *The Limits of Ancient Biography*, ed. Brian McGing and Judith Mossman (Swansea: Classical Press of Wales, 2006), 63–75; Richard Burridge, "Gospel: Genre," in *Dictionary of Jesus and the Gospels*, 2nd ed., ed. J. B. Green, Jeannine K. Brown, and Nicholas Perrin (Downers Grove, IL: InterVarsity Press Academic, 2013), 337–8; Michael F. Bird, *The Gospel of the Lord: How the Early Church Wrote the Story of Jesus* (Grand Rapids, MI: Eerdmans, 2014), 270–2; Justin M. Smith, *Why Bios? On the Relationship between Gospel Genre and Implied Audience*, LNTS 518 (New York: Bloomsbury/T&T Clark, 2015), 1–3; Craig S. Keener and Edward T. Wright, eds., *Biographies and Jesus: What Does It Mean for the Gospels to Be Biographies?* (Lexington, KY: Emeth Press, 2016); Jean-Noël Aletti, *Jésus, une vie à raconter: Essai sur le genre littéraire des évangiles de Matthieu, de Marc et de Luc* (Bruxelles: Lessius, 2016); and Michael R. Licona, *Why Are There Differences in the Gospels? What We Can Learn from Ancient Biography* (Oxford: Oxford University Press, 2017). Those who say Mark, while containing many similarities to ancient biographies, remains unique, include Graham Stanton, *Jesus of Nazareth in New Testament Preaching*, SNTSMS 27 (New York: Cambridge University Press, 1974), 117–36; Norman Perrin and Dennis C. Duling, *The New Testament: An Introduction*, 2nd ed. (New York: Harcourt Brace Jovanovich, 1982), 233; Joel Marcus, *Mark 1–8: A New Translation with Introduction and Commentary*, AB 27 (New York: Doubleday, 1999), 69; A. Y. Collins, *Mark*, 42; and Becker, *The Birth of Christian History*, 71. The following quotation from

the individual differences within the numerous biographies in the ancient world, while also maintaining familial similarities. When Mark transgresses these boundaries by, for example, incorporating other (nonbiographical) literary forms or themes (e.g., Mark 13), the Gospel is not alone in the *bios/vita* family tree.[19] Speaking to the relative flexibility of a genre, Seán Freyne's conclusion is fitting: "It is only by attending to the distortions as well as the similarities that it will be possible to discern the creativity and conventionality of Mark, Plutarch, or indeed any other ancient biographer."[20] In sum, biographies provide a close macro-literary analogy in the ancient world to Mark, a genre type in which Mark does not wholly fit but which the Gospel may creatively distort or "bend."[21]

Running parallel to this claim, scholarship on Greco-Roman biographies has long acknowledged that morality, as a value, is part and parcel of this literary genre.[22] This chapter will offer a brief discussion of moral formation in ancient biographies and then turn to several examples: Xenophon's *Memorabilia*, Philostratus's *Life of Apollonius*, Philo's *Life of Moses*, selections from Josephus's *Antiquities*, and, finally, Plutarch's *Lives*. The conclusion will address what the moral ecology of ancient biographies might suggest for Mark.

2.3 Biography and Morality

According to Graham Stanton, "Biographical writing was never purely historical, but was always ethical in intentions."[23] Greco-Roman biographies endorse character formation, often characterized by the imitation of a divine sage or politician. To be clear, this is not

---

Loveday Alexander summarizes this latter group's impulse: "[The gospel tradition is] a form whose external shape is strongly reminiscent of Greek *bios* but whose narrative mode and theological framework (connectives, narrative structure, use of direct speech, intertextuality) owe much more to the Bible" ("What Is a Gospel?" in *The Cambridge Companion to the Gospels*, ed. Stephen C. Barton [Cambridge: Cambridge University Press, 2006], 29).

[19] Hägg correctly contends that the size of one's genre-metric determines if and how the Gospels fit within the category of biography (*Art of Biography*, 97, 152).

[20] Freyne, "Mark's Gospel and Ancient Biography," 72. For language of genre flexibility, see also Momigliano, *Greek Biography*, 105–21; Richard Burridge, *What Are the Gospels? A Comparison with Graeco-Roman Biographies*, 2nd ed. (Grand Rapids, MI: Eerdmans, 2004), 59, 56–7, 269; and Keener and Wright, *Biographies and Jesus*, 6–8.

[21] The language of genre bending is a conceptual nod to Harold Attridge, "Genre Bending in the Fourth Gospel?," *JBL* 121 (2002): 3–21. This idea has been applied to Mark's genre by Charles Talbert, "Once Again: Gospel Genre," *Semeia* 43 (1988): 53–73; and John T. Carroll, *Jesus and the Gospels: An Introduction* (Louisville, KY: Westminster John Knox Press, 2016), 51.

[22] The term value is derived from Burridge (*What Are the Gospels?*, 119):

> Values are connected with the world-view being described or mediated; this may be one shared by the author and which he wishes to impart to the reader or audience, or it may be one internal to the work, which is merely being described. As a generic feature, however, it can be useful ... Works of the same genre will often breathe a similar atmosphere.

Charles Talbert uses the word "attitude" (*What Is a Gospel? The Genre of Canonical Gospels* [Philadelphia: Fortress Press, 1977], 115–31).

[23] Stanton, *Jesus of Nazareth*, 123. Or, as Pliny the Younger has it, "[Humans] learn better from examples, which have the great merit of proving that their advice is practicable" (*Pan.* 45.6 [Betty Radice, LCL]).

the *only* purpose of Greco-Roman biographies, but it is a frequent and pervasive one.[24] In this regard, Plutarch's reasons for recounting the story of Alexander prove most helpful:

> For it is not Histories [ἱστορίας] that I am writing, but Lives [βίους]; and in the most illustrious deeds there is not always a manifestation of virtue or vice, nay, a slight thing like a phrase or a jest often makes a greater revelation of character than battles where thousands fall, or the greatest armaments, or sieges of cities. Accordingly, just as painters get the likenesses in their portraits from the face and the expression of the eyes, wherein the character [τὸ ἦθος] shows itself, but make very little account of the other parts of the body, so I must be permitted to devote myself rather to the signs of the soul [τὰ τῆς ψυχῆς σημεῖα] in men, and by means of these portray the life of each, leaving to others the description of their great contests.[25]

It is clear from elsewhere in Plutarch that the "signs of the soul" in Alexander refer to moral formation produced by proper learning (*Alex.* 8.4; *Alex. Fort.* 1.4). In his analogy of the painter, quoted above, Plutarch contends that his portrait reveals the ἦθος of the subject. It is precisely Alexander's character that Plutarch intends to highlight, as is the case for many of the subjects in his biographies (e.g., *Per.* 2; *Pomp.* 8; *Cim.* 2; *Dem.* 1; *Sol.* 27). In the case of Solon, Plutarch states that a story's "chronology" (χρόνος) is far less important than its ability to correctly convey Solon's character (ἦθος), specifically for the purpose of emulation (e.g., *Per.* 1–2). In like fashion, the second-century author, Lucian, describes the purpose for his biography of Demonax as follows:

> It is now fitting to tell of Demonax for two reasons—that he may be retained in memory by men of culture as far as I can bring it about, and that young men of good instincts who aspire to philosophy may not have to shape themselves [τῶν παραδειγμάτων σφᾶς] by ancient precedents alone, but may be able to set themselves a pattern from our modern world and to copy [ζηλοῦν] that man, the best of all the philosophers whom I know about.[26]

Lucian writes about the noble philosopher Demonax for the purpose of moral imitation. Students of philosophy are invited, according to Lucian, "to shape themselves," not

---

[24] Consider also the work of David Tiede (*The Charismatic Figure as Miracle Worker*, SBLDS 1 [Missoula, MT: Society of Biblical Literature, 1972], 30–70), who culminates his study with the following remark:

> The most clearly defined stream of tradition that this study has identified is that of the depiction of the heroes of moral virtue in the philosophical tradition. Whether the figure in question is Plato's Socrates, Dio of Prusa's Diogenes, Plutarch's Alexander, or Philo's Moses, the elevated or divine status of the charismatic figure rests upon his characterization as a sage and possessor of virtue who can serve as a paradigm for moral edification. (Ibid., 291)

Tiede's artificial division of traditions about holy men has been refuted (cf. Cox, *Biography*, 30–4; Burridge, *What Are the Gospels?*, 18), but his detection of a moral emphasis throughout "divine man" traditions is right. See also Hadas and Smith's definition of an aretalogy, "a formal account of the remarkable career of an impressive teacher that was used as a basis for moral instruction" (*Heroes and Gods*, 3).

[25] *Alex.* 1.2–3 (Bernadotte Perrin, LCL).

[26] *Dem.* 1 (Harmon, LCL).

only from the precepts of theoretical ideas but also from the life of a specific person. While these directives to the reader are not ubiquitous, when they do appear, they reflect a common internal feature of many ancient biographies. The philosopher, statesmen, or hero elicits moral emulation from the reader: he teaches them how to live. Importantly, this feature is not restricted to Greco-Roman biographies alone; it also appears in, for example, Greco-Roman and Jewish historiography. The archetype of Jewish Hellenistic historiography, Josephus, offers an array of characters that the reader is directed to imitate. Josephus presents the unsuspecting necromantic woman of Endor, for instance, as a character worthy of emulation. Concerning her, Josephus reflects, "It is well, then, to take this woman for an example and show kindness to all who are in need, and to regard nothing as nobler than this or more befitting the human race or more likely to make God gracious and ready to bestow upon us His blessings."[27] In the ancient world, biographical discourse, even as it appears within historical or historiographical writings, aimed to shape a reader's character.[28] The Gospel of Mark appears to tap into this type of moral formation, but not in a straightforward way. Unlike the woman of Endor, who clearly models hospitality in the history of reception,

---

[27] *Ant.* 6.340-2 (Thackeray, LCL).

[28] Because moral formation in antiquity also involved the rhetorical practice of mimesis, I would like to clarify the use of "imitation" or "emulation" in this chapter. The Gospel of Mark makes no mention of mimesis. While it is a recurring subject in Greco-Roman education, it is does not appear in Mark in any obvious way. For ways in which mimesis does appear in traditional Greco-Roman models of education, see Richard McKeon, "Literary Criticism and the Concept of Imitation in Antiquity," in *Critics and Criticism: Ancient and Modern*, ed. R. S. Crane (Chicago: University of Chicago Press, 1968), 147–57; D. A. Russell, "De Imitatione," in *Creative Imitation and Latin Literature*, ed. David West and Tony Woodman (Cambridge: Cambridge University Press, 1979), 1–16; George A. Kennedy, *A New History of Classic Rhetoric* (Princeton, NJ: Princeton University Press, 1994), 41–5, 163–4; Raffaella Cribiore, *Gymnastics of the Mind: Greek Education in the Hellenistic and Roman Egypt* (Princeton, NJ: Princeton University Press, 2001); and Brad McAdon, *Rhetorical Mimesis and the Mitigation of Early Christian Conflicts: Examining the Influence That Greco-Roman Mimesis May Have in the Composition of Matthew, Luke, and Acts* (Eugene, OR: Pickwick, 2018). Quintilian is a prime example for this form of rhetorical mimesis (*Inst. Orat.* 1.1.36). I am not convinced that this kind of rhetorical practice is found in Mark, contra Dennis R. MacDonald, *The Homeric Epics and the Gospel of Mark* (New Haven, CT: Yale University Press, 2000); Dennis R. MacDonald, *My Turn: A Critique of Critics of "Mimesis Criticism,"* OPIAC 53 (Claremont, CA: Institute for Antiquity and Christianity, 2009); and Joel L. Watts, *Mimetic Criticism and the Gospel of Mark: An Introduction and Commentary* (Eugene, OR: Wipf and Stock, 2013). If imitation appears in this chapter, I refer to the imitation of one's teacher specifically. As in the words of Seneca, "the living voice and intimacy of a common life will help you more than the written word" (*Ep.* 6.5 [Gummere, LCL]). Andrew Pitts attempts to move beyond Dennis MacDonald by suggesting that, for example, "even if the evangelist frames his narrative in light of certain Homeric passages, that on its own does not require that Markan mimesis is purely aesthetic" ("The Origins of Greek Mimesis and the Gospel of Mark: Genre as a Potential Constraint in Assessing Markan Imitation," in *Ancient Education and Early Christianity*, ed. Matthew Ryan Hauge and Andrew W. Pitts, LNTS 533 [New York: Bloomsbury T&T Clark, 2016], 135). Unfortunately, in none of his suggestions does Pitts explore the possibility that rhetorical imitation in Mark could also apply to what George Kennedy calls "dramatic" imitation (cf. *Classical Rhetoric and Its Christian and Secular Tradition from Ancient to Modern Times* [Chapel Hill: University of North Carolina Press, 1980], 116–17). Like Kennedy, I am using imitation to describe the practice of emulating living models, as is commonly the case in Plutarch's *Lives* (e.g., *Per.* 1–2). See also Abraham Malherbe, "Exhortation in First Thessalonians," *NovT* 25 (1983): 238–56; Edward P. J. Corbett, "The Theory and Practice of Imitation in Classical Rhetoric," *College Composition and Communication* 22 (1971): 243–51; Allison, "Structure, Biographical Impulse," 149; Gerhard Schneider, "Imitatio Dei als Motiv der 'Ethik Jesu,'" in *Neues Testament und Ethik für Rudolf Schnackenburg*, ed. Helmut Merklein (Freiburg: Herder, 1989), 71–83; and

or Lucian's Demonax, "the best of all the philosophers," Mark's central character, Jesus, speaks in riddles (4:13), offends local farmers (5:17), and appears to disregard certain purity traditions of his day (5:41; 7:5, 24–26). Imitating this character appears, as evidenced by his disciples, quite challenging (8:31–33; 9:18; 10:35–45; 15:33–41). It is for this reason that a close examination of moral formation in ancient biographies is required in order to grasp the ways in which Mark's Gospel bends the reader's expectations of its central figure.

2.4 A Survey of Select Primary Sources

In this section I have selected an array of ancient biographical material in order to demonstrate their moral undercurrents. Obviously, many more biographical works could have been offered for early comparisons,[29] including the Gospels of Matthew, Luke, or John, or in late antiquity, where Christian iterations of biographies abound.[30] My selection of Philo's *Life of Moses* and portions of Josephus's *Antiquities* serves two purposes. Philo and Josephus represent two first-century Jewish story writers, the former a biographer and the latter a historiographer who integrates substantial biographical material. Additionally, I am responding to those who exclude Jewish biographical material in discussions of the Gospels.[31] While historiography is in a genre debate of its own, a number of notable episodes in Josephus's *Antiquities* present characters for moral consideration in a manner similar to ancient biographies.[32] In conclusion, I will turn my attention to Mark's account of Jesus.

Xenophon's Memorabilia

Discussions of ancient biographies frequently commence with Xenophon (*c*.430–*c*.350 BCE).[33] While he is not the first biographer,[34] he leaves a large imprint

---

Cornelis Brennema, *Mimesis in the Johannine Literature: A Study in Johannine Ethics*, LNTS 498 (New York: T&T Clark, 2018), 26.

[29] E.g., Porphry's *Life of Pythagoras*, Iamblichus's *Pythagorean Life*, Diogenes Laertius's *Lives of Imminent Philosophers*, or Arrian's *Discourses of Epictetus*.

[30] E.g., Athanasius's *Life of Anthony*, Eusebius's *Life of Constantine*, and Jerome's *Life of St. Paul the Hermit*. For Greek biography's influence on late antique Christian education, see Samuel Rubenson, "Philosophy and Simplicity: The Problem of Classical Education in Early Christian Biography," in *Greek Biography and Panegyric in Late Antiquity*, ed. Thomas Hägg and Philip Rousseau (Berkeley: University of California Press, 2000), 110–39.

[31] See the relevant critique of Burridge by Adela Yarbro Collins in "Genre and the Gospels," *JR* 75 (1995): 239–46.

[32] As in Plutarch's *Lives*, Josephus's examples are not always positive. This use of biographical literature for moral foils is not unlike Aristoxenus's *Life of Socrates* and *Life of Pythagoras*.

[33] Hägg, *Art of Biography*, 10. On the other hand, Burridge does not consider the *Memorabilia* to be a biography, due to its "excessive length, philosophical dialogue and lack of chronology" (*What Are the Gospels?*, 149). I would contend that the *Memorabilia* contains many generic features common to biographies, including the opening feature of title, identification of the central subject's name, topics pertaining to the subject's virtuous deeds, and the subject's death.

[34] Cox lists Skylax of Caryanda and Xanthus of Lydia as possible predecessors (*Biography*, 6); for a similar case, see also Leslie Kurke, *Aesopic Conversations: Popular Tradition, Cultural Dialogue, and the Invention of Greek Prose* (Princeton, NJ: Princeton University Press, 2011), 265–300.

on the development of biographies. According to the account in Diogenes Laertius (*Lives* 2.6.48), Xenophon received a personal call from Socrates to "follow me and learn" (ἕπου τοίνυν ... καὶ μάνθανε), which, whether historical or not, corresponds to Xenophon's first-person details of Socrates's life (*Mem.* 1.4.2; 2.4.1; 2.5.1). Of the works by Xenophon potentially relevant for the present chapter (e.g., *Memorabilia*, *Cyropaedia*, and *Agesilaus*), I devote the entirety of this section to the *Memorabilia*, Xenophon's apologetic account of the life of Socrates.

Xenophon's title is suggestive: ΑΠΟΜΝΗΜΟΝΕΥΜΑΤΩΝ (*Mem.* 1; 2.1; 3.1; 4.1). Xenophon collects his own "memoires" of Socrates, a term used by Justin Martyr to describe the Gospels (*Dial.* 106.3).[35] As Patricia Cox notes, "the process of 'mythologizing' a man's life by using fiction to convey truth became one of the enduring features of biography."[36] One aspect of this mythologizing is how Xenophon prioritizes a more episodic format over a strict chronology.[37] Contrary to the typical structure of an encomium, there are no details concerning Socrates's birth, education, or youth. Xenophon's goal, instead, is to present Socrates as the ideal moral teacher, refuting the charges brought against him.[38] Xenophon's production is nothing short of revolutionary. Or, as it is artfully phrased by Michael Flowers, Xenophon's "penchant for literary innovation" freed him from concern "about breaking any tacit rules or normative expectations."[39] At one of its earliest stages, biography is quite malleable.

As for its structure, the *Memorabilia* begins with a refutation of claims made against Socrates's character in the form of a defense (1.1–2); the latter half of the work illustrates Socrates's character in word and deed (1.3–4.8),[40] concluding with an account of Socrates's final days before his death (4.8.1–11). Xenophon's writings represent a shift away from more standard methods of historical writing to moral history.[41] As Thomas Hägg puts it, Xenophon seeks to "propagate certain social and moral values for which he found Socrates a suitable mouthpiece and his way of life the perfect illustration."[42] On the surface, it would seem that this aim is shared with the Gospel writers.

Xenophon's main character, Socrates, embodies the ideals of virtue and leadership (4.8.11). If one places Socrates alongside the line-up of characters about whom

---

[35] For more on the gospels as "memoires," see Larsen, "Accidental Publication," 362–87.
[36] Cox, *Biography*, 8. While Xenophon may not strive for veracity in the modern historical sense, he does narrate events as if he were present (*Mem.* 1.4.2; 2.4.1; 2.10.1; 4.3.2) or, at least, as if he overheard them (4.3.2).
[37] Hägg, *Art of Biography*, 25. One ought to keep in mind that biographers do not juxtapose mythology and history, per se, as in Lucian. *De Hist. Cons.*, 59–63.
[38] For more on Xenophon's goals in writing, see Shiner, *Follow Me!*, 37–8.
[39] Michael A. Flowers, "Introduction," in *The Cambridge Companion to Xenophon*, ed. Michael A. Flowers (Cambridge: Cambridge University Press, 2017), 10.
[40] For more on outline, see Hägg, *Art of Biography*, 25; M. D. Macleod, *Xenophon: Apology and Memorabilia I: With Introduction, Translation, and Commentary* (Oxford: Oxbow Books, 2008), 58–60.
[41] For the moral shift in historical writings, see Leo, *Biographie*, 89–90.
[42] Hägg, *Art of Biography*, 29; Clyde Weber Votaw, "The Gospels and Contemporary Biographies— Concluded," *AJT* 19 (1915): 219.

Xenophon writes, there is no contest (e.g., Agesilaus, Jason, or Cyrus the Younger).[43] Morality, for Socrates, concerns the examination of the self (ἐξετάζω; 2.5.1, 4; 3.7.9), facilitated by education (1.2.21–23; 2.6.39; 3.8.2–3; 3.9.2; 4.1.2), self-discipline (ἐγκράτεια; 1.5.1; 2.1.1; 4.5.1), and virtue (ἀρετή; 1.2.2; 1.2.64; 2.6.22; 3.9.5).[44] Socrates denies himself the title of teacher (*Mem.* 1.2.3; 1.2.8; cf. Plato, *Ap.* 19e). Instead, Xenophon presents Socrates as a moral example to those who surround him.[45]

The theme of Socrates and his pupils (συνόντες) is a strong thread running throughout the *Memorabilia*. In part, Xenophon defends the charge brought against Socrates: his corruption of the youth (1.2.64; 4.8.10).[46] Moreover, Socrates's more rancorous followers need to be explained.[47] For this reason, Aristippus, chief among them, is presented as undisciplined (2.1), hedonistic (2.1.1–10), and groping for power (1.2.60; 2.1.16–17).[48] The concern to defend Socrates against his followers is

---

[43] Melina Tamiolaki makes the case that Socrates is the paragon of virtue for Xenophon ("Virtue and Leadership in Xenophon: Idea Leaders or Losers?" in *Xenophon: Ethical Principles and Historical Enquiry*, ed. Fiona Hobden and Christopher Tuplin [Boston: Brill, 2012], 563–89). See also Richard Fernando Buxton, "Xenophon on Leadership: Commanders as Friends," in *The Cambridge Companion to Xenophon*, ed. Michael A. Flowers (Cambridge: Cambridge University Press, 2017), 323–37; and Vincent Azoulay, *Xénophon et les grâces du pouvoir: de la charis au charisme*, HAM 77 (Paris: Publications de la Sorbonne, 2004), 396–413.

[44] Consider Cicero's later comment about Socrates:

> But from the ancient of days down to the time of Socrates, who had listened to Archelaus the pupil of Anaxagoras, philosophy dealt with numbers and movements, with the problem whence all things came ... Socrates, on the other hand, was the first to call philosophy down from the heavens and set her in the cities of men and bring her also into their homes and compel her to ask questions about life and morality and things good and evil. (*Tusc.* 5.4.10 [King, LCL]; cf. *Mem* 1.1.15)

[45] This is likely for apologetic purposes. Ancient teachers, in theory, would be held responsible for the actions of their students. For Socrates's role as a teacher in Xenophon, see Donald R. Morrison, "Xenophon's Socrates as Teacher," in *Xenophon*, ed. V. J. Gray (Oxford: Oxford University Press, 2010), 195–227.

[46] Much of Xenophon's Socrates is crafted in contrast to the sophists (1.1.11). According to Louis-André Dorion, while the text refers to them as τῶν σοφιστῶν, these are more likely "Presocratics," chiefly represented by Anaxagoras, e.g., *Mem.* 4.7.6 ("Xenophon and Greek Philosophy," in *The Cambridge Companion to Xenophon*, ed. Michael A. Flowers [Cambridge: Cambridge University Press, 2017], 38–41).

[47] In order to distance Socrates from his reprobate offspring, Xenophon claims that Socrates, like a parent, is not to be blamed for his companion's moral deficiencies (a move Plato avoids, cf. *Ap.* 33a5–d9). As Tamiolaki notes, this does not accord with typical expectations of a teacher (Tamiolaki, "Virtue and Leadership in Xenophon," 585; cf. Shiner, *Follow Me!*, 43 n. 15). Should not the teacher be held responsible for (or exonerated by) the actions of his students? Xenophon's nuance, in this case, relies on the length of time Critias and Alcibiades spent under Socrates's tutelage. When the bird leaves the nest, it is no longer under the supervision (or the responsibility) of its mother (*Mem.* 1.2.17–18, 19–28; cf. Shiner, *Follow Me!*, 43). The apologetic move to exonerate the teacher from his disciples' actions may also occur in the Gospels, at least in Matthew and Luke (cf. David Daube, "Responsibilities of Master and Disciples in the Gospels," *NTS* 19 [1972–3]: 1–15). Xenophon's effort to dissociate Socrates from any particular person appears to be an unoriginal defense (cf. Dorion, "Xenophon and Greek Philosophy," 39).

[48] Cf. Diogenes Laertius, *Lives* 2.8.66–83. Recent scholarship has speculated about the actual philosophical connections between Socrates and Aristippus. In effect, while Xenophon couches this exchange as a disagreement of sorts, some claim that Aristippus may have learned hedonism from his teacher (David M. Johnson, "Aristippus at the Crossroads: The Politics of Pleasure in Xenophon's *Memorabilia*," *Polis* 26 [2009]: 204–22; Kurt Lampe, *The Birth of Hedonism: The Cyrenaic Philosophers and Pleasure as a Way of Life* [Princeton, NJ: Princeton University Press, 2015], 27–34).

accompanied by several idiosyncrasies: Socrates refuses the title of teacher, he does not have "disciples" (μαθηταί) but "companions,"[49] and he is often portrayed as picky in his selection of pupils.[50]

The content of Socrates's teaching includes straightforward moral values: honoring one's parents (2.2.14; 4.4.20), familial discord (2.3), making friends (2.4–6), the appropriate conduct of civil leaders (4.4.15–17; 4.6.12), avoiding idleness (ἀργία) and the pitfalls of wealth (4.1.5), and of course, maintaining self-control (ἐγκράτεια; 4.5.1).[51] To achieve such levels of moral excellence, one must, according to Xenophon, imitate Socrates (1.7.1–3; 3.5.14; 3.10 1–6; 4.3.18).[52] In the words of Xenophon, "by letting his own light shine, [Socrates] led his disciples [συνδιατρίβοντας][53] to hope that through imitation [μιμουμένους] of him they would develop likewise" (1.2.3).[54] Xenophon underscores that this imitation is achieved not only by one's words but also by one's deeds (4.4.1).

Finally, the linchpin of imitation for Xenophon is one's proximity to Socrates. This is best illustrated in the example of Euthydemus, the ideal student, who had received "the best education" (4.2.1). Upon first examination, Socrates considers him to be a suitable candidate for learning wisdom (4.2.1). He is handsome, committed to study, and attentive (4.2.8). The kind of "excellence" (ἀρετή) he desires is leadership, of the statesman or managerial quality, which Xenophon's Socrates considers the most noble (4.2.11).[55] Socrates launches into an intense series of questions, otherwise known as the Socratic elenchus, leading Euthydemus to despair, or aporia, eventually admitting he is incapable of answering Socrates's questions (4.2.23). Euthydemus resolves that he must spend "as much time as possible with Socrates" (4.2.40). It is at this point that Socrates reveals everything to him. After spending extensive time with him, Euthydemus becomes a near parrot of Socrates (4.6.1–11). Conversely, in the disappointing cases of Critias and Alcibiades, while they learn from Socrates and, at one point at least, perform honorably, they only do so under his supervision. It is their eventual departure from Socrates's orbit that pitches Critias and Alcibiades into corruption. They cease imitating their teacher upon departure (1.2.24).

In summary, Xenophon's *Memorabilia* offers moral formation in the example of Socrates, a so-called teacher, worthy of emulation. Socrates, according to Xenophon, does not profess a systematic doctrine but advises each student as they enter his sphere of influence. Because of this, Socrates is not responsible for the students who learn from him but soon after leave his tutelage. Regardless of his followers' actions,

---

[49] Xenophon uses a variety of terms, including συνόντες, συνδιατρίβοντας, and φίλοις.
[50] On Socrates's selectivity, see Morrison, "Xenophon's Socrates as Teacher," 199–206.
[51] E.g., *Mem.* 1.5.1; on Xenophon's use of ἐγκράτεια in the *Memorabilia*, see Macleod, *Xenophon: Apology and Memorabilia*, 149–50.
[52] Tamiolaki, "Virtue and Leadership in Xenophon," 581; Votaw, "The Gospels," esp. 223.
[53] *LSJ*, s.v., those with whom one may "pass or spend time."
[54] Consider Socrates's finals words in the *Memorabilia*: "I wronged no one at any time nor corrupted anyone, but strove to make my companions [τοὺς ἐμοὶ συνόντας] better" (4.8.10).
[55] Large portions of the *Memorabilia* deal with political leadership as the moral ideal. For the prominent theme of politics in Xenophon, see Vivienne J. Gray, *Xenophon's Mirror of Princes: Reading the Reflections* (Oxford: Oxford University Press, 2011), 5–69; and Houliang Lu *Xenophon's Theory of Moral Education* (Newcastle: Cambridge Scholars, 2015), 47–51.

Socrates embodies the political leader par excellence. In the words of David Morrison, "If Socrates had been just as clever a philosopher, and just as convinced of his own ignorance, but greedy, lecherous, and power-hungry, neither Xenophon nor Plato would have thought him a good man."[56] Reading Xenophon, one is taught to live as Socrates lived.

Philostratus's *Life of Apollonius*

Philostratus's *Life of Apollonius* (c.217–230 CE), is often compared with the Gospels and early Christianity.[57] By the turn of the seventeenth century, *Life of Apollonius* was evaluated by a majority of scholars as a polemical work against Christianity. Some appraised Philostratus more moderately, even positively, but many others reached less charitable conclusions.[58] It was not until the work of F. C. Baur in 1832 that a more scientific comparison between Apollonius and Jesus began. In the premodern period, the figure of Apollonius captivated attentive Christians as early as Origen (cf. *Cels.* 6.41).[59] By the fourth century, Hierocles, a supposedly fervent anti-Christian Roman official,[60] outlined the close similarities between Apollonius and Jesus in order to discredit the latter (*The Word of the Lover of Truth*; φιλαλήθης λόγος).[61]

The details of Philostratus's life (c.161–249 CE), as an author and writer, are unclear.[62] According to the *Suda*, there were at least three figures named Philostratus,

---

[56] Morrison, "Xenophon's Socrates as Teacher," 227.
[57] A small selection of works upon which this section draws includes H. Doergens, "Apollonius von Tyana in Parallele zu Christus dem Herren," *Theologie und Glaube* 25 (1933): 292–304; Ferdinand Christian Baur, *Apollonius von Tyana und Christus: Ein Beitrag zur Religionsgeschichte der ersten Jahrhunderte nach Christus* (Leipzig: L. F. Fues, 1876; repr., Hildesheim: G. Olms, 1966); G. Petzke, *Die Traditionen über Apollonius von Tyana und Das Neue Testament*, SCHNT 1 (Leiden: Brill, 1970), 10–16; Erkki Koskenniemi, *Apollonius von Tyana in der neutestamentlichen Exegese: Forschungsbericht und Weiterführung der Diskussion*, WUNT 2.61 (Tübingen: J. C. B. Mohr, 1994); Erkki Koskenniemi, "Apollonius of Tyana: A Typical ΘΕΙΟΣ ΑΝΗΡ?" *JBL* 117 (1998): 455–67; Robbins, *Jesus the Teacher*, 101–8.
[58] For a brief history of its reception, see Petzke, *Die Traditionen über Apollonius*, 10–16. Petzke cites the particularly entertaining conclusion of L. S. Tillemont that Apollonius was the "spawn of Satan" ("Ausgeburt des Teufels") sent during the time of Christ (ibid., 12).
[59] See also Arnobius, *Against the Gentiles*, 1.52.
[60] For more on Hierocles, see Aryeh Kofsky, *Eusebius of Caesarea Against Paganism*, JCPS 3 (Boston: Brill, 2000), 58–71; Petzke, *Die Traditionen über Apollonius*, 6–9.
[61] Preserved in Eusebius, *Against Hierocles*; cf. Lactantius, *Divine Institutes* 5.2–3; *On the Death of the Persecutors* 16.4. Eusebius seems ambivalent about the historical figure Apollonius. Most of his apology is directed toward Philostratus for misrepresenting Apollonius (43.3; 44.2; 44.3; 48.2). Hierocles cites the low level of education among Christians much like Celsus. Peter and Paul exaggerate details, but Philostratus has "reached a very high level of culture and honored truth," and writes so that "the acts of a virtuous man [ἀνδρὸς γενναίου], a friend of the gods" may not "go unknown" (2.2; "Eusebius's Reply to Hierocles" [Philostratus, *Apollonius of Tyana, Volume III: Letters of Apollonius. Ancient Testimonia. Eusebius's Reply to Hierocles*, ed. and trans. Christopher P. Jones, LCL 458 (Cambridge, MA: Harvard University Press, 2006)]).
[62] For historical evidence regarding Philostratus, see W. C. Wright, "Introduction," in *Philostratus Lives of the Sophists, Eunapius Lives of Philosophers*, LCL 134 (Cambridge, MA: Harvard University Press, 1921), ix–xli; Petzke, *Die Traditionen über Apollonius*, 1–5; Graham Anderson, *Philostratus, Biography and Belles Lettres in the Third Century A.D.* (Dover: Croom Helm, 1986), 1–22; Christopher P. Jones, "Introduction," in *Philostratus: The Life of Apollonius of Tyana*, LCL 16 (Cambridge, MA: Harvard University Press, 2005), 1–3; Adam M. Kemezis, *Greek Narratives of the Roman Empire under the*

further complicating the matter. The Philostratus responsible for the *Lives of the Sophists* may have also authored *Life of Apollonius*, since the former work refers to the latter (cf. *Lives* 570). From the *Lives of the Sophists*, we learn that Philostratus belonged to the self-designated "second sophistic" movement (δευτέρας σοφιστικῆς; *Lives* 481, 507):[63] a group of expert orators in whom "shines the light of perfect lucidity ... at once sublime and seductive, energetic and delightful."[64] Additionally, Philostratus claims to belong to an elite intellectual circle (*Life* 1.3; 8.29) that included Emperor Septimius Severus's wife, Julia Domna (cf. Dio Cassius, *Hist. rom.* 75.15.7; 78.18.2). If Philostratus belonged to such a prestigious group, then he would have been surrounded, and potentially influenced, by elites.[65] For this reason, scholars speculate the intended purpose of *Life of Apollonius*. If Philostratus is close to the emperor, has he produced imperial propaganda,[66] perhaps countering Christian literature or perhaps in defense of traditional Hellenism?[67] Regardless of his intentions, which are likely multivalent, Philostratus exhibits the high class and education Hierocles attributes to him (*Hier.* 2.2).

Using the sources available to him (*Life* 1.2–3), Philostratus writes a biography of the first-century itinerant Apollonius.[68] Apollonius is a character with whom the Roman world had developed a growing fascination, especially among upper-class elites (e.g., *Hist. Aug. Sev.* 29.2; Dio Cassius, *Hist. rom.* 78.18.4), and Philostratus's work is not the only biography about the famed itinerant philosopher.[69] In order to set apart his biography from others, he offers several reasons for writing. First, he describes his work as apologetic. According to Philostratus, some have disapprovingly "deprived" (ἀφαιροῦνται) Apollonius of his wisdom: Philostratus intends to correct such widespread ignorance with his accurate (ἐξακριβῶσαι) "chronology" (χρόνοις) of Apollonius's life (*Life* 1.2). Second, he claims to write in order "to bring profit to those

---

Severans: Cassius Dio, Philostratus and Herodian, GCRM (New York: Cambridge University Press, 2014), 150.

[63] For a full discussion of the "second sophist" movement, see Tim Whitmarsh, *The Second Sophist*, GR 35 (Oxford: Oxford University Press, 2005), 1–22.

[64] Philostratus is referring to the philosopher Aeschines in this passage (*Lives*, 510).

[65] For a historical discussion of Julia Domna's circle, see G. W. Bowersock, *Greek Sophists in the Roman Empire* (Oxford: Clarendon Press, 1969), 101–9.

[66] This is the argument made by Inge Mennen, "The Image of an Emperor in Trouble: Legitimation and Representation of Power by Caracalla," in *The Impacts of Imperial Rome on Religions, Rituals and Religious Life in the Roman Empire*, ed. L. De Blois, P. Funke, and J. Hahn, Impact of Empire 5 (Boston: Brill, 2006), 253–67; and O. D. Cordovana, "Between History and Myth: Septimius Severus and Leptis Magna," *GR* 59 (2012): 56–75.

[67] That Philostratus intends to defend traditional Hellenism, see Kemezis, *Greek Narratives*, 158–61.

[68] On the designation of Philostratus's *Life* as a biography, see Burridge, *What Are the Gospels?*, 150–84; and Kemezis, *Greek Narrative*, 158–63. Scholarship has questioned the historicity of the character Damis, from whom Philostratus claims to receive some of his information about Apollonius (1.3.1). It seems plausible that Damis is a literary invention of Philostratus (cf. E. L. Bowie, "Apollonius of Tyana: Tradition and Reality," in *ANRW* 2.16.2, 1652–67; and Erkki Koskenniemi, "The Philostratean Apollonius as a Teacher," in *Theios Sophistes: Essays on Flavius Philostratus' Vita Apollonii*, ed. K. Demoen and D. Praet, MS 305 [Boston: Brill, 2009], 322).

[69] Philostratus mentions the four-volume biography of Moeragenes, who "was greatly ignorant about the Master" (*Life* 1.3), and Origen cites Moeragenes as authoritative (*Cels.* 6.41). Alternatively, Kemezis argues that Philostratus rehabilitates "a figure of doubtful respectability in general" (*Greek Narratives*, 167). If this is the case, Philostratus's apologetic intentions are reminiscent of that of Xenophon's for Socrates in *Memorabilia*.

who enjoy learning" (τοῖς τε φιλομαθεστέροις ὠφέλειαν; 1.3). Philostratus writes for those who wish to learn from Apollonius's words and actions (*Life* 1.2: καθ᾽ οὕς εἶπέ τι ἢ ἔπραξε). Of the relevant pedagogical subjects from which to choose, Philostratus lists Apollonius's teachings on gods, customs, morals (ἐθῶν), and laws (1.2).

Among the variety of reasons Philostratus writes, one purpose is the moral formation of the reader. In this regard, Graeme Miles's fresh assessment of Apollonius as an "interpreter within a text" is apt. Miles avers that while Apollonius himself may be beyond literal imitation (e.g., one cannot also perform his miracles), "through the text's cues to emulate the interpretive practices of Apollonius, readers too are urged to assimilate themselves to the protagonist."[70] In other words, the text produced by Philostratus teaches one to interpret the world as Apollonius does.

Unlike Xenophon's Socrates, Apollonius receives the title of "teacher" (διδάσκαλος) on a few occasions (5.38.2; 6.18). His students receive the corollary description of "companions" (ἑταῖρος; 1.16.4; 3.17.2; 5.21.1), "followers" (ἑπόμενοι; 2.41), "disciples" (ὁμιλητής; 1.16.3; 4.23; 4.37.2), and "choir" (χορός; 4.36.1).[71] One may recall Socrates's ambivalence toward his disciples and conclude that Apollonius had a more committed following; however, the commitment of students in Philostratus's *Life* is also more often short-term.[72]

Apollonius's teaching occurs mainly in dialogues, but not without a combined emphasis on action. In this regard, an important feature of Philostratus's presentation of Apollonius is the practical life (e.g., "Apollonius's lectures in Olympia were on very useful [χρήσιμος] subjects [4.31; cf. 5.17]").[73] His disciples likewise imitate their teacher's practical example, as in the following description of his followers: "Their chief aim in philosophy was to follow whatever he said or did" (τὸ ἔπεσθαι λέγοντί τε καὶ πράττοντι; 5.21.1; cf. 1.2.3; 4.1.1; 6.3.2). In the assessment of Erkki Koskenniemi,

> his words were interwoven with his deeds. In this sense, all his actions, including his miraculous deeds, such as exorcism (IV 20), his appearance in a strife-torn city during his silent period (I 15) and especially his opposition against Domitian (books 7–8), were part of his mission as a teacher. A philosopher who did not pursue ascetic ideals was not a philosopher.[74]

---

[70] Graeme Miles, "Reforming the Eyes: Interpreters and Interpretation in the *Vita Apollonii*," in *Theios Sophistes: Essays on Flavius Philostratus' Vita Apollonii*, ed. K. Demoen and D. Praet, MS 305 (Boston: Brill, 2009), 157. Whitney Taylor Shiner claims that the work is didactic and entertaining, intended to "develop character" (*Follow Me!*, 109, 116). Similarly, Marc Van Uytfanghe suggests that Philostratus presents Apollonius as a "modèle à imiter" ("La Vie d'Apollonius de Tyane et le discours hagiographie," in *Theios Sophistes: Essays on Flavius Philostratus' Vita Apollonii*, ed. K. Demoen and D. Praet, MS 305 [Boston: Brill, 2009], 364); as does A. Billault, *L'Univers de Philostrate*, CL 252 (Bruxelles: Latomus, 2000), 125.

[71] Apollonius's followers also receive more generic description in places, e.g., γνώριμοι (acquaintances) in 4.47.

[72] Damis is the exception, of course. Apollonius's elite followers appear more committed in the episode where Philolaus is on his way to Rome (4.35–38) and the disciples plummet from thirty-four to eight. Consider also *Life* 8.21, in which Philostratus describes a young cohort of "Apollonians."

[73] Koskenniemi, "The Philostratean Apollonius as a Teacher," 329.

[74] Ibid.

Apollonius is imitable in both word and deed. The contours of this imitation include, proper political leadership (5.31-39), asceticism,[75] and the defense of traditional Greek culture (4.29).[76]

Finally, Philostratus's moral aims for his biography are well illustrated in an episode where Apollonius commends the great Aesop for his clever use of storytelling "to teach great lessons":

> [Apollonius asks] "And what do you think Aesop is?" "Nothing but a teller of stories [μυθολόγον]," [Menippus] replied, "and of fables." "Which kind of story is philosophical [σοφοὶ τῶν μύθων]?" "The poetic kind," Menippus replied, "since they are recited as if they were fact." "And what about Aesop's kind?" "They are frogs ... donkeys, and nonsense for old women and children to chew on." "And yet in my opinion," said Apollonius, "Aesop's seem more conducive to philosophy [σοφίαν]. Stories about heroes, to which all poetry is devoted, corrupt their listeners. ... Aesop by contrast had the wisdom first of all not to place himself in the common run of such poets, but traveled a certain path of his own. Moreover, like those who give an excellent dinner with rather modest food, he uses humble subjects to teach great lessons [ἀπὸ σμικρῶν πραγμάτων διδάσκει μεγάλα], and after setting out his tale rounds it off with a 'Do this' or a 'Don't do that.' He also was more devoted to truth [φιλαλήθους] than the poets."[77]

It seems that Philostratus, for the most part, understands himself to be doing something similar with Apollonius. In writing *Life*, Philostratus is forming the reader's character in a way "more devoted to the truth" than the poets (5.14.3; 5.16.1). In this regard, where Mark diverges is important. While the moral lessons in Philostratus or Aesop tend to be practical, even straightforward, Mark's Jesus speaks in parables.

Philo's *Life of Moses*

Philo's *Life of Moses* represents an important analogy to the Gospels in the first century: Philo is a Jewish biographer writing in Greek during the time of Jesus.[78] A careful analysis reveals cogent similarities between Philo's *Life* and contemporary

---

[75] On asceticism in Philostratus, and the larger biographical tradition, see Cox, *Biography*, 25-30.
[76] Koskenniemi rightly suggests that the competing traditions about Apollonius presented by Philostratus give us an inconsistent picture ("The Philostratean Apollonius as a Teacher," 330-1; cf. Erkki Koskenniemi, "The Function of the Miracle Stories in Philostratus' *Vita Apollonii Tyanensis*," in *Wonders Never Cease: The Purpose of Narrating Miracle Stories in the New Testament and Its Religious Environment*, ed. M. Labahn and B. J. Lietaert Peerbolte, LNTS 288 [New York: T&T Clark, 2006], 80-2).
[77] *Life* 5.14.2-3 (Jones, LCL).
[78] On the biographical character of Philo's *Life*, see Louis H. Feldman, *Philo's Portrayal of Moses in the Context of Ancient Judaism*, CJA 15 (Notre Dame, IN: University of Notre Dame Press, 2007), 23. Not all scholars agree that Philo's *Life* is a biography (see Licona, *Differences in the Gospels*, 4). For a full discussion of the issue, see B. C. McGing, "Philo's Adaption of the Bible in his 'Life of Moses,'" in *The Limits of Ancient Biography*, ed. B. C. McGing and J. Mossman (Swansea: Classical Press of Wales, 2006), 117-40.

biographies of the same era. Chief among these similarities is Philo's intentions for writing. In *On Abraham*, Philo explains,

> These are such men as lived good and blameless lives, whose virtues stand permanently recorded in most holy scriptures, not merely to sound their praises but *for the instruction of the reader and an inducement to him to aspire to the same.* (*Abr.* 1.4)[79]

Philo records the lives of Abraham, Joseph, and Moses to instruct the reader (*Moses* 1.158–162; 2.292).[80] In the case of Joseph, for example, Philo offers a model for the "statesman" (πολιτικός; *Jos.* 1.1), much like the models for leadership found in both Xenophon's Socrates and Philostratus's Apollonius, described above.[81] With regard to Philo's *Life*, he offers two distinct purposes for writing. First, he intends to spread the news of Moses that has, in his opinion, received relative neglect by Greek authors "to their widespread disgrace" (1.3; cf. Philostratus, *Life* 1.2).[82] Second, Philo intends to portray the "guiding pattern" (ὑφήγησις)[83] of "good men and also their lives" (1.3). In his two volumes, Philo frames Moses's words and deeds as worthy of praise and emulation (1.6–7; 1.9.48). In Philo's words, Moses "has set before us, like some well-wrought picture, a piece of work beautiful and godlike, a model [παράδειγμα] for those who are willing to copy [μιμεῖσθαι] it" (1.28.158).[84] Yet again, a similar appraisal may be found concerning the central characters in Lucian's *Demonax* or Plutarch's *Alexander*.

Philo's *Life* is also distinct from his biblical commentaries in that his intended audience appears to be non-Jews.[85] For this reason, his strategy becomes "almost evangelistic in calling the readers to follow the hero."[86] Philo's portrait of Moses seeks

---

[79] Italics added. Unless otherwise noted, the texts and translations of Philo belong to F. H. Colson and G. H. Whitaker, 12 vols., LCL (Cambridge, MA: Harvard University Press, 1929–53).

[80] I am not arguing that moral teaching is the sole purpose of Philo's *Life of Moses*. For the many reasons Philo writes, see Burridge, *What Are the Gospels?*, 145–8. Burridge notes how Philo's concluding remark, τοιοῦτος μὲν ὁ βίος, conveys "what sort of person Moses was" (ibid., 147; cf. Lucian, *Demonax*, 67). For a list of those who appraise Philo's *Life* similarly, see Hindy Najman, *Seconding Sinai: The Development of Mosaic Discourse in Second Temple Judaism*, SJSJ 77 (Boston: Brill, 2003) 100–7; Mireille Hadas-Lebel, *Philo of Alexandria: A Thinker in the Jewish Diaspora*, trans. Robyn Fréchet, SPA 7 (Boston: Brill, 2012), 144–5; Esteban Hidalgo, "A Redaction-Critical Study on Philo's *On the Life of Moses*, Book One," in *Biographies and Jesus: What Does It Mean for the Gospels to Be Biographies?*, ed. Craig S. Keener and Edward T. Wright (Lexington, KY: Emeth Press, 2016), 287–9; Jason M. Zurawski, "Mosaic *Paideia*: The Law of Moses within Philo of Alexandria's Model of Jewish Education," *JSJ* 48 (2017): 480–505; Maren R. Niehoff, *Philo of Alexandria: An Intellectual Biography*, AYBRL (New Haven, CT: Yale University Press, 2018), 110–11.

[81] On Philo's portrayal of Joseph, see Hadas-Lebel, *Philo of Alexandria*, 139–41; Niehoff, *Philo*, 121–5.

[82] Moses was a relatively well-known figure outside of Judaism in antiquity, cf. Feldman, *Portrayal*, 1–16; John G. Gager, *Moses in Greco-Roman Paganism* (Nashville, TN: Abingdon Press, 1972).

[83] *LSJ*, s.v., "leading, guidance … guiding pattern."

[84] For the case that Philo shares pedagogical aims with the classic Roman discourse of exemplarity in his presentation of Moses, see James M. Petitfils, "A Tale of Two Moseses: Philo's *On the Life of Moses* and Josephus's *Jewish Antiquities* 2–4 in Light of the Roman Discourse of Exemplarity," in *Reading and Teaching Ancient Fiction: Jewish, Christian, and Greco-Roman Narratives*, ed. Sara R. Johnson, Rubén R. Dupertuis, and Christine Shea, WGRWSup 11 (Atlanta, GA: SBL Press, 2018), 153–64.

[85] E. R. Goodenough's argument for Philo's non-Jewish audience ("Philo's Exposition of the Law and His De Vita Mosis," *HTR* 26 [1933]: 109–25) continues to persuade, see Feldman, *Portrayal*, 11–16.

[86] Burridge, *What Are the Gospels?*, 146.

to convince his audience of Moses's unparalleled excellence in the Greco-Roman world (from birth [1.9], throughout adolescence [1.18–24], and, finally, in his death [2.288–92]).[87] Second, quite atypical of Philo's known writings, he avoids allegory, likely a consequence of his intended readership.[88] Third, as a type of biography, *Life of Moses* exhibits characteristic moral concerns. As is the case in Plutarch's *Lives*, Philo sketches a "well-wrought picture" of an exemplary figure in order to reveal the contours of his ἦθος (cf. *Moses* 1.158). In this regard, Maren Niehoff has argued that Plutarch provides "the most significant parallel" to Philo's *Life*, noting how each share a "pedagogical aim."[89]

If Philo's Moses is a moral model for non-Jews, then what does imitation of Moses entail? The moral lessons found in *Life of Moses* include avoiding the pitfalls of wealth (1.29–30; 1.152–153), practicing piety (1.146, 189; 2.66), self-control (1.26; 1.154, 296–299), and the care of the soul (1.279; 2.108, 183).[90] As a leader, Moses operates for the benefit of his subjects (1.75, 151), a quality Xenophon highlights in Socrates.

Overall, Philo's moral pedagogy is evident throughout (cf. *Moses* 1.325, 329; 2.8–11, 17, 135, 183).[91] In one place, Philo recounts the story of the plagues in Exodus for a lesson in piety (εὐσέβεια). In the wake of the Egyptian plagues, the Hebrews are neither spectators, nor merely survivors, but learners (μαθημάτων) of "the finest and most profitable of lessons" (1.146). In another case, Philo narrates the life of Phinehas as an example for imitation at the "command of Moses" (1.300–304; *Leg.* 3.242).[92] Phinehas's righteous zeal purges the "defiled" nations, who mimic the "impiety" of their king (1.300). Scores follow his lead and only those in whom piety is found are saved.[93] As Louis H. Feldman notes, Philo's concept of piety, "the queen of the virtues" (*Spec.* 4.147; cf. *Virt.* 9.51, 33.175; *Abr.* 37.208), is a shared moral value in much of Greco-Roman philosophy (cf. Plato, *Protagoras* 330B; Aristotle, *De Virt.* 5.1250B.22–23).[94] Moses,

---

[87] Feldman's account demonstrates, at every turn, how Philo's Moses is palatable to a Greek audience (*Portrayal*, 35–59). Philo's intended audience may lead him to manipulate his sources in places. For example, his imperfect speech is because "he considered that human eloquence compared with God's was dumbness" (1.83). In this regard, Hidalgo has demonstrated how Philo expands, minimizes, or omits certain elements of the biblical account of Moses in order to bolster Moses's positive resume ("Redaction-Critical Study on Philo's Life of Moses," 287–8).

[88] With exceptions, as in *Life* 2.81–103; see Feldman, *Portrayal*, 25–6.

[89] Niehoff offers several compelling reasons for comparing the two: (1) Both begin as Platonic philosophers; (2) both write biographies later in life; (3) both distinguish "regular history" and biography; and (4) both illustrate a figure's character in narrative form (*Philo*, 128). More specifically, Niehoff writes, "Parallel to Philo, [Plutarch] sees the biography as an extremely useful form of literature that is concerned with the teaching of virtuous action. ... Like Philo, he anticipates a sympathetic audience that is open to being instructed" (*Philo*, 128–9).

[90] For a more exhaustive list, see Feldman, *Portrayal*, 235–57.

[91] One potential caveat is the intentions of each of the two books. At the beginning of book two, Philo explains that the former work served to highlight Moses's "education and career as a ruler" while the latter "is concerned with matters allied and consequent to these" (2.1). Feldman reconciles this, in part, by labeling book one a "Plutarchian" type and book two as a "Suetonian" type (*Portrayal*, 22).

[92] Philo says the people of Israel copied (ἐμιμήσαντο) this example (τοῦτο ... παράδειγμα): "and massacred all their friends and kinsfolk who had taken part in the rites of these idols made by men's hands" (*Moses* 1.303). For more on Phinehas as an exemplary figure in Jewish traditions, see Francis Watson, *Paul and the Hermeneutics of Faith*, 2nd ed. (London: Bloomsbury T&T Clark, 2016), 160–7.

[93] See also Philo, *Moses* 2.171–173.

[94] Feldman, *Portrayal*, 256–8.

as the mouthpiece of God, enacts God's judgment upon the land correlative to one's piety (or lack thereof; *Moses* 1.146; 2.36, 53, 202). In this way, Philo creates a Moses in whom philosophy and theology find no contradiction (e.g., 2.66, 216). He is the ideal neighbor (1.35; 2.28–33), worthy of emulation by Jew and non-Jew alike. One of the most conspicuous overlaps with the Gospel of Mark is Moses's role as an agent of God. Just as Moses enacts judgment in behalf of God, so, too, does Jesus (Mark 9:42–50).

Josephus's *Antiquities*

Though Josephus "sharply criticizes the inclusion in history of invectives or encomia" (e.g., *J.W.* 1.1–2), he seems to regularly transgress his own distinctions.[95] While Josephus's *Antiquities* differs greatly in form with his autobiography, he demonstrates the genre flexibility of both historiography and biography in this work. Polybius's description of Philopoemen of Megalopolis, with which this chapter began, illustrates the point (*Hist.* 10.21.2–8). Even those in the ancient world who considered themselves to be historians could utilize biographical vignettes for moral instruction.[96] Even so, *Antiquities* may strike the reader as a peculiar case for comparison. Surely, unlike *Life of Moses* or *Life of Apollonius*, Josephus is not writing a biography: in his own words, he composes a treatise (πραγματεία; cf. Polybius, *Hist.* 1.1; 1.17) that he considers to be precise in its details (ἀκριβής; 1.17). Quite different than the more explicit apologetic motives for writing *War*, Josephus claims to write *Antiquities* for those curious about the history of the Jews (1.7–8).[97] His work also does not focus on a single figure's span from life to death but rather on many figures, sometimes featuring only brief glimpses of these respective figures' lives. For these reasons, Josephus has been sidelined in the discussion of ancient biographies,[98] and especially Mark.[99]

---

[95] Ibid., 21, 27.

[96] See Eckstein, *Moral Vision in the Histories of Polybius*, 30–40, 282–3; P. G. Walsh, *Livy: His Historical Methods and Aims* (Cambridge: Cambridge University Press, 1961), 267; Momigliano, *Greek Biography*, 1–7; Bruno Gentili and Giovanni Cerri, *History and Biography in Ancient Thought*, LSCP 20 (Amsterdam: J. C. Gieben, 1988), 84; Louis H. Feldman, *Josephus's Interpretation of the Bible* (Berkeley: University of California Press, 1998), 3–13. Concerning Josephus's history, Steven Mason writes that "history shades into biography" ("Introduction to the *Judean Antiquities*," in Louis H. Feldman, *Flavius Josephus: Translation and Commentary, Volume 3: Judean Antiquities 1–4*, ed. Steve Mason [Boston: Brill, 2000], xxxii).

[97] Steve Mason notes how Josephus's motive for writing might compare to Seneca (*Contr.* 1.pref.1) or Quintilian (1.pref.1; *Josephus and the New Testament*, 2nd ed. [Peabody, MA: Hendrickson, 2003], 102). As Feldman notes, Josephus asserts a more apologetic tone in *Ag. Ap.* 1.1 (*Josephus's Interpretation of the Bible*, 160–2).

[98] See A. Y. Collins, "Genre," 239–46. Frickenschmidt's study includes a section on Josephus. Commenting on the moral characteristics of Josephus's writing, Frickenschmidt concludes that the Gospels do not "represent the nature of Jesus in the form of moral virtues and values ... [but] put theology in place of morality" (*Evangelium als Biographie*, 148). While theology is the central thrust of the Gospels, morality and theology are not mutually exclusive in Josephus. Frickenschmidt's comparison is apt so long as his conclusion is reversed: in the Gospels, much like Josephus, theology works in tandem with morality.

[99] Josephus is often compared with Luke-Acts: Gregory E. Sterling, *Historiography and Self-Definition: Josephus, Luke-Acts, and Apologetic Historiography*, NovTSup 64 (New York: Brill, 1992), 1–16. When Mark is compared to ancient biographical material, the moral storytelling techniques of Josephus ought to be considered as well. In this regard, Eve-Marie Becker compares Josephus and

However, Josephus goes on to explain that the "most important thing one might learn from this history ... is the ones who follow after the purpose of God ... succeed in everything in addition to belief and are honored by God with happiness" (*Ant.* 1.14).[100] It is precisely the model of "those who follow after the purpose of God" to which the reader is to pay attention. A few lines later, Josephus introduces the figure of Moses as a model for imitation. For the reader, Moses encourages one to "handle his own life well ... to consider first the nature of God, and, having seen in his mind the works of God, to imitate the best example of all and, as far as it is possible, to attempt to follow" (1.19; cf. *Ag. Ap.* 2.136).[101] In other words, from the outset of *Antiquities*, Josephus provides moral examples from God for the reader to imitate. Similar to Philo the virtuous deeds of Josephus's moral exemplars are theological (*Ant.* 1.22–24). In the words of Steve Mason, "Josephus assesses these lives [within *Antiquities*] for the moral instruction of his readers to prove his thesis about the effectiveness of the Jewish God."[102] Stated more boldly, Josephus's *Antiquities* is also theological. And while Josephus does not claim his work is apologetic, both the internal and external evidence points to the contrary (cf. *Ag. Ap.* 1.1). Like Philo's presentation of Moses, Josephus defends his Jewish heritage and practices while also offering biblical examples to non-Jews for moral emulation.[103]

Scholars have noted the "moralizing" tendencies in Josephus's *Antiquities*.[104] Unfortunately, the term "moralizing" carries a certain air of self-righteous finger-wagging that is not intended by Josephus. The term, in this context, means to reform one's character and conduct. As in the case of Xenophon or Philo, Josephus utilizes storytelling techniques, centered around individual characters, to teach his readers how they ought to live. He offers both positive examples (*Ant.* 1.53, 60–61, 66, 72) as well as negative ones (*Ant.* 5.296; 7.37–38; 9.282), occasionally counterweighing the negative examples with positive moral summaries (*Ant.* 6.344–350; 13.318–319).[105]

Of the moral examples included within Josephus's *Antiquities*, I offer two for discussion. The first is Saul, to whom Josephus devotes a considerable amount of

---

Mark, but on the grounds that Mark more closely resembles historiography: *Das Markus-Evangelium im Rahmen antiker Historiographie*, WUNT 194 (Tübingen: Mohr Siebeck, 2006), 301–40.

[100] Translations of Josephus, unless otherwise noted, are the author's.

[101] Note Feldman's comment: "Josephus thus connects the ἀρετή of Moses with the cosmos and God's nature" (*Flavius Josephus*, 8 n. 25). See also Petitfils, "A Tale of Two Moseses," 153–64. This line, once more, runs contrary to Frickenschmidt's conclusions about Josephus and theology (*Evangelium als Biographie*, 148). Josephus appears as interested in theology as Mark.

[102] Mason, *Josephus and the New Testament*, 117; see also Feldman, *Josephus's Interpretation of the Bible*, 82–131, who demonstrates Josephus's close affinity with encomium.

[103] Feldman, *Josephus's Interpretation of the Bible*, 132–62. For Josephus's non-Jewish audience, see Steve Mason, "'Should Any Wish to Enquire Further' (Ant. 1.25): The Aim and Audience of Josephus's *Judean Antiquities/Life*," in *Understanding Josephus: Seven Perspectives*, ed. Steve Mason, JSPSup 32 (Sheffield: Sheffield Academic Press, 1998), 64–103.

[104] The dissertation of Harold Attridge is pioneering in this regard (*The Interpretation of Biblical History in the Antiquitates Judaicae of Flavius Josephus*, Harvard Dissertations in Religion 7 [Missoula, MT: Scholars Press, 1976], 109–44). Mason, *Josephus and the New Testament*, 116–21, follows, as does Feldman, *Josephus's Interpretation of the Bible*, 197–8. John J. Collins, following Attridge, contends that this tendency in Josephus derives from the Deuteronomistic historians (*Between Athens and Jerusalem: Jewish Identity in the Hellenistic Diaspora* [Grand Rapids, MI: Eerdmans, 2000], 62).

[105] Mason, *Josephus and the New Testament*, 117.

attention (6.45–7.6).[106] In the assessment of Feldman, "Josephus regarded Saul as one of the foremost paradigms in developing the goals of his work."[107] Saul is a man of noble birth, from a virtuous lineage (*Ant.* 6.45), in possession of wisdom, courage, temperance, justice, and piety (*Ant.* 6.346).[108] After recounting Saul's death, Josephus writes, "But it is right for *those* to receive praise; however, the attributes of courage, bold adventurer, and despiser of danger might only be attributed rightly to the imitators of Saul [οἱ Σαοῦλον μιμησάμενοι; 6.347]."[109] As Harold Attridge notes, Josephus refers to the one "who knows that he will die for his efforts, who will truly deserve this title."[110] Saul's courage and strength, especially in the face of impending death, serve as a moral paradigm for the reader.[111]

Second, the woman of Endor presents a compelling case for moral modeling. While her occupation of necromancy is condemned in Jewish and Christian interpretation,[112] her virtuous actions receive praise in patristic exegesis.[113] Origen, for example, appears to draw a connection between the woman's actions and Christ "opening the way" to Hades.[114] As with Origen's exegesis, Josephus offers a positive appraisal of the woman's actions.

In recounting Saul and the woman, Josephus adds his characteristic details (*Ant.* 6.327–343; cf. 1 Sam 28:3–24). He tracks, at first, with the biblical account, referring to the woman as a "ventriloquist" (ἐγγαστρίμυθος),[115] who is able to raise up Samuel's spirit from the dead. Her reservations for summoning the dead are repeated by Josephus

---

[106] According to Feldman, "He devotes 2.19 times as much space (2,332 lines) to Saul (*Ant.* 6.45–7.6) as does the Hebrew text" (*Josephus's Interpretation of the Bible*, 509).

[107] Ibid., 510.

[108] Feldman offers a detailed analysis of Saul's depiction in Josephus (ibid., 514–35). Similar characteristics are also found in Josephus's portrayal of David (6.160), Samson (5.317), and Solomon (7.338).

[109] Italics and translation my own.

[110] Attridge, *Interpretation*, 114.

[111] Attridge also rightly observes that Josephus's encomium of Saul is concerned with his presentation in 1 Sam 28:16–20 because it ends on a negative note (ibid.). On the "noble death" motif, see ibid., n. 2.

[112] For a survey of the Jewish and Christian reception of 1 Sam 28, see K. A. D. Smelik, "The Witch of Endor: 1 Samuel 28 in Rabbinic and Christian Exegesis till 800 A.D.," *VC* 33 (1977): 160–79; Patricia Cox, "Origen and the Witch of Endor: Toward an Iconoclast Typology," *ATR* 66 (1984): 137–47; Pamela Tamarkin Reis, "Eating the Blood: Saul and the Witch of Endor," *JSOT* 73 (1997): 3–23.

[113] This is not always the case in premodern interpretations of the woman of Endor. For an example, see Theresa Angert-Quilter and Lynne Wall, "The 'Spirit Wife' at Endor," *JSOT* 92 (2001): 55–72. This is also not to say that the events surrounding the woman of Endor did not present a number of problems for early interpreters. As Cox notes, "for a whole tradition of interpreters, including such notables as Tertullian, Jerome, Eustathius, John Chrysostom, and Gregory of Nyssa the story of Saul, Samuel, and the Witch of Endor was a menacing text" ("Origen and the Witch of Endor," 139). Reis notes the positive reviews by both patristic and modern commentators ("Eating the Blood," 3–4). For a history of interpretation concerning the unfortunate use of the term "witch" for the woman of Endor, see Esther J. Hamori, *Women's Divination in Biblical Literature: Prophecy, Necromancy, and Other Arts of Knowledge*, AYBRL (New Haven, CT: Yale University Press, 2015), 110–17.

[114] For the original Greek, see Origen, "De engastrimutho," in *La maga di Endor: Origene, Eustazio, Gregorio di Nissa*, ed. Manlio Simonetti (Florence: Nardini, Centro Internazionale del Libro, 1989), 44–74. Cox observes, "The witch is a type of Christ, or so Origen's strange ending implies" ("Origen and the Witch of Endor," 144).

[115] Likely following the LXX.

(6.331, 338; cf. 1 Sam 28:9). Josephus's commentary begins at the end of the story, in which he makes a point of the woman's persistence and hospitality (6.339) despite her great poverty (6.341). The woman had every right to turn Saul away (6.340-341) but, instead, responds with friendliness to this stranger. For her act of kindness, Josephus contends that his readers should take her "for an example and show kindness to all who are in need and to regard nothing as nobler than this" (6.342). Josephus elevates this figure's act of hospitality (1 Sam 28:24-25) to an exemplary level. To be discussed more fully in Chapter 4, Mark's moral models, like Josephus's woman of Endor, are not always found in the central hero or brightest students, but in the story's marginal characters (cf. Mark 5:34; 7:29; 10:52).

In sum, Josephus integrates biographical discourse into his historiography for morally formative ends.[116] As with the material examined thus far, this is a common feature of ancient biographies and biographical discourse. Mason's turn of phrase is appealing in this regard: "For Josephus, history shades into biography."[117] Furthermore, similar to Philo in places, Josephus also writes a theologically shaded account of history. If one wishes to treat the Gospels as moral in tone, Josephus's moral appraisal of key figures, such as Saul or the woman of Endor, is worthy of consideration.

Plutarch's *Lives*

Finally, let us turn to Plutarch (45-120 CE). Of the biographies Plutarch composed, fifty are extant, likely written toward the end of his life.[118] Albrecht Dihle asserted that "Plutarch's biographies belong in the sphere of moral theory and parenesis, and the same is true for many other biographies that we know of only indirectly."[119] The "sphere of moral theory" that Dihle identified for Plutarch's biographies has since been applied to biographies more broadly.[120] Plutarch indicates as much in his own words: "These legendary and amusing things [ταῦτα μὲν οὖν τὰ μυθώδη καὶ γελοῖα] serve to teach of men's attitudes toward the gods" (*Num.* 15.6). However, because Dihle restricted his definition for the biographical genre to Plutarch's *Lives* exclusively, his conclusion for the Gospels as biographies was negative.[121] Nonetheless, Plutarch was the anchor for Dihle's hypothesis that *bioi* draw upon Aristotelian ethics.

---

[116] It is worth considering to what extent Josephus considers his own material to be "biographical." In his assessment, his work is free of "mythology" (*Ant.* 1.15-17); cf. Attridge, *Interpretation*, 43-57. I use the term "biographical discourse" instead of "biography" as the start of this chapter outlines (see Goarzin, "Presenting a Practical Way of Life," 115-29).

[117] Mason, "Introduction to the *Judean Antiquities*," xxxii.

[118] Licona, *Differences in the Gospels*, 16; Bernadotte Perrin, "Introduction," in *Lives Volume 1: Theseus and Romulus. Lycurgus and Numa. Solon and Publicola*, LCL 46 (Cambridge, MA: Harvard University Presss, 1914), xii.

[119] Albrecht Dihle, "The Gospels and Greek Biography," in *The Gospel and the Gospels*, ed. Peter Stuhlmacher (Grand Rapids, MI: Eerdmans, 1990), 369.

[120] Likewise, Leo's pioneering research classified Plutarch's biographies as peripatetic (*Biographie*, 315-21).

[121] Cf. Albrecht Dihle, *Studien zur Griechischen Biographie* (Göttingen: Vanderhoeck & Ruprecht, 1956); Dihle, "The Gospels and Greek Biography," 369; Albrecht Dihle, "Die Evangelien und die biographische Tradition der Antike," *ZTK* 80 (1983): 33-49; Burridge, *Imitating Jesus*, 28-32. Dihle is a figure commonly cited in the Gospels-are-not-biographies camp. In this regard, Dihle's work laid a foundation for appreciating the moral tenor of Greco-Roman *bioi*. Relying mainly

Regarding the moral tone of biographies, Plutarch's influence is far-reaching.[122] While ancient and modern biographies have obvious points of divergence, the popular eighteenth-century biography by James Boswell, *The Life of Samuel Johnson*, claims to find its roots in Plutarch, favoring conversation over chronology to "best display [Johnson's] character."[123]

Plutarch ventures to portray in his *Lives* the character of his subject. As in the case of Solon, "character" (ἦθος) supersedes "chronology" (χρόνος; *Sol.* 27).[124] Elsewhere, Plutarch cites a feud among a group of writers, in which Timaeus has attempted to discredit Plato and Aristotle (*Nic.* 1.4; 29.4). In a disapproving tone, Plutarch claims to avoid such trivial bickering by clarifying, once more, his intentions for writing. He can consult the annals of Thucydides's history whenever he pleases; he is more interested in "public decrees" that "pass down ... the appreciation of character and temperament [ἤθους καὶ πρόπου]" (1.5; cf. *Pomp.* 8.6). Plutarch has an unequivocal interest in the character of his subjects.

Plutarch's introduction to his *Life of Pericles* offers a clear example of his moral ecology (*Per.* 1-2).[125] Plutarch recounts a bizarre complaint by Caesar: "On seeing certain wealthy foreigners in Rome carrying young puppies and young monkeys about in their bosoms and fondling them, Caesar asked, we are told, if the women in their country did not bear children" (*Per.* 1.1). It would seem that these philotherianistic women, according to Plutarch's Caesar, have turned a proclivity to love children toward less worthy objects of affection, animals. In this analogy, Plutarch offers a cryptic, parabolic image to underscore a moral lesson. He explains that human beings are like sponges, possessing a "great fondness for learning," soaking up whatever object presents itself before the eyes and ears (in this case, a monkey or puppy). The objects that one meditates on, or even obsesses over, shape one's character. The "good objects," for Plutarch, should not be puppies, but "virtuous deeds [ἀρετῆς ἔργοις] ... that lead to imitation [ἀγωγὸν εἰς μίμησιν]."[126] Imitating such virtuous deeds does not come easy. "Nay, many times, on the contrary, while we delight in the work, we despise the workman" (*Per.* 1.4). This is why, for example, there are both excellent musicians and awful ones. How does one move from admiration of a subject to imitation of it?

on Plutarch, Dihle identified a chasm between Greek biographies and the Gospels (cf. Burridge, *What Are the Gospels?*, 88-90). This aspect of Dihle aside, what biblical scholars tend to overlook is Dihle's contribution to the study of biographies as moral literature. Building on the work of Leo before him, Dihle placed the antecedent of biographies in the Peripatetic school of Aristotle. Recent scholarship has since complicated his distinctions, painting a picture of much greater variety (cf. Momigliano, *Greek Biography*, exp. ed., 115; Cox, *Biography*, 6-7; Hägg, *Art of Biography*, 152-3). Even so, the degree to which morality frames the ecology of biographies in the ancient world as Dihle first observed is still worth considering.

[122] On the influence of Plutarch's *Lives* on the modern biography, see Tim Duff, *Plutarch's Lives: Exploring Virtue and Vice* (Oxford: Clarendon Press, 1999), 3-5.

[123] James Boswell, *The Life of Samuel Johnson, LL, D, Comprehending an Account of his Studies and Numerous Works in Chronological Order; A Series of His Epistolary Correspondence and Conversations with Many Eminent Persons and Various Original Pieces of His Composition Never Before Published: The Whole Exhibiting a View of Literature and Literary Men in Great-Britain, for Near Half a Century during which He Flourished* (London: Henry Baldwin for Charles Duly, 1791).

[124] τροπός is commonly used as well (*LSJ*, s.v., "way of life, habit, custom") as in *Rom.* 28.3; *Lyc.* 28.6.

[125] Translations of *Pericles*, unless otherwise noted, belong to B. Perrin (LCL).

[126] He repeats the same sentiment for imitating (μιμητικὸς) and emulating (ζηλοῦσθαι) in *Per.* 2.

According to Plutarch, it is "the Good" (τὸ καλὸν) that prods the observer to action: "It does not form his character by ideal representation alone, but through investigation." This investigation of a subject is precisely why Plutarch "decided to persevere in my writing of Lives" (*Per.* 2.4).[127] Here in Plutarch's *Pericles* we see a clear window into his intentions for writing his biographies. Plutarch understands himself as providing readers with an opportunity to reform their character through a careful investigation of his literary subjects.

This observation on the *Life of Pericles* is confirmed in much of the secondary literature on Plutarch. Françoise Frazier's work on Plutarch has brought attention to the moral nature of *Lives*. As Frazier notes, the etymology of *bios* is "not the fact of living, but the *manner* of living, the *mode* of life."[128] Likewise, Tim Duff comments on the "double reference" contained within the term *bios*: "Plutarch presents himself as, like a painter, 'shaping' the biographies he is writing. ... [B]ut 'life' also refers to the real lives of Plutarch's readers, whom he hopes to influence and morally improve."[129] In this sense, many of Plutarch's *Lives* teach his readers how to live in accordance with his ideal hero in a "mirror-like reflective quality."[130] Plutarch himself utilizes the language of "mirror" in *Timoleon*:

> I began the writing of my "Lives" for the sake of others, but I find that I am continuing the work and delighting in it now for my own sake also, using history as a mirror and endeavoring in a manner to fashion and adorn my life in conformity with the virtues therein depicted.[131]

To the end of moral formation, Plutarch's biographies idealize virtue,[132] self-restraint,[133] righteousness,[134] and education,[135] with an acute eye toward imitation of the subject's positive traits.[136]

---

[127] For a discussion of the textual difficulty of this passage, see Duff, *Plutarch's Lives*, 38.
[128] Translation and italics mine; the source is P. Chantraine, DELG., s.v. βίος, quoted in Françoise Frazier, *Histoire et Morales dans les Vies parallèles de Plutarque*, 2nd ed., CEASG 152 (Paris: Les Belles Lettres, 2016), 21. At times Frazier presses the evidence a bit too far, claiming that Plutarch is more of a "moralist" than a historian (ibid., 61–2), strongly differentiating history and biography (ibid., 99–129). Her conclusions about morality as a driving force in Plutarch's biographies are worth considering (ibid., 131–2), but Frazier's mutually exclusive dichotomy is not necessary; for example, "Either [history] does not interest Plutarch at all, or he replaces it with great, seemingly eternal, moral truths" (ibid., 370). Plutarch often compares his work with historians: e.g., *Rom.* 29.7; *Lyc.* 1.3–4; *Comp. Lyc. Num.* 3.6; cf. D. A. Russell, "On Reading Plutarch's Lives," in *Essays on Plutarch's Lives*, ed. Barbara Scardigli (Oxford: Clarendon Press, 1995), 81–90; Alan Wardman, *Plutarch's Lives* (Berkeley: University of California Press, 1974), 1–48.
[129] Duff, *Plutarch's Lives*, 17, 33–34.
[130] Ibid., 34. On Plutarch's readers, see Philip A. Stadter, *Plutarch and His Roman Readers* (Oxford: Oxford University Press, 2015), 1–12, 45–55; Wardman, *Plutarch's Lives*, 37–48.
[131] *Tim.* 1.1 (Perrin, LCL).
[132] E.g., *Lyc.* 27.3; *Num.* 3.5; 20.8; *Comp. Lyc. Num.* 1.2; *Sol.* 6.2; *Fab.* 3.6; *Pomp.* 1.3.
[133] E.g., *Rom.* 28.3; *Lyc.* 15.5; *Per.* 29.1–2; *Mar. Cat.* 6.1; *Ag.* 14.1.
[134] E.g., *Comp. Thes. Rom.* 1.4–5; *Lyc.* 3.4; *Comp. Lyc. Num.* 1.2, 4; *Ar.* 4.1; 6.1–3.
[135] E.g., *Num.* 3.5; 15.1; *Cras.* 2.6; *Mar. Cat.* 2.14, 8; *Dion* 10.1.
[136] E.g., *Lyc.* 27.3–4; 30.4; *Num.* 20.8; *Comp. Sol. Pub.* 1.1; *Per.* 2.2–3; *Comp. Per. Fab.* 1.1; *Ar.* 2.1; *Mar. Cat.* 19.5.

While many of Plutarch's extant *Lives* would provide an interesting point of comparison to Mark, a broad overview reveals Plutarch's interest in the formation of the reader and, at times, the formation of himself as a writer. Furthermore, Duff's "double reference," imbedded within the meaning of *bios*, acutely captures Plutarch's ability to shape both his literary subject and the reader simultaneously. As he plainly lays out in his introduction to *Pericles*, Plutarch claims that his literary subject's character is revealed through the reader's own investigation of it. The reader is formed through Plutarch's literary formation. This dynamic relationship between literary subject and reader, found in much of the biographical literature surveyed thus far, may also be found in the Gospel of Mark, especially as it pertains to one's manner of living. Chapter 3 will outline how Mark's own shaping of the life of Jesus shapes, in turn, those who hear or read it. Or one might say, as does the biographer Lucian, when reading a biography, the student of philosophy is invited "to shape themselves" (*Dem.* 1) in accordance with the life of the statesmen or philosopher.[137] It is worth repeating: the process of being shaped by a literary subject is a moral one.

2.5 Conclusion: What Does All This Mean for Mark?

This chapter presented a selection of ancient biographies and biographical discourses to establish a frequent preoccupation with the moral formation of the reader. By carefully constructing their historical figures, Xenophon, Philostratus, Philo, Josephus, and Plutarch intend, among a host of other motivations, a moral thrust to their compositions. The moral environment of Mark's Gospel belongs in conversation with these biographical compositions.

Additionally, this chapter has offered several examples from Josephus, neglected in biographical discussion of Mark. Josephus, as a Jewish historiographer, portrays his subjects for morally formative ends. Like Polybius before him, or like his contemporary, Plutarch, Josephus's *Antiquities* is an attractive example of the intersection between historiography and biography in early antiquity. Furthermore, Josephus and Philo occasionally direct the reader's attention to the God of Israel, as the source of their subject's moral character—a theological move also found within the Gospels.

At the same time, these works also contain notable differences from Mark. Such points of divergence should not preclude one from considering Mark's points of comparison with the *bioi/vitae* family. To the contrary, Mark's adaption of what amounts to a resilient and flexible genre in antiquity reveals unique aspects of Mark's theological and moral program. Stated another way, this study contends that the differences found in Mark may showcase a type of "genre bending" by the second evangelist. What for Rudolf Bultmann excluded the Gospels from a comparative analysis to biographies, for example, that they are too theological in nature, is the focal point of this study. The theology of Mark, to be addressed in Chapter 3, drives the moral formation of Mark's life of Jesus.

---

[137] Cf. Cox, *Biography*, 24.

Even so, several important dissimilarities should be noted. First, Mark does not appear to write a polemic. Theodore Weeden's thesis, in this regard, cannot be sustained.[138] While earlier versions of biographies, such as Xenophon's account of Socrates, possess clear apologetic goals, one cannot speak confidently of Mark in the same way. As noted in Chapter 1, those who find polemic or apologetic purpose in Mark's presentation of Jesus often do so from the vantage point of titular Christology. Briefly, while Mark does not defend Jesus's closest students as Xenophon does for Socrates—to the contrary, Mark's depiction of the disciples is ambivalent, if not overtly negative—this does not mean that Mark is "engaged in a polemic against the disciples."[139] Mark's mystifying portrayal of the disciples, in many ways unlike that of Matthew's and Luke's, appears to direct the reader's attention to God as well as to a subset of marginal characters. In this way, blind Bartimaeus (10:46–52) or the centurion (15:39), as two examples, possess insight into Jesus's identity in ways the disciples do not. Second, Mark has an indelible interest in apocalyptic eschatology.[140] From the start of his story (1:1–13) to the very end (13:1–37; 15:21–32), Mark's Jesus appears against a backdrop of Jewish apocalyptic eschatology, a feature that is only faintly present, if not completely absent, in the biographies of Xenophon, Philostratus, Philo,[141] Josephus,[142] and Plutarch.

Finally, and perhaps what is more important, Mark's Jesus has a tendency to subvert a central characteristic of the biographies examined thus far: moral modeling. Jesus in the Gospel of Mark appears to separate families (1:16–20) and to reject his own (3:31–35). According to the ethicist Zeno, such behavior would have been contrary to reason and morally questionable (Diogenes Laertius, *Lives* 7.108). Jesus speaks in parables in order to stupefy (4:12) to the point that even his closest followers misunderstand him (4:13; 8:17, 21; 9:10; 10:35–45). Yet again, the popular philosophy of the Stoics would have classified opaque speech and subsequent misunderstanding as vice and not virtue (*Lives* 7.93). The list goes on. Jesus orders a group of pigs to their death, upsetting an entire region of farmers (5:1–20); he destroys a fig tree (11:14) and appears to offer zero tolerance for divorce (10:11–12), standard eating customs (7:19), or temple regulations (11:16). Finally, there is no triumphant conclusion to Mark's tale: terror and astonishment seize Mary Magdalene, Mary the mother of James, and Salome

---

[138] Weeden, *Mark: Traditions in Conflict*, 1–26.
[139] Ibid., 26.
[140] Apocalyptic eschatology refines the question: what kind of eschatology? The use of apocalyptic signals a genre in which portions of Mark's Gospel participate. As Christopher Rowland has demonstrated, apocalypses do not always concern themselves with eschatology (*The Open Heaven: A Study of Apocalyptic in Judaism and Early Christianity* [New York: Crossroad, 1982]); conversely, eschatology need not be only apocalyptic in form. For this reason, both "apocalyptic" and "eschatology" are required in this sentence.
[141] Ken M. Penner provides a noteworthy treatment of Philo's eschatology: "In contrast to better-known Jewish eschatology from the first century in which a final battle and resurrection are brought about by an outside divine agent, Philo's eschatology stems from the gradual improvement of the soul" ("Philo's Eschatology, Personal and Cosmic," *JSJ* 50 [2019]: 383–402, here 402).
[142] The dominant scholarly position for Josephus is that he has little concern for Jewish apocalyptic eschatology. For evidence to the contrary, see Per Bilde, "Josephus and Jewish Apocalypticism," in *Collected Studies on Philo and Josephus*, ed. Eve-Marie Becker, Morten Hørning Jensen, and Jacob Mortensen, SANt 7 (Göttingen: Vandenhoeck & Ruprecht, 2016), 151–69.

(16:8). If biographers wrote to gain an audience, as is the case with Philo and Josephus, or to offer a paradigmatic sage for emulation, as in Xenophon, why does Mark not paint a more favorable, or at least more palatable, picture of its ideal teacher? As I will answer more fully in Chapter 3, it would seem that Mark's Jesus responds to a higher moral order. The kingdom of God has arrived (1:14–15), and Jesus consistently speaks and acts at the command of God. If Mark "bends" the genre of biography, it would seem that his Gospel subverts one of its central features. One might say that Mark is concerned with a theological type of imitation: doing the things that God wants, even if they seem absurd. As Chapter 5 will outline, one's inability to do the "things of God" is due, in part, to an evil so insidious and pervasive that God's help is not only needed but also required (10:27; 14:36). Seneca appears to come close to this idea in his understanding of divine obedience: "We are born in a kingdom—freedom is to obey god."[143] As Chapter 3 intends to explore, Jesus's words and actions are to be followed because he answers to God.

---

[143] *De Vita Beata* 15.7, trans. Brad Inwood, *Ethics and Human Action in Early Stoicism* (New York: Oxford University Press, 1985), 110. As the next few chapters will explore, Mark's notion of the "will of God" and its relation to the doer are of principal importance for how one understands Jesus's actions.

3

Moral Accountability according to Mark

And we know that whatever the law says, it speaks to the ones under the law, so that every mouth may be shut up and the whole world may be accountable [ὑπόδικος] to God.

Rom 3:19[3]

3.1 Introduction

This chapter builds upon a premise set forth by Leander Keck. In a short essay on Paul, Keck reframes the popular practices of Christian ethics, turning away from certain questions of modern philosophy, "What must/ought/should I do?" to ancient ones, "To whom am I accountable and for what?"[1] For Keck, the notion of accountability refers to "an acknowledged authority structure in which the self knows that it owes an account and expects a response."[2] In Paul's letters the moral category of "accountability" serves as a useful description for, among other examples, the pervasive topic of judgment (e.g., Rom 2:1–11, 3:5–6; 1 Thess 1:10) and Paul's self-understanding, as one answerable to God "not only for the integrity of his own word and life but also for that of these new communities" (e.g., 1 Cor 4:1–5; 10:14–22; Rom 14:1–9).[3]

For a chapter on moral accountability in Mark, it may seem odd to begin with Paul. In what follows, I intend to make clear that the Gospel of Mark presents a notion of

---

[1] Leander E. Keck, "The Accountable Self," in *Theology and Ethics in Paul and His Interpreters: Essays in Honor of Victor Paul Furnish*, ed. Eugene H. Lovering Jr. and Jerry L. Sumney (Nashville, TN: Abingdon Press, 1996), 1. A similar question shifting occurred in moral philosophy when G. E. M. Anscombe called for a type of virtue ethics ("Modern Moral Philosophy," *Philosophy* 33 [1958]: 1–19). On the notion of what an agent morally ought to do, Anscombe writes,

> It would be most reasonable to drop it. It has no reasonable sense outside a law conception of ethics; [Hume and other modern ethicists] are not going to maintain such a conception; and you can do ethics without it, as is shown by the example of Aristotle. It would be great improvement if, instead of "morally wrong," one always named a genus such as "untruthful," "unchaste," "unjust." We should not ask whether doing something was "wrong," passing directly from some description of an action to this notion; we should ask whether, e.g., it was unjust. (Ibid., 8–9)

Anscombe's appeal to a different, arguably more ancient, set of ethical questions, based more directly on "human flourishing," is comparable to that of Keck and of the present project.

[2] Keck, "Accountable," 2.

[3] Ibid., 10.

accountability similar to, though not as developed as, Paul's.[4] When it comes to moral responsibility in Mark, Jesus's own, at times confusing, actions are directed toward the God to whom he is accountable and from whom he receives his authority (e.g., Mark 1:11; 2:10, 27; 3:35; 4:41; 8:33). Moreover, the authority given to Jesus by God is questioned (11:27–33) or misattributed (3:30), suggesting that "accountability" is contested in Mark. Before moving into the specifics of Mark's moral life—the "for what" of Keck's question (to be considered in Chapter 4)—it is necessary to begin with that life's framework: the subject "to whom" Jesus and his disciples are held accountable.

This chapter begins with a brief overview of Mark's theological description of accountability. One of the issues to be addressed in this first section is the relative neglect of God's activity in Mark by twentieth-century scholarship. Compared to Paul or Matthew, Mark's tacit account of God's ownership and eventual judgment of the world is easy to overlook in favor of Mark's more pronounced Christology. For this reason, I dedicate the section, "A World in Conflict," to identifying select theological themes in Mark's prologue (1:1–15), including Mark's use of Scripture (1:2–3), God's role in the temptation episode (1:12–13), and the first words pronounced by Jesus (1:14–15). Each of these short pericopes illustrates Mark's keen interest in divine, moral action. In the second half of this chapter, "Moral Accountability in God's Family" and "Moral Accountability to God's Authority," I offer three images of the accountable God according to Mark: God the parent, God the authority, and God the judge.[5]

3.2 Moral Reasoning in Mark

Mark's moral life confronts the reader with divisive, even contradictory, moral options—saving or killing a life (3:4), being clean or unclean (7:19), eternal reward or punishment (8:35–38), belief or unbelief (9:24), paying taxes to or withholding them from Caesar (12:14)—within the context of a prevalent ontological binary of human and divine (7:8; 8:33; 10:27; 11:30; 12:17). One is either on the side of God or Beelzebul (3:20–27; 8:33), and to mix them up amounts to blasphemy (3:28–29). Taking a step back from this Markan attitude, I begin by asking whence these moral choices derive. Mark 3:35 offers a potential answer: "Whoever does the will of God is my brother and sister and mother." The pressing reality of God's kingdom and the impending consequences that it brings rotates on a moral axis ordered by the

---

[4] Another way to put this: Paul's notion of accountability to God is far more explicit than Mark's. This chapter's epigraph of Rom 3:19 illustrates Paul's overt description of accountability. For more evidence, one may turn to Paul's account of God's ownership of the world (Rom 4:17; 1 Cor 1:20–31; 3:9; 6:19) and coming judgment of it (Rom 1:18; 2:2; 9:22; 1 Cor 3:17; 5:13; 6:13; 1 Thess 1:10). These Pauline features are more allusive in Mark.

[5] The reason for my selection of these three images over other potential images for God is twofold. First, the images of authority and judge for God are indebted, once more, to Keck (see his "authorizing judge" in *Who Is Jesus?*, 163–77). Second, the image of parent derives from Meeks, *Origins of Christian Morality*, 172. In this regard, God's parental role is also found in scholarly discussions of early Jewish and Christian models of kinship.

will of God. Secondarily, doing God's will endows the moral agent with a special status of accountability. One is a responsible member of God's family.⁶ Mark's moral emphasis, I will argue below, is not so much on "doing" as it is on "belonging" to God. This section argues that this special status is the foundation for moral living in Mark.

To take another example, Jesus's question to the Pharisees in Mark 3:4, "Is it lawful on the Sabbath to do good or to do evil, to save a life or to kill?" is ethically loaded. Such a query situates the reader at a moral crossroads. On the one hand, the "good" and its incumbent mandate, "to save a life," offer the reader insight into the nature of morality in Mark: saving a life is good. Conversely, doing "evil" is provided clear definition by Mark's Jesus: "to kill" (ἀποκτεῖναι) is bad. However, to frame Mark's moral life *only* in this manner leaves the reader, at best, with moral casuistry.⁷ In other words, using the terms of Keck's definition of Pauline ethics, it is this "ought" that needs to be reframed; this line of reasoning, if left only to questions of "ought to" or "must," sidelines the "why" one must do good in the first place.⁸ *To whom* is the one doing good accountable? For Mark, the good is attached to a whom: "No one is good except one, God" (10:17–18; cf. 2:7).⁹ Mark's respect for life derives from the God who creates life (13:19). In this way, God constitutes the ultimate rubric against which Mark's moral life is to be evaluated, or so this chapter contends. Here, William Telford's memorable turn of phrase, "the primary thrust of the Gospel is Christological … and not ethical," should be paraphrastically turned on its head: the primary thrust of the Gospel is theological and, as a consequence, moral.¹⁰

---

⁶ This is especially clear in Mark 3:19b–30. The debate preceding the Beelzebul controversy concerns the origin of Jesus's authority.
⁷ William Telford does exactly this when he comments on Mark 3:4 and Mark's "contribution to ethical debate." He notes that "it is easier in our day to sympathize with a figure who appears to champion freedom over regulation, or human well-being over religious scruples" (*Theology*, 223). Telford does not go beyond this type of moral casuistry to the source of Jesus's ethical preference for human life: God.
⁸ Karl Barth intuits this difference in *CD* II/2

> When the ethical thinker who starts out from that general conception encounters the attestation of the command of God in the Christian doctrine of God he finds himself precipitated into a strange world because he is confronted by an enigmatic knowledge of the Whence? and Wither? of all ethical enquiry and reply. This violates at its nerve centre what usually passes for ethical reflection and explanation. (*Church Dogmatics, Volume II: The Doctrine of God, Part 2*, trans. G. W. Bromiley et al., ed. G. W. Bromiley and T. F. Torrance [Edinburgh: T&T Clark, 1957], 10–11)

That Barth has a similar axe to grind against moral casuistry, see Daniel L. Migliore, "Commanding Grace: Karl Barth's Theological Ethics," in *Commanding Grace: Karl Barth's Theological Ethics*, ed. Daniel L. Migliore (Grand Rapids, MI: Eerdmans, 2010), 6–9.
⁹ The same phrase appears in 2:7 (εἰ μὴ εἷς ὁ θεός) when the Pharisees question Jesus's authority to forgive sins.
¹⁰ Telford, *Theology*, 221. Here, some clarification is in order on the difference between the terms "Christological" and "theological." I tend to agree with M. Eugene Boring that "to dispute whether the Markan narrative is theocentric or Christocentric is a misplaced question" ("Markan Christology," 471). This section does not intend to elaborate on the scale of Mark's Christology (e.g., high or low). Instead, I am exposing the "polarity" of Mark's frequent juxtaposition between what is "God" and what is "human" (cf. 8:33; 14:36).

The Character of God in Mark: A Neglected Factor

Historically, the role of God in Mark, and in New Testament studies more broadly, has been overlooked.[11] For reasons outlined in Chapter 1, the motifs of discipleship and Christology stole the show for the better half of the twentieth century. In the last forty years, scholarship has turned toward evaluating the role of God in the second Gospel.

According to John Donahue's groundbreaking study, scholars conclude that Mark's interest in God is mild because, in comparison to Matthew, Luke, and Paul, Mark's references to God are less frequent by a significant margin.[12] Mark uses the term θεός forty-eight times;[13] of these, fourteen occur in the phrase βασιλεία τοῦ θεοῦ[14] and four in the phrase υἱὸς τοῦ θεοῦ.[15] Of the sixteen occurrences of κύριος, eight occur in the context of Old Testament citations.[16] Outside of these, one reference refers unequivocally to God (13:20; cf. 5:19; 12:9; 13:35).[17] Mark refers to God four times with the title "Father" (8:38; 11:25; 13:32; 14:36). The heavenly voice sounds twice (1:11; 9:7), with the implication that it derives from God. Finally, according to Donahue, there are at least thirty verbs that may be considered divine passives.[18] In the story of the paralytic, the man "was raised" (ἠγέρθη) before he picks up his mat (2:12). Donahue's study overlooks two key passive verbs in Mark 1:10 and 15:38, in which the heavens are "ripped open" and the temple curtain "was torn" by God.[19] Beyond these examples, there are a few other less obvious references to God, by Donahue's count.[20]

In addition to identifying an overlooked aspect of Markan scholarship, Donahue's study goes one step further: he applies the results of his observations to the motifs of discipleship and Christology. Donahue evaluates how two of the least neglected features of Markan studies are modified in light of his new control, God.[21] In the case

---

[11] As John Donahue has demonstrated, preoccupation with Christology has also led to a neglect of the study of God in Mark ("A Neglected Factor," 590). See also Boring, "Markan Christology," 451-71; Hanson, *The Endangered Promises*, 1-4; Danove, *Characterization of God*, 28-55; Hurtado, *God in New Testament Theology*, 18-20; Rindge, "Reconfiguring," 755-74.

[12] See Donahue, "Neglected Factor," 565-70. For example, consider Matthew's forty-four uses of "Father" and Luke's seventeen to Mark's four (8:38; 11:25; 13:32; 14:36), the named source of Peter's knowledge (Matt 16:17), or Zechariah and Elizabeth's righteousness (Luke 1:6).

[13] Mark 1:1, 14-15, 24; 2:7, 12, 26; 3:11, 35; 4:11, 26, 30; 5:7; 7:8-9, 13; 8:33; 9:1, 47; 10:9, 14-15, 18, 23-25, 27; 11:22; 12:14, 17, 24, 26-27, 29-30, 34; 13:19; 14:25; 15:34, 39, 43.

[14] Mark 1:15; 4:11, 26, 30; 9:1, 47; 10:14-15, 23-25; 12:34; 14:25; 15:43.

[15] Mark 1:1; 3:11; 5:7; 15:39; cf. 1:24.

[16] Mark 1:3; 11:9; 12:11, 29 (x2), 30, 36 (x2).

[17] The exceptions are the more ambiguous occurrences in 5:19; 12:9; and 13:35. In 5:19 Jesus is likely referring to himself. In 12:9 Mark refers to the owner of the vineyard with κύριος; since the son is killed (12:8), the term is likely a reference to God. In 13:35 the identity of the "master of the house" is unclear. However, in light of 13:32 ("no one knows ... except the Father"), it, too, is likely a reference to God.

[18] Donahue, "Neglected Factor," 566.

[19] Note the same verb, σχίζω, in both places.

[20] E.g., the spirit occurs six times (1:8, 10, 12; 3:29; 12:36; 13:11); "of the blessed one" (14:61), "from heaven" (11:31); presumably, the speaker in Mal 3:1 (Mark 1:2); Isa 56:7 (Mark 7:6); and Isa 29:13 (Mark 11:17) is God. More recently, Paul Danove, building on Donahue's work, presents an exhaustive case for "219 explicit and grammatically required implicit references to God in Mark 1:1-16:8" (*Characterization of God*, 30).

[21] Donahue, "Neglected Factor," 587.

of discipleship, Donahue demonstrates that "Jesus is not simply a model to be followed on the way of suffering, but a model of one who in the midst of suffering can address God as *abba*."[22] This chapter operates under a similar premise. A careful evaluation of God's role in Mark reveals a morally coded landscape with implications for popular motifs in Markan scholarship (e.g., Christology and discipleship). Christology is moral to the extent that Jesus is the effective agent of a particular kingdom (1:15). The same may be said of discipleship, in that leaving one's family (1:16–20), healing the sick (6:13), or casting out demons (3:15; 6:7) places moral demands on disciples by nature of their relationship to God.

3.3 A World in Conflict: Moral Accountability in Mark's Prologue

It should be noted that Mark is not unique in his presentation of God. God animates the moral universe of the broader Greco-Roman world as well. On the Stoics, Brad Inwood notes, "The ultimate standard of goodness and happiness is not the doing of conventionally moral actions. It is harmony with the will of Zeus."[23] In his *Life of Pericles*, Plutarch offers the reason he "decided to persevere in [his] writing of Lives":

> But virtuous action straightway so disposes a man that he no sooner admires the works of virtue than he strives to emulate those who wrought them … *The Good creates a stir of activity towards itself, and implants at once in the spectator an active impulse*; it does not form his character by ideal representation alone, but through the investigation of its work it furnishes him with a dominant purpose.[24]

In addition to virtuous action, Plutarch adds that "the Good" (τὸ καλόν) implants an "impulse" (ὁρμήν) within the spectator that, after proper investigation (τῇ ἱστορίᾳ), leads to character development. Ultimately, this "Good" supplies the drive for the moral agent's actions. For Mark, "the Good" derives from God (10:18). Similarly, in Philo's *Life of Moses*, Moses may serve as the premier example for virtue (e.g., *Moses* 1.6–7; 1.9.48; 1.28.158), but Moses's moral actions derive from the God to whom he answers (*Moses* 1.14; 1.17; 1.21).[25] Theocentricity—the centrality of God as such—governs Philo's presentation of Moses. The same may be said of Josephus, who connects Moses's virtue to God's: "Our legislator, on the contrary, having shown that God possesses the very perfection of virtue, thought that men should strive to participate in it" (*Ant.* 1.23–24 [Thackeray, LCL]; cf. 1.14; 1.19; *Ag. Ap.* 2.136).

---

[22] Ibid.
[23] Inwood, *Ethics and Human Action*, 212.
[24] *Per.* 2.3–4, italics added (Perrin, LCL).
[25] Philo frequently describes Moses's and others' actions "at God's command." Consider also Philostratus's Apollonius, who responds to the question, "What kind of philosophy do you practice?" He replies, "Theology, and to pray and sacrifice to the gods" (*Life* 4.40).

Additionally, there is the question of the term "apocalyptic" in Mark's presentation of God in his Gospel.[26] Mark's relationship with apocalyptic literature and theology has been the subject of much scholarly debate.[27] To be clear, I do not contend that Mark operates within only one literary framework, but that apocalyptic themes comprise key elements of Mark's composition, particularly within Mark's prologue. At the commencement of Mark's story, God's activity appears on an apocalyptically stylized canvas. Apocalypses regularly feature human life, according to John Collins, as "bounded in the present by the supernatural world of angels and demons."[28] As in the *Apocalypse of Abraham*, Azazel appears to have "heritage over those who are with you[,] … the men born by the clouds" (14.6–7).[29] For this reason, the frequently bifurcated moral choices in Mark (e.g., whether one's conduct comports with the human or the divine) may be considered manifestations of Mark's broader presentation of a world in conflict, a motif exemplified in the prologue.

The Beginning of the Gospel

The Markan prologue (1:1–15)[30] possesses many salient features that announce God's moral activity in the Gospel.[31] Mark's brief introduction contains the designation for

---

[26] Employing the term "apocalyptic" is fraught with scholarly debate. For a helpful summary of the state of the field, see Adela Yarbro Collins, "Apocalypse Now: The State of Apocalyptic Studies Near the End of the First Decade of the Twenty-First Century," *HTR* 104 (2011): 447–57. Collins, in this piece, provides a much needed update since the *Semeia* 14 definition, including the critiques by Christopher Rowland, David Aune, and Martha Himmelfarb of an eschatology-laden definition for apocalyptic.

[27] For brief summaries of the scholarly debate as it relates to Mark, see Elizabeth Shively, *Apocalyptic Imagination in the Gospel of Mark: The Literary and Theological Role of Mark 3:22–30*, BZNW 189 (New York: De Gruyter, 2012), 21–6; John K. Riches, *Conflicting Mythologies: Identity Formation in the Gospels of Mark and Matthew*, SNTW (Edinburgh: T&T Clark, 2000), 148–79.

[28] John J. Collins, *The Apocalyptic Imagination: An Introduction to the Jewish Matrix of Christianity* (New York: Crossroad, 1984), 9. According to Martinus de Boer, there are two tracks for the origin of evil in Second Temple Judaism ("Paul and Jewish Apocalyptic Eschatology," in *Apocalyptic and the New Testament: Essays in Honor of J. Louis Martyn*, ed. Joel Marcus and Marion L. Soards, JSNTSup 24 [Sheffield: JSOT Press, 1989], 169–90). Track one explains evil's origins by way of supernatural forces; track two, by way of human rejection of God. For an application of de Boer's theory to Mark, see Riches, *Conflicting Mythologies*, 13.

[29] Trans. Ryszard Rubinkiewicz, "Apocalypse of Abraham," in *OTP* 1.696. This is a strange passage, excluded in Codex Sylvester. G. H. Box and J. I. Landsman compared it with Wis 2.24; 1 En. 41:8–9; and 2 Bar. 42:7, referring to "predestinarian" ideas (*The Apocalypse of Abraham: Edited with a Translation from the Slavonic Text and Notes* [New York: Macmillan, 1918], 55). The Slavonic text appears to make this connection more explicit; so Rubinkiewicz "avec les Géants qui sont nés des hommes" (*L'Apocalypse D'Abraham en vieux slave: Introduction, texte critique, traduction et commentaire* [Lublin: Société des Lettres et des Sciences de l'Université Catholique de Lublin], 149).

[30] On the demarcation of vv. 1–15 for the prologue, see Leander E. Keck, "The Introduction to Mark's Gospel," *NTS* 12 (1956–66): 352–70; Gnilka, *Markus*, 1.39; Robert Guelich, "'The Beginning of the Gospel' Mark 1:1–15," *BR* 27 (1982): 5–15.

[31] Danove claims that the prologue of Mark "presents twenty-one references that establish eighteen distinct points of information about God" including (1) God's gospel (3x), (2) God's son, (3) God's holy scripture, (4) God's prophet, (5) God's sending, (6) God's messenger, (7) God's way (2x), (8) God's paths, (9) God's holy spirit, (10) God's tearing open of the sky, (11) God's spirit descending on/into Jesus, (12) God's voice, (13) God's beloved son, (14) God's spirit that sends Jesus into the desert, (15) God being pleased, (16) God's messengers serving Jesus in the wilderness, (17) God's fulfillment the time, and (18) God's kingdom (*Charaterization of God*, 50–1).

Jesus as one belonging to God ("God's Son" in 1:1),³² followed by a scriptural medley in which God is the central, if tacit, actor (1:2-3). John the Baptizer announces the ἰσχυρότερός to come after him (1:4-8), a term of importance later in the narrative (3:27).³³ God endorses Jesus's baptism by rending the heavens and pronouncing a blessing over "my son," only to have him cast into the wilderness to be tempted by Satan (1:9-13). Finally, the prologue concludes with Jesus preaching the "good news of God" concerning the "kingdom of God" (1:14-15). Needless to say, God's presence in Mark is sharply pronounced in the prologue. But is God's role a moral one? I now turn to Mark's use of Scripture in the prologue, in which God's "way" describes a moral pattern of life for God's family.

A Scriptural Medley (Mark 1:2-3)

Mark begins with a curious mishmash of Mal 3:1, Isa 40:3, and Exod 23:20, all of which he, or the source from which he draws, attributes to Isaiah the prophet (cf. Matt 3:3; 11:10; Luke 3:4; 7:27).³⁴ Two features of these Scriptural "allusions" will be the focus of my analysis: the role of God (the implied subject of ἀποστέλλω) and the moral function of "way" (1:2-3; cf. 12:14) in Mark's use of Scripture.³⁵

Mark 1:2, a composite text most certainly not from Isaiah,³⁶ displays similarities to both Mal 3:1 LXX (ἰδοὺ ἐγὼ ἐξαποστέλλω τὸν ἄγγελόν μου, καὶ ἐπιβλέψεται ὁδὸν πρὸ προσώπου μου) and Exod 23:20 LXX (καὶ ἰδοὺ ἐγὼ ἀποστέλλω τὸν ἄγγελόν μου πρὸ προσώπου σου, ἵνα φυλάξῃ σε ἐν τῇ ὁδῷ).³⁷ This conflation is recognized as early

---

³² The volume of studies devoted to the text-critical issue of υἱοῦ θεοῦ in Mark 1:1 is enormous. For a clear summary of the debate, see Max Botner, "The Role of Transcriptional Probability in the Text-Critical Debate on Mark 1:1," *CBQ* 77 (2015): 467-80. For a compelling case for the longer reading, including a thorough investigation of the patristic evidence, see Tommy Wassermann, "The 'Son of God' Was in the Beginning (Mark 1:1)," *JTS* 62 (2011): 20-50.

³³ See Marcus, *Mark 1-8*, 158. Notice also in 9:14-29 that the disciples lack the ability to cast out a demon (9:18).

³⁴ On the likelihood that all three references are in view, see Joel Marcus, *The Way of the Lord: Christological Exegesis of the Old Testament in the Gospel of Mark* (Louisville, KY: Westminster John Knox Press, 1992), 12-17; Rikki Watts, *Isaiah's New Exodus and Mark*, WUNT 2.88 (Tübingen: Mohr Siebeck, 1997), 61-90.

³⁵ On my use of allusions, see summary in Samuel Emadi, "Intertextuality in New Testament Scholarship: Significance, Criteria, and Intertextual Reading," *CBR* 14 (2015): 8-23, esp. 14-15. For my case, the allusions to Mal 3:1 and Isa 40:3 are justified in part by Jerome (*Ep.* 57.9; *Comm. Mal.* 3.1).

³⁶ Thomas Hatina offers seven scholarly positions for Mark's attribution of this passage to Isaiah: (1) Mark is ignorant of his sources; (2) Mark 1:2 was inserted later; (3) Isaiah is the prophet associated with messianic predictions in early Christianity; (4) the Isaianic quotation is longer than the others; (5) Isaiah was the most popular prophet in antiquity; (6) Mark uses a testimonium that did not properly reference the texts; and (7) Mark intended to connect all events in his Gospel to Isaiah's promise (*In Search of a Context: The Function of Scripture in Mark's Narrative*, JSNTSup 232 [New York: Sheffield Academic Press, 2002], 143). While any combination of these seven positions is plausible, Mark's later reference to Isaiah in 7:6 lends credence to position 5. If Mark is writing to an audience unfamiliar with certain Jewish laws and practices (e.g., 7:3-4, 19), then selecting a more popular prophet in antiquity would better serve his audience.

³⁷ Such conflation was not uncommon in Jewish tradition (see Klyne R. Snodgrass, "Streams of Tradition Emerging from Isaiah 40:1-5 and Their Adaptation in the New Testament," *JSNT* 8 [1980]: 24-45).

as Jerome, who cites Mal 3:1 but not Exod 23.³⁸ In context, Mal 3 contains an oracle of divine judgment regarding the day of the Lord (Mal 3:17; 4:1, 3, 5 LXX): Malachi sets forth a scene of eschatological judgment on behalf of God (3:18 LXX). In Malachi the "messenger" (מַלְאָכִי) is most likely Elijah (4:5 LXX), though the context is unclear.³⁹ With regard to the second possible allusion, Exod 23:20, the broader setting is God's discourse with Moses (Exod 20:22). God promises to provide an angel/messenger (מַלְאָךְ) who will lead the Israelites to the land of Canaan (23:20–33). It should be noted that the degree to which Mark invokes the entirety of these stories is difficult to determine with confidence.⁴⁰ Generally, the contexts of both passages reveal God as the actor who sends God's messenger, within the setting of either eschatological judgment (Mal 3:1) or future deliverance (Exod 23:20). This use of prophecy at the start of Mark's Gospel is one of the reasons James M. Robinson referred to Mark's introduction as "the inauguration of eschatological history."⁴¹ What happened long ago is unfolding now. Robinson's interpretation is supported by Irenaeus, who understood Mark 1:2 to announce the Gospel's "prophetic character."⁴²

Finally, Mark 1:2 contains the addition of the future verb κατασκευάσει.⁴³ Importantly, the object of this future preparation is "your way," to be discussed in detail below. Contextually, the pronoun σου may refer to Jesus's way (1:4–11); in Mal 3:1, "way" refers exclusively to God's way.⁴⁴ The parallelism with John the Baptist (if identified as "my messenger") suggests that "your" here refers to Jesus, but the obscurity should be noted.⁴⁵

Turning to Mark 1:3, the use of Isa 40:3 appears nearly identical to the LXX (φωνὴ βοῶντος ἐν τῇ ἐρήμῳ Ἑτοιμάσατε τὴν ὁδὸν κυρίου, εὐθείας ποιεῖτε τὰς τρίβους τοῦ θεοῦ ἡμῶν). One key difference is the alteration of "the paths of our God" to "his paths."⁴⁶ As was the case in the appearance of "your way" in 1:2, the antecedent is

---

³⁸ Jerome, *Ep.* 57.9; *Comm. Mal.* 3.1.
³⁹ Some understand the reference to "the Lord" in conjunction with "my messenger" in Malachi 3:1 to refer to God (see Andrew E. Hill, *Malachi: A New Translation with Introduction and Commentary*, AB 25D [New York: Doubleday, 1998], 286–9).
⁴⁰ C. H. Dodd's account of "testimony-books" makes the case that the use of the Hebrew Bible in the New Testament may recall the "whole context" of a passage (*According to the Scriptures: The Sub-Structure of New Testament Theology* [London: Nisbet, 1952], 126–7). According to Dodd, when certain verses or passages are quoted from Isaiah, "the total context … is in view." This is also the position of Watts: Mark presents "a positive scheme whereby Jesus' identity and ministry is presented in terms of Isaiah's New Exodus" (*New Exodus*, 4). Similarly, Marcus advocates for a Markan use of Isaiah that "does not appear in a vacuum" (*Way of the Lord*, 23). For a convincing case against the Exodus "metanarrative," see Hatina, *In Search of a Context*, 138–83.
⁴¹ James Robinson, *Problem of History in Mark*, SBT (London: SCM Press, 1962), 76. A. Y. Collins also refers to Mark's use of scripture as the "fulfillment of the divine plan" (*Mark*, 42); see also Adela Yarbro Collins, *Is Mark's Gospel a Life of Jesus?: The Question of Genre*, PMLT (Milwaukee, WI: Marquette University Press, 1990), 58–62.
⁴² προφητικὸς γὰρ ὁ χαρακτὴρ οὗτος (*Haer.* 3.11.8; SC 211, 169).
⁴³ A verb that is not uncommon in Second Isaiah: see Isa 40:19, 28; 43:7; 45:7, 9.
⁴⁴ In Exod 23:20, the "you" here would refer to the people of God.
⁴⁵ Marcus contends that the "your" here draws a close connection between Jesus and the "Lord" "without simply identifying Jesus with God" (*Way of the Lord*, 41). If one follows Jerome's reading (*Ep.* 57.9; *Comm. Mal.* 3.1), Malachi's context is preferred.
⁴⁶ On the uncertainty of a messianic reading here, see Snodgrass, "Streams," 34. In the textual apparatus, note the addition of "of your God" in Codex Bezae.

unclear.⁴⁷ If the intention is to connect Jesus with the "Lord," that is, God, the result is equivocal at best: whose way is "the way of the Lord"? Is it God's way, Jesus's way, or both? Some commentators identify the "Lord" in Mark 1:3 as Jesus exclusively,⁴⁸ while others identify the "Lord" as God exclusively.⁴⁹ Evidence for Mark's use of the term κύριος elsewhere is likewise split; sometimes the term is applied to God (5:19; 11:9; 12:11, 29, 30, 36), while other times it refers to Jesus (2:28; 11:3). While the exact meaning may be purposely elusive here (cf. 5:19), in Mark's prologue, God's "way" and "paths" are announced by the prophet Isaiah in a manner that closely aligns Jesus with God. This is depicted more clearly in the baptism scene (1:9–11). In v. 10, the heavens are "torn open" by God,⁵⁰ whose voice is then heard from heaven. This heavenly voice declares over Jesus a recapitulation of Mark's introduction: "You are my son." In other words, it is God's way with which Jesus aligns.

A prophetic use of Isa 40:3 also appears in Qumran's *Manual of Discipline*, where an ambiguous pronoun clearly refers to "the way of YHWH."⁵¹

> And when these have become a community in Israel in compliance with these arrangements they are to be segregated [יבדלו] from within the dwelling of the men of sin to walk to the desert [למדבר] in order to open there His path [דרך הואהא]. As it is written: 'In the desert prepare the way of the .... straighten in the steppe a roadway for our God [מסלה לאלוהינו]' (1QS 8:12b–14)⁵²

James H. Charlesworth argues that the term דרך "became a *terminus technicus* to denote the members of the community" in the sectarian literature of Qumran (1QHa 1:36; 1QM 14:7; 1QS 8:10, 18, 21).⁵³ This estimate coheres with early Christian usage of the term (e.g., Acts 9:2; 19:9; 22:4). The term "way," as it appears in 1QS, invokes special meaning, particularly in the phrase "perfection of the way" (בתמים דרך).⁵⁴ In addition to serving as a metonym for the community, the term דרך also refers to a

---

⁴⁷ The solution need not be "messianic exegesis," as suggested by Jocelyn McWhirter, "Messianic Exegesis in Mark 1:2–3," in *"What Does the Scripture Say?" Studies in the Function of Scripture in Early Judaism and Christianity, Volume 1: The Synoptic Gospels*, ed. Craig Evans and H. Daniel Zacharias, LNTS 469 (New York: T&T Clark, 2012, 158–78).
⁴⁸ See Hatina, *In Search of a Context*, 150.
⁴⁹ As is the case with Tolbert, *Sowing the Gospel*, 245. Vincent Taylor's position is mediatory: "Here it is used of God ... but it is possible that Mark has the Messiah in mind" (*The Gospel According to St. Mark*, 2nd ed. [London: Macmillan, 1966], 153).
⁵⁰ As Morna Hooker notes, the rending of the heavens and the descent of the spirit signify an eschatological event: "the descent of God to earth to assist his people" (*The Message of Mark* [London: Epworth Press, 1983], 11).
⁵¹ On the abbreviation for the tetragrammaton in this text, see James H. Charlesworth, "Intertextuality: Isaiah 40.3 and the Serek Ha-Yahad," in *The Quest for Context and Meaning: Studies in Biblical Intertextuality in Honor of James A. Sanders*, ed. Craig A Evans and Shemaryahu Talmon (Leiden: Brill, 1997), 212–13.
⁵² Trans. Florentino García Martínez and Eibert J. C. Tigchelaar, eds., *The Dead Sea Scrolls Study Edition: Volume One, 1Q1–4Q273* (Grand Rapids, MI: Eerdmans, 1997), 89. The ellipsis does not indicate that the text is incomplete or corrupt: this is a technical reference to the divine name in the DSS manuscript tradition.
⁵³ Charlesworth, "*Intertextuality: Isaiah 40.3* and the Serek Ha-Yahad," 215.
⁵⁴ Cf. 1QS 8:18, 21; 9:5.

series of precepts belonging to God (1QS 2:2; 3:10; 9:19, 21; 10:21; 11:13, 17). Furthermore, the occasional appearance of the circumlocution for YHWH ("...."), combined with the closing phrase "a roadway for our God" (מסלה לאלוהינו), indicates that the ambiguous pronoun here, "His" (הואהא), refers to YHWH.[55] The precepts and community comprising "the way," according to these selections from the Qumran corpus, belong to YHWH.

In conjunction with the appearance of the term "wilderness" (מדבר), Charlesworth also suggests that the intertext of Isa 40:3 served as support for the Qumranites' literal understanding of their call into the wilderness to study Torah. Likewise, George J. Brooke contends that, for Qumran, "going into the wilderness was an actual experience which fitted the eschatological hope that God would soon appear in glory to vindicate those who know and correctly practised the law."[56] If so, the use of the imperfect in 1QS 8:13 ("shall separate") may indicate an eschatological expectation of some kind (cf. the parallel text in 1QS 9:19–21). God's role in calling the Qumran community into the wilderness is set in terms of prophetic fulfillment. One may recall, at this point, Mark's use of "wilderness" (ἔρημος) throughout the prologue (1:3–4, 12–13; cf. 1:35; 6:31–32) in concert with the "way" in Mark 1:2–3.[57] In Mark, the combination of "way" with "wilderness" connects Mark's scriptural citations with the rest of the prologue. A wilderness is in Mark's immediate purview (1:12–13) and a "way" is conclusively announced (1:14–15). The brief comparison to Qumran demonstrates the following: Mark's Gospel, on the one hand, does not make claims for the type of ascetic exclusivism that one finds in the Qumran community. There is no evidence that Mark, or his readers, underwent self-imposed desert exile or that they operated by the strict ethical bylaws that we find in the *Manual of Discipline*. On the other hand, like the use of 1QS within Qumran reading communities, Mark and its intended audience may utilize the term "way" with moral import. A moral valence of the term "way," in the very least, was in the air. The way of God in Mark differs from the mores of this Essene sectarian group, if one considers Mark's inclusion of outsiders (5:1–20; 11:17; 12:28–34; 13:10) and elevation of women (5:21–43; 7:24–30; 12:41–44; 14:1–11; 15:40–41). With that said, Mark's use of Isa 40:3 seems to set God's activity in terms of a morally loaded way and God's future vindication of those who follow it.

Notably, the term ὁδός appears as a thematic link among all three of the scriptural allusions. The observation that ὁδός operates as an important motif in Mark has

---

[55] Charlesworth advises translating "Lord" for the odd use of the pronoun because it likely "represents the tetragrammaton" (ed., *The Dead Sea Scrolls, Hebrew Aramaic, and Greek Texts with English Translations: Volume 1, Rule of the Community and Related Documents*, PTSDSSP [Louisville, KY: Westminster John Knox Press, 1994], 37 n. 210).

[56] George J. Brooke, "Isaiah 40:3 and the Wilderness Community," in *New Qumran Text and Studies: Proceedings of the First Meeting of the International Organization for Qumran Studies, Paris, 1992*, ed. George J. Brooke and Florentino Garcia, STDJ 15 (Leiden: Brill, 1994), 132. Henry W. Morisada Rietz follows Brooke, "Interpreting Traditions: The Qumran Community and the Gospels," *Perspectives in Religious Studies* 37 (2010): 391–406.

[57] As Guelich notes, unlike Matt 4:1 and Luke 4:1, "Mark *repeats* the location (1:13a) in combination with the statement of the forty-day period when Jesus was tempted by Satan" ("Beginning," 9).

long been noted by scholars (e.g., 4:4, 15; 10:52; 12:14).[58] According to Joel Marcus, the appearance of "the way of the Lord" in Mark's prologue lends to an ethical interpretation: contrary to typical readings, in which human action is prioritized, Marcus rightly calls for a theocentric reading.[59]

Ernest Best understands the way in Mark to serve, primarily, as a description of discipleship, set forth by Jesus in 8:22–10:52 (8:27; 9:33–34; 10:17, 32, 46, 52).[60] According to Best, Jesus's way to death outlines a journey for discipleship, in which "Christians go the same way as their Lord but are always in the position of those who follow, never of those who have arrived."[61] Best's account of Jesus's way as both an attitude of "self-denial" and activity of "cross-bearing" moves closer to a moral account of the way, with the addition that it is *God's* way Jesus follows (1:2–3; 2:20; 5:19; 8:31; 10:38; 12:6, 9; 14; 14:27, 36; 15:34).[62]

Within a first-century biographical context, ethics tend to turn away from citation of detached ethical commands (i.e., one must follow Jesus) toward the framework in which those commands become intelligible: moral accountability to God. To illustrate this, consider the example Marcus cites from Mark 12:14. On the subject of paying taxes to Caesar, the Pharisees and Herodians attempt to trap Jesus. They approach Jesus, as Marcus correctly notes, on 'ethical" terms: how must one act in the given situation?[63] A nod to moral casuistry. Jesus responds on his own terms, "Hand over to Caesar, that which belongs to Caesar [τα Καίσαρος], and to God that which belongs to God [τὰ τοῦ θεοῦ]" (12:17). In this pericope, the "way of God" (12:14) boils down to a question of accountability, not of good behavior or imperial citizenship. God has rightful claim to that which belongs to God.[64] If Mark contains a "way" motif, then it is reasonable to infer that this way is, in the first instance, of God and that its moral characteristics entail accountability to God.[65]

---

[58] Snodgrass, "Streams," 36; Best, *Following Jesus*, 16; Marcus, *Way of the Lord*, 31–3; Rhoads, Dewey, and Michie, *Mark as Story*, 66–9; Werner H. Kelber, *Mark's Story of Jesus* (Philadelphia: Fortress Press, 1979), 17.
[59] Marcus, *Way of the Lord*, 29–31. One might compare ethical discourse that prioritizing human action to the doctrine of the "two ways" (1QS 3:13–4:26; T. Levi 19:1; T. Asher 3:1–4:5).
[60] Best, *Following Jesus*, 15–16.
[61] Ibid., 16, 248.
[62] Ibid., 39. While Best offers a balanced account of the *imitatio Christi* mode ("it cannot be said to dominate the thought of Mark," 39), he offers only glimpses of God's role (e.g., "Jesus points his disciples to God and himself walks the way of God," 248–9). Best is right to define discipleship as a moral pilgrimage, but it also must be defined in accordance with God's way (as in 1:2–3; 12:14). Best's discussion of Mark 1:2–3 and 12:14 offers little reflection on God's role in the way Jesus must follow (ibid., 16, 155).
[63] Marcus, *Way of the Lord*, 31 n. 71.
[64] Conversely, in Jesus's retort to the Pharisees (12:15b: "Why do you tempt [πειράζετε] me?"), Mark implicitly provides an example of immorality as well: confusing the "things of Caesar" with the "things of God."
[65] That the term way invokes ethical discourse is evidenced in Deut 5:32–33. 11:28; 1QS 3:13–4:8; Barn. 5; Did. 1.1; 5.1; 6.1; 1 Clem. 35.5; T. Asher 3:1–4:5. In these sources, "way" is frequently split between the righteous and the wicked. In Deut 11:28 it is God's way that leads to life. That Mark draws from Israel's ethical traditions, see Susan R. Garrett, *The Temptations of Jesus in Mark's Gospel* (Grand Rapids, MI: Eerdmans, 1998), 52.

The Temptation Scene (1:12–13)

The temptation scene contains one of several references to Satan in Mark (1:13; 3:23, 26; 4:15; 8:33).⁶⁶ It also contains one of several instances in which Jesus is tempted in Mark (8:11; 10:2; 12:15).⁶⁷ One purpose of this scene is to introduce the dominant moral adversary to God, Satan.⁶⁸ The frequent juxtaposition of moral quandaries in Mark, noted earlier, derives from a larger moral junction. Accountability to God in Mark, in other words, is apocalyptically contested territory. "Belonging" in Mark is jeopardized by forces at odds with "the things of God" (8:33; 12:17). Nowhere is this clearer than in Mark's temptation scene.

Leading up to this section, traces of moral struggle are already present. John the Baptist's designation of Jesus as the "stronger one" (1:7) has one clear parallel in Mark: 3:19b–30 (cf. 5:4).⁶⁹ In Mark 3, Jesus is accused of "having Beelzebul" the "ruler of demons" (v. 22). Mark alone attributes this controversy to the accusation that Jesus "has an unclean spirit" (3:30; cf. Matt 12:22–29; Luke 11:14–23). As Loren T. Stuckenbruck notes, it is defensible that by the first century "there was a mythological framework within which the idea of Jesus' demonic origin could be imagined."⁷⁰ As evidence, Stuckenbruck cites the Gen 6:4 tradition concerning the οἱ υἱοὶ τοῦ θεοῦ, which had developed into a story of fallen angels who tempt and torment humanity (1 En. 6–10; Jub. 5:1–8; Philo, *De Gig.* 1–2; T. Reub. 5:6–7). Whether or not the myth of fallen angels is constitutive of Mark's religious context here, a landscape of "unclean spirits" indisputably covers Mark's narrative. They inflict violence on and control over human bodies (1:26; 5:1–13; 7:24–30; 9:17, 20) and animals (5:13); they fear Jesus

---

⁶⁶ For a catalogue of temptation episodes and their conflation of Satan with Jesus's enemies, see Joachim H. Korn, *ΠΕΙΡΑΣΜΟΣ: Die Versuchung des Gläubigen in der griechischen Bibel*, BWANT 72 (Stuttgart: Kohlhammer, 1937), 79. Mary E. Andrews views temptation as a central theme to the Gospel stories ("Peirasmos: A Study in Form Criticism," *ATR* 24 (1942): 229–44).

⁶⁷ Jeffrey Gibson contends that Mark 8:27–33 and 14:32–43 should be considered temptations stories, even though the verb πειράζω is absent (*The Temptations of Jesus in Early Christianity*, JSNTSup 112 [Sheffield: Sheffield Academic Press, 1995], 212–37, 288–317); as does Garrett, *Temptations*, 76, 89–115.

⁶⁸ Outside of the temptation episodes, Satan's adversarial role is a predominant theme in the New Testament and early Christianity (Luke 13:16; 22:31; Acts 5:3; Rom 16:20; 1 Cor 5:5; Jas 4:7; Rev 2:13). It is also common in much of Second Temple Judaism, though with varying nomenclature (1 En. 6; Apoc. Abr. 20; 1QS 1:18, 24; 1QM 13:11–12; T. Dan 5:1; T. Naph. 8:4). Satan as adversary gains even more texture in late antiquity, as in Jacob of Sarug's homily, in which the temptation scene is described as an all-out brawl: "All the demons moved with war for the Son of God. ... [F]or forty days the slanderer arrayed his temptation as he was rousing hidden battles against the Savior" (*Jacob of Sarug's Homilies on Jesus' Temptation*, trans. Adam Carter McCollum, TCLA 38 [Piscataway, NJ: Gorgias Press, 2014], 43–4). For a thorough account of Satan's turn from a member of God's heavenly council (Job 1:6–12) to God's adversary, see Henry A. Kelly, "The Devil in the Desert," *CBQ* 26 (1964): 202–13; Elaine Pagels, "The Social History of Satan, the 'Intimate Enemy': A Preliminary Sketch," *HTR* 84 (1991): 105–28.

⁶⁹ See Ched Myers, *Binding the Strong Man: A Political Reading of Mark's Story of Jesus*, 20th anniversary ed. (Maryknoll, NY: Orbis Books, 2008), 127; Robinson, *Problem of History*, 77–8; Ernest Best, *The Temptation and the Passion: The Markan Soteriology*, SNTSMS 2 (Cambridge: Cambridge University Press, 1965), 12.

⁷⁰ Loren T. Stuckenbruck, *The Myth of Rebellious Angels: Studies in Second Temple Judaism and New Testament Texts* (Grand Rapids, MI: Eerdmans, 2017), 153.

(3:11; 5:7). The "stronger one" appears to recalibrate the moral compass of the world toward God and away from Satan.

Mark's temptation scene begins with "and immediately the spirit *cast him out* [ἐκβαλει] into the wilderness." Up to this point, the spirit has appeared twice in Mark: once as an agent in baptism (1:8) and, again, as a dove landing on (εἰς) Jesus (1:10; cf. Luke 3:22).[71] Thus far, it would appear that the spirit is the source of Jesus's power, qualifying him as the ἰσχυρότερός announced by John. Later in the narrative, the spirit is the means by which Jesus obtains extrasensory knowledge (2:8, "he recognized by/in his spirit"). Mark also reveals that this spirit is the one against whom an "eternal sin" may be committed (3:29). The act of blasphemy, confusing the holy spirit with an unclean one, has unforgivable consequences (3:30).[72] That the spirit is an agent of God is confirmed in the Hebrew Bible,[73] Qumran literature,[74] and apocalyptic texts.[75] Even in the *Life of Apollonius*, Apollonius is led by a "divine spirit."[76] In Mark 1:12, it is God's agent that casts Jesus out into the wilderness, an action typically reserved for the demonic. Indeed, Jesus and his disciples frequently cast out demons in Mark (1:34, 39; 3:15, 22–23; 6:13).[77] Nonetheless, and uniquely in Mark, Jesus's temptation appears forced upon him by God. In the words of C. E. B. Cranfield, "We think of a moral compulsion by which the Spirit made it clear to Jesus that the acceptance of his Servant-vocation must lead him."[78] If time is up (1:15) and the world exists in a state of demonic disarray (1:21–28), then the spirit's compulsion of Jesus is morally motivated.

Next, we learn that Jesus is "in the wilderness forty days tempted by Satan."[79] The word for "tempting/testing" (πειράζω) appears four times in Mark (1:13; 8:11; 10:2; 12:15). The forces against which Jesus contends extend beyond Satan to the Pharisees,

---

[71] On reading the baptism and temptation scene together, see Garrett, *Temptations*, 55–6.
[72] This condition for blasphemy is also defined by Jesus's adversaries in Mark (2:7; 14:64).
[73] E.g., in the LXX: "spirit of the Lord" (Judg 3:10; 1 Kgs 18:12; Isa 61:1); "spirit of God" (Gen 1:2; Num 24:2; 1 Sam 19:20; Ezek 11:24); "holy spirit" (Ps 50:13; Isa 63:11).
[74] E.g., 1QS 3:13–4:26; 1QHa 12:32–33; 20:14–15; 21:34.
[75] E.g., Dan 5:12; 6:3; 2 Bar. 6:3; 21:4.
[76] δαίμων, as in Philostratus, *Life* 1.18.
[77] Matthew and Luke describe the spirit in less aggressive terms: the spirit "leads" Jesus (Matt 4:1; Luke 4:1). While I do not intend to read an Adam typology here per se, it is interesting that Philo uses ἐκβαλλω for God's banishment of Adam from paradise in *Cher*. 1.1. Outside of the New Testament, the verb's connotation can be strongly negative (e.g., Josephus, *Ant*. 5.7.8; 6.2.1).
[78] C. E. B. Cranfield, *The Gospel According to Saint Mark: An Introduction and Commentary*, CGTC (Cambridge: Cambridge University Press, 1959), 56.
[79] The presence of "wild beasts" in Mark 1:13 deserves brief attention. The term θηρίον appears in Genesis LXX (e.g., 1:24, 25, 30; 2:19, 20; 3:1, 14; and 6:19), leading some to read an Adam typology in Mark (cf. Joachim Jeremias, "Ἀδάμ," in *TDNT* 1.141; Joachim Jeremias, *Neutestamentliche Theologie. Erster Teil Die Verkündigung Jesu* [Gütersloh: Gütersloher Verlagshaus, 1971], 74; W. A. Schulze, "Der Heilige und die wilden Tiere. Zur Exegese von Mc 1,13b," *ZNW* 46 [1955], 280–3). Others cite the beasts in the wilderness mentioned in the Testaments of the Twelve Patriarchs (T. Iss. 7:7; T. Ben. 5:2; T. Naph. 8:4), under the assumption that the Testaments predate the Gospels (e.g., Best, *Temptation*, 9; Gibson, *Temptations*, 67–8). It is possible, however, that the Testaments borrow from the Gospels (see M John-Patrick O'Connor, "The Devil will Flee: James 4:7, the Jesus Tradition, and the Testaments of the Twelve Patriarchs," *JBL* 138 [2019]: 883–97). If one takes up A. Y. Collins's position, as I do, Mark's potential use of Isaiah for "wild beasts" would strengthen Mark's apocalyptic landscape and in particular Jesus's conflict with the demonic (see Isa 13:21 LXX; A. Y. Collins, *Mark*, 153).

scribes, and Herodians.⁸⁰ On Mark's use of πειράζω in 1:13, many conclude that the word illustrates Jesus's "trustworthiness."⁸¹ But trustworthiness to whom? As Susan Garrett summarizes, "[it is] God who put Jesus into the wilderness to be tested. God has declared Jesus to be his son, and now God arranges for Satan to test Jesus to see whether he is worthy of that assessment."⁸² By comparison, prominent figures in Judaism were subjected to temptation. In the Martyrdom and Ascension of Isaiah, Manasseh becomes an agent of Beliar: "Isaiah said to Hezekiah the king ... 'and Beliar will dwell in Manasseh, and by his hands I will be sawed in half'" (1:9–10).⁸³ While the word "temptation" does not appear, Manasseh's evil actions (1 Kgs 21:1–18; 2 Chron 33:1–9) are attributed to Satan (Mart. Isa. 2:2; cf. 5:1–16).⁸⁴ Similarly, the author of the Testament of Joseph introduces the story of Joseph (Gen 39) with the preface that "in ten temptations [God] showed me trustworthy" (T. Jos. 2:7).⁸⁵ While the figure of Beliar appears less frequently in the Testament of Joseph, he is named as the source of temptation (T. Jos. 7:2–4).⁸⁶ In another example, Abraham receives frequent veneration for his ability to overcome temptation in Second Temple and rabbinic literature (cf. Apoc. Abr. 13.7–14; Jub. 17:17; Pirke Aboth 5.4). In the book of Jubilees, Abraham is found faithful after ten tests (19:8). In the author's retelling of Gen 22, it is Prince Mastema, not God,⁸⁷ who initiates the testing of Abraham's faith (17:15–18:12). In each of these accounts, God's champion undergoes a diabolical test to prove his faith. In Mark, Jesus's filial status with God, declared prior to the temptation (1:1, 11), suggests that God, more than proving Jesus's faithfulness in this episode, demonstrates God's possession of Jesus and authority over Satan.⁸⁸ As in the words of the farmer in the

---

⁸⁰ Contra Best, *Temptation*, 15.
⁸¹ For an overview, see Jeffrey Gibson, "Jesus' Wilderness Temptation according to Mark," *JSNT* 53 (1994): 3–34, esp. 11. Birger Gerhardsson derives this meaning from the Hebrew word *nisāh*, "testing of the partner in the covenant" (*The Testing of God's Son [Matt 4:1–11 & Par]: An Analysis of Early Christian Midrash*, CBNTS 2 [Lund: Gleerup, 1966], 25–7). Relying on the early reception of the temptation by the author of Hebrews (2:18; 4:15), H. Seesemann understands such testing as "obedience through suffering," ("πεῖρα κτλ.," in *TDNT* 6.33). Andrews emphasizes Jesus as the exemplary model of one who was "without sin" ("Peirasmos," 41).
⁸² Garrett, *Temptations*, 59.
⁸³ Translation by M. A. Knibb, "Martyrdom and Ascension of Isaiah," in *OTP* 2.157. For a critical text of the Ethiopic, see Paolo Bettiolo et al., eds., *Ascensio Isaiae Textus*, CCSA 7 (Trunhout: Brepols, 1995), 46–7.
⁸⁴ The Martyrdom and Ascension of Isaiah is a composite text, with at least three divisions (1:1–3:12 and 5:1–16; 3:13–4:22; and 6–11). The Christian additions and editing of this text are usually obvious, especially in chs. 6–11. The sections referenced above likely derive from a Jewish original, with minor Christian interpolations (see Knibb, "Martyrdom," 143).
⁸⁵ Author's translation, based on M. de Jonge, *The Testaments of the Twelve Patriarchs: A Critical Edition of the Greek Text*, PVTG 1.2 (Leiden: Brill, 1978), 146.
⁸⁶ The phrase πνεῦμα τοῦ Βελιάρ is idiomatic in the Testaments of the Twelve Patriarchs (cf. T. Iss. 7:7; T. Jos. 7:4; T. Ben. 6:1).
⁸⁷ Cf. God as one who tests in Gen 22:1–2 or Deut 8:2.
⁸⁸ In this regard, Garrett places too much emphasis on human choice, claiming that even Jesus "proves that he is indeed worthy to be called God's 'beloved son.' For he has chosen the way of God rather than a path of his own desiring" (*Temptations*, 172). Garrett's observation must be reversed: Jesus prevails *because* he is God's son. On my reading, Garrett's use of Jdt 8:25–27 may be reinterpreted. As in Jdt 8:27 (NRSV), "For he has not tried us with fire, as he did them, to search their hearts, nor has he taken revenge upon us; but the Lord scourges *those who draw near to him*, in order to admonish them" (italics add). It is not, then, "that God tests to investigate"; rather, those who are near to God will undergo testing by nature of their proximity to God (ibid., 28).

parable of the wicked tenants, "They will"—or should—"respect my son" (12:6). In the temptation, God displays ownership over Jesus.

Jesus's interaction with Satan in Mark 1:12-13 also sets a precedent for the unclean spirits Jesus encounters throughout Mark (1:23; 3:11; 5:2, 13; 6:7, 13; 7:25; 9:25). The designation of Beelzebul as the "ruler of demons" (3:22) makes this association clear enough. Beyond Jesus's identification with adversarial agency, Jesus's first healing story in Mark is an exorcism (1:21-28), followed by a summary statement that Jesus "cast out many demons" (1:32, 34, 39; cf. 6:13). Exorcism is a specific task given to the disciples by Jesus on two occasions (3:15; 6:7); even more, it is only one of four tasks given to the disciples.[89] Whitney Taylor Shiner, in his detailed study of discipleship in Greco-Roman call stories, notes that the transfer of authority over spirits from teacher to student "is quite alien to the philosophical" material.[90] The disciples are given authority not by nature of what they do but by nature of the one to whom they belong: Jesus appoints the twelve "to be with him" (ἵνα ὦσιν μετ'αὐτοῦ). This becomes the major point of deviation for Judas, who "hands him over" (3:19; 14:10). Judas's betrayal is described in terms of a refusal to belong. Jesus is turned over to the ones to whom he does not belong, and eventually forsaken (15:34). The temptation scene, in sum, serves to further underscore a moral precedent handed down to the disciples from Jesus.[91] Authority in Mark exists over and against an antithetical moral force.[92] The opposite of what is good is alignment with Satan.

A Time Crunch: The Kingdom of God Has Come Near (1:14-15)

Evil's shadowy grip carries over into the next section as the reader learns that John was "handed over" (1:14): a verb used in Mark to describe Jesus's betrayal (3:19; 9:31; 10:33; 14:10, 11, 18, 21, 41-42, 44). Satan's swift departure in Matthew and Luke is not recorded by Mark (cf. Matt 4:11; Luke 4:13): evil still lingers. Jesus picks up where John left off, "preaching" in Galilee (κηρύσσων in 1:7) the "good news" of God,[93] simultaneously drawing the Gospel's introduction to a close and anticipating the ministry of Jesus to follow. While Mark's use of ἤγγικεν to describe the presence of God's reign has received much attention,[94] the focus of this section will be on the moral connotations for the fulfillment of time.

---

[89] According to Mark 3:14-15, the disciples are appointed (1) to be with Jesus, (2) to be sent out, (3) to preach, and (4) to cast out demons.
[90] Shiner, *Follow Me!*, 189.
[91] Whether or not the disciples in Mark succeed in doing so is another question. Other than 6:13 and 6:30, the disciples' only explicit attempt at exorcism appears to be a misfire (9:18).
[92] Once again, Best's conclusion that exorcisms in Mark are only "mopping-up" what has already been accomplished in the temptation scene ignores Satan's presence elsewhere in the narrative (*Temptation*, 15; see Mark 4:15; 8:33).
[93] While both John and Jesus "preach," Mark's John never "evangelizes" (εὐαγγελίζω; cf. Luke 3:18).
[94] Dodd's reliance on Mark 1:14-15 for his "realized eschatology" sparked much debate (*The Parables of the Kingdom* [New York: Scribner's Sons, 1958], 44-5). For two positions to the contrary, see R. H. Fuller, *The Mission and Achievement of Jesus: An Examination of the Presuppositions of New Testament Theology*, SBT 12 (London: SCM Press, 1954), 20-35; and Werner G. Kümmel, *Promise and Fulfilment: The Eschatological Message of Jesus*, trans. Dorothea M. Barton, SBT 23 (London: SCM Press, 1957), 20-4.

Mark's vigorously debated phrase "the time has been fulfilled" (πεπλήρωται ὁ καιρὸς) is removed by Matthew and Luke.[95] Oscar Cullmann memorably analyzed the concept of time in New Testament theology, claiming that καιρός "has to do with a definitive *point of time* which has a fixed content," specifically related to the "history of redemption."[96] For Cullmann, it is God's "divine decision" that orchestrates the καιρός time.[97] Gerhard Delling posits that the association of time with the gods appears as early as Aristotle.[98] Additionally, there is a strand of patristic tradition that reads Mark 1:15 in connection with Gal 4:4 ("but when the fullness of the time [τὸ πλήρωμα τοῦ χρόνου] came, God sent out his son").[99] While the different Greek words undercut Cullmann's point (χρόνος and καιρός), early Christian reception may indicate that Paul's theological understanding of time is closely connected to Mark 1:15. Further support for a theological understanding of time may be found, as Joachim Gnilka notes, in the apocalyptic use of temporal concepts.[100] An apocalyptic *Endzeit* nuance would correspond to Mark 10:30; 13:33; and elsewhere in early Christianity.[101] Even without this evidence, Mark's divine passive for the fulfillment of time announced at the beginning of Mark would imply God's divine orchestration: the time has been fulfilled (by God).[102] Additionally, time carries moral implications as one finds in the Epistle of Barnabas:

> And so by carefully investigating what is here and now, we must seek for the things that can save us. We should flee, entirely, all the works of lawlessness; otherwise, they may overwhelm us. And we should hate the error of the present age [τὴν πλάνην τοῦ νῦν καιροῦ], that we may be loved in the age to come. ... [T]he final stumbling block is at hand, about which it has been written, just as Enoch says. For this reason the Master shortened the seasons and the days [τοὺς καιροὺς καὶ τὰς ἡμέρας], that his beloved may hurry and arrive at his inheritance. (4:1–3)[103]

---

[95] Werner H. Kelber offers five ways in which Matthew alters Mark 1:14–15. First, Matthew moves this statement to ch. 4, no longer making it Jesus's "inaugural address." Second, while Mark has used the term "gospel" twice up to this point, Matthew refrains until 4:23. Third, Matthew presents Jesus's message as dependent on John the Baptist's (Matt 3:2; 4:17; potentially mitigated by 3:14–15). Fourth, Matthew omits the saying about "time" altogether. Fifth, Matthew reverses the order of the sayings (*The Kingdom in Mark: A New Place and a New Time* [Philadelphia: Fortress Press, 1974], 10).

[96] Oscar Cullmann, *Christ and Time: The Primitive Christian Concept of Time and History*, trans. Floyd V. Filson (Philadelphia: Westminster Press, 1950), 39, italics in original.

[97] Ibid.

[98] Gerhard Delling, "καιρός," in *TDNT* 3.455–6; cf. Aristotle, *Eth. Nic.* 1.6.3.

[99] Origen, *Comm. Joan.* 10.2.5–9. For a brief survey of the patristic treatment of Mark 1:14–15, see Ma'afu Palu, *Jesus and Time: An Interpretation of Mark 1.15*, LNTS 468 (New York: T&T Clark, 2012), 44–54. Palu misses the reference found in the Byzantine catena, *Cat. Marc.* 273.19–31, likely a summary of Origen, in the view of William R. S. Lamb (ed. and trans., *The Catena in Marcum: A Byzantine Anthology of Early Commentary on Mark* [Leiden: Brill, 2012], 231 n. 73).

[100] Gnilka cites Dan 7:22; Ezek 7:12; 9:1; and 1 Pet 1:11 as "consistent with the prophetic apocalyptic language" of time (*Markus*, 1.66). On the basis of early reception, however, one need not exclude, as Gnilka does, Gal 4:4 simply because Paul uses a different word for time.

[101] Cf. Luke 12:56; 18:30; Rev 12:14. See also the Epistle of Barnabas, which invokes Danielic language for "time" (4:1, 9; 15:5). For more, see BDAG s.v., καιρός, as "special crisis."

[102] Cf. Danove's comment, "God fulfills [πληρόω] the time" (*Characterization of God*, 51).

[103] Trans. Bart D. Ehrman, ed., *The Apostolic Fathers*, 2 vols., LCL (Cambridge, MA: Harvard University Press, 2003).

On the surface, the tone of this text strongly implies a time of crisis. As a result, one must choose good moral conduct. Time, or the lack thereof, dictates one's actions. Considered a little more deeply, the text offers us information about the ethos of the community that reads it. As Julien C. H. Smith has argued, the two-ways teaching in Barnabas may serve to unify the communal identity of the readers around the authority of a single teacher over against the teaching of dissenters.[104] In this way, for the community reading Barnabas, "there are two ways of teaching authority: *my* way, which is the way of light, and the way of *their* teachers, which is the way of darkness" (cf. 18:1).[105] In this sense, the eschatological hour is not the time to clean up one's act, so to speak, but the time to choose sides.[106] Morality is more than one's "hate of error" but accountability to a singular, authoritative teaching.[107]

Returning to Mark 1:14–15, this reading seems permissible within the Markan context. In addition to Mark's pervasive insider and outsider scheme (epitomized in 4:11),[108] God's good news, announced by Jesus, arrives in the form of two moral imperatives: repent and believe. The way of God governs the prologue and creates a moral crisis in which antithetical moral forces are made right by God. For this reason, the moral divide suggested in Mark's prologue does not concern paraenesis primarily, but moral accountability.[109] In the Hebrew Bible, repentance may connote a turning to God away from evil, according to G. R. Beasley-Murray (see Isa 46:8 LXX).[110] Coupled with the term "believe," an important theological concept scattered throughout Mark (5:36; 9:23, 42; 11:23; 13:21; 15:32), these imperatives appear grounded in a reality that God's kingdom has arrived. The moral actions of repenting and believing derive principally from human apprehension of the reality that God has arrived to call the world to account.[111]

In summary, Mark's prologue announces a world belonging to God. Jesus is God's son, who announces God's way, as foretold by God's prophets in conflict with God's adversary. Any moral activity in the Gospel proceeds from this reality. Furthermore, Mark's bifurcated moral choices (e.g., does one save or kill a life?) stem from a world beset by conflict. Satan's temptation of Jesus sets the tone for constant struggle throughout the narrative. The "things of God" war against the "things of humans," and

---

[104] Julien C. H. Smith, "The Epistle of Barnabas and the Two Ways of Teaching Authority," *VC* 68 (2014): 465–97.
[105] Ibid., 488 (italics in original).
[106] As Kelber has it, "it is Galilee where the mission of Jesus is continued. There the Kingdom of God is pitted against the Kingdom of Satan in a struggle which will decide the fate of history" (*The Kingdom in Mark*, 23).
[107] A similar phenomenon is evidenced in the literature of Qumran. The Righteous Teacher possess the mysteries of the prophets, while the Wicked Priest does not (1QpHab 7.3–8; 12.7–9).
[108] For more on the insider/outsider motif in Mark, see Laura C. Sweat, *The Theological Role of Paradox in the Gospel of Mark*, LNTS 492 (New York: Bloomsbury, 2013), 28–62.
[109] Contra Kelber, who calls Mark 1:15b "paraenesis" (*The Kingdom in Mark*, 12).
[110] G. R. Beasley-Murray, *Jesus and the Kingdom of God* (Grand Rapids, MI: Eerdmans, 1986), 75.
[111] Keck's language for moral warrants supports my point. "Warrants assume that one is more likely to do what is right if one knows why it is right and how that rightness is grounded in the kind of reality that matters. Characteristically, the New Testament writers appeal to the new reality created by the Christ-event" ("Rethinking," 11).

the arrival of God's kingdom reveals that the time has come for God to call the world to account.

3.4 Moral Accountability in God's Family

Another aspect of moral accountability in Mark concerns the family unit. There are several key sections in Mark that reveal a new family order: families are ruptured in answer to God's call (1:20, 30; 3:19b–35; 6:1–6, 18; 8:36–37; 10:1–12; 12:24–27; 13:12) and reordered around new "little" priorities (e.g., children in 9:42; 10:13–16; cf. 4:30–32). Names are changed (3:16), familial nomenclature is bestowed (2:5; 5:34; 10:24), mothers are valorized (15:40; 16:1), and the intimate location of the home regularly appears (2:1; 5:19; 7:24; 8:26).[112] In what follows, my contention is that this new family, with God as the parent (8:38; 11:25; 13:32; 14:36; cf. 12:6), reflects a restructured order of accountability that is fundamentally moral in character.

In antiquity, depending on the group with which one identified, family ties comprised the moral fabric of society. As in the accusation brought against Socrates, he "made his companions not only disgrace their fathers but also their other family members as well" (Xenophon, *Mem*. 1.2.51 [author translation]). According to Iamblichus's fourth-century CE account, Pythagoras, on the other hand, demanded good family relations of his followers before they could join his ranks (*Pythagorean Life* 17.71). This stringent account of familial ethics also accords with Zeno's teaching (Diogenes Laertius, *Lives* 7.109). As Bruce Malina notes, "honor is assumed to exist within one's own family of blood."[113] This social expectation may be found in Jewish groups in the Mediterranean world as well. In the Letter of Aristeas, one guest of King Ptolemy II defines family as an unbreakable bond in the face of great suffering (241–242). So, too, Philo, who classifies honoring one's parents as the highest duty, second only to honoring God, and disrupting families, by way of adultery, as the greatest evil (*Decal*. 24.127–131; 31.165–166). With this in mind, Jesus's very first action, following Mark's prologue, is to call Simon, Andrew, James, and John to leave their occupations, and presumably, their families (1:30; 10:28–31; 13:12).[114] Moreover, when Jesus's own family gets in the way of his teaching, he appears to disown them (3:33; 6:3). This is perhaps why, by the second century, early Christians became known by some as home-wreckers (*Cels*. 3.55).[115]

---

[112] See Elizabeth Struthers Malbon's study on home as space in Mark: *Narrative Space and Mythic Meaning in Mark*, BS 13 (Sheffield: JSOT Press, 1991), 106–40.

[113] Bruce J. Malina, *The New Testament World: Insights from Cultural Anthropology*, 3rd rev. ed. (Louisville, KY: Westminster John Knox Press, 2001), 36.

[114] We learn Simon is married in Mark 1:30 (cf. 1 Cor 9:5). His departure from his family, even if just his spouse, would have had legal ramifications (cf. Gaius, *Inst*. 1.127; 2.156; Justinian, *Dig*. 50.16.195). For more on the legal aspects of the *pater familias*, see Gottfried Schneider, "Pater familias," *Brill's New Pauly: Encyclopaedia of the Ancient World*, ed. Hubert Cancik and Helmuth Schneider (Boston: Brill, 2007), 10.595–98. Joseph H. Hellerman considers Peter's actions here "betrayal" (*The Ancient Church as Family* [Minneapolis, MN: Fortress Press, 2001], 66).

[115] As Mona Tokarek LaFosse rightly notes, Celsus draws on "a generalization in the ancient Mediterranean that women and children were susceptible to superstition and easily duped," but, as LaFosse goes on to suggest, "it is striking that women and children are highlighted, and

To be fair, Jesus's teachings in Mark do not always provoke rejection of accepted family values (7:10–13; 10:19); nonetheless, some of the evidence suggests that Jesus's words and actions would have been perceived as immoral in a first-century milieu.[116] One had duties and obligations to one's families that prohibited absolute abandonment.[117] Why, then, would Jesus call his disciples to leave their families? And further, why would he show disregard for his own?

The classic study by Martin Hengel, *The Charismatic Leader and His Followers*, offers several potential explanations.[118] First, the disrupted family motif appears in certain apocalyptic texts, as reflected in Matt 10:21 and Luke 21:16, "Brother will betray brother to death and a father his child, and children will rise up against their parents and they will kill them" (cf. Mic 7:6; Zech 13:3; 1 En. 99:5; 100:1; 2 Bar. 70:6). On the one hand, this reading seems plausible, especially considering the apocalyptic tones of the prologue discussed above and the harsh abandonment clause in Mark 13:12. On the other hand, outside of ch. 13, Mark does not provide the reader with the same cataclysmic, world-ending details. Second, scholars have suggested that the motif of abandoning one's family might fit the function of a teacher–pupil relationship. As in the Socratic tradition, "the teacher summons and lures young men into the role of disciple-companion."[119] While this is plausible, as Shiner observes, Mark's call-stories lack many characteristic features of Greco-Roman call-stories.[120] Moreover, these disciples are leaving not only their father Zebedee (1:19–20) but also their families as well. Third, the disruption of family motif may recall the messianic prophets or "zealot charismatics," recorded by Josephus (e.g., *Ant.* 18.4.1),[121] especially in times of crisis (e.g., *J.W.* 7.7). While Mark's Gospel contains several clues tying it closely to the Jewish War and times of great social upheaval (Mark 11:17; 13:7–9, 14, 22), it would seem a stretch to conclude that the remainder of the Gospel portrays Jesus as a charismatic zealot.[122] Even if the extenuating circumstances of war are envisioned in Mark, this would have been a time for families to draw together, not to be torn apart (cf. Mark 13:17).[123] Finally, some philosophers' calls to conversion petitioned

---

implies that they were present in a way and with such numbers that outside observers took notice" ("Women, Children, and House Churches," in *The Early Christian World*, 2nd ed., ed. Philip F. Esler [New York: Routledge, 2017], 385).

[116] Of course, communities existed in antiquity who were withdrawn from society, such as certain Essenes (Joesphus, *J.W.* 2.8.2), Philo's Theraputae (*De Vita Contemplativa*), the Qumranites (e.g., 1QS 6), and the Epicureans (Diogenes Laertius, *Epicurus*, 10.143). My case builds upon the rule, not the exception: abandoning one's family by Greco-Roman or Jewish standards was morally unacceptable.

[117] Aristotle provides an exhaustive view of the household in his *Politics*. Household management was a matter of virtue (see *Politics* 1.5.3).

[118] *The Charismatic Leader and His Followers*, trans. James Greig (New York: Crossroad, 1981), 15–37.

[119] Robbins, *Jesus the Teacher*, 118. Hengel notes this same pattern in the calling of Elisha by Elijah in 1 Kgs 19:19–21 (*Charismatic Leader*, 16–18)

[120] Shiner lists a "lack of motivation," "lack of moral criteria," and "lack of moral change" (*Follow Me!*, 183–98). My own case is that Mark's moral criteria for Jesus's calling is a prevailing accountability to God.

[121] Hengel, *Charismatic Leader*, 18–24.

[122] For the Jewish War setting, see Marcus, *Mark 1–8*, 28–37.

[123] On the galvanizing of families during times of war, see Suzanne Dixon, *The Roman Family* (Baltimore, MD: Johns Hopkins University Press, 1992), 27–8.

family disruption.[124] Epictetus, for instance, recalls a type of family abandonment in the conversion of a Cynic philosopher:

> And how is it possible for a man who has nothing, who is naked, without home or hearth, in squalor, without a slave, without a city, to live serenely? Behold, God has sent you the man who will show in practice that it is possible. "Look at me," he says, "I am without a home, without a city, without property, without a slave; I sleep on the ground; I have neither wife nor children, no miserable governor's mansion, but only earth, and sky, and one rough cloak. Yet what do I lack?"[125]

Hengel's options are not mutually exclusive: a combination of apocalyptic motifs, teacher–pupil dynamics, and a call to conversion may all be in play in such texts as Mark 1:16-20; 3:13-19; 6:1-6; 10:28; and 13:12-13a. If so, mitigating circumstances, such as the ones listed above, would allow for a reevaluation of natural family ties.[126] In Mark's case, it seems that the major circumstance in question is the arrival of God's kingdom and a moral order higher than what was conventionally assumed (1:14-15).

God the Parent[127]

By rupturing family ties, Mark's Gospel upsets some firm social expectations in antiquity. As the previous section demonstrated, this type of upheaval of one's family was not unprecedented in the first century. Times of socioeconomic crisis or the beguiling harangue of a moral philosopher may have enticed someone to leave his home. Whatever social factors were contributory to Mark's Jesus's call, the grounds by which familial disjunction becomes morally permissible, according to Mark, is the arrival of God's kingdom. A new moral order supersedes the present one.

The image of God as parent is common in Second Temple Judaism and Greco-Roman literature.[128] Mark utilizes the image of father more sparingly than do Matthew and Luke (Mark 8:38; 11:25; 13:32; 14:36; cf. 12:6).[129] In early Judaism and Christianity,

---

[124] Gerd Theissen refers to this type as "itinerant charismatics" or "wandering charismatics" (*Social Reality and the Early Christians: Theology, Ethics, and the World of the New Testament*, trans. Margaret Kohl [Minneapolis, MN: Fortress Press, 1992], 40). According to Theissen, marginal groups would have greater incentive to leave their families due to political upheaval, economic struggle, or natural disaster (ibid., 60-93). While this solution is entirely possible, especially considering Jesus's minimalist commands for the disciples' journey (6:7-12), extrapolating social factors remains speculative. What is certain is Mark's theological framing of leaving one's family.

[125] *Diss.* 3.22.45-49 (Oldfather, LCL). For more on conversion among the moral philosophers, see Abraham J. Malherbe, *Paul and the Thessalonians: The Philosophic Tradition of Pastoral Care* (Philadelphia: Fortress Press, 1987), 21-8.

[126] So Hellerman: "When one is forced to choose between loyalty to God and loyalty to one's blood family, the former must prevail" (*Church as Family*, 68). Consider Philo: "We are evacuating our cities, withdrawing from our houses and lands; our furniture and money and cherished possessions and all the other spoil we will willingly make over" (*Legat.* 32.232 [Colson, LCL]).

[127] For my selection of the three images that follow, see n. 5 above.

[128] For a survey of the literature from the Hebrew Bible and Second Temple Judaism, see Hellerman, *Church as Family*, 59-64. Hellerman refers to this as the "surrogate patrilineal kin group" (ibid., 59).

[129] For comparative data from Matthew and Luke, see n. 12 above.

the paternal language assigned to God often designated a role of ownership. In the Testament of Abraham, God spares creation from a sinless Abraham, who desires to destroy all those who sin upon the earth (10:1–15).[130] It is God as parent who oversees and protects God's children. That the Gospel writers envision God as replacing the role of the earthly parent is prevalent in the sources (e.g., Matt 7:7-11; Luke 12:28). As Wayne Meeks puts it, "the first Christians (like other sects of Jews) were taught to conduct their moral life under the all-seeing eye of a God who was simultaneously a stern patriarch and a forgiving and caring parent."[131]

Within a first-century household, the father's role formed the basis of the family's identity.[132] This language of ownership, typically referring to the father's ownership of the child, could extend beyond the biological family structure in antiquity as well. As Caroline Johnson Hodge rightly observes within ancient philosophical schools, "the members of these groups, who often explicitly distance themselves from traditional patrilineal structures (such as *genos*, *oikos*, and *polis*), imagine themselves to be related and organized by a kinship of the soul, mind, or spirit."[133] This is the case for the followers of Epicurus, who becomes the "father" of his students (cf. Lucretius, *De Rer.* 3.9; Diogenes Laertius, *Lives* 10.10). This type of constructed kinship could exist in philosophical schools but also in religious sects. Qumran, for example, appears to have a similar type of paternal kinship within their community. Those who are insiders receive titles, such as "sons of light" (1QM 1:1–15; 1QS 3:13) or "brothers" (1QM 13:1; 15:4; 1QS 6:26), while outsiders are referred to as "sons of darkness" (1QM 3:6, 9; 1QS 1:10). God is the "Father" of this community (1QHa 17:35–36),[134] while the Righteous Teacher is designated by God to reveal the meaning of divine mysteries (1QpHab 7:3–8).[135]

Returning to the Gospel of Mark, God's paternal role appears to operate within a similar framework of constructed or "fictive" kinship. God is the parent of Jesus (1:1, 11; 9:7), and whoever, in turn, follows God's will becomes a surrogate child of God (3:35). God alone is the one who forgives sins (2:7; 11:25), knows when "that day" will come (13:32), and the one to whom Jesus prays for a way out (14:36).

---

[130] In this episode, the venerable Abraham, who is known for advocating against mass destruction (Gen 18:22–33), "has no mercy on sinners" (T. Abr. 10:14). God, as creator of the world, must protect God's creation even from Abraham.

[131] Meeks, *Origins of Christian Morality*, 172.

[132] Importantly, as Caroline Johnson Hodge notes, this "identity—whether based on kinship or some other essentializing characteristic—is constructed from the start" (*If Sons, Then Heirs: A Study of Kinship and Ethnicity in the Letters of Paul* [New York: Oxford University Press, 2007], 21). For Hodge's case, Paul utilizes this construct of identity by patrilineal descent for Gentile inclusion. For more on the predominant role of the father in the home in the classical age of Rome, see Geoffrey S. Nathan, *The Family in Late Antiquity: The Rise of Christianity and the Endurance of Tradition* (New York: Routledge, 2000), 15–54.

[133] Hodge, *Heirs*, 38.

[134] Note Eileen M. Schuller and Carol A. Newsom's translation: "Until old age you yourself sustain me. Truly, my father did not acknowledge me, and my mother abandoned me to you, but you are a father to all the children of your truth and you rejoice over them as a woman who loves her nursing child, and like a foster-father you sustain all your creatures in (your) bosom" (*The Hodayot [Thanksgiving Psalms]: A Study Edition of 1QHa*, EJL 36 [Atlanta, GA: Society of Biblical Literature, 2012], 57).

[135] The Righteous Teacher may also assume the role of father as in 1QHa 15:23.

In 10:28–31, Peter declares that "we have left everything and followed you." In response, Jesus outlines the extent of Peter's desertion: "houses or brothers or sisters or mothers or fathers or fields" have been forsaken for "me and the gospel." The reward for such a high-stakes departure, according to Mark's Jesus, is "houses and brothers and sisters and mothers and children and fields"—but, noticeably, not fathers.[136] According to Gerhard Lohfink, fathers are left out of Mark 10:30 because "patriarchal domination is no longer permissible in the new family."[137] Whether or not this is the case, it seems that Mark's paternal lacuna may be filled by God alone (cf. Matt 23:9). Robert L. Brawley's short essay on the role of God in Mark summarizes the point well:

> A part of Mark's portrayal of God as father is that when family members evaluate Jesus as insane (3:21), Jesus supplants blood kinship with fictive kinship. Incidentally, fictive kinship is real. That is, when Jesus speaks of sisters, mothers, and brothers, he is naming genuine relationships with metaphors. His criterion for kinship is doing God's will.[138]

In other words, when Jesus assigns familial titles in Mark (e.g., "child" in 2:5; 10:24; "daughter" in 5:34), he is including real people within God's new family. Paternal accountability is supplanted by God.

Finally, it should be noted that Mark's Jesus does not take family abandonment lightly. In Mark 7:1–23, Jesus criticizes a certain group of Pharisees and scribes for their apparent misuse of Scriptural tradition. In vv. 7–9, Jesus zeros in on the command to honor one's parents. It appears that a certain tradition of "Corban" (Hebrew: קרבן), a vow intended to transfer property to God by way of the temple (Lev 1:2, 3, 10; Num 7:3), had been abused by some children seeking ways around Deut 5:16 and Exod 20:12. In Moshe Benovitz's assessment, "[The Pharisees and scribes'] elegant turn of phrase enables the son to bar his parents from using his property."[139] In certain cases,

---

[136] This is a Markan idiosyncrasy: cf. Matt 19:29–30; Luke 18:29–30.

[137] Gerhard Lohfink, *Jesus and Community: The Social Dimensions of Christian Faith*, trans. John P. Galvin (Philadelphia: Fortress Press, 1984), 49.

[138] Robert L. Brawley, "Generating Ethics from God's Character in Mark," in *Character Ethics and the New Testament: Moral Dimensions of Scripture*, ed. Robert L. Brawley (Louisville, KY: Westminster John Knox Press, 2007), 62.

[139] Moshe Benovitz, *KOL NIDRE: Studies in the Development of Rabbinic Votive Institutions*, BJS 315 (Atlanta, GA: Scholars Press, 1998), 23. The meaning of this passage has produced some disagreement. Origen suggests that the tradition is "obscure" (ἀσαφέστερον) in the Gospels. On the word of a Jewish friend, Origen explains that the practice originated between creditors and debtors. The creditor, in certain cases, could declare unpaid debt a gift to God, transferring the debtors account to the "poor fund" (τὸν τῶν πενήτων λόγον; *Comm. Matt.* 11.9; SC 162, 310–21). J. Duncan M. Derrett agrees with Origen ("KOPBAN, Ο ΕΣΤΙΝ ΔΩΡΟΝ," *NTS* 16 [1969–70]: 364–8). J. H. A. Hart contends that a Nazirite (or "quasi-Nazirite") vow is in view, which would have redirected the vassal's funds to the temple, preventing a child from supporting his own parents. Hart argues that Jesus commends the practice of Corban as radical devotion to God: one's commitment to God may even jeopardize honoring one's parents ("Corban," *JQR* 19 [1907]: 615–50). However, our sources offer no hint of a Nazirite vow here, and Jesus more clearly condemns the practice (Mark 7:8–9). Interpreters as early as the nineteenth-century priest John Lightfoot connect Corban to the rabbinic practice of *qonam*, a votive consecration "devoted to holy use," but Lightfoot does so only

the policy took effect simultaneously with the violation; therefore, theoretically, the child could insulate his property from parental use, and, if his parents accessed it, he could tie them up in ligation without ever having to donate the property to the temple (cf. *m. Ned.* 48a). Such circumstances incite Jesus to accuse this group of Pharisees and scribes of both "abandoning" and "rejecting" the commandment of God (τὴν ἐντολὴν τοῦ θεοῦ). In moral terms, the child is effectively relinquishing all accountability to authority (both to parents and to God), claiming sole authority over his own life and belongings (7:12).

In Second Temple Judaism, the commands to honor God and to honor one's parents were close counterparts. As in Josephus, "honor to parents the Law ranks second only to honor to God. ... It requires respect to be paid by the young to all their elders, because God is the most Ancient of all" (cf. Ps.-Phoc. 3; Jos. Asen. 11:11–13; 11Q19 54:19–21).[140] Even so, there were exceptions to this policy other than the Corban tradition. Philo, for example, explains that the command to honor parents can be abused by parents (*Decal.* 23.120). In this passage, Philo reprimands parents who consider themselves equal to God. In a similar vein, Jesus appears to condemn the replacement of God's command with human tradition. Picking up on language from Isa 29:13, it is the human element of the tradition's authority—τὴν παράδοσιν τῶν ἀνθρώπων—that crosses the line (7:7–8). Much like Philo's concern, in what amounts to a moral offense, God and humans must not be conflated. The juxtaposition in Mark 7 is that of humans and God. One may find ways around accountability to earthly parents, but no one dodges accountability to God.

In summary, accountability to God is expressed in terms of a new family in Mark. Those who leave fathers and mothers for the sake of God's call become surrogate members of God's family (3:35; 10:30). This family extends not only to the disciples but also to those who are physically sick (1:34; 2:5; 5:34). Moreover, leaving one's parent, an otherwise immoral action in antiquity, is permitted on the grounds that a higher moral order must be recognized, entailing a superior moral warrant. The decision to leave one's family is not a flippant one as Jesus's discourse on the Corban tradition reveals. Rather, it is the decision to place the self as its own moral compass, evacuating God's parental role that classifies an action as immoral. The orientation of the self, over and against God, as true north on a moral compass is one source of evil. The consequences for said immorality (7:21–23) will be outlined in Chapter 5.

---

in passing with little added commentary (*Horae Hebraicae et Talmudicae: Hebrew and Talmudic Exercitations upon the Gospels, the Acts, Some Chapters of St. Paul's Epistle to the Romans, and the First Epistle to the Corinthians* [Oxford: Oxford University Press, 1859], 2.226). Benovitz provides a nuanced statement of the most probable case:

> The son declares that any and all of his property from which his parents derive benefit is consecrated for the Temple service. This vow cannot be fulfilled: if his parents do derive benefit from any of his property, it will be too late to transfer the property to the Temple. But in fact, the son has no intention of consecrating the property. (*KOL NIDRE*, 22)

[140] *Ag. Ap.* 2.206 (Thackeray, LCL). On honoring parents in Second Temple Judaism, see Hellerman, *Church as Family*, 63–4.

3.5 Moral Accountability to God's Authority

The concepts of power (5:30; 6:2, 5; 9:1, 39; 12:24; 13:26; 14:62) and authority (1:22, 27; 2:10; 3:15; 6:7; 11:28–29, 33) regularly appear in Mark.[141] These terms indicate that God is the authority over Jesus and the source of his power. In Mark, authority also indicates power *against* someone or something (e.g., Satan in 1:13; the scribes in 1:22; the human heart in 7:21). In ancient moral philosophy, the term "authority" (ἐξουσία) could carry moral connotations. In Aristotle's *Politics*, a tyrant should not act simply because he has the authority (ἐξουσία) to do so, but out of consideration for honor (5.9, 1315a24).[142] Elsewhere, in defense of just government, Aristotle says, "For the authority [ἐξουσία] to go about however one wishes is not able to protect against the carelessness [φαῦλον] in every man's character" (6.2, 1318b40). Likewise, Zeno describes authority in terms of rightful belonging according to the law ("everything belongs to the wise"; Diogenes Laertius, *Lives* 7.125) and freedom as "authority of independent action" (ἐξουσίαν αὐτοπραγίας).[143] Mark, of course, does not contain a sophisticated examination of political authority or individual freedom. Nevertheless, authority was a moral term, and, in Mark, the ultimate moral authority is God.

God as the Source of Jesus's Authority

When the authority of Jesus is in question, the reader is redirected to its source. In Mark 1:21–28, the subject of Jesus's authority first appears. Jesus enters a synagogue on the Sabbath and begins to teach. Right away, those listening react to his authority as a teacher. As Brian K. Blount observes, while "teacher" is a favorite designation for Jesus in Mark,[144] Jesus offers little sustained teaching; he "perform[s] the Reign of God."[145] Beyond a simple lesson in good behavior, Mark's Jesus uses his authority to expel spirits, cleanse lepers, and forgive sins (2:10).

Second, Jesus's teaching is pitted against that of the scribes (καὶ οὐχ ὡς οἱ γραμματεῖς). These scribes appear as Jesus's opponents throughout the Gospel.[146] According to Ben Sira, scribes enjoy a life of intellectual leisure (Sir 38:24); however, in Josephus, scribes are low-level government officials (*Ant.* 7.14.7).[147] Among the available depictions for

---

[141] The words δυναμις and ἐξουσία, at times, possess the overlapping meaning of "power," as in Plutarch, *Lyc.* 3.4; 7.2; *Num.* 2.7; cf. *LSJ* s.v. "δυναμις" and "ἐξουσία."

[142] μὴ δι' ἐξουσίαν. On Aristotle's view of tyrants, see Andrés Rosler, *Political Authority and Obligation in Aristotle* (Oxford: Clarendon Press, 2005), 25–6.

[143] Diogenes Laertius, *Lives* 7.121; cf. Diogenes Laertius, *Lives* 5.86–88, where it appears that Heraclides's work Περὶ ἐξουσίας may be an "ethical dialogue" of some kind (διάλογοι ὧν ἠθικὰ).

[144] Mark 4:38; 5:35; 9:17, 38; 10:17, 20, 35; 12:14, 19, 32; 13:1; 14:14; cf. 10:51.

[145] Brian K. Blount, "Jesus as Teacher: Boundary Breaking in Mark's Gospel and Today's Church," *Interpretation* 70 (2016): 184–93, here 188. Before Blount, Achtemeier made the same point ("He Taught them Many Things," 465–81, see esp. 473–6).

[146] Mark 2:6, 16; 3:22; 7:1, 5; 8:31; 9:11, 14; 10:33; 11:18, 27; 12:28, 32, 35, 38; 14:1, 43, 53; 15:1, 31. Scribes are also included among those who come under the authority of God (12:32–33).

[147] For a survey of the characteristics of scribes in Second Temple Judaism, see Anthony J. Saldarini, *Pharisees, Scribes and Sadducees in Palestinian Society: A Sociological Approach* (Wilmington, DE: Michael Glazier, 1988), 254–76.

scribes in the first century, Mark presents them as an authoritative foil to Jesus.¹⁴⁸ In 1:22, the scribes, who are, generically, figures of authority, are denied their authority. While Jesus is teaching, a man with an unclean spirit stumbles into the gathering and blurts out Jesus's identity: "the holy one of God" (1:24).¹⁴⁹ While the spectators are baffled over Jesus's new teaching (τί ἐστιν τοῦτο;), it is the unclean spirit who reveals its source: Jesus's authority is from God (τοῦ θεοῦ).

The designation of the spirit as unclean is also noteworthy.¹⁵⁰ While characteristic of the Synoptics, this term for the demonic is relatively scarce in Greco-Roman sources. Plato understands ἀκάθαρτος in moral terms (i.e., an evil and polluted soul; *Phaed.* 81b). This moral connotation may be retained by Luke who refers to spirits as evil (cf. Luke 7:21; 8:2; Acts 19:12), but Mark's usage is less clear. A closer analogy may be found in the literature of Qumran. Thus, 11QPsᵃ 19:15–16, "Let not Satan rule over me, nor an unclean spirit [רוח טמאה]; neither let pain nor the evil inclination take possession of my bones."¹⁵¹ In Mark, the contrast is between an unclean spirit and the terms "holy one" and "Sabbath."¹⁵² In other words, Jesus makes this person clean as a moral service (see Lev 14:1–20). As a result, those observing are led to believe that the unclean spirits obey (ὑπακούουσιν) Jesus. Obedience here underscores the nature of Jesus's authority: unclean spirits must submit to him even to their own demise.

The controversy over Jesus's authority continues in the narrative: his credentials to forgive sins are called into question (2:1–12), his companions are smeared as known reprobates (2:13–17) and violators of tradition (2:18–28), and even his acts of compassion are deemed unlawful (3:1–6). By the time we arrive at Mark 3:19b–30, in which a group of scribes from Jerusalem outright questions his authority, one wonders if Jesus's adversaries will permit him to do or say anything at all. In this scene, the scribes' indictment again centers on Jesus's authority: "He has Beelzebul, and by the ruler of demons he casts out demons." The term ἄρχων is used elsewhere in the New Testament of malignant spiritual forces (Rom 8:38; Eph 6:12).¹⁵³ The scribes, in essence, ask, "Who is Jesus's sovereign? To whose kingdom does he belong?" According to the Testament of Solomon, "Beelzeboul" is the prince of demons (6:9) who controls a

---

148 For the case that Mark is ignorant of the historical Pharisees and scribes, see Michael J. Cook, *Mark's Treatment of the Jewish Leaders* (Leiden: Brill 1978).

149 Marcus suggests that the use of the divine name here is "an attempt to gain magical control over him through disclosure of his identity" (*Mark 1–8*, 192). This is certainly possible. In some magical texts, evil is caused to flee by way of an incantation, a ritual act, or the name of either an evil spirit or God. In the Testament of Solomon, evil spirits flee at the sign of the cross or at the mention of the spirit's name (17:5; 18:6). Josephus preserves similar demonic expulsion stories regarding Solomon (*Ant.* 8.2.5 §§ 45–49), in one place describing Solomon's extraction of a demon through specific odors (cf. Tob. AB 6:18). Likewise, in *PGM* IV.154–285, a section dealing with necromancy and divination, a god or demon is dismissed by speaking the name of the "great god." If this is the case for Mark 1:24, then we have yet another iteration of evil's combative struggle with God's rightful authority over the world.

150 For a clear overview of "unclean" terminology, see Clinton Wahlen, *Jesus and the Impurity of Spirits in the Synoptic Gospels*, WUNT 2.185 (Tübingen: Mohr Siebeck, 2004), 1–8.

151 Trans. J. A. Sanders, *DJD* 4 (Oxford: Clarendon Press, 1965), 78.

152 On the relationship between demons and impurity at Qumran, see Philip S. Alexander, "Demonology of the Dead Sea Scrolls," in *The Dead Sea Scrolls after Fifty Years: A Comprehensive Assessment*, ed. Peter W. Flint and James C. Vanderkam (Boston: Brill, 1999), 2.348–50.

153 See Gerhard Delling, "ἄρχω, ἀρχή," in *TDNT* 1.482–4.

demonic army at his pleasure (6:1–11) and is thwarted by God alone (6:8).[154] Similarly, Jesus frames his response in terms of loyalty: "If a kingdom is divided against itself, that kingdom is not able to stand" (3:24). The answer to the scribes' question regarding Jesus's authority is to identify the kingdom (βασιλεία) to which he belongs. Satan's kingdom stands in opposition to God's (1:15).[155] As in T. Dan 6:1–11, two kingdoms war against each other. Satan and his spirits tempt Israel toward evil, while God and God's law attract Israel toward righteousness. Those who do God's will belong to God's family (Mark 3:31–35).[156]

Finally, in Mark 11:27–33, the chief priests, scribes, and elders launch another set of challenges to Jesus's authority. Up to this point in the story, their bewilderment over the source of Jesus's power has been accruing interest, including his authority to forgive sins (2:1–12) and to cast out demons (3:19b–30). The location of this cross-examination is the temple, the setting of the previous episodes (11:11–25).[157] Fittingly, the temple, God's abode (1 Kgs 8:27–30), is the place where Jesus's authority is questioned.[158] The chief priests, scribes, and elders' twofold question concerns "what kind of authority" (ποίᾳ ἐξουσίᾳ) Jesus possesses and whence he received it (τίς σοι ἔδωκεν τὴν ἐξουσίαν ταύτην). Characteristically, Jesus replies with a riddle (cf. 2:19, 25; 3:23) about the authority of John's baptism. Jesus's retort recalls the parallels between John the Baptist and Jesus drawn in the prologue (1:1–8; cf. 8:28). John's "baptism of repentance" (1:4) parallels Jesus's command to "repent and believe" (1:15). Here, the authority by which John and Jesus operate is directed toward God. Once more, moral accountability is presented in a juxtaposition: John's baptism is either "from heaven" (ἐξ οὐρανοῦ) or "from human origin" (ἐξ ἀνθρώπων). Here, as elsewhere, Jesus's authority originates from God and nowhere else (Mark 1:2–3; 3:24–27; 12:13–17).

God as Judge

The theme of judgment in Mark implies God's authority over the world. As Keck notes, quoting William James, "because God 'means it, and … recognizes it' the coming

---

[154] For an introduction to the problem of dating the Testament of Solomon, see D. C. Duling, "Testament of Solomon," in *OTP* 1.935–59. Satan as a commander or "prince" of a demonic army is not unusual in Second Temple Judaism (e.g., 1 En. 6:1–8; Jub. 10:18; 48:15; T. Dan 5:6). For more on Satan's names, see W. D. Davies and Dale C. Allison, *A Critical and Exegetical Commentary on the Gospel According to Saint Matthew*, ICC (New York: T&T Clark, 1991), 2.195–6, 2.335–6.

[155] The passage in question contains a dispute over the activity of Satan in Mark. Best gives considerable attention to Mark 3:27 in which Satan, as the "strong man," is bound and therefore no longer at work in the world (*Temptation*, 11–12). Marcus, on the other hand, claims that the parable outlines "the way things actually are": Satan's activity is still present in Mark well beyond 3:27 (*Mark 1–8*, 282). In agreement with Marcus, Riches notes that the parable of the sower (4:15) makes it hard to deny the fact that "Satan's power is still strong" throughout Mark (*Conflicting Mythologies*, 153).

[156] It is often acknowledged that Mark 3:19b–35 represents a Markan intercalation. For an overview, see James R. Edwards, "Markan Sandwiches: The Significance of Interpolations in Markan Narratives," *NovT* 31 (1989): 193–216.

[157] Sharyn Echols Dowd refers to this pericope as a "double intercalation, since the question about Jesus' authority should logically follow the temple cleansing (*Prayer, Power, and the Problem of Suffering: Mark 11:22–25 in the Context of Markan Theology*, SBLDS 105 [Atlanta, GA: Scholars Press, 1988], 38).

[158] See ibid., 46–51.

judgment is the ultimate sanction."[159] For Keck, a sanction is an external, sometimes punitive, consequence to coerce moral action from the doer. In Paul's case, "the Day of the Lord" encroaches upon the present hour, though the apostle does not know its exact time of arrival (1 Thess 5:2).[160] Similarly, Mark refers to "that day or hour" that only the Father knows (13:32).

The topic of God's judgment in Mark has been virtually ignored by those who claim to offer an "ethic" for Mark,[161] perhaps because judgmental tones in Mark are less pronounced than in Matthew and Luke.[162] Even if implicit, Jesus's proclamation of the kingdom of God necessarily entails an impinging time of judgment (1:15; 9:47).[163] The topic of future judgment appears in a handful of locations in Mark (8:35-38; 9:42-50; 12:9; 13:14-19).[164] On two occasions, the demons fear God's authority to destroy (ἀπολέσαι) them (1:24; 5:7; cf. 3:11). In the case of Mark 8:35-38, it seems that the moral sanction of shame is employed,[165] but loss of life (ἀπολέσει αὐτήν) may also imply final judgment.

Mark's use of ἀπολλυμι, "destroy," for future judgment occurs four times (1:24; 8:35; 9:41; 12:9).[166] The term's use in pronouncements of God's future judgment is not

---

[159] Keck, "Rethinking," 14. See William James, *The Will to Believe and Other Essays in Popular Philosophy*, ed. Frederick H. Burkhardt, F Bowers, and I. Skrupskelis (Cambridge, MA: Harvard University Press, 1979), 98.

[160] That this day invokes judgment is clear in the Hebrew Bible (e.g., Job 20:28; Lam 2:1; Zeph 1:18). As M. Eugene Boring puts it, "When Paul thinks of the coming of the Kingdom of God, he thinks of God reestablishing the divine rule over a rebellious humanity, bringing unity to a divide creation" (*I & II Thessalonians: A Commentary*, NTL [Louisville, KY: Westminster John Knox Press, 2015], 178). For more on the day of the Lord, see Marius Reiser, *Jesus and Judgment: The Eschatological Proclamation in Its Jewish Context*, trans. Linda M. Maloney (Minneapolis, MN: Fortress Press, 1998), 27.

[161] In Allen Verhey's treatment of ethics in Mark, judgment is virtually ignored (*Great Reversal*, 74-82). Dan Via contends that Mark does not give judgment—the "consequences of unethical acts"—"the same kind of attention" as what he classifies as norms, intentions motives, enablement, or circumstances (*Ethics of Mark's Gospel*, 32). Wolfgang Schrage thinks Mark's "ethical statements (e.g., 9:41) … do not often include an eschatological motif (e.g., eschatological reward)" (*The Ethics of the New Testament*, trans. David E. Green [Philadelphia: Fortress Press, 1988] 139). Frank Matera prefers Mark's talk of reward over punishment: "Overall, the Markan Jesus, unlike the Matthean Jesus, is more concerned with describing the reward of those who are saved than the fate of those who are lost" (*The Legacies of Jesus and Paul: New Testament Ethics* [Louisville, KY: Westminster John Knox Press, 1996], 31). Additionally, the topic of judgment in Mark has been neglected in Markan studies more broadly. On 9:42-50, for example, most interpreters are satisfied with an explanation of sexual misconduct (cf. A. Y. Collins, *Mark*, 452; Dale Allison, *Jesus of Nazareth: Millenarian Prophet* [Minneapolis, MN: Fortress Press, 1998], 178-82; Will Deming, "Mark 9.42-10.12; Matthew 5.27-32, and B. Nid. 13b: A First Century Discussion of Male Sexuality," *NTS* 36 [1990]: 130-41). This conclusion comes, in part, by way of Matt 5:27-30. Even Shively, who claims that "the whole of Mark is an apocalyptic narrative" (*Apocalyptic Imagination*, 5), offers no discussion of 9:42-50 (cf. 288).

[162] Cf. Matt 10:15, 28; 11:22; 12:42; 13:20; 18:6-9; 22:13; 24:51; 25:31-46; Luke 9:54; 10:12, 14; 11:31-32; 12:2, 4-5, 47-48; 13:5, 28; 14:24; 16:19-31; 18:8; 20:47.

[163] See Reiser, *Jesus and Judgment*, 236-8.

[164] See also the language as "taking away" (4:25), "eternal sin" (3:28-29), and the woe spoken against Judas (14:21). For Mark, Reiser lists 3:28-29; 4:24-25, 29; 6:11; 8:38; 9:43-49; 10:25, 31; 12:1-12, 40; 13:4, 13, 20, 24-27; 14:62 (ibid., 303).

[165] Keck, "Rethinking," 14; David F. Watson, *Honor among Christians: The Cultural Key to the Messianic Secret* (Minneapolis, MN: Fortress Press, 2010), 66-72.

[166] More commonly, outside of the New Testament, the word means to destroy or to kill: cf. LSJ s.v. "ἀπολλυμι." In the New Testament, the word appears in eschatological contexts (1 Cor 10:10; 15:18; 2 Thess 2:10; Jas 4:12).

unusual in the Greek of prophetic literature (e.g., Mic 5:10; Obad 8; Zeph 2:13; Isa 13:9). Furthermore, God's final destruction of demons is a common fate in Second Temple texts (1 En. 21:10; 41:9; 53:1–6; Apoc. Abr. 31.1–4; T. Moses 10:1). In the Book of Watchers, for example, the fallen stars and angels face a similar judgment:

> And I came to an empty place … a chaotic and terrible place. And there I saw seven stars of heaven bound together in it, like great mountains, burning with fire. At that moment I said, "For which sin are they bound, and for what reason were they cast in here. … These are the stars of heaven which have transgressed the commandments of the Lord and are bound in this place. … This place is the prison house of the angels; they are detained here forever. (1 En. 21:1–10)[167]

So, too, in the Book of Similitudes, the coming judgment includes both human beings (53:1–6; 67:8–9) as well as the "messengers of Satan" (54:6; 55:4). In each case, God enacts and executes this final, future judgment.

By far Mark's most extensive discourse on judgment occurs in 9:42–50 (see Chapter 5). When interpreting this text, many draw parallels to one's ethical responsibility.[168] Regarding its broader context, Vincent Taylor makes the plausible suggestion that vv. 37–50 are connected "under a catechetical impulse by the aid of catchwords intended to assist the memory."[169] Martin Dibelius classified the material in Mark 9:42–50 as a collection of punitive Jesus sayings.[170] As a result, this section is commonly assigned to pre-Markan oral transmission.[171] For the most part, the complexities of the textual variants bear witness to the thrust, and chief anxiety, of the passage: Gehenna.[172] For example, the verb ἀπελθεῖν is occasionally altered in v. 43,

---

[167] Trans. E. Isaac, "1 Enoch," in *OTP* 1.24.

[168] Via refers to "unethical acts," (*Ethics of Mark's Gospel*, 81–3); C. S Mann, to "sacrificial attitudes" (*Mark: A New Translation with Introduction and Commentary* [Garden City, NY: Doubleday, 1986], 382). Ecclesial responsibility to the body of Christ is suggested first by Origen (*Comm. Matt.* 13.9, 24) and later by John Donahue and Daniel J. Harrington, *The Gospel of Mark*, SPS (Collegeville, PA: Liturgical Press, 2002), 287; and Helmut Koester, "Mark 9:43–47 and Quintilian 8.3.75," *HTR* 71 (1978): 151–3. The Byzantine archbishop Theophylactus suggests cutting out friends or family that cause one to go astray (*The Explanation by Blessed Theophylact of the Holy Gospel According to St. Mark*, trans. Christopher Stade [House Springs, MO: Chrysostom Press, 1993], 80). Many suggest that sexual misconduct is in view (see n. 161 above), while others suggest general vigilance over one's behavior (cf. Ernest Best, *Mark: The Gospel as Story* [Edinburgh: T&T Clark, 1983], 89; Cranfield, *Saint Mark*, 314).

[169] Taylor, *St. Mark*, 408–9. Boring calls it "a loosely structured unit composed of mostly independent sayings" (*Mark: A Commentary*, 279).

[170] Dibelius categorizes this material as an "extended commandment" flavored "with a threat" (*From Tradition to Gospel*, 247).

[171] Ernest Best, *Disciples and Discipleship: Studies in the Gospel of Mark* (Edinburgh: T&T Clark, 1986), 40–2. See also Allison and Davies, *Saint Matthew*, 2.761. By contrast, Harry Fledderman contends that Mark 9:33–50 "shows signs of much more extensive Marcan redaction and composition" ("The Discipleship Discourse [Mark 9:33–50]," *CBQ* 43 (1981): 57–75). So, too, Robert Fowler, who posits that 9:38–50 "at the level of discourse" is told "with a steady and consistent narrative voice" (*Let the Reader Understand* [Minneapolis, MN: Fortress Press, 1991], 100).

[172] For extended discussion of the textual variants in 9:42–50, see (Joel Marcus, *Mark 8–16: A New Translation with Introduction and Commentary*, AB 27A [New Haven, CT: Yale University Press, 2009], 691–4).

suggesting an attempt to configure whether one enters, departs (v. 43), or gets thrown (vv. 45, 47) into the fires of Gehenna.[173] The aorist passive of βληθῆναι in vv. 45 and 47 appears to be yet another instance of the divine passive: one is thrown into hell by God (see also Isa 66:24; 4 Ezra 7:35-44; Sib. Or. 2:283-296).[174]

Finally, it should be noted that God's judgment in Mark 9:42-50 is not generic (i.e., against "the wicked"). God's punitive action is directed against those who cause "little ones who believe in me" to stumble (9:42). Ian Henderson makes the likely suggestion that Mark 9:42-50 functions as an "oracular curse on leaders-in-waiting," sentencing them to excommunication if they lead little ones astray.[175] The narrative context implies that Jesus's remarks take place in an intimate gathering of his disciples (9:33) with children in the room (v. 36). In this way, much as in the case of the unclean spirit (1:21-28) or in the healing of the paralytic (2:1-12), God's protection extends over those who are unable to assert authority for themselves.[176] The moral obligation of the doer will be the subject of Chapter 4; for now, let it suffice to say that moral accountability, especially as it manifests in divine judgment texts in Mark, refers to the agent to whom the moral actor belongs. Children belong to God in Mark (5:23; 7:26-27; 9:17, 35-37; 10:13-16).[177] One's moral obligation to this group will be discussed further in Chapter 4, and God's judgment against those who violate such obligations will be subject of Chapter 5.

3.6 Conclusion

This chapter has defined the moral life according to Mark in terms of moral accountability. From the outset, God declares Jesus's filial status in accordance with God's way, a morally loaded term. God's kingdom asserts a moral claim upon humanity—to repent and believe—over against alliance with the activity of God's adversary. Mark's declaration that the time has been fulfilled by God further underscores a moral urgency. Moral fissures crack throughout the narrative as unclean spirits, disease, and human self-aggrandizement pose grave threats to God's reign. For this reason, any description of Mark's Gospel that claims to be moral in outlook must take seriously the images of

---

[173] According to the apparatus of NA[28]: D ⁎ (a f) have βληθῆναι and ℵ*(r¹) have εἰσελθεῖν; similar variants occur in v. 47.

[174] In the Sibylline Oracles, the agent is clearly God: "[The] everlasting God will punish terribly from above with whips of flame, having bound them around with fiery chains and unbreakable bonds. Then, in the dead of night, they will be thrown under many terrible infernal beasts in Gehenna" (trans. John J. Collins, "Sibylline Oracles," in *OTP* 1.317–472, here 352). For more on the reception history of Gehenna, see Joachim Jeremias, "γέεννα," in *TDNT* 1.657–58; Mareike V. Blischke et al., "Gehinnom (Gehenna)," in *EBR* 9.1068–81.

[175] Ian Henderson, "'Salted with Fire' (Mark 9:42–50): Style, Oracles and (Socio)Rhetorical Gospel Criticism," *JSNT* 80 (2000): 44–65.

[176] On the low social status of children in the Roman Empire, see Nathan, *Family*, 133–9.

[177] On Mark 9:36, Judith M. Gundry comments, "Jesus' hug, therefore, can be seen as an adoptive embrace, an assumption of a parental role" ("Children in the Gospel of Mark, with Special Attention to Jesus' Blessing of the Children [Mark 10:13–16] and the Purpose of Mark," in *The Child in the Bible*, ed. Marcia J. Bunge, Terence E. Fretheim, and Beverly R. Gaventa [Grand Rapids, MI: Eerdmans, 2008], 156).

God as parent, authority, and judge. Moreover, these features reconstrue the exhausted motifs of Christology and discipleship. Jesus's questionable action to disown his family is mandated by God's superseding moral order. Jesus's harsh words of judgment (9:42–50) derive from divine protection of God's surrogate children. Noticeably, Mark's boundaries for kinship extend beyond blood relatives. Discipleship in Mark, a topic notoriously plagued with incongruencies, is not exclusively doing as Jesus does (e.g., *imitatio Christi* in 8:34); more basically, it is pledging loyalty to Jesus's God. As their failed exorcism demonstrates, the disciples struggle to follow their master's example (9:18). For this reason, "doing as Jesus does" presents an incomplete picture of Mark's discipleship motif; discipleship endows a special status of belonging to the God to whom Jesus himself belongs. When the disciples fail to acknowledge this status, as in Mark 9:29, their power dissipates. The nature of one's accountability to God requires the virtue of faith in God (2:5; 4:40; 5:34; 9:24; 10:52; 11:22): turning away from "the things of humanity" toward "the things of God" (8:33). As Mark 8:33–34 indicates, this human way of thinking is associated with the satanic and radical opposition to God.

Karl Barth's definition for "theological ethics" turns on a similar notion of the creature's accountability to God:

> The problems of ethics generally—the law or good or value which it seeks as a standard by which human action and modes of action are to be measured, and according to which they are to be performed ... is no problem at all in the ethics immanent in the Christian concept of God, in the doctrine of the command of God. For in virtue of the fact that the command of God is the form of His electing grace, it is the starting-point of every ethical question and answer.[178]

In Mark's Gospel, the "starting point" for ethics, the conduct of the moral life, is accountability to God: the moral agent's choices derive from one's loyalty to God's family and one's disposition as an agent obligated to render an account to God's authority and subject to his judgment. Belonging to God provides the standard for moral activity in Mark.

This, however, answers only part of the question for the moral life. In Chapter 4, the content of one's accountability, and specifically the virtues it entails, will be addressed. For what, exactly, is the moral agent accountable as God's child? Let us now turn to the actions that this status of accountability produces in the moral agent.

---

[178] CD II/2, 519. As Migliore interprets Barth, this attitude for Christian ethics is neither violent nor forced:

> If Barth refuses to posit the absolutely autonomous moral agent as the basis of his ethics, he equally rejects the idea of the arbitrary will of God as its basis. Far from being an abstract moral idea, or the will of a capricious or arbitrary tyrant, the God who commands is the gracious God who has chosen from all eternity to be God for humanity. ("Commanding Grace," 10)

Likewise, God's accountability in Mark is not arbitrary: the moral sanction of eternal judgment is professed in defense of little children (9:42), surrogate membership in God's family extending to those who are ill (2:5), and God's way, which denounces the immoral activity of those in contest with God (1:12–13).

4

The Accountable Self according to Mark

And the LORD *said unto Cain, Where is Abel thy brother? And he said, I know not: Am I my brother's keeper?*

Gen 4:9 (KJV)

4.1 Introduction

In the previous chapter, Leander Keck's probe into Pauline ethics provided the groundwork for establishing accountability to God as a centerpiece in Mark's moral program. In review, Keck argues that to discern Paul's ethics, we must rid ourselves of questions of "ought to" or "must," a common preoccupation for modern ethicists. Instead, Pauline ethics are driven by the question of belonging. Keck suggests the category of the "accountable self" as a mode for understanding Paul, a term he pits in opposition to the "deciding self." According to Keck, the deciding self "puts a premium on the deed as the result of careful choice; the accountable self's central concern with 'To whom am I accountable, and for what?' puts the emphasis on the doer's vulnerable relation to the sovereign Other."[1] If the moral agent is accountable to God for her actions, as a member of God's family, then the "chosen act's impact on the fellow believer's relation to God can never be overlooked or minimized."[2] The entailment of these deeds and their impact on a "fellow believer," by Mark's account, are the subject of the present chapter. What are the identity markers of the members of God's "fictive," yet genuine, family? For what, exactly, is this new family held accountable?

Side by side with the community at Qumran, Howard Clark Kee posits a set of values, such as "severing family ties," "no reliance on possessions," forgiveness, and love of neighbor, which define the moral responsibilities of the Markan community.[3] Kee's suggestions for the community's ethos remain instructive. As in the case of Jesus's healing of the paralytic (2:1–12), "it was not sufficient to overcome the disease"; forgiveness of sins was presumed or admonished as "a basic practice" for the community as well.[4] On the notion of "basic practices," Kee is correct: the moral agent's internalization of forgiveness is

---

[1] Keck, "Accountable Self," 12. See also Keck, *Who Is Jesus?*, 175.
[2] Keck, "Accountable Self," 12.
[3] Kee, *Community*, 151–62.
[4] Ibid., 157.

a necessary practice to maintain the believer's relationship to God and to neighbor (Mark 11:25). Similarly, Dan Via offers a set of ethical guidelines in Mark, pinpointing faith as "the possibility of ethical achievement."[5] However, unlike these accounts, this chapter seeks to frame the moral agent's responsibilities strictly in terms of accountability. As the previous chapter demonstrated, one's actions are inextricably tied to the God to whom one gives an account. This chapter expands this account to encompass accountability to one's neighbor.[6]

Alasdair MacIntyre, who influentially rehabilitated a virtue approach to ethics in contrast to certain strands of modern philosophy, describes accountability as follows: "I am not only accountable, I am one who can always ask others for an account, who can put others to the question. I am part of their story, as they are part of mine."[7] The accountable self, in MacIntyre's terms, belongs to a community, shaped by a shared narrative in which the individual inherits a tradition of relating to the world. The identity of this community, outlined in the previous chapter, seeks a teleological good for the benefit of its members: the good life is defined as God's will (3:35) or way (1:1-2; 12:14) and the arrival of God's reign (1:15; 4:11; 9:1, 47; 10:14-15; 12:34). According to MacIntyre, the communal self is defined as "someone's son or daughter, someone else's cousin or uncle; I am a citizen of this or that city. ... [T]he story of my life is always embedded in the story of those communities from which I derive my identity."[8] Put negatively, the "detached self," the self that attempts to detach from its own social and historical identity, runs the risk of living "an illusion with painful consequences."[9] In Mark's terms, the self is accountable to the community established by God the parent, authority, and judge, inclusive of new brothers, sisters, and mothers (e.g., 3:32, 35; 10:29-30). The choice to rebel against God's new community exists in Mark as well, carrying its own set of painful consequences (8:34-38; 9:42-50; 12:9).

Naturally, God's family brings with it a set of virtues and practices. MacIntyre contends that the tradition (e.g., "the narrative phenomenon of embedding") may eventually "decay, disintegrate, and disappear."[10] What keeps a tradition alive, as a "not-yet-completed narrative," is the *practice* of certain internalized virtues believed to move one toward the "determinate conception of the good life."[11] In the case of Mark,

---

[5] Via, *Ethics of Mark's Gospel*, 96-7.
[6] Via comes close with his account of God as the source and enabler of "required conduct" (ibid., 85). However, Via's account of ethics relies on a type of moral reasoning this project seeks to avoid: "Overall we might say that Mark is quite concerned about what the disciple ought to do and be and how the disciple is enabled to" (ibid., 83). The focus on the disciples' deeds as such (e.g., marriage and divorce) obscures the reason *why* the disciple should so act in the first place. To the contrary, it is the coming reign of God, the force of which is now exerted by Jesus, that enables the virtue of faith.
[7] Alasdair MacIntyre, *After Virtue: A Study in Moral Theory*, 3rd ed. (Notre Dame, IN: University of Notre Dame Press, 2007), 218. See also Edmund Pincoff's analysis of "Quandary Ethics" and its distinction from early philosophers: "When Aristotle discusses moral deliberation it is not so much in the interest of finding grounds for the solution of puzzles as of determining when we may assign responsibility" ("Quandary Ethics," *Mind* 80 [1971]: 552-71, here 554).
[8] MacIntyre, *After Virtue*, 220.
[9] MacIntyre offers the example of the German citizen born after the Second World War. If he decides "that what Nazis did to Jews has no moral relevance to his relationship to his Jewish contemporaries" he has chosen "rebellion against [his] identity" (ibid., 220-1).
[10] Ibid., 222.
[11] Ibid. This is why the virtues, according to MacIntyre, must be "secondary." Depending on the embedded narrative with which one identifies, one's definition for virtue may vary. As MacIntyre bluntly puts it,

these virtues include trust in and love of the God who governs the world and who cares for those who would otherwise have no power to care for themselves (1:21–28; 2:1–12; 5:21–43; 10:13–16; 12:30–31, 41–44). The practice of such virtues as love of God or neighbor includes forgiveness, compassion, demon-exorcism, and prayer.[12] The first half of this chapter establishes the nature of certain virtues defined by God's new family in Mark—principally, faith, love, and humility. The second part of this chapter examines moral practices as they relate to the outworking of these core virtues.[13]

4.2 Virtues in Mark

The Gospel of Mark contains a set of virtues coterminous with the arrival of God's kingdom. It goes without saying that Mark does not contain a philosophical account of the virtues like that of Aristotle, Thomas Aquinas, or Albert the Great; nevertheless, the Gospel, as a biography, carries with it an identifiable disposition for the moral life. Owing to such a disposition, the moral life possesses a set of values, or as I call them here, "virtues," which necessarily accompany and express it. Once one has been made aware of God's in-breaking kingdom, then the moral choice to "repent and believe" immediately and inextricably follows. In Aristotle's words, "it is evident that this [end] must be the Good [τἀγαθὸν] and the most virtuous [ἄριστον]. Will then the knowledge of it have great implications for one's way of life [πρὸς τὸν βίον]?"[14] For Mark, knowing God's way also has "great implications" for one's way of life, centered not on the deeds of the believer ("the deciding self") but on the believer and her relationship to God and to the other members of God's family ("the accountable self").

Faith

According to Christopher D. Marshall, words for faith (e.g., πίστις, πιστεύω) occur seventeen times in Mark 1:1–16:8, a disproportionately frequent number compared to other popular Markan terms (e.g., gospel, Son of Man, Galilee).[15] If one includes Mark's antithetical cognates, ἀπιστία or ἄπιστος, there are a few more instances (6:6; 9:19, 24).[16] The term may be translated, generally, as

---

Aristotle "would have been horrified by St Paul" (ibid., 159). However, Aristotle and the writers of the New Testament both share a teleologically framed definition of the good, and both internalize certain virtues for one's achievement of the human *telos*, whether or not the *telos* is understood anthropologically (Aristotle) or theologically (New Testament). See also Keck, *Who Is Jesus?*, 151–82.

[12] Likewise, practices become a necessary component of defining virtue according to Aristotle (see *EN* 2.1.8; 1103b20). The emphasis here is not on the deed but on the formation of the doer.

[13] A similar approach is taken by Robert Ewusie Moses in *Practices of Power: Revisiting the Principalities and Powers in the Pauline Letters*, ES (Minneapolis, MN: Fortress Press, 2014), 40–2. Moses defines Paul's use of "powers" in connection to a larger story. In Col 2:15, for example, the practice of baptism presumes the story of Christ's divestment of the "powers at the cross" (ibid., 41). Similarly, for Mark, the practice of demon-exorcism connects to the larger story of God's defeat of Satan.

[14] *EN* 1.2.2; 1094a22. Author's translation.

[15] Christopher D. Marshall, *Faith as a Theme in Mark's Narrative* (New York: Cambridge University Press, 1989), 1. Marshall includes the textual variant of ὀλιγόπιστοι in 8:17.

[16] One might add the related term, πιστικῆς, in 14:3.

"trust."[17] As in Plutarch's *Life of Caius Marius*, Bataces, the priest of the Great Mother Cybele, reports an omen of good fortune from the goddess. After some brief chaos breaks out, the Senate awards trustworthiness (τῷ λόγῳ τοῦ ἀνθρώπου πίστιν παρέσχεν) to his report.[18] The same may be said of the Septuagintal usage: in Exod 19:9 God speaks to Moses so that the people may "trust you forever" (σοὶ πιστεύσωσιν εἰς τὸν αἰῶνα).[19] In New Testament usage, trust typically denotes an ideal relationship with God, founded on "absolute *pistis*."[20]

A clear example of trust occurs in Mark 11:22, when Jesus instructs his followers to "have trust in God" (ἔχετε πίστιν θεοῦ) in regard to the impossible task of moving a mountain.[21] The currency of trust in this passage is repeated twice more (vv. 23–24), in the context of "doubt in one's heart" and "prayer." God is the one in whom trust is placed (cf. 11:25).[22] Beyond this, a person's trust (or lack thereof) in Jesus's divine prerogatives seems to be a prerequisite to one's healing (2:5; 5:34; 9:23; 10:52). In 6:1–6a, in which the cognate term ἀπιστίαν appears (6:6a), Jesus's lack of power (οὐκ ἐδύνατο ἐκεῖ ποιῆσαι οὐδεμίαν δύναμιν) is due to his hometown's skepticism of his credibility and origin (cf. 11:31). In 9:42 it is the little ones "who believe in me" whom God fiercely defends; in 9:23 all things are possible for the one who believes (πάντα δυνατὰ τῷ πιστεύοντι). Glimpses of how one trusts in God's gospel (1:15) are interwoven throughout Mark.

In her exhaustive treatment of trust (πίστις and *fides*) in the Greco-Roman world, Teresa Morgan argues that πίστις carries a distinctly sociological and ethical nuance:

> In imagining the divine-human relationship as creating a *politeia* structured by virtues, a new society through which, if it does not in practice replace all one's exiting social relationships, all one's other relationships are reinterpreted, and in which *hoi pisteuontes* live in accordance with both divine law and natural law, Christians had many precedents and parallels to draw on in the world around them, from popular morality to political theory.[23]

---

[17] *LSJ*, s.v., πίστις. For an exhaustive treatment of *pistis/fides* in Greco-Roman religion, see Teresa Morgan, *Roman Faith and Christian Faith: Pistis and Fides in the Early Roman Empire and Early Churches* (Oxford: Oxford University Press, 2015), 123–75.
[18] *Mar.* 17.5; see also Morgan, *Roman Faith*, 146.
[19] Ibid., 186, see also 176–211. For a similar appraisal of Josephus and Philo, see Dennis R. Lindsay, *Josephus and Faith: Πίστις and Πιστεύειν as Faith Terminology in the Writings of Flavius Josephus and in the New Testament*, AGAJU 19 (New York: Brill, 1993), 60–2, 80. A prominent example in Hellenistic Judaism is Gen 15:6 LXX: καὶ ἐπίστευσεν Αβραμ τῷ θεῷ, καὶ ἐλογίσθη αὐτῷ εἰς δικαιοσύνη. On the reception of this text and Abraham's faith, see Watson, *Hermeneutics of Faith*, 201–47.
[20] Morgan, *Roman Faith*, 365.
[21] On the objective-genitive reading, see Thomas Söding, *Glaube bei Markus: Glaube an das Evangelium, Gebetsglaube und Wunderglaube im Kontext der markinischen Basileiatheologie und Christologie*, SBB 12 (Stuttgart: Katholisches Bibelwerk, 1985), 324–5.
[22] Söding regards this text as a thoroughly "theocentric" reflection of not belief in God but trust (*Vertrauensglaube*) in God (ibid., 325).
[23] Morgan, *Roman Faith*, 499.

As Morgan rightly notes, studies related to ethics in the New Testament have had "little to say about the theological virtue *pistis*."[24] Many communal pockets in the ancient world, such as the cult of Isis or the popular philosophy of the Stoics, shared a set of moral virtues (e.g., love or justice) that made up the fabric of their social group (e.g., Plutarch, *Fort. Alex.* 1.6, 329b).[25] If this is largely the case in a first-century milieu, then trust, specifically trust in God (Mark 11:22), would naturally serve as an ideal virtue for early Jewish and Christian communities embedded in the Greco-Roman world. In the case of Philo's account of Abraham, Francis Watson fittingly identifies trust in God as Abraham's "supreme virtue" for Philo.[26] In context, Philo writes,

> Faith in God [ἡ πρὸς θεὸν πίστις], then, is the one sure and infallible good, consolation of life, fulfilment of bright hopes, dearth of ills, harvest of goods, inacquaintance with misery, acquaintance with piety, heritage of happiness, all-round betterment of the soul which is firmly stayed on Him who is the cause of all things and can do all things yet only wills the best. ... [N]ot only do the oracles attest his possession of the queen of virtues [βασιλίδα τῶν ἀρετῶν], faith [πίστιν] in the existent, but he is also the first whom they speak of as elder.[27]

While the second evangelist's Jesus never pontificates about faith with the eloquence of Philo, the centrality of trust in the healing episodes suggests that πίστις is a virtue descriptive of those who belong to God's family. Trust concerns accountability to God and not what a person ought to do.

At this point, it is necessary to delineate who, in Mark, possesses the virtue of trust. Mark 9:14–29 contains the most extensive description of faith/lack of faith as it pertains to healing. This pericope has generated much discussion regarding the two-source theory because it occurs in all three of the Synoptics (Matt 17:14–20; Luke 9:37–43a) but with considerable redaction by Matthew and Luke.[28] Most noticeably, Matthew and Luke remove the term ἴσχυσαν in Mark 9:18 and replace it with ἠδυνήθησαν (Matt 17:16; Luke 9:40), and the words of the father in Mark 9:21–24 are also excised.[29] The Markan cry of the father in v. 24 is for help: πιστεύω βοήθει μου τῇ ἀπιστίᾳ. The father's declaration of trust, however limited, sharply contrasts with the lack of power exhibited by the disciples (v. 18);[30] their lack of perception (v. 28) prompts Jesus's exasperation

---

[24] Ibid., 500.
[25] Ibid., 488–98.
[26] Watson, *Hermeneutics of Faith*, 230.
[27] *Abr.* 46.268–70 (Colson, LCL).
[28] On the redaction- and source-critical problems in this passage, see Gregory E. Sterling, "Jesus as Exorcist: An Analysis of Matthew 17:14–20; Mark 9:14–29; Luke 9:37–43a," *CBQ* 55 (1993): 467–93. Paul J. Achtemeier observes that Matthew's abbreviations of Mark are not atypical of Matthew's style ("Miracles and the Historical Jesus: Mark 9:14–29," *CBQ* 37 [1975]: 473–4).
[29] According to Sterling, a few more differences include the removal of Mark's setting (the scribes in dispute with the disciples); both Matthew and Luke add διεστραμμένη as an adjective to describe this "generation" (Matt 17:16; Luke 9:41); and Mark's explicit resurrection language is removed in v. 27 ("Jesus as Exorcist," 474). For more on the agreements with Matthew and Luke against Mark in this episode, see Frans Neirynck, ed., *The Minor Agreements of Matthew and Luke against Mark, with a Cumulative List*, BETL 37 (Leuven: Leuven University, 1974), 126–30.
[30] In Matt 17:20, the disciples have faith, just not enough (ὀλιγοπιστίαν).

with this "faithless generation" (v. 19). Surprisingly, it is the bereft father who invests trust in God: "I believe." Moreover, the episode concerns the family dynamics of a father and son (v. 17). As the previous chapter highlighted, filial relationships in Mark are not inconsequential: God's parental role in Mark demonstrates concern for both natural and surrogate children. Sometimes the call of God disrupts the natural family unit (1:16–20; 3:31–35; 10:29–30); in other cases, as in 9:14–29, ruptured families are restored (cf. 5:21–43; 7:24–30). In either case, faith is theocentric and not anthropocentric. Those in Mark who exhibit faith place their trust in God.

An episode in the story of Apollonius of Tyana presents the healing of a child with similar thematic elements, including a nod to moral living (*Life* 4.20; cf. 1.9; 3.38). In *Life* 4.20, a demon causes an unsuspecting boy to laugh, weep, and sing for no reason (cf. Mark 9:17, 25). Upon exiting the youth, the demon puts up a fight, uttering sounds "in fear and in anger" (cf. Mark 9:26). Once the boy's health is restored in the presence of an approving crowd (cf. Mark 9:25), Apollonius receives their respect (αἰδῶ). After regaining his health, the young man takes on Apollonius's ethos (ἤθη), mimicking his style and clothing. As a common feature of biographies, Philostratus depicts right action as the imitation of the philosopher Apollonius.[31] Not so in Mark 9:14–29: the disciples fail to do as Jesus does (9:18), and it is the father, not the boy, who places trust in God to heal his child. By requesting assistance, the father hands over the moral duty of parental oversight to God. The father's practice of faith is directed toward God the parent in behalf of his son.

In Mark 5:21–43, another episode regarding the virtue of faith appears. An example of Markan intercalation,[32] the stories of Jairus's daughter and the infirm (μάστιγος) woman contain striking parallels: the mention of daughters (vv. 23, 34–35), the number twelve (vv. 25, 42), fear (vv. 33, 36), and faith (vv. 34, 36). The first part of the story, vv. 24–34, has received much attention for its magical tones, treatment of purity laws (e.g., Lev 15; *m. Zab.* 5.1), the medical nature the woman's illness, and Mark's overall depiction of women.[33] Matthew and some manuscripts of Luke remove the extenuating

---

[31] Cf. *Life* 1.2; Miles, "Reforming the Eyes," 157. For more on imitation in Philostratus's *Life*, see the section "Philostratus's *Life of Apollonius*" in Chapter 2. See also the demon-exorcism episode in *Life* 3.38 to be discussed below.

[32] Acknowledged as early as Ernst von Dobschütz, "Zur Erzählerkunst des Markus," *ZNW* 27 (1928): 193–8.

[33] For an overview of the popularity of this text, both ancient and modern, see Marla J. Selvidge, *Woman, Cult, and Miracle Recital: A Redactional Critical Investigation on Mark 5:24–34* (Lewisburg, PA: Bucknell University Press, 1990), 17–30. For an example of reading the woman's faith against that of the disciples', see Joan L. Mitchell, *Beyond Fear and Silence: A Feminist-Literary Approach to the Gospel of Mark* (New York: Continuum, 2001), 66–75. According to Katharina von Kellenbach, the type of reading that focuses on the woman's impurity as an oppressive Jewish regulation based on evidence from Lev 15 carries tones of anti-Judaism (*Anti-Judaism in Feminist Religious Writings*, AARCC 1 [Atlanta, GA: Scholars Press, 1994], 74). Alternatively, Susan Haber claims that Jesus's concern for the woman's health, and only secondarily her status of impurity, strengthens feminist readings of this text for "Jesus' ministry to women with women's issues" ("A Woman's Touch: Feminist Encounters with the Hemorrhaging Woman in Mark 5.24–34," *JSNT* 26, no. 2 [2003]: 171–92, here 191). Charlotte Fonrobert offers an equally mediating position: as in the two, very different traditions of reception in the *Didascalia Apostolorum* and Dionysius of Alexandria, Mark 5:24–34 is not "by itself necessarily affirming of women" ("The Woman with a Blood-Flow [Mark 5.24–34] Revisited: Menstrual Laws and Jewish Culture in Christian Feminist Hermeneutics," in *Early Christian Interpretations of the Scriptures of Israel: Investigations and Proposals*, ed. Craig A.

detail that the woman spent all her money on doctors before reaching Jesus.[34] In other words, in Mark's account, the hemorrhaging woman has more clearly run out of options.[35] It is not only her touch that elicits Jesus's power (δύναμιν), especially considering the disciples' comment about a bustling crowd around Jesus, but also her faith. The subject of the woman's faith was of great interest to the early church.[36] Origen, for example, connects this story to Mark 6:1–6, regarding the role of faith in Jesus's ability to perform many miracles.[37] The combination of divine passives to describe her healing (v. 29: ἐξηράνθη, ἴαται) confirms that it is God's power, communicated through Jesus, that heals her. In Mark, Jesus is neither aware of her presence nor in control of his power, a feature Matthew removes (Matt 9:18–26)—further evidence that God is the active force behind Jesus's actions in this episode. In Wendy Cotter's assessment, Mark 5:21–43 illustrates "the *character* of Jesus' power, the way Jesus uses it, the way he seems unable to refuse anyone who calls on it."[38] Cotter's claim needs one major

---

Evans and James A. Sanders, JSNTSup 148 [Sheffield: Sheffield Academic Press, 1997], 121–40). According to the history of reception, the pericope has been used to include and exclude women. As for the magical tones in this text, especially regarding Jesus's use of Aramaic in 5:41, see David Aune, "Magic in Early Christianity," in *ANRW* 2.23.2, 1533–9. See Candida Moss's important note: "The power comes out of [Jesus] (ἐξ αὐτοῦ) not out of his garments. ... This is not an act of simple magical transference from garment to woman; the woman's touch pulls power out of Jesus himself" ("The Man with the Flow of Power Porous Bodies in Mark 5:25–34," *JBL* 129 [2010]: 507–19, here 510). For the medical dimensions of this text in antiquity, see M. Hengel and R. Hengel, "Die Heilungen Jesu und medizinische Denken," in *Der Wunderbegriff im Neuen Testament*, ed. A. Suhl (Darmstadt: Wissenschaftliche Buchgesellschaft, 1959), 338–74; and Adela Yarbro Collins, who argues convincingly from Aristotle (*HA* 3.19, 521a.25–27) and Soranus of Ephesus (*Gyn.* 3.10–11) that "flow of blood" is the preferred translation for ῥύσις αἵματος (Mark 5:25) (*Mark*, 280–1). To add to Collins's observation, this translation is also supported by the story of Porcia in Plutarch's *Life of Brutus*: she cuts her thigh to prove her loyalty to Brutus, such that a "great flow of blood" (ῥύσιν αἵματος πολλὴν) comes out of her (13.5; cf. Philo, *De Fug.* 34.188).

[34] The detail that she spent all she had on physicians in Luke 9:43 (ἰατροῖς προσαναλώσασα ὅλον τὸν βίον) is missing from at least p[75], B and (D), according to NA[28], potentially indicating a rewriting of Mark 5:26 (δαπανήσασα τὰ παρ᾽ αὐτῆς πάντα). According to Bruce M. Metzger, the evidence of the earlier and diverse attestation is "well-nigh compelling" for the shorter reading (*A Textual Commentary on the Greek New Testament*, 2nd ed. [Stuttgart: German Bible Society, 1994], 121).

[35] Elizabeth Struthers Malbon misleadingly classifies her as one with "bold faith" ("Fallible Followers: Women and Men in the Gospel of Mark," *Semeia* 23 [1983]: 29–48, here 36). Faith in Mark cannot be measured as either little or bold (cf. Matt 17:20). As Mary Ann Beavis notes, the woman comes to Jesus 'fearing and trembling' (v. 33)—hardly an example of 'bold faith'" ("Women as Models of Faith in Mark," *BTB* 18 [1988]: 3–9, here 6). According to Fonrobert, "fear in the gospel of Mark [is] always a reaction when the significance of Jesus is recognized" ("Blood-Flow," 132 n. 30), an interpretation derivative of Peter Trummer, *Die blutende Frau: Wunderheilung im Neuen Testament* (Freiburg: Herder, 1991), 98.

[36] Eusebius mentions a statue in her honor at Caesarea Philippi, *Eccl. Hist.* 7.18. According to Epiphanius's account (quoting Irenaeus), the Valentinians gravitate toward the woman's story but only with regard to the number twelve (*Pan.* 1.35.20). For more examples, see Selvidge, *Woman*, 17–22.

[37] *Comm. Matt.* 10.19; SC 162, 232. Notice also Origen's connection between faith and God's power: "And Matthew and Mark, it seems to me, making perfectly clear the prominence of divine power [θείας δυνάμεως], wished to establish that even in unbelief it has power, but not as much power as it has in the trust [ἐν πίστει] of the ones who are shown kindness" (author's translation).

[38] Wendy Cotter, "Mark's Hero of the Twelfth-Year Miracles: The Healing of the Woman with the Hemorrhage and the Raising of Jairus's Daughter (Mark 5.21–43)," in *A Feminist Companion to Mark*, ed. Amy-Jill Levin (Sheffield: Sheffield Academic Press, 2001), 77–8. However, the evidence is not always consistent in Mark. A possible exception is found in Mark 7:24–30, where Jesus seems at first to refuse the woman's request.

modification: this story illustrates the character of *God's* power. It is God's power that flows to the woman, without Jesus's knowledge and seemingly without his consent. The person who calls on God's power here, like the epileptic child above, would be considered marginal in Greco-Roman society.[39] A woman's faith grants her not only healing but also membership into God's family: she is called "daughter" (5:34; cf. 2:5).[40]

In the sandwiching tale of Jairus's daughter (5:21–24a, 35–43), the theme of faith remains a central motif. Upon learning that Jairus's daughter has died, Jesus responds with two imperatives: do not fear, only believe (v. 36). Notice, yet again, the familial boundaries demarcated in this text: faith and family membership are often tied together in Mark. Much like the father of the epileptic boy (9:14–29), a biological parent's inability to save his daughter requires him to turn her care over to God. As Marshall notes, even though Jairus is "clearly a man of high standing," described as an ἀρχισυναγώγων,[41] with a large house and a company of mourners (vv. 38–40), "a power greater than himself" has overtaken his daughter.[42] Other points of contact with the story of the epileptic boy include the onlookers' pronouncement of the girl's death (5:35, 39; cf. 9:26) and the description that she gets up (ἔγειρε) and walks (ἀνέστη; 5:41–42; cf. 9:27). Philostratus's *Life* contains a similar miracle story (4.45),[43] and Mark's use of Aramaic is reminiscent of Apollonius's secret spell;[44] however, the girl in Philostratus's account never appears to be dead, and the virtue of trust, in either Apollonius or the gods, is not mentioned.

In conclusion, models for faith in Mark are embodied by those in great need (2:5; 9:24; 10:52).[45] Furthermore, returning to Keck's definition for the accountable self, faith denotes the doer's relationship to God and God's power (11:22).[46] In the case of the epileptic boy and Jairus's daughter, parents hand over their authority and care to

---

[39] Haber, "A Woman's Touch," 171–92, notes that the woman's marginalization does not entail an anti-Jewish attitude. Furthermore, as Winsome Munro has demonstrated, Mark's use in 15:40–41 of ἠκολούθουν, his typical synonym for discipleship, may indicate "the prominence of women and female leadership in the primitive church, as it is known to Mark" ("Women Disciples in Mark?," *CBQ* 44 [1982]: 225–241, here 241).

[40] According to a quotation persevered in Thomas Aquinas's *Catena Aurea*, John Chrysostom comments, "He calls her daughter because she was saved by her faith; for faith in Christ makes us His children" (*Catena Aurea: Commentary on the Four Gospels Collected out of the Works of the Fathers*, 4 vols., ed. John Henry Newman [Oxford: John Henry Parker, 1842], 2.99).

[41] Cf. *LSJ* s.v., ἀρχισυναγώγων as "ruler of synagogue" or "master of guild."

[42] Marshall, *Faith*, 95.

[43] See A. Y. Collins, *Mark*, 278–9.

[44] A brief word on Mark's Ταλιθα κουμ in 5:41 is in order. Several important textual variants include Ταλιθα κουμι (A, Θ), Ταβιθα (W), ραββι θαβιτα κουμι (D). An old Latin script has the variant *tabea acultha cumhi*. The appearance of Ταβιθα is best explained by scribal confusion with Acts 9:40 (following Metzger, *Textual Commentary*, 87). To retrovert the Greek back into Aramaic would result in *ṭĕlîtāʾ qûm*, where *ṭĕlîtāʾ* is in the emphatic state (see "*ṭalyĕytāʾ*," in *DJBA*, 504–5). While the Greek form has the G-stem, 2ms imperative, the grammatically correct rendering appears in Alexandrinus (2fs form: *qûmî*); even so, κουμ is likely original, possibly an indication that the Gospel writer's knowledge of Aramaic is limited (cf. 7:34; 15:34).

[45] As Gerd Theissen puts it, "In all the Marcan miracle stories the motifs of faith and difficulty are associated" (*The Miracle Stories of the Early Christian Tradition*, trans. Francis McDonagh, ed. John Riches [Philadelphia: Fortress Press, 1983], 136).

[46] These concepts are even more closely related in the Vulgate, where δύναμις is rendered with the doubly layered *virtus* (e.g., Mark 5:30; 9:39 Vulg.; 9:38 Greek). Aquinas gravitates to the use of *virtus* in Mark 5:30 in his exposition of the text in *Catena Aurea* 2.98.

God. Also found in the healing episode of the paralytic (2:1–12), the guardian's trust in behalf of those who cannot care for themselves activates God's power (2:5; 5:36; 9:24). In the case of the hemorrhaging woman (see also blind Bartimaeus 10:46–52), utter desperation leads one to call upon God's healing power. Marshall accurately characterizes this as a "radical powerlessness," exhibited in the faith episodes of 2:1–12; 5:21–43; 9:14–29; and 10:46–52.[47] Once more, Marshall's radical powerlessness fits nicely with Keck's descriptions for Pauline ethics. If the deciding self puts a "premium on the deed as the result of careful choice," the paradigmatic characters in Mark who illustrate faith do just the opposite. They have little or no choice.[48] One might say that trusting God is not their best option; it is their *only* option. The accountable self, in this sense, is modeled by and for particularly vulnerable people in Mark's Gospel.[49]

Love of God

The Jewish philosopher Maimonides describes loving God as the ultimate virtue:

> I refer to a man who directs all the powers of his soul solely toward God, may He be exalted; who does not perform an important or trivial action nor utter a word unless that action or what word leads to virtue or to something leading to virtue. ... This is what the Exalted requires that we make as our purpose when He says: *And you shall love the Lord your God with all your heart and with all your soul.* He means, set the same goal for all the parts of our soul, namely, *to love the Lord your God.*[50]

According to Maimonides, the love of God is a primary virtue expressed in the Hebrew Bible (Deut 6:4–5). That loving God (and its sister virtue, loving the neighbor, to be discussed below) was a prominent virtue in early Judaism may be readily demonstrated in the writings of Philo.[51] In *On the Virtues*, Philo describes true friendship as "the love that is heavenly and undefiled and being of God, out of whom all virtues are born"

---

[47] Marshall, *Faith*, 133.
[48] Keck, "Accountable Self," 12. For a full account of minor characters as exemplary figures in Mark, see Joel F. Williams, *Other Followers of Jesus: Minor Characters as Major Figures in Mark's Gospel*, JSNTSup 102 (Sheffield: JSOT Press, 1994). Bartimaeus is Williams's central example (170). See also Elizabeth Struthers Malbon, "The Major Importance of Minor Characters in Mark," in *The New Literary Criticism and the New Testament*, ed. Elizabeth Struthers Malbon and Edgar V. McKnight, JSNTSup 109 (Sheffield: Sheffield Academic Press, 1994), 58–86, and esp. 83).
[49] In contrast, Mary Ann Tolbert notes the use of a faith-word in Mark 15:31–32. Those who mock Jesus demand a miracle to believe, but Jesus offers them none. People with power, in this example, demand faith; they do not practice it. As Tolbert so elegantly puts it, "Miracles will not come to those who seek them *in order to* believe; for the Gospel of Mark, *miracles occur as the fruit, not the cause of faith*" (*Sowing the Gospel*, 182, italics in original). Those who demand a sign for faith "are Satan's feeding ground most surely" (ibid.).
[50] Maimonides, "Eight Chapters," in *Ethical Writings of Maimonides*, trans. Raymond L. Weiss and Charles E. Butterworth (New York: New York University Press, 1975), 75–6, italics in original.
[51] According to Dale Allison, other early references to the double love command include T. Iss. 5:2; 7:7; T. Dan 5:3; Aristeas *Ep.* 229; Philo *Virt.* 51; 95; *Spec. Leg.* 2.63; *Abr.* 208 ("Mark 12.28–31 and the Decalogue," in *The Gospels and the Scriptures of Israel*, ed. Craig A. Evans and W. Richard Stegner, JSNTSup 104 [Sheffield: Sheffield Academic Press, 1994], 270–8).

(cf. *Virt.* 18.95; *Deus* 14.69; 34.156).[52] Again, when Philo summarizes the Torah, he appears to do so in a manner similar to Jesus in Mark 12:28-31:

> Now we have known some who associate themselves with one of the two sides [of the Decalogue] and are seen to neglect the other. They have drunk of the unmixed wine of pious aspirations and turning their backs upon all other concerns devoted their personal life wholly to the service of God [τὸν οἰκεῖον βίον θεραπείᾳ θεοῦ]. Others conceiving the idea that there is no good outside doing justice to men have no heart for anything but companionship with men. ... [T]hese may be justly called lovers of men [φιλανθρώπους], the former sort lovers of God [φιλοθέους]. Both come but halfway in virtue [ἀρετήν].[53]

For Philo, the virtue of loving God is part and parcel of the virtue of loving humanity. Early Christians likewise placed love of God in high, moral regard (cf. Rom 5:5; 8:39; 2 Thess 3:5; 1 John 4:8; Jude 21).[54] According to Justin Martyr, the standard for "all that is just" (ὅλου δίκαια) and "all righteousness" (πᾶσαν δικαιοσύνην) was revealed to the entire world (παντὶ γένει ἀνθρώπων) by God in the words of Jesus in Mark 12:28-31.[55] The virtue of loving God, according to Justin Martyr, stands opposed to all sinful activity. Loving God is also not a requirement placed upon the moral agent: that she *ought to* love God. Rather, as Philo has it, love is a chief characteristic of God. For this reason, much like faith, love reveals to whom the moral agent belongs.

Returning to Mark, Jesus's quotation of the Shema in 12:28-31 stands at the center of this section's discussion—and it is not without scholarly controversy. The debate over Mark's inclusion of a "love ethic" in the modern era begins with Victor Paul Furnish.[56] Furnish rightly notes Mark's "own special point and meaning" in 12:28-34: the question is posed by a scribe, not a lawyer (Matt 22:35; Luke 10:25), Jesus replies with both Deut 6:4 *and* 6:5 (Matt 22:37; Luke 10:27), and Jesus and the scribe have an extended dialogue in which Jesus finally declares that the scribe is "not far" (οὐ μακρὰν) from the kingdom of God (cf. Luke 10:28).[57] Furthermore, the content of Deut 6:5 is different in Mark: Mark supplies, in addition to one's heart, soul, and strength, "out of all your mind [ἐξ ὅλης τῆς δυνάμεως]," but the scribe repeats back "out of all

---

[52] Author's translation (*Virt.* 10.55).
[53] *Dec.* 22.108-110 (Colson, LCL). So Allison: "This interpretation, which is offered as though well-known and obvious, makes plain that the summary of the Torah, the Decalogue, may itself be summarized by two demands, the demand to love God and the demand to love one's neighbor" ("Mark 12.28-31," 272).
[54] For a brief overview of the reception of the Decalogue in early Christian circles as a rubric for "basic moral conviction," see Hermut Löhr, "The Decalogue in the New Testament Apocrypha: A Preliminary Overview and Some Examples," in *The Decalogue and its Cultural Influence*, ed. Dominik Markl, HBM 58 (Sheffield: Sheffield Phoenix Press, 2013), 57-71.
[55] *Dial.* 93; PG 6, 697. Cf. Tertullian, *Adv. Marc.* 5.8; *De Res.* 9; *De Iei.* 2.
[56] Furnish, *Love Command*, 19.
[57] In Luke's account, on the other hand, Jesus replies by saying "do this, and you will live" (τοῦτο ποίει καὶ ζήσῃ). No mention is made of the kingdom of God. Furthermore, Luke's chief concern appears to be showing mercy (ἔλεος) toward one's neighbor: a term with higher theological import for Luke than for Matthew or Mark (Luke 1:50, 54, 58, 72, 78; 10:37).

your understanding [συνέσεως],"⁵⁸ for which he is applauded for answering "wisely."⁵⁹ After establishing the text's meaning, Furnish surprisingly voids Mark of any serious interest in the love command: "the love command and related themes play no great role in Mark's Gospel."⁶⁰ Instead, for Furnish, Mark is overridingly concerned with the oneness of God. For the most part, Richard Hays follows Furnish's interpretation.⁶¹ To be sure, strictly on the grounds of frequency of appearance, love occurs significantly less often in Mark than in Matthew, Luke, John, or Paul.⁶² Nonetheless, does Mark present a more significant love ethic than Furnish and Hays recognize? Mark's unique phrase concerning the double love command, as "much more sufficient than burnt offerings and sacrifices" (12:33), is removed by Matthew and Luke.⁵³ Might this offer a clue to Mark's view of the law and, in turn, Mark's view of the love command?⁶⁴ Mark's Gospel values the command of God, accentuating that it originates with God and not with humans (7:8; 10:9).

Mark's concern with the oneness of God certainly claims the lion's share of this passage: this study would agree that God and God's accompanying characteristics are central to Mark. To that end, the quotation of Deut 6:4-5 may signal a debate about monotheism,⁶⁵ a concern operative elsewhere in Mark (2:7; 10:18). However, this is not the exclusive use for the Shema in Second Temple Judaism. As *m. Berakoth* 1.1-4 and *m. Tamid* 5.1 demonstrate, the Shema may have had a social function in daily prayer as well.⁶⁶ Moreover, later Christian interpreters, such as Aquinas, gravitate toward the moral dimensions of the text. Aquinas argues from this text that "love is an

---

⁵⁸ According to Steve Moyise, the variants in Matthew (heart, soul, mind) and Luke (soul, strength, mind) can be explained by variants in Codices A and B of the LXX (A: heart, soul, might; B: mind, soul, might) and the MT (heart, soul, might). Harder to explain, however, are the variants on the lips of the scribe (heart, understanding [συνέσεως], strength) ("Deuteronomy in Mark's Gospel," in *Deuteronomy in the New Testament*, ed. Maarten J. J. Menken and Steve Moyise, LNTS 358 [New York: T&T Clark, 2008], 35). For the case that Matthew follows Mark and does not make corrections in alignment with the MT, see Davies and Allison, *Matthew*, 3.242.
⁵⁹ Νουνεχῶς is a New Testament *hapax legomena*. Luke 10:28 has ὀρθῶς instead. As Furnish notes, the word combination in Mark 12:28-34 gives Mark "a decidedly rationalistic aspect" (*Love Command*, 29).
⁶⁰ Ibid., 74.
⁵¹ Richard B. Hays, *The Moral Vision of the New Testament: Community, Cross, New Creation: A Contemporary Introduction to New Testament Ethics* (San Francisco: HarperSanFrancisco, 1996), 84.
⁵² If one tallies up the appearance of the verb ἀγαπάω, for example, Mark has five occurrences, compared to nine in Matthew, thirteen in Luke, and thirty-seven in John; however, if one considers the length of Mark in comparison to Matthew and Luke, the term's fewer occurrences is statistically less significant.
⁵³ As William Loader notes, this "inclusive antithesis" is a common theme in the prophets (Isa 1:11-17; 56:7; Hos 6:6; 1 Sam 15:22; *Jesus' Attitude towards the Law: A Study of the Gospels*, WUNT 2.97 [Tübingen: Mohr Siebeck, 1997], 100).
⁵⁴ To clarify again, I refer to Mark the Gospel, not Mark the author.
⁵⁵ E.g., Ps.-Clem. 3.57; 16.7; cf. *Aristeas* 132. According to Marcus, the scribe's proclamation that "'there is no other besides him' (12:32) is an important Jewish principle that was frequently used against Christians, who were accused of making Jesus equal to God" (*Mark 8-16*, 844). See also Wayne Meeks, *First Urban Christians: The Social World of the Apostle Paul* (New Haven, CT: Yale University Press, 1983), 91.
⁵⁶ This tradition is as late as the third century with no clear textual attestation prior. For the case that the Shema may not have enjoyed widespread liturgical use before the third century, see Paul Foster, "Why Did Matthew Get the Shema Wrong? A Study of Matthew 22:37," *JBL* 122 (2003): 321-31.

act of the will. ... [A]ccordingly we are commended to direct our whole attention to God."[67] In this regard, Via accurately suggests that, while Mark 12:28–34 is undeniably preoccupied with the oneness of God, monotheism and the command to love are not mutually exclusive.[68] Both are theological in that they describe characteristics of God. In Philo's terms, if all virtue derives from God, then to assert, on the one hand, that God is one and, on the other, that one must love God is to affirm two sides of the same coin (*Virt.* 18.95). Love of the one God moves the scribe into God's kingdom (12:34).[69]

A few other instances in Mark affirm this reading. Jesus's relationship with God is described as "beloved" on three occasions (1:11; 9:7; 12:6). The word ἀγαπητός is not insignificant for Mark and may carry allusions to Isa 42:1 (cf. Isa 44:2 LXX), Ps 2:7, and Gen 22 LXX.[70] Those who read Gen 22 alongside Mark 1:11 typically find an early foreshadowing of Jesus's death, although one does not need an intertext from Genesis to determine this (cf. 12:6).[71] In fact, the label of "beloved" in Mark 12:6 (removed by Matthew, retained by Luke) further clarifies the term's meaning: beloved exemplifies Jesus's special status as God's son and one loved by God.

Another instance of Mark's use of love appears in Mark 10:21. Of the Synoptics, only in Mark does Jesus look upon the rich man and "love him" (ἠγάπησεν; 10:21; cf. Matt 19:21; Luke 18:22). According to C. E. B. Cranfield, Jesus's love in this passage, "regardless of the worthiness or unworthiness of its object, shows itself by helping its object."[72] As Furnish notes, in dissension, the word may alternatively mean "admiration" or "affection for his young questioner."[73] Evidence to the contrary may be found among several ancient interpreters who pick up on Jesus's love for the rich man. In a fragmentary comment on Luke 18:20, Origen refutes a claim of certain Marcionites that the "law of Christ is hostile" by drawing on the concept of love found in Mark 10:21.[74] Similarly, Clement of Alexandria, reflecting on whether or not the wealthy can be saved, draws attention to Jesus's love for the rich man (10:21) alongside the intertext of Mark 12:28–31.[75] As Clement and Origen demonstrate, the concept of God's love

---

[67] *Summa* 2.2. quest. 44, art. 5. Trans. Fathers of the English Dominican Province, *Summa Theologica: First Complete American Edition in Three Volumes* (New York: Benziger Brothers, 1947). The moral imperative to love is also picked up by Augustine, *Doc. Chris.* 1.22.

[68] Via, *Ethics*, 86.

[69] What begins as a few discourses regarding the temple (11:11–25) ends with a parable of the temple's destruction (13:1–2). However, the context need not indicate that the scribe must interpret "Jesus as the basis of a new temple" (Loader, *Jesus' Attitude*, 102). This section is more broadly concerned with God: God's house (11:17), God's power (11:22; 12:24), God's authority (11:27–33), God's son (12:6), God's "things" (12:17), and God's love (12:28–31).

[70] Marcus contends that the use of ἀγαπητός is best explained by Isa 42:1 and Ps 2:7, on the grounds that there are strong linguistic connections between ἀγαπητός and ἐκλεκτός (cf. Luke 9:35; *Way of the Lord*, 51). Jeffrey Gibson more readily sees an Isaac typology behind the "beloved" language and Jesus as the "Willing Sacrifice" (*Temptations*, 78).

[71] Thus, Sharon Dowd and Elizabeth Malbon: "So the very first hint of jeopardy to the life of the Markan Jesus alludes to the sacrifice of a beloved son made by a father to demonstrate commitment to God" ("The Significance of Jesus' Death in Mark: Narrative Context and Authorial Audience," *JBL* 125 [2006]: 271–97, here 274); cf. Malbon, *Mark's Jesus*, 77; Gibson, *Temptations*, 78; Michael L. Cook, *Christology as Narrative Quest* (Collegeville, MN: Liturgical Press, 1997), 95.

[72] Cranfield, *Saint Mark*, 329.

[73] Furnish, *Love Command*, 72.

[74] Origen, *Frag. Luc.* 78; GCS 9, 271 (οἵ τὸν νόμον ἀλλότριον εἶναί φασι χριστοῦ).

[75] Clement, *Quis. Div. Sal.* 4.27–30; cf. Chrysostom, *Matt. Hom.* 63.

may be comparatively underdeveloped in Mark, but it is not absent. These ancient commentators also provide early precedent for reading Mark 10:21 with 12:28-31.

In sum, it would seem that, although infrequent, love occupies a virtuous space in Mark, to the extent that love is theological; it is a character trait of God. The scribe's declaration that the command to love God with all one's being is "more important than all the burnt offerings and sacrifices" leads Jesus to conclude that he is not far from God's kingdom. In this way, Mark's Jesus relativizes some opinions of the traditional sacrificial protocols of his day, redirecting supplicants' attention directly to God. Once more, the accountable self is defined in relationship to God.[76] As in Philo's summary of the Decalogue, Mark's Jesus condenses the law into two love commands: love of God and love of neighbor. Furthermore, this same love is modeled by Jesus in his attitude toward the rich man. Loving God motivates the moral agent to love one's neighbor. As George Keerankeri has argued, Mark 12:28-34 reveals the doing of God's will *as* the "fulfillment of the love command" in Mark. If so, Mark's passion narrative and three passion predictions (8:31-32b; 9:30-32; 10:32-34) reveal Jesus's love of God in that Jesus obeys the will of God.[77] If Keerankeri is right, Mark's theme of doing God's will may also be tied to the virtue of loving God. In this way, the moral life in Mark reframes ethical inquiry: no longer deed-oriented, doing God's will refers to a status of belonging, one who is loved by God.

Paradox and Destruction of the Self in Mark

A rather unorthodox feature that Mark places at the forefront of his Gospel is perplexity and misunderstanding or, as I have titled it here, paradox. In addition to the messianic secret (1:34, 44; 3:11; 5:43; 8:30; 9:9, 30), the disciples are plagued with misunderstanding (4:13, 41; 5:31; 6:52; 8:14, 21; 9:18, 34; 10:13, 38); the central character, Jesus the son of God, ushers in the reign of God to his eventual demise (Mark 14-16). Beyond that, much of what Jesus says fosters confusion instead of clarity (4:11-12; 8:21; 10:24). One may recall that the famed Apollonius spoke to his listeners with more intelligibility (*Life* 5.13: "at once, his word become clear"; cf. 5.17);[78] one cannot say the same for Jesus's parables or aphoristic sayings (8:34-37; 10:43-45). Even the original ending of the Gospel leaves readers scratching their heads (16:8). If, as Laura Sweat contends, Mark's Gospel operates under a certain guise of paradox, might

---

[76] To be sure, Mark's Jesus does *not* eliminate the ritual practices of early Judaism; like Philo, he simply underscores their divine animus.

[77] George Keerankeri, *The Love Commandment in Mark: An Exegetico-Theological Study of Mk 12,28-34*, Analecta Biblica 150 (Roma: Editrice Pontificio Istituto Biblico, 2003), 189-238.

[78] In fact, when Apollonius corrects Damis's false assumptions, he immediately recognizes the folly of his ways:

> So affected was Damis by these arguments that he says his own previous remarks made him hide his face, and he begged Apollonius's pardon for his failure to understand him, and for unthinkingly offering him such advice and arguments. Apollonius cheered him up by saying, "Never mind. I said all this not to rebuke you, but to give you an impression of myself." (*Life* 1.35; [Jones, LCL])

No such course-correction of previous misunderstandings by the disciples is found in Mark.

this invite moral reflection as well?[79] What virtue might be learned while in a state of perpetual misunderstanding? Among the more prominent paradoxes in Mark, Sweat offers three general categories: "God's activity as both concealing and revealing," "that even scripture itself demonstrates a paradoxical understanding of God's action," and the relationship between waste and "extravagant generosity."[80] These polar realities, according to Sweat, highlight "the mysterious character of God's action in the Gospel of Mark."[81] I would add that paradox also highlights a virtue for moral formation in Mark: humility to trust God even with limited understanding and to cross boundaries created by one's in-group. Via's study of Markan ethics advises similarly:

> If Mark is to be considered as one authoritative source for constructive Christian ethics, not only must the Markan norms be taken into account but also the paradoxical, ironical, presentation of ethical enablement must be an element in the Christian understanding of existence with its moral project.[82]

In Mark, what one knows is constantly limited by what one does not, and those with more limited understanding or meager social status seem to be closer to understanding God's kingdom than their social superiors (e.g., 9:33–37; 10:13–16). As in the case of faith and love, paradox appears to be theological in nature as well.

As far as moral philosophy is concerned, humility, as it relates to something unknowable, is perhaps the moral category closest to paradox in the Christian tradition (e.g., Augustine, *Civ. Dei* 1.Pr.; Aquinas, *Summa* 2.2. quest. 161).[83] Yet, in antiquity, humility was seen as weakness to some, or in the very least, far from a proper moral virtue:

> For not only is there nothing puffed up, vainglorious, or proud in taking a high tone about oneself at such a moment [e.g., to defend oneself], but it displays as well a lofty spirit and greatness of character [μέγεθος ἀρετῆς], which by refusing to be humbled [ταπεινοῦσθαι] humbles [ταπεινούσης][84] and overpowers envy.[85]

---

[79] Sweat, *Paradox*, 27. Before Sweat, Narry F. Santos argued that "paradox is a rhetorical device used by Mark throughout the narrative dramatically to jolt and challenge his readers to depart from the accepted opinion that servanthood is incompatible with authority" (*Slave of All: The Paradox of Authority and Servanthood in the Gospel of Mark*, JSNTSup 237 [Sheffield: Sheffield Academic Press, 2003], 3). In a similar vein, Jerry Camery-Hoggatt refers to this phenomenon as irony that creates a "crisis of loyalty" in the reader (*Irony in Mark's Gospel: Text and Subtext*, SNTSMS 72 [New York: Cambridge University Press, 1992], 31–5; cf. Donahue, *The Gospel in Parable*, 196–7).

[80] Sweat, *Paradox*, 28–89. Sweat offers a cogent treatment of these themes (ibid., 93–158): Jesus's apparent waste at Bethany (14:1–11), Jesus's subtle challenge of scripture in his Gethsemane prayer (14:32–42), and the concealment and revelation contained in the ambiguous words of the centurion (15:39).

[81] Ibid., 177.

[82] Via, *Ethics of Mark's Gospel*, 191.

[83] On Augustine's influence on humility in the Christian moral tradition, see Joseph J. McInerney, *The Greatness of Humility: St. Augustine on Moral Excellence* (Eugene, OR: Pickwick, 2016).

[84] While not in Mark, the term ταπεινόω appears with a moral valence in much of the New Testament: e.g., Matt 18:4; 23:12; Phil 2:8; 4:12; Jas 4:10; 1 Pet 2:8.

[85] Plutarch, *De laude* 540d (De Lacy and Einarson, LCL); cf. Aristotle, *EN* 1124b25.

The early Jewish and Christian approach to humility was counterintuitive by the standard of some philosophical ideals in the ancient word.[86] To take a modern example, Simone Weil channels Mark's account of paradox and its interplay with humility when she writes,

> Idiots, men without talent, men whose talent is average or only a little more, must be encouraged if they possess genius. We need not be afraid of making them proud, because love of truth is always accompanied by humility. … A village idiot is as close to truth as a child prodigy. The one and the other are separated from it only by a wall. But the only way into truth is through one's own annihilation; through dwelling a long time in a state of extreme and total humiliation.[87]

To Weil, Mark's Jesus might chime in: "The one who wishes to save his life must destroy [ἀπολέσει] it" (8:35). For the accountable self, the image of an autonomous, deciding creature is constantly deconstructed by Mark's presentation of God The larger context of Mark 8:34–38 suggests that the self, to be properly accountable, must be annihilated. In v. 34, Jesus issues an open call to discipleship: those who desire to follow "after me" (ὀπίσω μου; cf. 1:17, 20) must first deny themselves (ἀπαρνησάσθω ἑαυτὸν). According to St. Basil, Jesus's words imply "the entire forgetfulness of the past and surrender of one's will—surrender which is very difficult, not to say quite impossible."[88] Jesus's elliptical aphorism does not end there: those who "lose" (ἀπολέσει) their lives will "save" (σώσει) them. Most English translations obscure the meaning of ἀπόλλυμι by translating it here as "lose." According to *LSJ*, the range of meaning for ἀπόλλυμι includes "demolish," "ruin," or "cease to exist." In Mark, ἀπόλλυμι occurs a total of nine times, most often in reference to one's permanent annihilation (1 24; 3:6; 4:38; 8:35; 9:22, 41; 11:18; 12:9; cf. 2:22). The complete loss of one's own will is necessary to submit to God's (3:35), as Jesus himself displays (14:36).[89]

As another example, consider when Peter approaches a confession of truth in 8:29 ("You are the Christ"). The Gospel explains that Peter's confession was not by human faculties (8:33; and as Matt 16:17 explicates). In one moment, Jesus's identity is supposedly clear; in the next, Peter's veiled understanding fails to translate into

---

[86] Meeks describes humility in the Christian tradition in terms of a central, paradoxical proclamation of an executed God (*Origins of Christian Morality*, 15, 86–8). A positive account for humility is not exclusively Christian. Philo offers an account of humility (ταπεινόω) as both positive and negative (*Post.* 13.46–48; 21.74).

[87] See "Human Personality," in *Simone Weil: An Anthology*, ed. Siân Miles (New York: Penguin Books, 2005), 87. In this passage, Weil combats Aristotle's "men of talent" in that such approbation accounts only for those gifted with intelligence. On Weil's moral writings, see Robert Coles, *Simone Weil: A Modern Pilgrimage* (Woodstock: Skylight Paths, 2001), 89–109.

[88] Basil of Caesarea, *Ascetical Works*, trans. Sister M. Monica Wagner, FC 9 (Washington, DC: Catholic University of America Press, 1962), 246.

[89] Helen K. Bond makes the convincing case that, much like the death of a philosopher, Jesus's death embodies his teachings: "Jesus' lonely and voluntary death has theological significance in for Mark: it acts as a ransom and offers those who follow him a new way to relate to God" ("A Fitting End? Self-Denial and a Slave's Death in Mark's Life of Jesus," *NTS* 65 [2019]: 425–42, here 438).

appropriate conduct. Peter stands opposed to Jesus's journey to the cross. Most of Mark's narrative must unfold until Peter's self finally surrenders (14:66–72).[90]

Mark's Gospel, oscillating between two extremes—between what is human and divine, what is known and unknown—eludes the grasp of certainty.[91] For this reason, Frank Kermode selected Mark to emphasize the complexities of interpreting literature for insiders and outsiders. Kermode settles on the Transfiguration to illustrate his main point: "Mystery and stupidity make an important conjunction or opposition; but it must be seen with all the others, denial and recognition, silence and proclamation, clean and unclean, indoors and out, lake and mountain, one side and the other side. ... [A]t the end of the book the resurrection is proclaimed to those who keep silent."[92] *Something* is revealed to Peter, James, and John on a high mountain, but the message is obtuse, veiled in a frightening and overshadowing cloud (9:6–7). The disciples haven't the slightest clue what it means (9:9–10). Here, as elsewhere in Mark, two polarizing realities ("concealment and revelation") combine to produce the virtue of humility.[93] What Sweat, and others, refer to as paradox engenders humility. As already noted, humility comes at the complete surrender of the self (8:34–38). Without surrender of the self, paradox may also engender hostility and rejection (14:27, 43–52, 63–72; 15:6–15, 25–32).

The parable of the sower offers a glimpse of this Markan paradox at work.[94] The act of sowing is a clear analogy for preaching the gospel (λόγον in 1:45; 2:2; 4:15–20, 33; 5:36; 13:31) and an indelible concern for Mark (1:1, 14–15; 8:35; 10:29; 13:10; 14:9). Furthermore, the content of the parable has strong resonances with much of the Gospel elsewhere.[95] The sower's first scattering falls "along the path" (παρὰ τὴν ὁδόν), a term

---

[90] The complete surrender of the self to God is a concept reminiscent of Paul's theology (Rom 7:14–25; 1 Cor 6:19b–20; 12:18). This raises questions of human agency in Mark and in the ancient world more broadly. J. Albert Harrill argues that, in the Roman world, granting one's subordinate agency was a "deeply moral" value. Utilizing slavery discourse in Greco-Roman literature, Harrill contends that Paul's self in Rom 7 is wrestling with God's power and authority: "Converts must likewise accept God's point of view so fully as to anticipate the divine personal will. ... The Pauline view of God's mastery recognizes the subjectivity and agency of the converted religious self and sees that true authority consists, not in obeying individual commands ... but in total directness toward God" ("Paul and the Slave Self," in *Religion and the Self in Antiquity*, ed. David Brakke, Michael L. Satlow, and Steven Weitzman [Bloomington: Indiana University Press, 2005], 61–2). Harrill's claims may be applied to Mark: the autonomous self chooses self-annihilation in favor of accountability to God. For feminist readers, however, this suggestion poses a significant problem. For the abuse of ethics of Christ-like submission, see Anna Mercedes, *Power For: Feminism and Christ's Self-Giving* (New York: T&T Clark, 2011), 22–38. For this reason, any application of "surrendering" requires cautious consideration.

[91] Following Kermode, Via refers to this story as an "impression point" in Mark, in that it "translates into narrative the schematic opposition proclamation/silence—or revealed/concealed" (*Ethics of Mark's Gospel*, 175).

[92] Frank Kermode, *The Genesis of Secrecy: On the Interpretation of Narrative* (Cambridge, M.A.: Harvard University Press, 1979), 143.

[93] Sweat, *Paradox*, 28–62.

[94] Via: "It contains the harshest and most extreme expression of the concealed revelation motif" (*Ethics of Mark's Gospel*, 182–3).

[95] Tolbert, who interprets Mark 4:3–9 as a parable for the entire Gospel, suggests that the parable functions as a proemium for various characters in Mark, including the disciples and those healed (rocky soil), the scribes and Pharisees (scattered seed on the path), and the rich man (thorny soil) (*Sowing the Gospel*, 153–64). Beavis lists even more examples: the thematic parallel of hardening (6:52; 8:16–21), the private setting of Jesus's explanation (7:17–23; 13:3), the repeated themes of

of relative moral significance in Mark, already noted (1:2–3; 4:4, 15; 10:52; 12:14) and, according to Jesus's interpretation, a location vulnerable to Satan's attacks (4:15; cf. Jub. 11:10–23).[96] Second, in Jesus's explanation for the seed among rocky soil, those who face "trouble" (θλῖψις; cf. 13:19, 24) and "persecution" (διωγμός; cf. 10:30) immediately "stumble" (σκανδαλίζω; 6:3; 9:42–47; 14:27, 29): a snare that will later entrap *all* the disciples (14:27). The central intertext, Isa 6:9, concerns "seeing" (βλέποντες) and "not seeing" (μὴ ἴδωσιν), "hearing" (ἀκούοντες) and "not understanding" (μὴ συνιῶσιν). One may recall a number of parallels at this point: the two healings of blind men that bookend Jesus's teaching discourse in Mark (8:22–26; 10:46–52), the appearance of Jer 5:21 in Mark 8:18,[97] the faculty by which one loves God according to the wise scribe (συνέσεως), and the imperative to see that fills Mark 13 (vv. 5, 9, 23, 33).[98] Finally, as Sweat adroitly claims, the content of Mark 4:1–20 concerns theology more than Christology: it is ultimately God who both "hides and reveals."[99] The parable of the sower provides a fair snapshot of the Markan theme of paradox and, more broadly, of Markan theology. If one accepts the proposition that Markan theology operates with a certain paradoxical quality, as shown above, then the virtue of humility is not far behind—but only when the agent surrenders to God (8:34–38; 14:36). Otherwise, when confronted with paradox, characters may act in fear (6:50; 16:8) or violence (6:3; 12:1–12; 14:53–65). An illustration of this may be found in the stilling of the storm pericope (4:35–41), in which the disciples make a rational request of their leader—please save us from imminent destruction (4:38)! Upon Jesus's compliance, he rebukes them for having "no faith" (οὔπω ἔχετε πίστιν). The disciples are faced with an impossible task: complete surrender to God even at death's door. In terms of moral

---

insiders and outsiders and seeing and hearing, the reference to "parables" (cf. 3:23; 7:17; 12:1; 13:28), and Jesus's use of Scripture (*Mark's Audience: The Literary and Social Setting of Mark 4:11–12*, JSNTSup 33 [Sheffield: Sheffield Academic Press, 1989], 87–130).

[96] The tradition in Jubilees expounds upon apparent textual troubles in Gen 15, in which God promises a land to Abram's "seed" (זרע; 15:17). According to Cory Crawford, God's promises to Abraham's seed are reinterpreted to mean his agricultural seed in Jub. 11 ("On the Exegetical Function of the Abraham/Ravens Tradition in Jubilees 11," *HTR* 97 [2004]: 91–7). In both Mark 4 and Jub. 11, the thwarting agents are Satan and the ravens of Mastema. In the case of Satan, his activities are mentioned only sparingly in Mark (1:13; 3:23, 26; 4:15; 8:33).

[97] Mark's Jesus diagnoses the disciples' failure to understand in terms of hardened hearts (6:52; 8:17); in this text they more clearly fit the bill for those who have eyes and do not see and ears and do not hear (cf. Donald H. Juel, *A Master of Surprise: Mark Interpreted* [Minneapolis, MN: Fortress Press, 1994], 59; Robbins, *Jesus the Teacher*, 138; Telford, *Theology*, 133). Within the tradition, God hardens hearts (Exod 4:21; 7:3; 10:20; Isa 6:10; John 12:40; Rom 9:17–18; 11:17, 25; 2 Cor 3:14); however, other texts imply human agency in the process (1 Sam 6:6; Eph 4:18; Heb 3:8). As Paul explicates in Rom 9–11, a hardened heart would indicate God's right to act however God sees fit. Unfortunately, Mark is much less clear. The use of the passive form of πωρόω in 6:52 and 8:17 may suggest a divine passive, such that God hardens the disciples' hearts. Their general lack of understanding may also point to the scope of evil in Mark, as we see in Peter in 8:33.

[98] Much like the imperatives in Mark 13, as Arland Hultgren observes, this is the only parable in Mark that begins with sense-preceptory commands to listen and to look (ἀκούετε, ἰδού; *The Parables of Jesus: A Commentary* [Grand Rapids, MI: Eerdmans, 2000], 190).

[99] Sweat observes that the lack of clarity has a "theological point" that "both accuses and saves God from the charge of keeping some from repentance and forgiveness by withholding some gifts and granting others" (*Paradox*, 39). For an example of those who turn to Christological solutions for Mark's "mystery," see James G. Williams, *Gospel against Parable: Mark's Language of Mystery*, BLS 12 (Sheffield: JSOT Press, 1985), 44.

accountability, they are asked to do nothing, simply trust in God. Without surrender of self, what Mark's Jesus calls "repentance" (1:15), paradox cannot cultivate humility.

As a positive illustration of the surrendered self, Mark's pericopes concerning children are instructive (9:33–37; 10:13–16).[100] Once more, true accountability centers not on an individual's action—one "ought to" choose to surrender to God—but on the status of belonging. The reader is told that children belong to God and enter into the kingdom of God (9:37; 10:14–15; cf. 4:30–32). Those who harm them face grave consequences from God (9:42–50). Thus, one may ask, what deed have these children done to earn such a status? In both cases, the children are subject to the agent acting upon them. In 9:36, Jesus "takes" (λαβών) a child, "sets" (ἔστησεν) the child among them, and then "picks [the child] up into his arms" (ἐναγκαλισάμενος). In 10:13–16, a similar sequence occurs: "[people] brought to him children" (προσέφερον αὐτῷ παιδία) for him to bless; he "picks them up in his arms" (ἐναγκαλισάμενος) and "blesses" (κατευλόγει) them, while "placing" (τιθεὶς) his hands on them. Especially in contrast to the rich man (10:17–31), these children have virtually nothing to offer. The rich man obviates his entrance into God's kingdom because of his unwillingness to perform a deed, divestiture from his wealth. In contrast, children, who have neither said nor done anything, enter by nature of their dependence on those who pick them up.

Two remaining elements tend to unsettle interpreters in the parable of the sower.[101] First, Mark's oft-noted insider–outsider scheme is laid out in v. 11: "To you the mystery

---

[100] One might also consider Joseph of Arimathea who "boldly" approaches Pilate to request the body of Jesus (15:43). As a respected member of the council (εὐσχήμων βουλευτής), Joseph may have been culpable in the death of Jesus, according to William John Lyons, a point Luke tries to refute (23:51; cf. Matt 27:57; John 19:38; "On the Life and Death of Joseph of Arimathea," *JSHJ* 2 [2004]: 29–53). Furthermore, it is possible that Mark's Joseph acts not in his own interest but out of "a more communal sense of duty," out of respect for the dead. Joseph's commitment is to a greater moral duty (ibid., 37; cf. Deut 21:23) and compels him to approach Pilate. He acts not because he "ought to" but because he is accountable before God to his neighbor.

[101] Interpreters struggle with the theological implications of Mark 4:11–12. For this reason, a number of redaction critics, according to Beavis, view these verses as a "Marcan addition, containing ideas important to the evangelist" (*Mark's Audience*, 84; cf. Joachim Jeremias, *Parables of Jesus*, 2nd ed. [New York: Charles Scribner's Sons, 1972], 12 n. 11). The quotation of Isa 6:9 in 4:12–13 is introduced with ἵνα (cf. ὅτι in Matt 13:13), implying that Jesus speaks to those outside in parables *in order that* they may not perceive or understand. William Wrede pulls no punches in his analysis: Mark ascribes to Jesus a view, "the cruelty of which vies with its oddity and purposelessness" (*Messianic Secret*, 62). Likewise, T. W. Manson: "The stumbling block here is the ἵνα. As the text stands it can only mean that the object, or at any rate the result, of parabolic teaching is to prevent insight, understanding, repentance, and forgiveness. On any interpretation of parable this is simply absurd" (*The Teachings of Jesus: Studies in Its Form and Content*, 2nd rev. ed. [Cambridge: Cambridge University Press, 1967], 76). See also Michael D. Goulder, "Those Outside (Mk 4:10–12)," *NovT* 33 (1991): 295–7. Jesus's closest followers are excluded on the grounds that they do not perceive or understand what he is saying. In yet another example of Markan paradox, Markan characters regularly portrayed as outsiders, the chief priests and scribes, possess greater perspicacity than the Twelve. When Jesus concludes the parable of the vineyard in Mark 12:1–12, the chief priests, scribes, and elders (11:27) "recognized that he spoke the parable concerning them." While 4:13–20 may cushion the blow, God's choice to include some to the exclusion of others undercuts Mark's missionary purposes delineated in the parable of the sower (4:1–12). The "why" here is far from satisfying: Jesus teaches the "way of God" (12:14) with "new" authority from God (1:27; 11:27–33), but the details of this way are not always made known, even to Jesus (14:36; 15:34). As Sweat advises, the "promise" of 4:22 is a helpful place to land: "There is nothing hidden that will not be revealed, nor made secret except to be made plain" (*Paradox*, 62). Mark's parable maintains that God is the central actor who conceals

of the kingdom of God [τὸ μυστήριον τῆς βασιλείας τοῦ θεοῦ] has been given [by God], but to the ones outside [ἔξω] everything comes [from God] in parables." The irony of this statement is layered. Those supposedly inside, the disciples, and "those around him" (οἱ περὶ αὐτὸν), fail to understand not only this parable but also Jesus's actions elsewhere (e.g., 8:21: "Do you not yet understand?"); those supposedly outside, the crowd (4:1),[102] possess a better understanding of Jesus's purpose and mission (1:40; 5:28; 10:47; 12:34; 15:39). Donahue suggests that the insider–outsider schemes in Mark are not between the disciples and the crowd but are "existential, religious categories, determined by the kind of response one makes to the demands of Jesus."[103] In a similar move, Mary Ann Tolbert recommends reading Mark 3:21–35 alongside the parable of the sower such that those outside correspond "to that class of people who, for whatever reasons, do *not* do the will of God."[104]

To develop the observations of Donahue and Tolbert, such application of mystery is not uncommon in early Judaism and Christianity. As in the third-century *Tripartite Tractate*, "to those who fall outside, [the Logos] revealed himself quickly and in a striking way."[105] This same division may be found in the Qumran corpus: God has revealed to the Righteous Teacher alone "all the mysteries" of the prophets (1QpHab 7:3–8), and even the children of light are led astray by the angel of darkness "according to the mysteries of God" (1QS 3:21–23). The same may be said of certain apocalyptic texts, as in 2 Bar. 48:2–3: "You do not reveal your mysteries to many."[106] In line with Marcus's suggestion, the duality of those inside and outside bear striking similarities to apocalyptic literature, concerning "God's strange design" in revealing God's activities.[107] The moral divide present from the outset of the Gospel continues

---

and reveals: God's choice to include some and exclude others is exclusively God's prerogative. Moral accountability in Mark, once more, means accountability to God—a God whose ways are beyond human comprehension. For Paul, the authority of God occupies much of his discussion in Rom 9–11. After thoroughly exploring the problem of gentile inclusion, going back and forth a few times (see esp. 9:30–33; 11:1–5, 28–32), Paul ends on a note of mystery (11:33–36). God chooses even Pharaoh, an "outsider," to demonstrate God's power (9:7). On Paul's theology vis-à-vis earthly rulers, Beverly R. Gaventa concludes, "Paul's protection of the community from outsiders—from the human rulers—is also protection from themselves, from their own proclivity to hubris, to making more of their own judgments than is appropriate" ("Reading Romans 13 with Simone Weil: Toward a More Generous Hermeneutic," *JBL* 136 [2017]: 7–22, here 20). This is precisely the point in Mark: God's right to choose, even when baffling, overrides human preferences.

[102] Beavis lists a litany of theories for the identity of "those outside" including any who are not among the disciples (see J. Behm, "οἱ ἔξω," in *TDNT*, 2.576), or not among the twelve specifically (Meye, *Jesus and the Twelve*, 44, 135), non-Christians (e.g., Nineham, *Saint Mark*, 135), the Jews generally (evidenced already in Eusebius. *Eccl. Theo* 2.20.11 [the "mysteries of God" μὴ τῷ Ἰουδαίων λαῷ παρεδόθη ταῦτα]), the Jewish authorities, and Jesus's own family (Mark 3:31; see Beavis, *Mark's Audience*, 70–2).

[103] Donahue, *The Gospel in Parable*, 44.

[104] Tolbert, *Sowing the Gospel*, 160, italics in original.

[105] *Tri. Trac.* 90:10, trans. Harry W. Attridge and Dieter Mueller, in *The Nag Hammadi Library in English*, ed. James M. Robinson, 4th rev. ed. (New York: Brill, 1996). In a variety of so-called Gnostic texts, outside-and-inside themes proliferate (cf. *Thomas* 22, 40; *Thund.* 20:20–25; Gosp. Phil. 68:4–10). As Marcus correctly observes, these comments tend to revolve around the act of creation ("Mark 4:10–12 and Marcan Epistemology," *JBL* 103 [1984]: 560). As in the text On the Origin of the World, light is "inside" while the darkness is "outside" (e.g., *Orig. Word* 98.25–26).

[106] As quoted in Marcus, "Marcan Epistemology," 560.

[107] Ibid., 567.

here in Mark 4:3–9. For Marcus, this division explains, for a small persecuted community, why they face continual hardship and hostility.[108] However, in Mark, it is not an epistemological revelation exclusively.[109] The reality that those who were once outside have now been brought in serves a moral and social function as well. The social function of insulating a small, persecuted community may be in view in the Qumran corpus or the *Tripartite Tractate*, but Mark's content appears to transgress these types of in-group boundaries. Those who are brought inside now include "all the nations" (11:17; 13:10). To recognize that biological family members (3:31–35) have been replaced with surrogate ones, including demoniacs (5:1–20) or the child of a Syrophoenician woman (7:24–30), requires a social and moral change of mind facilitated by the virtue of humility. Mark's Jesus's call to repentance offers us a hint of this change (1:15), as do the disciples by way of a foil (8:17, 33; 10:35–45; 14:27–31, 50). In the case of Peter, a change of mind (οὐ φρονεῖς) is in order (8:33), in which he surrenders his faculties to the things of God.

A nonmember of the disciple's social group (ὅτι οὐκ ἠκολούθει ἡμῖν) may even gain membership by doing no more than taking a stance against God's enemies (9:38–41). Mary Ann Beavis directs our attention, at this point, to the Pauline communities.[110] They should be open to outsiders (1 Cor 14:23), a fact with which Paul's letters perennially struggle (1 Cor 1:10–11; Gal 2:11–21; Rom 14:10; 15:9–12).[111] A similar attitude toward outsiders may be expected of Mark's audience as well. Those who are accountable to God extend their allegiances beyond conventional in-groups and social norms.

In summary, Mark's Jesus proclaims a message that his own followers, those inside, fail to grasp. Instead, it is those outside who occasionally understand the meaning of God's kingdom in the narrative. The language of mystery provides an accurate description of the simultaneous action of God to conceal and reveal, as well as God's inclusion of those outside and exclusion of those supposedly inside (e.g., Jesus's own family). This section has attempted to describe the tension of hiddenness and revelation in Mark as engendering humility within readers: an attitude of

---

[108] Ibid., 573.

[109] In agreement, Beavis offers a "social setting" for the parable of the sower. She suggests "an early Christian missionary group with an imminentist [sic] eschatology, an interest in apocalyptic esoterica, which was politically and religiously alienated, and facing persecution" (*Mark's Audience*, 169–70). The community was exhorted to open themselves up to "potential converts" in the face of persecution (171). Similarly, Francis Watson claims that the social function of Mark's messianic secret theme is twofold: "It reinforces the community's sense of eliteness by attributing its separation from society as to the saving activity of God," and "it explains the potentially threatening fact of the unbelief of the majority as being itself the result of divine activity" ("Social Function of Mark's Secrecy Motif," *JSNT* 24 [1985]: 63). While Watson is right to note the social dimension of this theme, secrecy in Mark seems to reinforce inclusion of, not separation from, the nations.

[110] Beavis, *Mark's Audience*, 171.

[111] Paula Fredriksen's treatment of early Christian missionaries and "pagan sympathizers" is helpful. "The Kingdom's pagans were a special and a purely theological category: they were ex-pagan pagans ... [and] are included *as* gentiles (*Paul: The Pagan's Apostle* [New Haven, CT: Yale University Press, 2017], 74–5). In other words, according to Fredriksen, there is room in God's plan for gentiles *qua* gentiles, without conversion to Judaism (as a "God-fearer" might demonstrate). A less developed version of this type of boundary-crossing may be present in Mark.

acceptance of God's plan of inclusion toward unexpected persons. To return to Keck's formulations, the moral framework of the "deciding self" accentuates the deed. The accountable self, on the other hand, accentuates the person to whom one gives an account. In Mark, a prime example of the accountable self is in the children whom Jesus picks up and blesses (9:36; 10:16). Theologically speaking, the Markan quality of paradox demonstrates that the choice of inclusion belongs to God, which requires complete surrender of the self to God's way and will. Learning humility may mean adjusting traditional modes of inclusion, including cultic demarcations of what is clean and unclean (Mark 5:1-20), the law (7:1-23), and even one's own expectations for Jesus (8:32; 10:35).[112] Paradox undermines the deciding self's emphasis on the deed, especially deeds of self-interest, even annihilating the self in order to redirect one's attention to the decision maker (8:34-38). God's family now includes those who were once outside. For this reason, humility and acceptance are not defined by a set of good deeds but by one's relationships: "Who are my mother and my brothers?"

4.3 Virtuous Practices

As suggested in the section above, Furnish's verdict on Mark's indifference to the love command may have been rendered precipitately. Furnish's analysis, like previous ethical inquiries into the Gospels before him, concentrates on Jesus's words instead of his deeds.[113] On Mark's use of compassion in 1:41 and 8:2, Furnish dismisses outright any moral modeling by Jesus: "This healing [episode in 1:41], like the others in Mark, is presented mainly as a manifestation of Jesus' divine power, not of his compassion."[114] However, according to the double love command in Mark 12:28-34, one is equally accountable to one's neighbor (12:31, 33). Love of God without love of neighbor, to quote Philo, comes "but halfway in virtue" (*Dec.* 22.110). In Kee's words, "the chief virtue which the Markan community is exhorted to manifest is love of neighbor."[115] Consequentially, one's failure to recognize God or God's family members may be classified as a vice in Mark. Søren Kierkegaard refers to this type of love as the duty to love the one you see, something the disciples repeatedly fail to do.[116] Jesus himself models this type of love in Mark 10:45 when he announces that the Son of Man came "to give his life as a ransom for many." In this section, three virtuous practices will be considered: healing, demon-exorcism, and prayer.

---

[112] Mark's Jesus draws upon trends for inclusiveness already present within Judaism. Mark's Gospel provides a snapshot of larger conversations concerning gentile inclusion in the Second Temple period (see Matthew Thiessen, *Contesting Conversion: Genealogy, Circumcision, and Identity in Ancient Judaism and Christianity* [New York: Oxford University Press, 2011], 67-86).

[113] See Burridge, *Imitating Jesus*, 27.

[114] Furnish, *Love Command*, 72-3.

[115] Kee, *Community*, 158.

[116] Søren Kierkegaard, *Works of Love*, trans. Howard and Edna Hong (New York: Harper Perennial, 2009), 157-70.

Love of Neighbor in the Act of Healing

On the subject of healing in the ancient world, one might turn to the *Hippocratic Writings*'s memorable dictum: "In disease, two things must be done: be useful, or do not harm."[117] On several occasions, Jesus's compassion reflects a moral responsibility to one's neighbor as outlined by Lev 19:18 (Mark 1:41; 6:34; 8:2; 9:22).[118] According to Mark's Jesus, "the strong [ἰσχύοντες] have no need for a physician, but the ones who are sick [κακῶς]" (2:17). The semantic range for κακῶς encompasses not only illnesses but the moral category of evil as well.

Before cleansing a leper (1:40–45), Jesus is moved with compassion at the leper's request: "If you wish you can cleanse me" (1:40).[119] The leper appeals to Jesus's desire (ἐὰν θέλῃς), a theme in other Markan episodes (3:13; 10:36, 44, 51; 14:36). The leper's request for purification not only correlates with Jesus's typical expulsion of unclean spirits but also undermines the ritual boundaries in Mark over which Jesus frequently crosses.[120] Elsewhere, in the two feeding episodes, Jesus has compassion on the crowds (6:34; 8:2). In the Testament of Zebulun, one is instructed to "have compassion on his neighbor" (8:3; Ὅσον γὰρ ἄνθρωπος σπλαγχνίζεται εἰς τὸν πλησίον), an act Jesus undoubtedly models here. Without explicit mention of σπλαγχνίζομαι, Jesus is moved toward action on account of a supplicant's begging on a few more occasions (5:1–20, 21–43; 6:56; 7:24–30, 31–37; 8:22–26; 10:46–52). Jesus reports that God has mercy on the Gerasene demoniac (5:21), and Jesus also displays mercy toward Bartimaeus (10:47–48). According to Stephen Voorwinde, "Mark captures a wider range of Jesus's emotions than any other Gospel."[121] Perhaps Voorwinde is right: Jesus may appear more emotive in Mark's Gospel than the others; however, more than an emotive Jesus, Mark's healing episodes also depict a moral responsibility to love one's neighbor.

To render a clearer picture of Jesus's compassion, I now turn to the Markan summary statements. I do so for two reasons: (1) These summaries contain brief synopses of Jesus's work and ministry; and (2) Schmidt's opinion is that these sections showcase

---

[117] *Hp. Epid.* 1.5, as quoted in Jacques Jouanna, *Greek Medicine from Hippocrates to Galen*, trans. Neil Allies, ed. Philip van der Eijk, SAM 40 (Boston: Brill, 2012), 263.

[118] Cotter concludes that the miracle stories of the Gospels illustrate "certain virtues" for the reader, including *philanthrōpia* (*The Christ of the Miracle Stories: Portrait through Encounter* [Grand Rapids: Baker Academic, 2010], 9–10). Cotter states, "The narrator has taken pains to provide situations where the encounter with petitioners will allow Jesus to reveal not only his power, but also his 'soul,' as Plutarch would say" (ibid., 7).

[119] That Jesus's movement to compassion, not anger, is more likely the original reading, see Nathan C. Johnson, "Anger Issues: Mark 1.41 in Ephrem the Syrian, the Old Latin Gospels and Codex Bezae," *NTS* 63 (2017): 183–202. Note also that Mark's characterization of Jesus in 1:41 flatly contradicts Furnish's assessment above.

[120] Juel refers to this theme in Mark as "transgressing boundaries" (*A Master of Surprise*, 39–41); cf. Brian K. Blount, *Then the Whisper Put on Flesh: New Testament Ethics in an African American Context* (Nashville, TN: Abingdon Press, 2001), 50–63. Cotter concludes that Jesus, in Mark 1:40–45, teaches the virtues of compassion and gentleness (*Christ of the Miracle Stories*, 41).

[121] Voorwinde also notes Mark's Jesus "sighs" in two episodes (7:34; 8:12; *Jesus' Emotions in the Gospels* [New York: T&T Clark, 2011], 60–1). According to Michael Card, Mark paints "the most varied image of the emotional life of Jesus" (*Mark: The Gospel of Passion*, BIS [Downers Grove, IL: InterVarsity Press, 2012], 25).

a "compositional technique of the Evangelist."[122] Two other form critics, Rudolf Bultmann and Martin Dibelius, agree.[123] In other words, one might say that these summary sections are more or less distinctly Markan, especially considering the habit of Matthew and Luke to truncate or remove them altogether. According to Schmidt, the following sections may be included among these so-called summary statements: 1:14–15, 21b–22, 39; 2:13; 3:7–12; 5:21; 6:6b, 12–13, 30–33, 53–56; 10:1.[124] William Egger adds 1:32–34, 45; 2:1–2; 4:1–2 (and deletes 5:21 and 6:12–13 from Schmidt's list).[125] For Egger, the summary statements—especially 1:14–15, 39, 45; and 2:1—provide a general overview of the activities of the historical Jesus, to which Mark adds his own theological tint.[126] If Schmidt and Egger are right, then these summary statements offer a reasonable glimpse into the Gospel's interpretation of the major events in Jesus's life. For those not predisposed to redaction criticism, summaries, by nature of their form, still offer broad overviews of Jesus's activities in an otherwise very short story. While a majority of these summary statements concern Jesus's teaching (1:21b–22; 2:13; 4:1; 6:6b, 30; 10:1) and, for Egger, the proclamation of the good news (1:14–15; 1:45; 2:1; 6:11–12), others include Jesus's acts of compassion, such as casting out demons (1:32–34, 39; 3:7–12; 6:13) and healing the sick (1:32–34; 3:7–12; 6:13, 55–56). In many cases, the practice of demon-exorcism is coupled with healing the sick. In Mark 1:34, Jesus cured many (ἐθεράπευσεν) and cast out demons (ἐξέβαλεν); in 3:11–12 he cured the sick (ἐθεράπευσεν) and rebuked unclean spirits (πολλὰ ἐπετίμα); in 6:13 the disciples cast out many demons (ἐξέβαλλον) and anointed (ἤλειφον) and healed many who were sick (ἐθεράπευον). The exception to these parallels occurs in 6:53–56, in which the masses bring their sick on mats to touch him (ἥψαντο αὐτοῦ) to be healed by him (ἐσῴζοντο): no mention is made of demonic exorcism. One may reasonably conclude that Jesus's miraculous acts of healing move beyond mere gestures of power (contra Furnish) to acts of genuine compassion: a conclusion strengthened when one notes the appearance of these statements in proximity to vignettes about Jesus's

---

[122] Karl Ludwig Schmidt, *Der Rahmen der Geschichte Jesu: literarkritische Untersuchungen zur ältesten Jesusüberlieferung* (Berlin: Trowitzsch, 1919; repr., Darmstadt: Wissenschaftliche Buchgesellschaft, 1969), 82 n. 2. Kee takes a similar approach (*Community of the New Age*, 60).

[123] Dibelius: Mark "invented a framework of remarks which rather mentioned than narrated the proceeding without any closer details" (*From Tradition to Gospel*, 224). See also Bultmann, *History*, 340–1. C. H. Dodd, decided, contra Schmidt, that the *Sammelberichte* derive from tradition ("The Framework of the Gospel Narrative," *ExpTim* 43 [1931–2]: 396–400).

[124] Schmidt, *Der Rahmen*, 33, 50, 59, 82, 158–9, 161, 163, 188, 238.

[125] Wilhelm Egger, *Frohbotschaft und Lehre: Die Sammelberichte des Wirkens Jesu im Markusevangelium*, FTS 19 (Frankfurt: Josef Knecht, 1976), 23. Differing from the positions of Schmidt, Bultmann, and Dibelius, Egger finds pre-Markan tradition in these summary statements; however, it is a tradition that Mark reworks for his theological agenda. Using examples from Apollonius of Tyana, Charles W. Hedrick claims that, far from simply summarizing the activity of Jesus, these statements also exaggerate the measure and reach of Jesus's ministry ("The Role of 'Summary Statements' in the Composition of Mark: A Dialog with Karl Schmidt and Norman Perrin," *NovT* 26 [1984]: 289–311). For that reason, Hedrick ill-advisedly adds to Schmidt's compilation even more: 1:5, 28; 2:15; 4:33–34; 6:1; 9:30–32; and 10:32.

[126] Egger refers to this tendency as Mark's 'Mosaik von Motiven" (*Frohbotschaft und Lehre*, 158). That Mark's summary statements carry the theological freight of the evangelist is also espoused by Taylor, *St. Mark*, 165.

compassion (1:40; 6:34).[127] Moreover, Jesus appears unable to refuse his supplicants. While compassion intermittently motivates him, in places like 6:53–56 where Jesus's reaction is not mentioned, the crowd's begging (παρεκάλουν αὐτὸν) is met with no resistance. In fact, when the disciples attempt to prevent children from approaching him (10:13–16), Jesus responds, "For the kingdom of God belongs to [ἐστὶν] such as these." In antiquity, Jesus's obligation toward the sick accords with Galen's use of φιλάνθρωπος to describe some doctors' attitude toward their patients:

τινὲς μὲν γὰρ ἕνεκα χρηματισμοῦ τὴν ἰατρικὴν τέκνην ἐργάζονται, τινὲς δὲ διὰ τὴν ἐκ τῶν νόμων αὐτοῖς διδομένην ἀλειτουργησίαν, ἔνιοι δὲ διὰ φιλανθρωπίαν ὥσπερ ἄλλοι διὰ τὴν ἐπὶ ταύτῃ δόξαν ἢ τιμήν.[128]

For some, on account of profit, do they practice the art of medicine, and others, exempt from the obligation of public service passed down, do so *because of love for humanity*, just as others do so on account of glory and honor. (Author translation)

According to Jacques Jouanna, Galen finds in Hippocrates "the model of doctors who treat men for the love of men and not for the love of money or reputation."[129] The moral impulse among some doctors in antiquity to treat their patients provides an analogy for the moral obligation depicted in Jesus's compassion toward the sick (cf. Philo, *Dec.* 22.108–110). Stated more emphatically, healing the sick was considered, in some cases at least, a moral activity (cf. Mark 2:17).

In short, in addition to Mark's explicit healing episodes (cf. 1:40–45; 2:1–12; 7:24–30; 9:14–29; 10:46–52), Mark's summary statements imply that Jesus had compassion for the sick on many more occasions. They also suggest a compulsory responsibility that Jesus passes on to his disciples (6:6b–13). Jesus acts with compassion toward those who are sick, demon-possessed, and fragile. The immediacy with which Jesus extends healing toward those in need, and his ostensible inability to refuse them, may also reflect a moral imperative as one finds in Galen. Mark's Jesus, and occasionally his disciples (6:13, 30), display accountability to God *for* one's neighbor in the form of healing, a practice that extends to demonic expulsions as well.

Love of Neighbor in Exorcisms

Another central activity of Jesus in Mark's Gospel is exorcism (1:21–28, 32–34, 39; 5:1–20; 7:24–30; 9:14–29).[130] It is also a task that Jesus passes on to his disciples (3:15; 6:7,

---

[127] According to Galen's short treatise *Quod optimus medicus sit quoque philosophus* ("That the Best Doctor Is Also a Philosopher"), all doctors were expected to possess some "ability" (δύναμιν) or power (*Claudii Galeni Opera Omnia*, ed. K. G. Kühn [Leipzig: Knobloch, 1821], 1.56). For an analysis of Galen's use of δύναμις in this text, see Jouanna, *Greek Medicine*, 276. Cotter's monograph also makes a similar case for Jesus's miracles, namely that they showcase Jesus's virtues more than simply Jesus's power (*Christ of the Miracle Stories*, 1–15).

[128] *De placitis Hippocratis et Platonis* 9.5.5 (*Claudii Galeni Opera Omnia*, ed. K. G. Kühn [Leipzig: Knobloch, 1823], 5.750–1). Cf. Galen's reference to medical practices as τέχνην οὕτω φιλάνθρωπον in *Quod opt. med.* (*Claudii Galeni*, 1.56).

[129] Jouanna, *Greek Medicine*, 281–2.

[130] As Graham Twelftree notes, "Not only does the conducting of miracles appear to dominate the activity of the historical Jesus; the exorcisms in particular loom large as one of the most obvious and

13).¹³¹ The story of the anonymous exorcist (9:38–41) indicates that those who stand in opposition to Satan align themselves with God. In other words, one who expels demons is closer to God than the one who does nothing to help the possessed. This practice also resembles healing formulae in the Second Temple period: "[Beel]zebub ... I adjure you by the name of YHWH ... O Fever and Chills and Chest Pain" (4Q560 1.4).¹³² Or consider Josephus's account of David: "For [Saul's troubles] were charmed by [David] and against the affliction of the demons; whenever they came upon him, he was the only physician [μόνος ἰατρὸς] ... who could make Saul himself again."¹³³ The act of demon-exorcism, then, reveals not only God's power but also God's healing. In light of this pervasive action toward those in need, exorcism ought to be understood as a virtuous practice. Accountability extends not only to one's neighbor who is ill but also to one's neighbor who is afflicted by the demonic.

In antiquity, the power of an exorcist derived from who they were (e.g., Apollonius, Rabbi Simeon, Solomon) or because of what they said or did.¹³⁴ As in the case of Apollonius, he is able to perform exorcisms by nature of his charisma (*Life* 4.20), as is also the case with Rabbi Simeon ben Yose (*b. Me'il.* 17b). The central figure possesses a "charismatic force" or special object (e.g., Solomon's ring in T. Sol. 1:5–7) to cast out demons. Why would someone perform these actions in the first place? In exorcism accounts in the Greco-Roman world, there is a moral responsibility for expelling demons.

In the case of Apollonius of Tyana, demons exert control over their victims (*Life* 3.38; 4.20). In *Life* 3.38, a desperate woman confronts a group of wise men. She pleads with them for the safety of her demon-possessed son. In her plea, she describes the demon's character (ἦθος): the demon is "phony" (εἴρωνα) and "deceitful" (ψεύστην). The relatively rare term, εἴρωνα, appears twice in Aristotle's *Nicomachean Ethics* (*EN* 1108a23; 1124b30) to describe the character of one who self-deprecates: its opposite meaning, in both places, is truthfulness.¹³⁵ As the tale goes, the demon has seized the young boy, taking control of his mental faculties and personality to the mother's grief. Eventually, on her own, the mother pries out the true identity of the demon: the ghost of a lovesick man from war, who tortures young men so that they may never fall in

---

important aspects of his ministry" (*In the Name of Jesus: Exorcism among Early Christians* [Grand Rapids, MI: Baker Academic, 2007], 46).

¹³¹ See summary in Andreas Hauw, *The Function of Exorcism Stories in Mark's Gospel* (Eugene, OR: Wipf and Stock, 2019), 1–11.

¹³² Trans. Douglas L. Penny and Michael O. Wise, "By the Power of Beelzebub: An Aramaic Incantation Formula from Qumran (4Q560)," *JBL* 113 (1994): 627–50. Consider also the engraved *lamella*, dated to the early second century, in which the name of Jesus is used to cure a headache: Roy Kotansky, "An Early Christian Gold *Lamella* for Headache," in *Magic and Ritual in the Ancient World*, ed. Paul Mirecki and Marvin Meyer RGRW 141 (Boston: Brill, 2002), 37–46.

¹³³ *Ant.* 6.168–169, author translation. For an account of Josephus's demonology, see Hauw, *Exorcism Stories*, 34–7.

¹³⁴ This categorization is indebted to Graham Twelftree, *Jesus the Exorcist: A Contribution to the Study of the Historical Jesus*, WUNT 2 54 (Tübingen: J. C. B. Mohr, 1993), 22–47.

¹³⁵ The term is rather ambiguous as it appears in *Nicomachean Ethics*. In *EN* 1124b30, εἴρωνα more clearly refers to a man of good character (the "great-souled" man) who speaks "truthfully" (ἀληθευτικός) except when he "self-deprecates" before commoners. In *EN* 1108a23, Aristotle contrasts εἴρωνα with "truth" (ἀληθὲς).

love. Once the demon reveals his identity, he threatens to kill the mother's son if she attempts to rescue the boy. Out of despondency, the mother seeks help from a group of wise men. The wise men, the subject of the larger section in which this episode appears, typically advise the local king as if they themselves were gods. They are, according to Philostratus, the moral voice for the local government (*Life* 3.10). In this case, they decide in the mother's favor: they hand over a demonic-expulsion letter to the mother for the demoniac to read.[136] The wise men act to protect the boy's safety: "[The demon] will not kill him" (3.38).

In the Acts of Peter, a late-second- to early-third-century text, another demonic episode details a young boy's possession by a "very evil spirit" (v. 11: *daemonium nequissimum*).[137] The story is reminiscent of Apollonius (*Life* 4.20).[138] In this tale, the demon clearly harms the boy: he exerts the capacity to "hurt him" (cf. Mark 9:22) by throwing him against a wall. The evangelistic overtones of the story (the central character, Marcellus, eventually believes in the name of "Jesus Christ the Son of God") are coupled with compassion: Peter acts in the interest of keeping the boy unharmed. Peter commands the demon to "go out of that young man and hurt him no more." In short, the activity of demons is morally reprehensible; exorcists extend compassion to the host.

In the Genesis Apocryphon (1QapGen 20; cf. Gen 12:17), Pharaoh is tormented by a "chastising spirit" (רוח מכדש), also described as an "evil spirit" (רוח באישא), that removes his desires for sexual pleasure (20.16–18). After two years of torment, Pharaoh calls wise men, magicians, and physicians to remove the spirit from his household, but to no avail. It is only Abraham's prayer and the laying on of his hands that expels the spirit (20.28–29). The function of demonic possession in this text is explicitly moral but curiously inverted: it is the evil spirit's presence that keeps Sarah chaste before Pharaoh's advances (cf. Philo, *De Abr.* 19.96–98).[139]

Finally, the Testament of Solomon is replete with demonic exorcism accounts with moral overtones. The story begins with Solomon recalling the building of the temple and the demon Ornias's tormenting of the foreman's little boy (1:2). Ornias pilfers his wages and rations such that the boy is sure to starve to death. When Solomon finds this out, he is outraged and marches into the temple to pray. In response to Solomon's prayers, the angel Michael gives him a ring by which he imprisons all the demons (1:7). One by one, Solomon interrogates each demon, rendering them powerless (4:12). Solomon then reenlists the demons for service in his temple-building project. Much could be said of the demons' odious activities, including causing jealousy (6:4), foaming

---

[136] A written magical formula for demonic expulsion was common, as in P. Oxy VI 886. See David Jordan, "Two Papyri with Formulae for Divination," in *Magic and Ritual in the Ancient World*, ed. Paul Mirecki and Marvin Meyer, RGRW 141 (Boston: Brill, 2002), 25–36.

[137] "Sehr böser Dämon." Critical text and German translation from Marietheres Döhler, ed., *Acta Petri: Text Übersetzung und Kommentar zu den Actus Vercellenses*, TUGAL 171 (Boston: de Gruyter, 2018), 239.

[138] Döhler lists the three major similarities: the demon's characteristic laughter, the miracle workers' correct identification of a demon in the possessed, and a knocked-over statue (ibid., 239).

[139] The use of evil spirits as an instrument for God's purposes may be found 1 Sam 16:1–23 and *Liber Antiquitatum Biblicarum* 60:2–3. God's creation of the spirits, both good and evil, is attested in 2 En. 29:1 and Jub. 2:2.

at the mouth and grinding the teeth (καὶ ἀφρίζειν καὶ τρίζειν τοὺς ὀδόντας, 12:2; cf. Mark 9:18, 20),[140] natural disasters (7:5–7), and murder (9:2). As Todd E. Klutz's study highlights, "the moral aspects of the *Testament*'s message have been almost entirely overlooked" by scholarly interest in magic.[141] On nearly every page, demons torment people's health. As in the episodes examined in Philostratus's *Life of Apollonius* and the Acts of Peter, so also here: good health or the removal of bodily harm is a common moral imperative for exorcisms.[142] While a display of power or magic is also present, those who cast out demons do so out of a moral obligation to the demon-possessed person.

Returning to Mark, the Gerasene[143] demoniac is among the best attested demonic episodes in the Gospels, appearing in all three of the Synoptic accounts (Matt 8:28–34; Mark 5:1–20; Luke 8:26–39). That this pericope deals with demon-exorcism is repeatedly brought to the reader's attention, not only in the exorcism itself (vv. 1–13) but also afterwards, with the refrain "the one who had the demon" (δαιμονίζομαι; 5:15–16, 18).[144] The designation of "unclean spirit" is common within Mark (1:23, 26–27; 3:11, 30; 5:2, 8, 13; 6:7; 7:25; 9:25) and need not recall a specific intertext.[145] The section overflows with references to the unclean: the man lives among the dead (Num 5:2; 9:7) and the demons enter into pigs (Lev 11:7; Deut 14:8; *Gen. Rab.* 44.23).[146] As we have already noted in Chapter 3, "the unclean" may serve as a catch-all metonym for that which is morally bad (as in 11QPsª 19.15–16). Surprisingly, however, demonic possession is not the only morally negative element in this tale: as far as the history of interpretation is concerned, Jesus's permissive attitude toward the demons' request

---

[140] This, of course, is likely a Christian interpolation. See D. C. Duling, "Testament of Solomon," in *OTP* 1.940–3, here 973.
[141] Todd E. Klutz, *Rewriting the Testament of Solomon: Tradition, Conflict and Identity in a Late Antique Pseudepigraphon*, LSTS 53 (New York: T&T Clark, 2005), 53.
[142] As Klutz observes, "the interest in human illness and health care is found in so many of the document's individual literary units that it must be seen as standing in the foreground of the implied author's ideological concerns (ibid., 54).
[143] Geresa is "thirty-seven miles southeast of the sea of Galilee" (Marcus, *Mark 1–8*, 342), so Matthew appears to correct Mark here to Gadara (8:28). Origen blames the Greek copies of the New Testament for this problem. He argues that the name "Gerasenes" comes from "Gergesa" (Γέργεσα), which he interprets to bear a "prophetic" meaning, "the place of the casting out" (*Comm. Joan.* 6.41; GCS 10, 150).
[144] Matthew removes the wording; Luke replaces it with τὸν ἄνθρωπος ἀφ᾽ οὗ τὰ δαιμόνια ἐξῆλθεν and ὁ ἀνὴρ ἀφ᾽ οὗ ἐξεληλύθει τὰ δαιμόνια in 8:35, 38.
[145] Nicholas Elder's creative suggestion that the term "unclean" "was interpreted in light of the watchers' and giants' uncleanness" is not exegetically necessary ("Of Porcine and Polluted Spirits: Reading the Gerasene Demoniac [Mark 5:1–20] with the Book of Watchers [1 Enoch 1–36]," *CBQ* 78 [2016]: 430–46). Already in Plato, the term "unclean" carries negative moral weight (*Phaed.* 81b) that Luke makes explicit (Luke 7:21; 8:2; Acts 19:12). Similarly, Origen understands the man's unclean dwelling place, among the tombs, to indicate that he is a sinner (ἁμαρτωλοῖς γὰρ οἱ τάφοι οἰκίαι εἰσίν; *Comm. Joan. Cat.* 79; GCS 10, 547). Other suggested intertexts include Isa 65:1–7 MT, which mentions eating pig's flesh and sitting in tombs (v. 4; cf. Gnilka, *Markus*, 1.203), or Exod 14:1–15:22 LXX, in which the Egyptians flee (14:27) and drown in the sea (14:28–30), causing the nations to react in fear (15:14–15; cf. Marcus, *Mark 1–8*, 349; J. Duncan M. Derrett, "Contributions to the Study of the Gerasene Demoniac," *JSNT* 3 [1979]: 6–8).
[146] So Derrett: "This may be why contemporary Jews did not bother about the loss of the swine in this case" ("Spirit-Possession and the Gerasene Demoniac," *Man* 14 [1979]: 290)

(5:13), his destruction of the local economy of pig farmers (vv. 13, 17),[147] and his refusal of the man's request to join his ranks (5:18) also raises serious moral problems for readers. In fact, Dibelius refused to assign this text to Christian origin because this passage "lacks the Gospel ethos," especially Jesus's final dismissal of the man, which, according to Dibelius, runs "contrary to the mission of Jesus."[148] Bertrand Russell finds a moral flaw in Christ in this episode: "It certainly was not very kind to the pigs to put the devils into them."[149] The famed Apollonius, according to Philostratus, would never hunt a poorly treated animal out of respect for its life (*Life* 1.37). Jesus's activity in Mark, one might say, does not conform with some moral expectations, which is yet another reason why Jesus's actions cannot be easily conformed to "ethics." Jesus's actions in this episode also complicate flat-footed models of "imitating Christ" as a blanket ethic for Mark. Instead, this episode, with all of its abrasive features, teaches an important value and practice for the moral life in Mark. Much like losing one's life (8:34–35) or leaving one's family "for my sake" (10:29), God's kingdom prioritizes the mental health of one's neighbor—even if he is an outsider, in this case, a gentile—over considerations of economy and the humane treatment of animals.

Investigations of Mark 5:1–20 often assess veiled references to Roman occupation of Palestine, especially the term "legion."[150] Stephen D. Moore, allegorizing the text, suggests that the destruction of the pigs unveils the Romans as "the filthy swine that they are."[151] The underlying moral impulse in Moore's reading, however, is too narrow. While Rome may be tangentially in view here, the moral demands of God extend

---

[147] The Byzantine commentary on Mark suggests that Jesus values human life over the pigs and that demons, if given the opportunity, would otherwise kill people: "He allowed them to enter the pigs, so that from the pigs the anger of the demons should be made plain and they should know his power, and that those who made so many pigs disappear in a flash were not unable to do the same thing to human beings" (ET: Lamb, *Catena*, 286).

[148] Dibelius, *From Tradition to Gospel*, 101. On a pre-Markan version of this tale, Franz Annen's monograph has gained traction among some (*Heil für die Heiden: Zur Bedeutung und Geschichte der Tradition vom besessenen Gerasener (Mk 5,1–20 parr.)*, FTS 20 [Frankfurt am Main: Knecht, 1976]; cf. Jostein Ådna, "The Encounter of Jesus with the Gerasene Demonic," in *Authenticating the Activities of Jesus*, ed. Bruce Chilton and Craig A. Evans, NTTS 28 [Boston: Brill, 1999], 279–302).

[149] Bertrand Russell, *Why I Am Not a Christian and Other Essays on Religion and Other Subjects*, ed. Paul Edwards (New York: Simon and Schuster, 1957), 19.

[150] The observation is not new (e.g., Paul Winter, *On the Trail of Jesus* [Berlin: de Gruyter, 1961], 129). Several scholars have reassessed Mark 5:1–20 in postcolonial or political terms: Richard Dormandy, "The Expulsion of Legion: A Political Reading of Mark 5:1–20," *ExpTim* 111 (2000): 335–7; Christopher Burdon, "'To the Other Side': Construction of Evil and Fear of Liberation in Mark 5.1–20," *JSNT* (2004): 149–67; Stephen D. Moore, *Empire and Apocalypse: Postcolonialism and the New Testament*, BMW 12 (Sheffield: Sheffield Academic Press, 2006), 24–44; Joshua Garroway, "The Invasion of a Mustard Seed: A Reading of Mark 5.1–20," *JSNT* 32 (2009): 57–75; Warren Carter, "Cross-Gendered Romans and Mark's Jesus: Legion Enters the Pigs (Mark 5:1–20)," *JBL* 134 (2015): 139–55. This explanation for legion is unnecessary. As Dietmar Neufeld notes, "a simpler explanation suggests that it may be a threatening hint indicating strength in numbers, designed to deter Jesus from expelling the demons from the man" (*Mockery and Secretism in the Social World of Mark's Gospel*, LNTS 503 [New York: Bloomsbury T&T Clark, 2014], 159). So also Robert H. Gundry, who contends that the "text explicitly associates Legion with numerousness" (*Mark: A Commentary on His Apology for the Cross* [Grand Rapids, MI: Eerdmans, 1993], 260). Rudolf Pesch reaches a similar conclusion: *Der Besessene von Gerasa: Entstehung und Überlieferung einer Wundergeschichte*, SB 56 (Stuttgart: Verlag, 1972), 33.

[151] Moore, *Empire and Apocalypse*, 29.

beyond the walls of the empire. The critical issue in this text is Jesus's assertion of his moral authority, in a manner similar to his first exorcism (1:23–27). When the demons use his name ("Jesus, Son of the Most High God"), Jesus responds, in turn, by demanding the demons' name. One recalls Solomon's escapades in the Testament of Solomon, particularly his method of first demanding the name of a demon to secure control over it. Jesus's demand for the demons' name, regardless of any veiled reference to Rome, gains power over them (cf. *PGM* IV.1017–19, 3039).[152] Notably, Jesus attributes this power to God (5:19).[153] Second, the demons beg Jesus not to torment them (μὴ με βασανίσῃς), a fate awaiting the unclean spirits at the final judgment (1:24; cf. Rev 20:10). Jesus, by the demons' admission, serves as a proxy for God's judgment. Jesus appears to grant their request by sending the demons into the herd of two thousand pigs to the animals' unfortunate demise. A fate no worse awaits those who mistreat children (9:42–50). Most immediate and obvious, the destruction of the swine triggers the fascination of the masses (v. 16: καὶ περὶ τῶν χοίρων), who are filled with fear (cf. 5:15; 16:8). In the passage's conclusion, Jesus directs their attention to God, to whom he offers tribute for the demoniac's freedom. Once more, the account is thoroughly theocentric. If a veiled reference to the Roman imperium is present, it is subservient to God's authority in healing the demoniac. Through the accountable agent, Jesus, God decides to heal this gentile demoniac at a high cost.

Turning down his request to "be with him" (5:18; cf. 3:14), Jesus instructs the now healed man instead to relate to those in his home (ὕπαγε εἰς τὸν οἶκόν σου πρὸς τοὺς σούς) "what the Lord has done for you" (5:19). By going home, a term of significance in Mark, especially after one's healing (2:11; 7:30; 8:26),[154] the man's right-mindedness confronts his neighbors (12:31), those who know him (πρὸς τοὺς σούς). Furthermore, the man's home is located in gentile territory.[155] Jesus includes among one's neighbors a gentile demoniac. It would seem, then, that Jesus once more acts on behalf of God, not only as God's judge (in this case, of the demons and the pigs) but also as a proxy of God's mercy. Caring for one's neighbor, even a demon-possessed gentile, means

---

[152] As Roger David Aus notes, naming of demons occurs in the rabbinic tradition as well (e.g., *b. Me'il* 17b; *b. Pesah* 112b: *My Name is "Legion": Palestinian Judaic Traditions in Mark 5:1–20 and Other Gospel Texts*, SJ [Lanham, MD: University Press of America, 2003], 12–13). See also Twelftree, *Exorcist*, 84.

[153] The reference to κύριος likely refers to God (cf. 1:3; 11:19; 12:19, 29–30), even though the man attributes his good health to Jesus (5:20).

[154] Commenting on Mark 5:1–20 and 7:24–30, Malbon refers to these as patterns of opposition: "The lives of swine-keeping Gerasenes and the Syrophoenician women appear chaotic from the point of view of the Jewish life ordered by laws regulating not only worship and work but also daily food" (*Narrative Space*, 157). As the previous chapter noted, Mark's moral choices are also pitted in polar opposition: belief or unbelief (9:24), clean or unclean (7:19), human or divine (7:8; 8:33; 10:27; 11:30; 12:17), and eternal reward or consequence (8:35–38). Jesus transgresses these boundaries of opposition to demonstrate a higher moral responsibility to one's neighbor.

[155] Ian J. Elmer contends that the Gerasene demonic is an "exemplar" for gentile converts to Jesus's mission. Elmer reads the exorcism story of 5:1–20, in gentile territory, as a counterpart to Jesus's first exorcisms in Jewish territory (1:21–28, 32–34, 39). Once he returns to his homeland, Jesus can do next to nothing (6:1–6). That, in effect, "juxtapose[es] the success of the Gentile mission over against the failure of the Jewish mission" ("Fishing the Other Side: The Gentile Mission in Mark's Gospel," in *Attitudes to Gentiles in Ancient Judaism and Early Christianity*, ed. David C. Sim and James S. McLaren, LNTS 499 [New York: Bloomsbury/T&T Clark, 2013], 168).

adhering to a higher moral demand even to the detriment of one's economic livelihood. Moral accountability involves service to the mental health of one's neighbor to the end that that his entire community may be evangelized.

The request of the Syrophoenician woman evokes similar themes (7:24–30). This story concerns an unclean spirit's occupation of a woman's daughter. The family boundaries recall the theme, already noted, of parents acting on behalf of their children (5:21–43; 9:14–29).[156] Moreover, the unclean pigs in 5:1–20 correspond to Jesus's derogatory reference to dogs (7:27) in this text.[157] More similarities include the location home (5:19; 7:24, 30),[158] the posture of falling at Jesus's feet (5:6; 7:25), a refusal of request (5:19; 7:27), and reference to gentile territories (5:1, 20; 7:24, 31).[159] According to Joachim Jeremias, Mark 7:24–30 is the "only solid evidence" in the Gospels for Jesus among the gentiles.[160] Initially, Jesus is hesitant to grant her request: the children

---

[156] Kelly R. Iverson lists several parallels between the story of Jairus's daughter and the Syrophoenician woman: both supplicants approach Jesus, fall at his feet (5:22, 33; 7:25), they intercede for their daughters, and the healing occurs in the home (5:23; 7:26; *Gentiles in the Gospel of Mark: "Even the Dogs Under the Table Eat the Children's Crumbs,"* LNTS 339 [New York: T&T Clark, 2007], 47).

[157] For the modern reader, both texts may offend. The woman is called a Ἑλληνίς: Hans Windisch notes here that Greeks were notoriously "hostile to the Jews" (s.v., *TDNT*, 2.507) and vice versa. According to Josephus, "among the Phoenicians the Tyrians are notoriously our bitterest enemies" (*Ag. Ap.* 1.13; [Thackeray, LCL]). The potentially derogatory use of the term "dog" appears in some of our sources (cf. Isa 56:11; Jer 15:3; Sir 13:18; 1 En. 89:42; Jos. Asen. 10:13; Phil 3:2). However, the common interpretatation that the term "dog" is derogatory for gentiles has since come into question (for a summary and overview, see Ryan D. Collman, "Beware of the Dogs! The Phallic Epithet in Phil 3:2," *NTS* 67 [2021]: 105–20, esp. 110–15. For the opinion that what we have in Mark is still more or less derogatory, see Matthew Thiessen, "Gentiles as Impure Animals in the Writings of Early Christ Followers," in *Perceiving the Other in Ancient Judaism and Early Christianity*, ed. Michael Bar-Asher Siegal, Wolfgang Grünstäudl, and Matthew Thiessen, WUNT 394 [Tübingen: Mohr Siebeck, 2017], 19–32). Elizabeth Schlüsser Fiorenza recommends reading Mark 5:1–20 together with 7:24–30: "Since dogs and swine were considered unclean animals they could be used figuratively to characterize pagans" (*In Memory of Her: A Feminist Theological Reconstruction of Christian Origins* [New York: Crossroad, 1994], 137). Similarly, Jonathan A. Draper, analyzing a comparable line in the Didache (9:5), suggests that ritual purity of the community helps to explain the term dog ("'You Shall Not Give What is Holy to the Dogs' [*Didache* 9.5]: The Attitude of the *Didache* to the Gentiles," in *Attitudes to Gentiles in Ancient Judaism and Early Christianity*, ed. David C. Sim and James S. McLaren, LNTS 499 [New York: Bloomsbury/T&T Clark, 2013], 242–58). In Mark, an impurity tradition about unwashed hands is reevaluated in light of Scriptural tradition (7:2, 13): perhaps the same overturning of certain attitudes toward gentiles occurs with the "word" of the woman. Nonetheless, the text still offends: "At best, he associates her with a stray mongrel that has wandered into the house" (F. Scott Spencer, *Dancing Girls, Loose Ladies, and Women of the Cloth: The Women in Jesus' Life* [New York: Continuum, 2004], 62). It should be noted that the mudslinging goes both ways. Peter Shäfer notes similar derogatory tendencies toward Jews in antiquity. The first-century Latin satirist, Petronius, writes, "The Jew may worship his pig-god [porcinum numen] and clamour in the ears of the heights of heaven" (Peter Shäfer, *Judeophobia: Attitudes toward the Jews in the Ancient World* [Cambridge, MA: Harvard University Press, 1997], 77).

[158] Susan Miller notes how the Syrophoenician woman "risks her security" by approaching Jesus in a private home because "respectable women were not expected to go out unaccompanied or to approach strangers, particularly men" (*Women in Mark's Gospel*, JSNTSup 259 [New York: T&T Clark, 2004], 93). According to Miller, an exception to this perception of women in antiquity might include educated, upper-class women in Rome (see also Gillian Clark, *Women in the Ancient World* [Oxford: Oxford University Press, 1989], 17–21).

[159] Jeremias compares the two texts on similar grounds but considers it "doubtful" that the two stories are of the same type (*Jesus' Promise to the Nations: The Franz Delitzsch Lectures for 1953*, trans. S. H. Hooke, SBT 24 [London: SCM Press, 1958], 30).

[160] He lists Matt 8:5–13 and Mark 5:1–20 as other possible exceptions (ibid., 35).

deserve to be fed first (cf. Matthew's "only" in 15:24). Mark's Jesus has just fed a large crowd (6:30–44), but, as Kelly Iverson notes, "there was still plenty left over."[161] Because of her word (διὰ τοῦτον τὸν λόγον), Jesus is compelled to comply (cf. 5:29).

If one turns to the previous pericope, similar themes of purity and impurity swirl about (7:1–15). In this episode, Jesus accuses the Pharisees and scribes of rendering the word (τὸν λόγον) of God powerless (7:13; cf. 7:8). In 7:24–30, it is the *word* of this woman, a term often used in Mark for the gospel (1:45; 2:2; 4:15–20, 33; 5:36) that overturns some traditional views of gentiles. If it is the human heart that ultimately defiles (7:21), then neither this woman nor her daughter may be discounted because of their ethnicity. Once more, Mark depicts Jesus as acting in a compulsory manner: God's demand to care for one's neighbor, even this Hellene woman, appears to almost twist Jesus's arm on account of a higher moral requirement. God demands care for this woman's child regardless of any preexisting cultural boundaries. Imitating Jesus, as a moral demand, again falls short: Jesus, at first, appears to refuse the woman's request. Instead, it is God's power and mercy that persists.

In summary, the act of demon-exorcism in Mark may be classified as a moral practice. The moral self is accountable to God not only for one's own health and belongings, but also for her neighbor's. God's house of prayer is "for all nations" (11:17), and it would seem that Mark intends, in 5:1–20 and 7:24–30, at least, to make explicit the nature of this inclusion. The Gerasene demoniac and Syrophoenician woman's location in gentile territory further identifies who, exactly, constitutes one's neighbor (cf. 13:10).[162] Jesus's own stubbornness toward the Syrophoenician woman embodies some traditional perceptions for clean and unclean; however, God's kingdom in Mark cannot be stopped. Similar to the hemorrhaging woman, her request in behalf of her child elicits God's power apart from Jesus's willful cooperation. The sphere of God's family extends to daughters outside of some traditional cultural and ethnic boundaries, to whom the self is now accountable.[163]

Prayer

Another virtuous practice in Mark that receives comparatively little discussion in the secondary literature is prayer.[164] One's communication with God in prayer is

---

[161] Iverson, *Gentiles*, 51.
[162] As Matthew Thiessen notes, Second Temple Judaism offered a variety of solutions for "the Gentile problem," including the expectation that Gentile inclusion would trigger an eschatological event of God (Isa 55:5 LXX; Tob 14:6; 1 En. 90:37–38; *Paul and the Gentile Problem* [New York: Oxford University Press, 2016], 19–42).
[163] To clarify once more, I am not claiming that Jesus invents gentile inclusion. Mark's Jesus participates in a long-established debate about gentile inclusion already present in Second Temple Judaism (see, e.g., Thiessen's discussion of Jubilees in *Contesting Conversion*, 67–86).
[164] One of the issues here, raised by Dowd, is the placement of Mark 11:22–25 after the intercalation of 11:12–14, 15–19, 20–21 because "their placement after Peter's recognition that the cursed fig true has withered (11:21) seems to interpret the fig tree pericope as a straightforward example of the kind of power promised to believing prayer" (*Prayer, Power*, 4). In other words, the believer's ability to destroy (or to perform extraordinary feats) is invoked by the simple task of prayer, a theme prominent in the so-called prosperity gospel. (For the misuse of Mark 11:23–24 in this tradition, see Kate Bowler, *Blessed: A History of the American Prosperity Gospel* [New York: Oxford University Press, 2013], 66, 122, 141.) Christfried Böttrich identifies even more issues with interpreting

an action of the accountable self that defines her vulnerable status before God. In Mark's Gethsemane account, Jesus's prayer to God reorients his will toward God's (14:36): "but not what I will, but what you will" (ἀλλ᾽ οὐ τί ἐγὼ θέλω ἀλλὰ τί σύ). Prayer, one might object, is intrinsically deed-oriented ("the deciding self"), on the grounds that the believer is expected to pray as a right moral action. Thus, Matthew's injunction, "therefore pray in this way" (οὕτως οὖν προσεύχεσθε ὑμεῖς), or the parable in Luke concerning a "necessity always to pray" (τὸ δεῖν πάντοτε προσεύχεσθαι; Luke 18:1). Might prayer, construed in this way, be considered a moral deed, an "ought to"? In several of Augustine's writings against the Pelagians, the degree to which prayer is a human action is a frequent subject of debate. In one section, Augustine writes,

> But if any man says that we ought not to use the prayer, "Lead us not into temptation" (and he says as much who maintains that God's help is unnecessary to a person for the avoidance of sin, and that human will, after accepting only the law, is sufficient for the purpose), then I do not hesitate at once to affirm that such a man ought to be removed from the public ear, and to be anathematized by every mouth.[165]

For Augustine, prayer "expresses human powerlessness," especially in Matt 6:12–13.[166] As in his comments above, any contention that human beings are able to avoid temptation, to pull themselves away from evil, is an affront to these words of the Lord's Prayer.[167] Prayer, according to Augustine, redirects our very desires (cf. *Ep.* 130.9). Karl Barth's reflections on prayer echo a similar theological commitment: "Wherever there is the grace of God, human beings pray. God works in us, for we know not how to pray as we ought" (cf. Rom 8:26).[168] Prayer, understood in this way, aligns with the virtues

---

this text, including the rationalist trouble in the nineteenth century with Jesus's talking to a tree (e.g., H. E. G. Paulus, *Das Leben Jesu als Grundlage einer reinen Geschichte des Urchristentums I* [Heidelberg: C. F. Winter, 1828], 97–9), the liberal exegetical concern in the twentieth century that Jesus, as a moral exemplar, curses anything at all, and the modern environmentalist concern with tree planting (*Baumpflanzaktion*), not tree cursing ("Jesus und der Feigenbaum: Mk 11:12–14, 20–25 in der Diskussion," *NovT* 39 [1997]: 329; cf. Russell, *Not a Christian*, 19).

[165] *De Perfect. Just. Hom.* 21.44 (Peter Holmes, *NPNF1* 5.549).

[166] Anthony Dupont, "The Prayer Theme in Augustine's *Sermons ad Populum* at the Time of the Pelagian Controversy: A Pastoral Treatment of a Focal Point of his Doctrine of Grace," *ZAC* 14 (2010): 379–408, here 383.

[167] In Dupont's assessment, "human beings have a fundamental need for prayer" (ibid., 405). Prayer, in the Augustinian sense, may be defined as a deed in relation to God, not a deed in and of itself. Through prayer, one invites God's action into her own powerlessness to act.

[168] Karl Barth, *Prayer*, ed. Don E. Saliers, trans. Sara F. Terrien, 50th anniversary ed. (Louisville, KY: Westminster John Knox Press, 2002). Barth's account of prayer illustrates its paradoxical nature as a human action. Consider Daniel Migliore's comment that prayer for Barth "is centrally petition: asking, wishing, desiring, expecting" ("Freedom to Pray: Karl Barth's Theology of Prayer," in *Prayer*, 98). In this way, prayer is the substance of Christian ethics, in that it precedes all right action: "Prayer and Christian ethics are inseparable" (ibid., 100). An earlier Barth, in his commentary on Romans, defines prayer—and all religion—as "the tragic paradox" (Karl Barth, *The Epistle to the Romans*, trans. Edwyn C. Hoskyns [New York: Oxford University Press, 1968], 252). If prayer be defined as a *human* achievement, it necessarily "stands under the radical judgment of God" (Ashley Cocksworth, *Karl Barth on Prayer* [New York: Bloomsbury/T&T Clark, 2015], 4). In other words, as a human action, prayer is not free from the power of sin (here following Paul's view of the law in Rom 7:7–13). A later Barth, as Migliore's comment above illustrates, would define

of faith and love in that it cannot be separated from the believer's relationship with God or neighbor.

Overshadowed by prayer themes in Luke–Acts (Luke 1:10, 13; 3:21; 9:18; 11:1–14; 18:1–8, 9–14; Acts 1:14; 2:1–4; 4:23–31; 8:15–17) and the more obvious absence of the Lord's Prayer, Mark has received relative neglect on the subject. As Peter T. O'Brien observes, "the Second Evangelist shows little interest in the subject."[169] While indeed less frequent, Mark's Jesus teaches about prayer on six occasions (9:29; 11:17; 11:22–25; 12:40; 13:18; 14:38) and models prayer on four more (1:35; 6:46; 14:32–42; 15:34). Sharyn Echols Dowd's study of prayer in Mark correctly contends that Mark "recounts the story of Jesus in order to shape the beliefs and actions of the community which takes its identity from him."[170] For Dowd, a pillar of this community's formation is prayer. Of the pericopes examined so far in this chapter, prayer has already played a role: the disciples' inability to heal the epileptic boy reveals their prayerlessness (9:29). Stated another way, the forces of evil are combated by prayer in Mark. Furthermore, the act of prayer connects Jesus with God (1:35; 6:46; 14:32, 35, 38, 39) and may also be subverted for personal gain (12:40).

Prayer is a major theme in Mark 11:22–25, an intercalated component of the larger section on the temple (vv. 11–25).[171] The section begins with Jesus's interaction with a fig tree. Hungry, Jesus "sees" (vv. 13, 20) a fig tree and demands a product it cannot give: figs out of season (v. 13).[172] Origen is troubled by Jesus's demand here. Manifestly reading Mark (Ὁ δὲ Μᾶρκος), Origen's solution is tropological: he considers the fruit not found by Jesus to be the fruits of the spirit outlined by Paul in Gal 5:22.[173] Taking

---

prayer more clearly in terms of "petition," not in terms of human subjectivity or achievement but as the action preceding all other human action, drawing humans into "a life of promise and hope" (see Mark Anthony Husbands, "Barth's Ethics of Prayer: A Study in Moral Ontology and Action" [PhD diss., Toronto: University of St. Michael's College 2005], 268). Cf. Oliver O'Donovan, who argues that "prayer is the very heart of moral teaching" in that one's actions are oriented toward God ("Prayer and Morality in the Sermon on the Mount," *SCE* 22 [2000]: 21–33, here 33).

[169] Peter T. O'Brien, "Prayer in Luke-Acts," *TynBul* 24 (1973): 111–27. For an overview of the scholarly neglect of prayer in Mark, see Dowd, *Prayer, Power*, 2–5.

[170] Dowd, *Prayer, Power*, 25. As Dowd states elsewhere, "prayer in the Markan narrative and in the Markan community functions as the practice in which the tension between power and suffering is faithfully maintained" (ibid., 164).

[171] C. Clifton Black observes at least six connections between the two texts:

1. Judgment appears in the words of Jesus against the tree (v. 14), against the temple practices (vv. 15–17), and in the chief priests and scribes' words against Jesus (v. 18).
2. This judgment is absolute: the tree is cursed to its roots, forever (vv. 14, 20), and not even a σκεῦος may be carried through the temple (v. 16).
3. Both Peter and the crowd appear amazed at the events (vv. 18, 21).
4. Jesus "answers" both the tree and his disciples (vv. 14, 22).
5. Prayer appears as a subject in Jesus's rebuke of the temple and exhortation to the disciples (vv. 17, 22–24).
6. The reference to mountain in v. 23 and the mountain on which the temple rests (*Mark*, ANTC [Nashville, TN: Abingdon Press, 2011], 239–40).

One might also consider the mountain mentioned in Isa 56:7 LXX.

[172] A detail removed by Matthew (21:19). For a history of modern attempts to explain Jesus's hunting for figs out of season, including "winter figs," figs left over from the season before, or "abnormal foliage," see William Telford, *The Barren Temple and the Withered Tree. A Redaction-Critical Analysis of the Cursing of the Fig-Tree Pericope in Mark's Gospel and Its Relation to the Cleansing of the Temple Tradition*, JSNTSup 1 (Sheffield: JSOT Press, 1980), 3–6.

[173] *Comm. Matt.* 16.29; GCS 40, 571–2.

our cues from Origen, a moral tone may be closer to Mark's meaning. Regardless of what Jesus expects to find on this tree, the mention of season (καιρὸς) recalls an eschatological time announced by God (1:15; 10:30; 13:33). In other words, time is up, and the tree has nothing to show for it. Origen's reading is attractive for this reason: figs represent the virtues of the good life, not found in the current buying and selling practices in the temple (11:15–16). As a result, Jesus condemns the tree to never bear fruit again (εἰς τὸν αἰῶνα), so loudly that the disciples hear him (v. 14). Whereas Matthew portrays an immediate destruction of the tree (21:19), Mark delays the effect of Jesus's words until the next day (11:20), reinforcing the intercalation. Following the temple-clearing episode (vv. 15–19), the fig tree reappears, thanks to Peter's sharp eye, this time "withered from the roots" (ἐξηραμμένην ἐκ ῥιζῶν; vv. 20–21).[174] As in Jesus's parable of the sower, those who have no root wither away (τὸ μὴ ἔχειν ῥίζαν ἐξηράνθη; 4:6). In conclusion, a seemingly disjointed teaching on prayer follows (vv. 17, 24–25).[175] As mentioned in the section on faith above, the miraculous act of moving a mountain is correlated with trust in God (11:22).

Within the temple-clearing scene, Mark uses another absolutism that Matthew removes: "He did not permit anyone to carry an object through the temple" (11:16; cf. 10:11; 12:33). Jesus's teaching contains the central proof text for the scene, a conflation of Isa 56:7 LXX (ὁ γὰρ οἶκός μου οἶκος προσευχῆς κληθήσεται πᾶσιν τοῖς ἔθνεσιν) and Jer 7:11 LXX (μὴ σπήλαιον λῃστῶν ὁ οἶκός μου, οὗ ἐπικέκληται τὸ ὄνομά μου ἐπ᾽ αὐτῷ ἐκεῖ, ἐνώπιον ὑμῶν;), which is not unlike Mark's conflation of Scripture in the prologue (1:2–3). In context, Isa 56 reassures the outsider (ἀλλογενὴς) and eunuch of eternal inclusion in "my house" so long as they "choose the things I want" (ἐκλέξωνται ἃ ἐγὼ θέλω; 56:4).[176] The inclusive nature of Isa 56 is strengthened by Mark's "for all nations," removed by Matthew and Luke.[177] The second half of the intertext, Jer 7:11, reframes these assurances in terms of judgment. Jeremiah calls for right action in a manner similar to the intertext of Isa 40:3 found in in the prologue: "Straighten out your ways [τὰς ὁδούς] and your practices, and in so doing, act with justice" (Jer 7:5 LXX). The oracle ends in judgment against the temple for a failure to do so (7:13–15).[178] Mark 11:22–25 is less about the deed of praying, or even its outcomes (e.g., moving a mountain; destroying the Temple), and more about the alignment of the believer's will to God's (cf. 1 Cor 13:2). As in Isa 56, it is "choosing things I [that is, God] want" that guarantees a place in God's house. In this case, God appears to want radical inclusion: "My house will be called a house of prayer *for all nations*." In another example, practicing forgiveness, the topic with which the pericope closes (cf. 9:50),

---

[174] Peter reports this as a "curse" of the fig tree; however, as Dowd points out, Peter may be incorrect. Jesus's action may also be seen as a prayer (*Prayer, Power*, 58).

[175] So, Telford: "The Markan epilogue bears little, if any, connection to what is reported in the story" (*Withered Tree*, 106).

[176] See A. Y. Collins, *Mark*, 530.

[177] This expectation was not uncommon in Second Temple Judaism, as J. R. Daniel Kirk notes, cf. Tob 13:8–11; 14:5–7; 1 En. 90:28–39 ("Time for Figs, Temple Destruction, and Houses of Prayer in Mark 11:12–25," *CBQ* 74 [2012]: 515).

[178] Jack R. Lundbom refers to the genre of Jer 7 as "Temple Oracles" directed at "the devout who have come to worship Yahweh" (*Jeremiah 1–20: A New Translation with Introduction and Commentary*, AB 21A [New York: Doubleday, 1999], 470).

is an act God performs and that Jesus mandates for the disciples (11:25). In a similar vein, the miracles performed in Mark are performed by the hand of God. Prayer, much like faith, orients one toward God's will.[179]

In addition to 11:22–25, the second major text on prayer in Mark appears in the Gethsemane scene in Mark 14:32–42. One of the major problems in this text for early interpretation is the depiction of Jesus as powerless and at odds with God's will. The passage begins, in v. 33, with Jesus, for the first time, alarmed (ἐκθαμβεῖσθαι)[180] and distressed (ἀδημονεῖν).[181] To this Jerome avers, "Let those who think that the Savior feared death and in fear of his passion said, 'Let his cup pass from me'—let them turn pink with shame."[182] In a similar move Origen claims that Jesus's hesitation represents pity on those who would soon be persecuted as a result of his death.[183] In Mark, Jesus's petition to God is desperate: "if it were possible [δυνατόν; cf. v. 36] that the hour may pass from him" (v. 35; cf. vv. 36, 39). So also, Ambrose: "Do not open your ears to those treacherous people who suggest that it was out of infirmity that the Son of God prayed, as though he had to ask for something that he was powerless to achieve himself."[184] On the other hand, there are strands of interpretation, such as the one found in the Pseudo-Athanasian dialogues, that prefer to emphasize Jesus's alarm and distress as evidence of his authentic humanity.[185] While this type of reading does not sit well with either Origen or Jerome, who seem unable to fathom Jesus in such agony,[186] this is not the first time in Mark that Jesus has struggled despite impending divine action (5:30; 7:24–30). As with the other virtues and practices examined in this chapter, prayer is fundamentally theological in nature.

---

[179] This is the insightful conclusion of Dowd at the end of her study: "The Markan community holds to the worldview that 'everything is possible for God'" (*Prayer, Power*, 122).

[180] ἐκθαμβέω has two meanings in Mark: either "awe" (9:15) or "alarm" (16:5–6). cf. *LSJ*, s.v., ἐκθαμβέω. Matthew has "sorrowful" (λυπεῖσθαι).

[181] Retained in Matt 26:37.

[182] *Comm. Matt. Lib. IV* on Matt. 26:39; CCSL 77, 244; trans. Kevin Madigan, "Ancient and High Medieval Interpretations of Jesus in Gethsemane: Some Reflections on Tradition and Continuity in Christian Thought," *HTR* 88 (1995): 157–73, here 164. Martin Luther disagrees: "The humanity was left alone, the devil had free access to Christ, and they deity withdrew its power and let the humanity fight alone" (*Luther's Works: Volume 12, Selected Psalms I*, ed. Jaroslav Pelikan [Saint Louis, MO: Concordia, 1955], 127). Likewise, John Calvin: "If we are ashamed that Christ should experience fear and sorrow, our redemption will perish and be lost" (*Commentary on a Harmony of the Evangelists: Matthew, Mark, and Luke*, trans. William Pringle [Grand Rapids, MI: Eerdmans, 1949; repr., Grand Rapids, MI: Baker, 1989], 3.226).

[183] *Cels.* 2.25.

[184] *Exp. Evang. Sec. Luc.* 5.42; CCSL 14, 150; trans. Madigan, "Ancient and High Medieval Interpretations," 158.

[185] *Dial. Contra Mac.* 28; PG 28, 1332. These fourth-century dialogues are staged conversations between a fictive "Orthodox" voice and a dissenting voice (e.g., Anomoeans, Apollinarians, Macedonians). In the text referenced here, the dissenting position represents the Macedonians, who claim that Jesus's alarm and distress in Mark 14:33 indicate he is a "soulless body" (σῶμα ἄψυχον) and only godlike (θεότης). For the dialogues' use and reception, see Alasdair Heron, "The Two Pseudo-Athanasian Dialogues Against the Anomoeans," *JTR* 24 (1973): 101–22.

[186] Origen, in *Comm. Matt.* 90; GCS 38, 205–6, states that Jesus felt distressed "according to human nature [*humanam naturam*], which is subject to such passions, not however, according to the divine power [*divinam virtutem*/τὴν θείαν φύσιν], which is quite distant from passion of this kind" (trans. Richard Layton, *Didymus the Blind and His Circle in Late-Antique Alexandria: Virtue and Narrative in Biblical Scholarship* [Urbana: University of Illinois Press, 2004], 122).

Returning to the text of Mark, it seems that prayer has at least two functions in 14:32–42. First, prayer orients Jesus's will toward God's. In his prayer, Jesus confesses that with God "all things are possible" (πάντα δυνατά), a theological confession that appears four times in Mark—twice in the Gethsemane prayers (14:35–36), once in Jesus's response to the plea of the father of the epileptic boy (9:23), and again when Jesus explains to Peter how difficult it is for some to enter the kingdom of God (10:27). In the latter text, the disciples ask, "Who is able [δύναται] to be saved?" To this, Jesus retorts, "With God all things are possible [δυνατά]." Like these texts, God's power is at the forefront of Jesus's prayer. Some have argued that the Markan Aramaism, αββα (14:36; cf. 3:17; 5:41; 7:11, 34; 15:22, 34), which Matthew and Luke remove (Matt 26:39; Luke 22:42; cf. John 12:27), signifies an intimate address to God (cf. Mark 5:37; 9:2; Gal 4:6; Rom 8:15).[187] More clearly, Jesus reaffirms his own identity, outlined from the start of the Gospel, as God's son (1:1) and asks for God's assistance.

Second, Jesus admonishes the disciples to pray "so that you may not enter into temptation" (ἵνα μὴ ἔλθητε εἰς πειρασμόν; 14:38). The mention of temptation recalls Jesus's episode with Satan in the prologue (1:13; cf. 8:11; 10:2; 12:15). Not only this, but Jesus's question to Peter in v. 37 ("Did you not have the strength [ἴσχυσας] to stay alert for one hour?") recalls Peter's susceptibility to Satan's ploys (8:33) and Jesus's strength over Satan (1:7; 3:27; cf. 9:18). Prayer, much like the act of demonic exorcism, provides access to God's power as well as power over God's adversary. As Calvin states on Mark 14:34, "hence we infer that the true test of *virtue* is only to be found when the contest begins."[188]

The Gethsemane scene is also replete with eschatological language. The repetitive imperative to "stay awake" (14:34, 37–38) is prominently featured in the doorkeeper pericope in Mark 13 (vv. 34–35, 37; cf. 13:33) in reference to sleeping (v. 36) and a swiftly approaching time (13:33).[189] In vv. 35, 37, and 41, the hour (also featured in 13:11 and 32) and the cup may have eschatological tones as well (cf. 10:38–39). In the Testament of Abraham, death's bitter cup (τοῦ θανατοῦ πικρὸν ποτήριον) appears on three occasions (T. Abr. 1:3; 17:16; 19:16).[190] In the Hebrew Bible, cups may be

---

[187] As argued, e.g.f, by Larry W. Hurtado, "The Place of Jesus in Earliest Christian Prayer," in *Early Christian Prayer and Identity Formation*, eds. Reidar Hvalvik and Karl Olav Sandnes, WUNT 336 (Tübingen: Mohr Siebeck, 2014), 40. On the other hand, the term αββα appears in the more common emphatic state, and Matthew and Luke's removal accord with their treatment of Mark's redundancies. Arguing against Jeremias's special or "new" use (*The Prayers of Jesus* [London: SCM Press, 1967], 53–4; cf. also 4Q372; 4Q560), Mary Rose D'Angelo claims that the term αββα, more generally, "evoked the relation of humanity to God in terms of kindred and likeness, and the providence of God for humanity" ("Abba and 'Father': Imperial Theology and the Jesus Tradition" *JBL* 111 [1992]: 611–30, here 622).

[188] Calvin, *Harmony*, 3.226, italics in original.

[189] As noted by Pesch, *Naherwartungen*, 199–202; Werner H. Kelber, "Mark 14:32–42: Gethsemane: Passion Christology and Discipleship Failure," *ZNW* 63 (1972): 171; Garrett, *Temptations*, 91–5.

[190] From the long recension. In 1:3 it is "the bitter cup of death" (τοῦ θανατοῦ πικρὸν ποτήριον), in 17:6 it is "the cup filled with poison" (ποτήρια μεμεστωμένα φαρμάκων), and in 19:16 it is "the cup filled with poisonous destruction" (ποτήρια δηλητήρια φαρμάκα μεμεστωμένα). Dale Allison suggests that the more common "suffering of God's wrath or judgment" pictured in Gethsemane, and the Hebrew Bible is not featured in the Testament of Abraham; instead, it is "the personification of the end that inevitably comes to all human beings" (*Testament of Abraham*, CEJL [New York: Walter de Gruyter, 2003], 72–3). In either case, a future end is in mind.

associated with salvation (Ps 115:4 LXX), but more commonly with God's wrath (Ps 10:6 LXX; Isa 51:17, 22). In short, the eschatological hour has arrived, and a moral divide stands before Jesus and his followers. Ultimately, it is prayer that enables Jesus to do God's will. Framed in terms of accountability, prayer is not a neutral, "deciding" act. Prayer aligns one with God and against God's enemies.

In summary, the act of prayer further emphasizes the role of the accountable self in Mark. Prayer reorients the accountable agent to God. When prayer is subverted for purposes to the contrary, such as the exploitation of widows' houses, Mark's Jesus offers sharp condemnation (12:40). Jesus's own modeling of prayer exhibits a degree of powerlessness without access to the God to whom he prays. In this sense, prayer is always theological. In 14:32-42, the act of praying enables Jesus to do what he otherwise could not do. Jesus's discourse in 11:11–25 tells the readers to whom, exactly, the moral act of prayer belongs: "all nations." Finally, the eschatological context of prayer indicates that accountability in Mark is contested. Much like demonic exorcism (9:38–41), prayer solidifies one's status of belong to God and God's family over and against the power of evil (14:38).

4.4 Conclusion

In the ancient word, nearly every aspect of the moral life taught a person or community how to live. While some of these sayings were difficult to accept, someone like Philo wrote to *gain* an audience, not to lose one: Moses "has set before us, like some well-wrought picture, a piece of work beautiful and godlike, a model [παραδειγμα] for those who are willing to copy [μιμεῖσθαι] it" (*Life of Moses* 1.28.158). One might say the same of Xenophon's *Memorabilia*. Xenophon strives to depict Socrates as a model worthy of imitation, not as someone who corrupts the youth (1.2.64; 4.8.10).[191] Josephus portrays Saul as a brave and courageous king par excellence: "The attributes of courageous, greatly adventurous, and despiser of danger, might only be attributed rightly to the imitators of Saul" (οἱ Σαούλου μιμησάμενοι; *Ant*. 6.347).

When placed among these ancient writers, Mark offers a different picture in his life of Jesus. This chapter addresses the problematic claim of an "ethic" of imitation in Mark. By the presentation of the disciples alone, "doing as Jesus does" in Mark is fraught with problems: the disciples fail to expel demons (9:18), fall asleep at Jesus's greatest hour of need (14:32–42), dismiss children as insignificant (10:13–16), and vie for positions of power (10:35–45). Jesus himself appears to wrestle with God's will (14:32–42) and God's inclusivity (7:24–30), and his fate, which may also await those who follow him (8:34–35; 10:39; 13:12), is crucifixion.[192] This Jesus presents a staunch

---

[191] According to Hägg, Xenophon seeks to "propagate certain social and moral values for which he found Socrates a suitable mouthpiece and his way of life the perfect illustration" (*Art of Biography*, 29; cf. Votaw, "The Gospels," 219).

[192] A theology of suffering that encourages one to "do as Jesus does" without ethical consideration of "why," "what," and "for whom" creates a host of problems. To quote Mercedes,

> So long as females, racial minorities, and persons with less money are taught to be submissive while white, monied males are taught to be strong, Christian self-giving ethics will have

moral commitment to God, even when the circumstances may dictate other, perhaps more standard, moral commitments, such as honoring one's family (10:29–30) or maintaining ritual purity (7:1–23). Unlike the followers of Socrates (cf. Euthydemus in *Mem.* 4.2.1), the characters who appear to model faith in God in Mark are the fringe characters.[193] Parents surrender their moral right to children (5:36; 9:24);[194] those unhinged by demonic possession are made well (5:15); those who are blind see God's mission more clearly (10:52). For these reasons, and more, Jesus tends to relativize moral customs of his day. He destroys a local economy (5:1–20), invites his disciples to leave their families (1:16–20), rejects his own (3:31–35), and defames an outsider (7:27). Doing as this Jesus does without considering why would result in grave consequences for the doer. Perhaps this is why his parables are told in order to leave the hearer dazed and confused (4:12): his very actions repeatedly confound. For a small sectarian group, the virtue of loving God cannot be separated from the practice of loving neighbor or the posture of humility toward God's inclusion of others. These neighbors include those outside of some traditional cultural boundaries, those deep in gentile territory (5:1–20), the antagonistic scribes (12:34), and even political persecutors (15:39).

This chapter began by asking for what, exactly, the moral agent in Mark is accountable and how this impacts her relationship with fellow believers. The virtues of a believer examined in this chapter include faith, love, and humility, the internalization of which leads to the practices of healing, demonic exorcism, and prayer. One's love of God finds expression in the practice of healing one's neighbor. As Aristotle has it, "in a word, our moral dispositions are formed as a result of the corresponding activities."[195] Aristotle's sentiment might be turned on its head: our activities are formed by a moral disposition toward God and the virtues of God's kingdom. The moral life in Mark depends on absolute trust in God, which may come as no surprise. The real surprise arrives when the reader learns for whom the believer is accountable. One's trust in God does not serve the self (Mark 7:1–23) but functions for someone else: a parent for a sick son or daughter (5:21–43; 7:24–30; 9:14–29), a group of friends for a paralytic (2:1–12). Love and trust extend to those outside one's biological family: Jesus leaves his own family (3:31–35), Peter his wife (1:30), and the sons of Zebedee their father (1:20). The accountable self is inundated with nonsensical demands to lose itself (8:34–38) and to include in one's family those who, according to the standards of Greco-Roman society, have little to give in return or offend the benefactor (7:24–30). Likewise, moral action, such as prayer, must never puff up one's self-worth (12:40) but reorient one's very desires toward God's (14:32–42). Prioritizing these "little ones" defy *human* faculties, thus requiring a complete surrender to *divine* capabilities (8:33).[196] God's way in Mark

---

different effects on different persons—especially when the spokespersons for these messages are at the top of the hierarchy. In such a patriarchal, racist, and classist context, no message about self-giving is politically neutral. (*Power For*, 12)

[193] Once more, for a thorough account of the role of minor characters in Mark, see Malbon, "Major Importance of Minor Characters," 58–86; and Williams, *Other Followers*, 89–206.
[194] Cf. Gaius, *Inst.* 1.127; 2.156; Justinian, *Dig.* 50.16.195.
[195] *EN* 2.1.8; 1103b20 (Rackham, LCL).
[196] A character study of Mark's minor characters, especially in contrast to the disciples, may be found in Rhoads, Dewey, and Michie, *Mark as Story*, 130–6. Rhoads, Dewey, and Michie include in this

leaves those inside on the outs if they do not turn and repent: once more, God's way now includes all the nations. Finally, there are also, to use Keck's term, "sanctions" for one's failure to follow God's initiatives. In cases examined so far, we have already seen the subversion of prayer (12:40) and God's commandments (7:1–23) in service to the self. Evil and God's judgment are the subject of the next chapter. As virtues derive from God in Mark, evil also has a source, albeit a much more insidious one.

category, among others, the friends of the paralytic, the leper, Jairus, the Syrophoenician woman, the children, the poor widow, and Joseph of Arimathea.

5

Evil in the Gospel of Mark

5.1 Introduction

In studies related to the ethics of Mark, the role of evil and the topic of eternal judgment have received remarkably short shrift.[1] One reason for such avoidance is that references to eternal judgment appear infrequently in Mark compared to Matthew (10:15, 28; 11:22; 12:42; 13 20; 18:6–9; 22:13; 24:51; 25:31–46) and Luke (10:12–14; 11:31–32; 12:2, 4–5, 47–48; 13:5, 28; 14:24; 16:19–31; 18:8; 20:47). Even so, Mark's Jesus does not make light of the final consequences that accompany evil activity (8:38; 9:42–50; 12:9; 13:14–19). Consider, once more, Jesus's question in Mark 3:4, which concerns both doing good (i.e., saving a life) and doing evil (i.e., murder). As Chapter 3 of the present study has shown in Mark's prologue, God's moral program in Mark begins in contested territory: ultimate good meets adversity. Evil is pronounced from the start of the second Gospel, such that even God's champion, Jesus, is not free from the temptations of Satan (1:12–13). Later on, Jesus's own human frailty challenges his best intentions (14:33). Even on a good day, his pupil, Peter, falls prey to Satan's predatory tactics (8:27–33). No discussion of the moral life of Mark would be complete without an account of the evil that may thwart it.

This final chapter will offer such an account in terms of moral agency. In review, the terms are set not by moral casuistry (what must I do?) but by moral accountability (to whom do I belong?). Accountability, then, remains the chief metric by which I will assesses immoral activity. For Mark, the one who does not belong to God or to God's family belongs to Satan. This type of absolutism for insiders and outsiders is not uncommon in Jewish apocalypticism (1QS 3:19–26; 1 John 3:7–10). Mark's presentation of evil is well illustrated in the anonymous exorcist pericope (9:38–41) in which Jesus declares, "Whoever is not against us, is for us" (ὅς γὰρ οὐκ ἔστιν καθ᾽ ἡμῶν, ὑπὲρ ἡμῶν ἐστιν).[2] Important to Jesus's meaning is the context: the act of exorcising demons is a characteristic of God's family. In short, exorcism of evil displays belonging.

---

[1] Tat-siong Benny Liew identifies an interesting trend in Markan studies: those who emphasize Mark's apocalyptic world tend to downplay political dimensions while those who emphasize Mark's sociopolitical world tend to downplay apocalyptic dimensions. In either case, judgment receives only partial treatment. For more on "the great divide," see *Politics of Parousia: Reading Mark Inter(con)textuality*, BIS 42 (Boston: Brill, 1999), 46–63.

[2] Luke's account of the use of Jesus's name by itinerant exorcists is quite different (Acts 19:13–15).

By casting out demons, the anonymous exorcist has chosen a side. He does not belong to Satan (cf. 3:23); therefore, he must belong to God.

The present chapter is divided into two parts. The first part deals with the superhuman or demonic characteristics of evil in Mark. God's actions respond to the cosmic scope of evil and the work of Satan that appear to have gained traction at an alarming rate, entrapping all things human.[3] Evil, in this account, is the result of demonic, superhuman forces. The second half of this chapter will consider a more anthropological account of evil. According to Mark, evil is not only an external force but also comes from within (7:21).[4] Overall, this chapter seeks to answer the following question: What kind of person belongs to Beelzebul (3:20–34)? In Chapter 4, I argued that those who belong to God possess characteristics of God's family, such as faith, love, and humility, as well as engage in practices of God's kingdom, such as love of neighbor, demonic exorcism, and prayer. In the present chapter, this inquiry is reversed: those who belong to evil possess characteristics of the evil one, such as greed, misanthropy, and pride. Like the demonic in Mark, those who belong to evil seek out death instead of life. In this way, evil has its accompanying practices, such as taking advantage of the poor and worship of the self over God.

The basis of my twofold division is indebted to John K. Riches's *Conflicting Mythologies*. One of Riches's central claims is that the Gospels of Matthew and Mark offer two competing cosmologies concerning the "origins and resolution of evil."[5] In Pauline studies, such a bifurcated explanation for the origins of evil was posited by Martinus de Boer.[6] In a nod to de Boer, Riches outlines his thesis for Mark as follows:

> The Gospel of Mark does not present a single ethos, or indeed a single unified view of reality: it can be read in different ways, as a narrative of conversion and radical transformation, or as a narrative of commission and restoration; as the story of the purging of the world from pollution by unclean spirits, or as the

---

[3] On the use of the term "cosmic" in reference to evil activity in Mark, see Robinson, *Problem of History*, 33.

[4] A helpful overview of these two views of evil in Second Temple Judaism may be found in Miryam T. Brand's *Evil within and Without: The Source of Sin and Its Nature as Portrayed in Second Temple Literature*, JAJSup 9 (Göttingen: Vandenhoeck & Ruprecht, 2013): "These texts reflect the idea that sin is inherent to the human, originates from external influences, or is a combination of these two factors" (25). Additionally, for a helpful overview of the development of the rabbinic doctrine of the *yetzer ha'rah* out of earlier source material, see Ishay Rosen-Zvi, *Demonic Desires: Yetzer Hara and the Problem of Evil in Late Antiquity*, Divinations (Philadelphia: University of Pennsylvania Press, 2011).

[5] *Conflicting Mythologies*, xiii. The traditional divide in Markan studies, as Riches sees it, is between the positions exemplified by Ernest Best, on the one hand, and James Robinson and Joel Marcus, on the other. According to Riches, Best locates evil within the "hearts and minds of men and women," while scholars such as Robinson and Marcus give more attention to the "cosmic struggle between Jesus and Satan" (xii). Best interprets Mark's account of evil primarily as an anthropological struggle; he locates victory in the hearts of humans and takes as final the binding of Satan (Mark 3:27; cf. Best, *Temptation*, 11–13). Best notes that the demonic "slowly fades out of Mark" (ibid., 22). Robinson, on the other hand, interprets Mark's account of evil as an apocalyptic struggle between Jesus and Satan. Robinson then focuses on the demonic accounts in Mark's narrative to establish "Jesus' unrelenting opposition in the exorcism narrative … for life and communion on behalf of the possessed person" (*Problem of History*, 42).

[6] See de Boer, "Paul and Jewish Apocalyptic Eschatology," 169–90.

story of the parodic, strange restoration of Israel's glory and the coming of its light to the Gentiles. Behind these two different, if interwoven, stories ... are two fundamentally opposed mythologies ... One account suggests that the root of such evils lies in some form of angelic invasion and pollution of the world; the other prefers a primal myth of human disobedience.[7]

As Chapters 3 and 4 have already established, in Mark's Gospel the world is torn apart by unclean spirits who control and torment bodies. For the first half of this chapter, I argue that the human incapacity to do good is due, in part, to malevolent, superhuman forces. In turn, God's correlative judgment of evil is reserved for these forces, namely Satan and his diabolical allies (1:24; 5:7). In the second half of this chapter, I will outline the other mythological strand identified by Riches ("a primal myth of human disobedience"). I will argue that there is also a corresponding account of evil in Mark that stresses the human capacity for greed and pride. These two views may conflict or conflate with one another. Accounts of evil classified in the former, cosmic-invasion category may also manifest symptoms in the latter, anthropological category. Consider, for example, Pilate's self-serving motive for handing Jesus over (15:6-15; cf. 7:22)[8] or, similarly, Herod's motive for beheading John (6:19-20). Pride, as a symptom of the human capacity to do evil, has deadly consequences in both cases. However, one may also observe that these human dispositions to do evil point to the hand of Satan. In Mark, both accounts of evil are up and running, and both compete with God for humanity's moral accountability in the world.

5.2 The Personification of Evil in Mark

Some of the exegetical work for establishing an antithetical moral force in Mark appears in Chapter 3 of this book. To briefly recapitulate, the Gospel of Mark begins in contested territory (1:12-13). From the beginning, the temptation of Jesus reveals God's ownership of Jesus, as God's son (cf. 1:11), and God's authority over Satan. This contest is dramatized in the Markan exorcism pericopes (1:21-28; 5:1-20; 7:24-30; 9:14-29, 38-41) and in Jesus's commissioning of the disciples to do likewise (3:14-15; 6:7). Moreover, the image of God as judge, and Jesus's derivative authority, appear in frequent contention in Mark. Jesus's authority in Mark is pitted against the scribes (1:21-28), misattributed to Satan (3:19b-35), and brought into question (11:27-33). God's judgment is reserved for God's enemies, including those who harm little ones (9:42-50) and those who murder his son (12:1-12). The source of Jesus's authority

---

[7] Riches, *Conflicting Mythologies*, 145.
[8] On the Johannine characterization of Pilate, Cornelius Brennema concludes that Pilate "represents those in positions of authority who compromise truth and justice to safeguard their career and ensure survival; those who start well on a quest for truth but eventually abandon it because other things (career, image, and so on) take precedence" ("The Character of Pilate in the Gospel of John," in *Characters and Characterization in the Gospel of John*, ed. Christopher W. Skinner, LNTS 461 [London: Bloomsbury/T&T Clark, 2013], 253). One wonders if the seed of such a characterization of Pilate begins in Mark.

is the thrust of these inquiries: Under whose sovereignty does Jesus serve? God or Satan? To which realm is he accountable? To heaven's or to earth's? The question of belonging is the axis upon which morality turns in Mark. Answered positively, Jesus receives his authority and power from God. Alignment with God's intent drives the moral self in Mark. The polar, anthropological alternative—the question "of human origin" (11:30)—is the subject of this next section. Who opposes God in Mark?

The Role of Satan in Mark

Since the temptation scene has already been discussed in detail (see the section "The Temptation Scene (1:12–13)" in Chapter 3), this section will focus on Mark's account of evil in 3:19b–35. According to Elizabeth Shively, this pericope showcases Mark's apocalyptic account of evil: "Using symbols available to him from Jewish tradition and apocalyptic thought, Mark imagines a world in which Satan is the strong ruler over a united kingdom of demons that fights against the Spirit."[9] Shively utilizes "apocalyptic topoi" to describe evil in Mark.[10] These terms refer to the coded language found in at least some apocalyptic texts in the Second Temple period.[11] While it is valid to question how closely portions of Mark's Gospel track with Jewish apocalyptic literature, Jesus's activity in Mark 3:19b–35 appears to be "cast in terms of the binding of this figure [of Satan] and his exorcisms are part of this work."[12] Shively may overstate her case for the entirety of Mark,[13] but her assessment of the apocalyptic symbolism in Mark 3 is a helpful starting point for our purposes. Indeed, a growing number of scholars view the Beelzebul controversy in Mark 3:19b–35 as essential for understanding Jesus's role in Mark.[14]

---

[9] Shively, *Apocalyptic Imagination*, 1. For a similar appraisal of Mark, see Marcus, *Mark 1–8*, 72–3.
[10] She also employs the term "cosmic imagery" (*Apocalyptic Imagination*, 26).
[11] Shively groups the evidence to favor her position: "The characters in the story inhabit a world in which the agents of persecution are not simply bodily or human, but supernatural" (ibid., 147, see 84–147). While Daniel, 1 Enoch, Jubilees, and the Testament of Solomon may depict, to use Shively's term, human "victimization" by the demonic (146), de Boer has demonstrated that the evidence in Second Temple Judaism is more mixed ("Paul and Jewish Apocalyptic Eschatology," 169–90). J. P. Davies offers a detailed account of the various forms of "apocalyptic" one may find in Second Temple Judaism: *Paul among the Apocalypses? An Evaluation of "Apocalyptic Paul" in the Context of Jewish Christian Apocalyptic Literature* (New York: Bloomsbury/T&T Clark, 2016). For example, Davies notes that 2 Baruch and 4 Ezra "resist dualism" (128), which are two texts Shively does not treat in detail (*Apocalyptic Imagination*, 84–149, 233).
[12] Grant Macaskill, "Apocalypse and the Gospel of Mark," in *The Jewish Apocalyptic Tradition and the Shaping of New Testament Thought*, ed. Benjamin E. Reynolds and Loren T. Stuckenbruck (Minneapolis, MN: Fortress Press, 2017), 61.
[13] "Mark employs apocalyptic *topoi* to interpret Jesus' ministry as a skirmish in a dualistic cosmic contest in which Spirit-empowered Jesus wages war against Satan to rescue people held captive by demonic powers" (*Apocalyptic Imagination*, 39). As stated previously, my position is closer to Riches's conflicting accounts of evil in Mark. While demonic control of humans is certainly in Mark's purview, evil comes from within as well (7:21).
[14] Cheryl Pero describes it as a "spring board for the topic of demonic possession and exorcism in the Gospel of Mark" (*Liberation from Empire: Demonic Possession and Exorcism in the Gospel of Mark*, Studies in Biblical Literature 150 [New York: Peter Lang, 2013], 69); Hauw follows, *Exorcism Stories*, 91. Consider also Stephen Moore's comment: "Jesus' earlier boast that his plundering of the property of the 'strong man' portends the end of Satan's empire (3:23-7) could then be read as equally portending the end of Rome's empire" ("Mark and Empire: 'Zealot' and 'Postcolonial' Readings,"

Mark 3:19b-35

The setting of this pericope is the "home" (v. 19b: καὶ ἔρχεται εἰς οἶκον) and, quite naturally for such a setting, the question of Jesus's origin (3:31-33).[15] In other words, the overarching inquiry of this text is this: Where does Jesus live? Whose sphere of influence does he inhabit? Similar thematic concerns are also found throughout the passage (note Mark's use of οἰκία in 3:25, 27). That the strong man parable is sandwiched inside the narrative setting of family conflict is paramount to the parable's interpretation. The English translation of οἱ παρ᾿ αὐτοῦ as "his family" (NRSV, NIV, CEB) in v. 21 is contingent upon the narrative intercalation of Jesus and his family of origin. For this reason, Mark's apparent interest in Jesus's family is lost in both Matthew (12:22-32, 46-50) and Luke (8:19-21; 11:14-23; 12:10).[16] Mark's story begins with an overbearing crowd (cf. 2:2; 5:31) and a blistering accusation by Jesus's own family: "They were saying, 'He is mad!'" (ἔλεγον γὰρ ὅτι ἐξέστη).[17] Among the Synoptics, Mark alone contains the accusation that Jesus is out of his mind, further emphasizing the tension over Jesus's accountability depicted within the parable to follow.[18] While the term ἐξέστη may mean, in some cases, astonishment (Mark 2:12; Luke 2:47), the meaning here is closer to madness (cf. Xenophon, *Mem.* 1.3.12).[19] The accusation appears to reflect a characteristic of the demonic, often found in Mark: that which drives people out of their minds (1:26; 5:5; 9:18). This sets up the accusation by the scribes: 'He has Beelzebul" (3:22). The use of ἔχω here suggests possession, as in the unclean spirit episodes.[20] Jesus, like the unclean spirits throughout Mark, is accused of acting according to the domicile of Satan. Such activity includes violence (1:26; 5:5) with intent to kill (7:24-30; 9:22).

---

in *The Postcolonial Biblical Reader*, ed. R. S. Sugirtharajah [Malden, MA.: Blackwell, 2006], 194). Geert van Oyen calls 3:19b-35 "the heart of the meaning of Jesus' actions against the demons" ("Demons and Exorcisms in the Gospel of Mark," in *Demons and the Devil in Ancient and Medieval Christianity*, VCSup 108 [Boston: Brill, 2011], 110). See also Twelftree, *In the Name of Jesus*, 112-16.

[15] As previously mentioned, Mark's use of home is not insignificant. John Painter notes how other people's homes are a common space in Mark for Jesus to conduct his miracles ("When Is a House Not a Home? Disciples and Family in Mark 3.13-35," *NTS* 45 [1999]: 498-513). For further discussion, see Section 3.4: "Moral Accountability in God's Family."

[16] James Edwards correctly notes that both Matthew (12:22-32, 46-50) and Luke (8:19-21; 11:14-23; 12:10) alter Mark's sequence here ("Markan Sandwiches," 209). Painter notes how the intercalation is critical for understanding the meaning of this Markan text ("When Is a House Not a Home," 503), as does George Aichele, "Jesus' Uncanny 'Family Scene'," *JSNT* 74 (1999): 29-49.

[17] My translation reflects the majority position. In contrast, David Wenham offers textual support for the reading: "For they said it was out of control with enthusiasm," "it" referring to the crowd ("The Meaning of Mark 3:21," *NTS* 21 [1975]: 295-300). This reading seems difficult to justify in light of the Markan intercalation noted above.

[18] Jack T. Sanders notes how this saying in Mark 3:21 is wrongfully overlooked in historical Jesus research, because it is a saying *about* Jesus instead of a saying *of* Jesus. If anything, this line in Mark may demonstrate tension between Jesus and his family of origin and Jesus's role as a charismatic leader ("The Criterion of Coherence and the Randomness of Charisma: Poring through Some Aporias in the Jesus Tradition," *NTS* 44 [1998]: 1-25). According to Henry Wansbrough, Matthew and Luke remove it because "they cannot stomach the accusation against Jesus" (("Mark III.21—Was Jesus Out of His Mind?" *NTS* 18 [1972]: 233-5).

[19] In this passage, Socrates describes the effects of a poisonous spider bite: it drives one insane (καὶ τοῦ φρονεῖν ἐξίστησι).

[20] Robinson also notes how the use of possession language in the demonic episodes is indicative of belonging in Mark (*Problem of History*, 35)

The scribes claim that Jesus resides among the immoral, and as a consequence of his residence, his authority does not come from God.

Images of the Demonic in Second Temple Period

According to various literary sources in antiquity, demonic possession resulted in complete surrender of human faculties to the governing demonic host (Philostratus *Life* 3.38; 1QapGen 20.16–18). The old adage—the devil made me do it—in this case accurately describes an assumption about human liability. In 1 Enoch, the fallen angel Azazel torments humanity, leading it astray (8:1–4). In Jubilees, Mastema and his evil spirits proliferate sin upon the earth, the source of massive bloodshed (11:4–9). Likewise, the angel of darkness corrupts humanity in the Qumran corpus (1QS 3:20–21; 1QM 13:10–12).[21] In the Testaments of the Twelve Patriarchs, immoral activity is regularly depicted as the result of tormenting spirits. In T. Benj. 3:3–4, for instance, spirits "demand" (ἐξαιτέω) the right to afflict humanity:

> Φοβεῖσθε κύριον καὶ ἀγαπᾶτε τὸν πλησίον. Καὶ ἐὰν τὰ πνεύματα τοῦ βελιὰρ εἰς πᾶσαν πονηρίαν θλίψεως ἐξαιτήσωνται ὑμας, οὐ μὴ κατακυριεύσῃ ὑμῶν πᾶσα πονηρία θλίψεως, ὡς οὐδὲ Ἰωσὴφ τοῦ ἀδελφοῦ μου. Πόσοι τῶν ἀνθρώπων ἠθέλησαν ἀνελεῖν αὐτόν, καὶ ὁ θεὸς ἐσκέπασεν αὐτόν. ὁ γὰρ φοβούμενος τὸν θεὸν καὶ ἀγαπῶν τὸν πλησίον αὐτοῦ ὑπὸ τοῦ ἀερίου πνεύματος τοῦ βελιὰρ οὐ δύναται πληγῆναι, σκεπαζόμενος ὑπὸ τοῦ φόβου τοῦ θεοῦ.

> Fear the Lord and love [your] neighbor. And if the spirits of Beliar demand to torment you with every evil affliction, every evil affliction will certainly not have authority over you, as in the case of Joseph my brother. How many people wished to kill him, and God guarded him. For the one who fears God and loves his neighbor is not able to be overpowered by the futile spirit of Beliar, being shielded by the fear of God.[22]

In this passage, deviant human action is attributable to the whim of demonic power. However, those who belong to God are under God's protection. The Testaments refer to Beliar as a figure that will be "bound" by God, such that God's children have power "to tread upon evil spirits" (T. Levi 18:12; cf. Mark 3:27; 16:17–18).[23] The binding imagery in the strongman parable may have a similar nuance. It is only by first binding (δέω) the strong man that his "possessions" (τὰ σκεύη) may be plundered. One may safely

---

[21] With respect to Jubilees, James C. VanderKam observes, "*Jubilees* connects the demons/evil spirits with many kinds of sins, but bloodshed and idolatry are prominently consistent among them. In general the demons/evil spirits are the agents of Mastema in causing evil of every sort in human society" ("The Demons in the *Book of Jubilees*," in *Demons: The Demonology of Israelite-Jewish and Early Christian Literature in Context of Their Environment*, ed. Armin Lange, Hermann Lichtenberger, and K.F. Diethard Römheld [Tübingen: Mohr Siebeck, 2003], 345).

[22] Author's translation. Greek text from de Jonge, *The Testaments of the Twelve Patriarchs*.

[23] On the close (and complicated) relationship between the Jesus tradition's depiction of Satan and the depiction of Beliar in the Testaments of the Twelve Patriarchs, see O'Connor, "The Devil Will Flee," 883–97.

assume that the strong man's "possessions" are the content within his house (3:27); in this case, it is the unclean spirits. As in the Testament of Solomon, the figure of Beelzeboul, as the "prince of all the demons," coordinates his malevolent lackeys to do his dirty work (2:9). One need not look far for similar evidence in Mark: the trouble with the Gerasene demoniac is that no one was able to bind him (5:3; οὐδεὶς ἐδύνατο αὐτὸν δῆσαι) because no one had the strength (οὐδεὶς ἴσχυεν) to subdue him. It is only when the stronger one arrives that the unclean spirits obey. As mentioned above, John the Baptist's designation for Jesus as the "stronger one" is connected to God's power over the demonic (1:7).[24] It is no coincidence, then, that one of the chief aims of Jesus's adversaries in Mark is to "bind him" (15:1; cf. 6:17).[25] In Mark, God's power functions to reclaim human bodies from an adversary, such that even the body of Jesus is targeted by his enemies. In Mark 3:19b–35, his adversaries claim that his body is out of control and, thus, neither his own nor God's.

Evil spirits are often antithetical to God in Second Temple literature.[26] Azazel, Mastema, Beliar, Satan, and the like are not motivated to destroy humanity purely out of unhinged misanthropy. They are often narrative foils set in opposition to God and God's will. In Mark, Robinson refers to frequent demonic opposition as the "hostility" in the narrative.[27] God intends a punitive future for the demons, and they are at least marginally aware of it (1:24; 5:7). The moral terrain in Mark is split: with virtually no wiggle room, the things of God stand opposed to the things of humans (8:33). For this reason, even though the anonymous exorcist's allegiance is unclear to the disciples, his active resistance to the demonic aligns him with God (9:38–41).

While this type of moral duality pervades Mark's moral life, it is important to keep in mind that release from demonic possession is only one feature of the soteriology found in apocalyptic texts. J. P. Davies's survey of the duality in apocalyptic literature invites a caution worth recounting. Davies demonstrates how the cosmologies in the literary sources of the Second Temple period are often diverse.[28] The opposition between God and the forces of evil is only one facet of these rather complex dualities. One iteration of the flat-footed duality that Davies contests is polarized accounts of evil in apocalyptic literature. To understand evil as exclusively manifested in superhuman forces (and not in human disobedience) is reductionistic. For example, 1 Enoch's

---

[24] See the section "The Temptation Scene (1:12–13)" in Chapter 3. Robinson also connects John's words in the prologue to 3:27. "This relation of the designation 'strong' to the struggle with Satan finds its confirmation and nearest parallel in the exorcism debate, the only other place in Mark where the term 'strong' occurs" (*Problem of History*, 30). Robinson overlooks the additional use of "strong" in 5:4.
[25] Because of the overlapping imagery of the demonic and Jesus's adversaries, Elaine Pagels contends that the figure of Satan was utilized as a veiled metaphor for Jesus's enemies: "Satan serves to characterize *human* opposition to Jesus and his followers" ("The Social History of Satan, Part II: Satan in the New Testament Gospels," *JAAR* 62 [1994]: 17–58, here 19).
[26] Opposition to God is not the only function for evils spirits. On the nuance of evil figures in Second Temple Judaism including occasional partnership with God, see Reed Carlson, "Provocateurs, Examiners, and Fools: Divine Opponents to the Aqedah in Early Judaism," *CBQ* 83 (2021): 373–89.
[27] Robinson, *Problem of History*, 36–7.
[28] Davies notes the complex dualisms in 1 Enoch that resist dichotomies as evidenced in the multilayered heavenly ascent motif: "If apocalyptic cosmology were characterized by a strict dualism, there would be no place for heavenly ascents" (*Paul among the Apocalypses*, 127).

Book of Watchers is traditionally understood to present evil as the consequence of an "angelic invasion."[29] Even here, however, the evidence is mixed. While 1 En. 12–16 attributes evil to the spirit realm and its giants (9:1, 6–9; 10:7–9; 15:8–16:2), the Book of Watchers also ascribes evil to human transgression (e.g., 1 En. 32:6). In other words, according to Davies,

> two aetiologies for sin and evil are placed side-by-side. This is a common feature of the apocalypses. On the one hand the primordial, corrupting rebellion of angels; on the other the human transgression of God's command beginning in Eden. Humankind is both victim and perpetrator of evil, and God's judgment has been prepared for both angelic rebellion and human transgression.[30]

For this reason, while Shively's account of Mark's apocalyptic imagination is informative, it is incomplete (on which I shall discuss more in Section 5.3: "Human Responsibility in Mark"). Whether manifested in demonic spirits or in human disobedience, evil is uniformly opposed to God. Duality in Mark exists between God and evil.[31]

Finally, demons often inflict harm upon their victims. In Chapter 4 we examined several examples of this type of demonic misanthropy (cf. Philostratus, *Life* 3.38; 4:20; Acts Pet. 11; 1QapGen 20; Testament of Solomon). One might also consider David's role as an exorcist in biblical retellings of 1 Sam 16. The MT reads that "an evil spirit from YHWH tormented [... [וּבִעֲתַתּוּ] [Saul]" (16:14), which the LXX changes to "choked" (ἔπνιγεν). These more violent aspects of Saul's tormenting spirit are retained and elaborated upon in other traditions (LAB 60:1–3; Josephus, *Ant.* 8.2–5). For this reason, Geert van Oyen's conclusion regarding the demonic episodes in Mark is fitting: "Thus, although the fight between Satan and God seems to be a supernatural combat myth, it is a matter of life and death for every human person on earth. Stories about demons are stories about human beings."[32] God's role in Mark as parent, authority, and judge is pitted against that which destroys. The layered dimensions of evil indicate that the moral stakes are high for the accountable self, such that repentance requires complete surrender of the self to God (1:15; 8:34–38; 9:42–50; 10:31, 45; 14:36; 15:16–41).

Human Frailty in Mark: The Disciples as a Case Study

Another observation is in order regarding human frailty in Mark. If one thread of Markan cosmology is demonic invasion and its concomitant torment of human bodies, then what does this mean for the moral life? Keeping in mind that this Gospel, concordant with the literary milieu of the Second Temple period, offers a mixed or "conflicting" account of evil, the thesis of this section is as follows: if Satan is in competition with God for control of the world, then human fragility depicts, in microcosm, a struggle

---

[29] See de Boer, "Paul and Jewish Apocalyptic Eschatology," 174.
[30] Davies, *Paul among the Apocalypses*, 161.
[31] See Brand, *Evil within and Without*, 25.
[32] Oyen, "Demons and Exorcisms," 116.

with such evil. Unlike other accounts of the human capacity to resist evil in early Christianity (cf. Eph 6:11; Jas 4:7; 1 Pet 5:8-9; *Herm. Man.* 12.45, 4; 12.47, 7; 12.48, 2), human willpower in Mark appears feeble at best. The threat is so alarming that Jesus himself, God's son and champion, wrestles with God's directives (14:33). As Joel Marcus puts it, "the whole issue is summed up in the terse pronouncement in 10:26-27: salvation is impossible for human beings but not with God."[33]

There are several interesting examples of human fragility in Mark: Peter's (8:31-33; 14:66-72), Herod's (6:14-29), Judas's (14:10-11), that of select characters in the healing episodes (5:21-43; 9:14-29) especially in relation to fear (5:15, 33, 36; 6:50), and Jesus's fragility (14:33). One could make the case that some of these instances of human fragility reflect demonic malevolence: in the case of Peter, for example, Mark's Jesus makes this connection explicit (8:33). In the case of Judas, Luke and John offer the overt explanation that he acts under the influence of Satan (Luke 22:3; John 13:2). Howard Clark Kee states that John's death is not at the hand of Herod but "at the hands of the hostile powers."[34] Herod's decision to kill one whom he respects with ambivalence (6:20) recalls Mark's definition of immoral activity (3:4), the general objective of the demonic (5:5; 9:22), and the overarching plot of Jesus's adversaries (3:6; 12:12).

Among the available options, I will focus here on the notorious 'fallible disciples" motif. Running contrary to the insistence by some that Mark presents an *imitatio Christi* ethic for discipleship,[35] my contention is that (1) the disciples struggle on numerous occasions to follow the Markan Jesus and fail to meet the imitation criteria,[36] and (2) one purpose of this image of discipleship is to impress on the reader an account of the magnitude of evil. If we accept that Mark's literary genre comports in large part with ancient biography, as Chapter 2 lays out, then why would Mark undermine one of its central facets? My contention is that Mark has an apocalyptically shaded account of evil.

As Chapter 2 notes, in addition to presenting the central figure of a biography as a paradigmatic moral model, one common feature of biographies was to depict the teacher's early followers as credible. If the conductor is good, so, too, is his choir. Conversely, poor performers for Socrates at least, are distanced from their teacher in order to preserve his reputation. In the case of Xenophon's account of Socrates, Aristippus is undisciplined (*Mem.* 2.1) and hedonistic (*Mem.* 2.1.1-10; cf. 1.2.60;

---

[33] Marcus, *Mark 1-8*, 72.
[34] Kee, *Community*, 88. Kee's evidence is limited, however. He cites the comparative example of Elijah in Mark 9:13 to demonstrate that John's death serves as "a forerunner of Jesus" in 6:14-29 (ibid).
[35] See, e.g., Burridge, *Imitating Jesus*, 183-4.
[36] An interesting counter to my claim is presented by Michal Beth Dinkler, "Suffering, Misunderstanding, and Suffering Misunderstanding: The Markan Misunderstanding Motif as a Form of Jesus' Suffering," *JSNT* 38 (2016): 316-38. If the disciple's frequent misunderstanding is a form of suffering that contributes to Jesus's own suffering, then they do, in the end, imitate their teacher (Mark 8:34-38). Dinkler asks, "If Jesus' sufferings are meant to be emulated by his disciples, and being misunderstood by 'insiders' is a form of suffering, then does Jesus' call for his disciples to 'follow' him (ἀκολουθέω, 8.34) imply that being misunderstood is constitutive of discipleship?" (330). I would add that more than misunderstand him, the disciples occasionally derail his mission (8:32; 9:18-19; 14:5-7) and denounce (14:66-72) and abandon him (14:50-51; 16:8). In other words, especially in comparison to Greco-Roman biographies, they are poor students. Those who appear to be better suited to follow Jesus are the minor characters in Mark (2:5; 5:19, 34, 36; 7:29; 9:24; 10:52; 12:43; 14:6).

2.1.16–17). Aristippus's portrayal is likely an attempt to distance Socrates from Aristippus's vices. On the other hand, Socrates's star pupil, Euthydemus, is handsome, committed to study, and attentive (*Mem.* 4.2.8). Euthydemus professes the politics of Socrates in a manner worthy of praise. As depicted by Philostratus, Apollonius's early followers are similarly laudable (*Life* 5.21.1; cf. 1.2.3; 4.1.1; 6.3.2).

This pattern is also present in other Gospels. In Matthew, the disciples obey their teacher (8:18–22; 9:9; 21:6; 26:19; 28:7, 16–20) and understand his teaching (13:51; 14:33; 16:12), though not always (15:16; 26:6–13).[37] They are not entirely void of faith: Matthew describes their faith as "little" (8:26; 14:31; 16:8; 17:20). Matthew is straightforward: "The disciples went and did just as Jesus instructed them" (21:6). To Jesus's question "Did you understand these things?" the disciples reply with an unequivocal "Yes" (13:51). In Luke-Acts, the disciples model prayer (Luke 11:1; Acts 1:14; 2:42; 4:24; 6:4; 10:9) and obedience (5:5, 11; 7:29–30; 9:15); they also receive divine assistance for understanding (24:45; cf. 7:43). Again, the straightforward description of the disciples' compliance should be noted in Luke 9:15, "and they did so" (καὶ ἐποίησαν οὕτως). Even the occasion for the disciples' misunderstanding is given an explanation in Luke: "It was hidden from them" (9:45).

Mark's Gospel presents a more ambivalent account of the disciples, with several occasions to call their credibility into question.[38] While the Markan disciples obey Jesus (Mark 1:16–20; 2:14; 9:20; 11:2–4) and receive commission from him to preach and to exorcise demons (6:6b–13), they also appear unqualified for the task (9:18; 14:66–72). Episodes include frequent misunderstanding of Jesus's teaching (6:52; 7:18; 8:17–18, 21; 9:32), maladroit dismissals of would-be-disciples of Jesus (5:31; 9:38; 10:13–16; 14:4–5), constant squabbling over internal power dynamics (9:34; 10:35–45), reactions of fear instead of faith (4:40–41; 6:50; 9:32; 10:32; 16:8), and total abandonment of their teacher (14:50). For these reasons and more, many have concluded that Mark's portrait of the disciples is fallible.[39] My contention is that the disciples' inability to follow Jesus's words and actions attests to the prominence of evil in the narrative. Peter, the chief spokesman and representative of the disciples in Mark

---

[37] For more on the comparison between Matthew, Mark, Luke, and John's account of discipleship, see Black, *Disciples*, 36–45.

[38] So Black:

> In summary, then, misunderstanding, antagonism, and failure are not unique to the disciples in Mark, but neither are faith, insight, and allegiance to Jesus. To the extent that these latter attributes, not only their negative counterparts, are displayed by figures other than the twelve—that is, to the degree that "discipleship" is evinced by those not directly called or trained to be disciples—that status of Peter and his cohorts appears correspondingly equivocal. (*Disciples*, 45)

[39] Also known as the misunderstanding motif. A few examples include Robert C. Tannehill: "The surprisingly negative development of the disciples' story requires the reader to distance himself from them and their behavior" ("The Disciples in Mark: The Function of a Narrative Role," *JR* 57 [1977]: 386–405, here 393); Marcus: "The disciples' question [in Mark 8:4] is also important because its incredible obtuseness fits into a developing Markan theme" (*Mark 1–8*, 496); Donahue and Harrington: "One of the more startling phenomena in Mark is the negative portrait of disciples, especially the chosen Twelve" (*Mark*, 32); R. T. France: "But more often [the disciples] are negative models, in their fear and faithlessness (4:40; 6:49-50), their selfish ambition (9:34; 10:35-45), their spiritual failure (9:14-29) and their ultimate desertion of their master" (*The Gospel of Mark: A Commentary on the Greek Text*, NIGNTC [Grand Rapids, MI: Eerdmans, 2002], 28–9); Rhoads,

(3:16; 5:37; 9:2; 10:28; 11:21; 13:3; 14:29, 33, 37), is the one whom Jesus associates with Satan (8:33). Peter is tasked, like the rest of the disciples, with preaching the good news (3:14; 6:6b–13). However, in Mark's first three narrations of Peter's opportunity to evangelize, he denies his master instead (14:68, 70–71). What are the grounds for this association with Satan? Peter is mindful, not of godly things, but of human things (φρονεῖς τὰ τοῦ θεοῦ ἀλλὰ τὰ τῶν ἀνθρώπων). The realm of "human things" is precisely the territory that is contested in Mark. As in the Rule of the Community, those who are spiritually blind belong to the "spirit of wrongdoing" (ולרוח עולה).[40] In the Parables of Enoch, the human condition is marked by a general lack of wisdom (1 En. 42:1–3), reminiscent of the disciples' frequent incomprehension. A similar appraisal of humanity may be found in the psalms of the Hodayot (1QHa 9:23–25), in which incomprehension of God's way is attributed to a "spirit of error" (רוח התועה). The same may be said of the disciples' overall fragility in Mark: even Jesus's closest followers are not free from demonic malfeasance.

In summary, a similar appraisal of demonic activity that one finds in much of the literature of Second Temple Judaism appears in Mark. Evil spirits control human bodies and in some instances seek to destroy them (1:26; 5:5; 9:18). As in the case of Jubilees, one role of Mastema's evil spirits is "to shed blood upon the earth" (11:4). Demons serve the purpose to harm and to destroy. After his survey of demonic material in Mark, David L. Bartlett observes, "The demonic is beyond human control and beyond the conscious control of the one who is possessed … the demonic is positively hurtful, it is not only super-human, it is anti-human, dehumanizing."[41] Furthermore, demonic activity, as a form of evil, opposes God. Much like my case for accountability in Mark in Chapter 3, Mark's apocalyptic dualism unveils a contested territory in which God must reclaim humanity from the throes of the demonic and, as we will see below, from human disobedience. Finally, the infamous misunderstanding motif in Mark's portrait of discipleship may be explained in terms of the Markan attitude toward evil. The disciples' frequent inability to follow Jesus successfully, especially in contrast to Matthew and Luke, reveals the nature of human fragility in Mark. Even among Jesus's closest followers, *no one* can be saved apart from God's power (10:26–27).

5.3 Human Responsibility in Mark: An Account of Vice

In addition to personifying evil, Mark's Gospel also presents the reader with a set of human attitudes and practices that place one outside of God's family. On the one hand, those who belong to Satan, exhibit qualities of possession. Immorality, that is, action contrary to God's way in Mark, is a consequence of extraterrestrial invasion of human bodies. On the other hand, humans also exhibit certain attitudes and practices that

---

Dewey, and Michie: "In Mark, the failures of the disciples constitute the primary device by which the narrator reveals Jesus' standard for discipleship" (*Mark as Story*, 125).

[40] 1QS 4:1–11; cf. 4Q167 1:8, 2:6; 4Q387 frag. 3 col. 2:4.
[41] David L. Bartlett, "Exorcism Stories in the Gospel of Mark" (Ph.D. diss, New Haven, CT: Yale University, 1972), 302.

qualify as immoral sans demonic activity. In de Boer's words, this latter type, "forensic apocalyptic eschatology," appears in literature in which "human beings willfully reject or deny the Creator, who is the God of Israel, thereby bringing about death and the perversion and corruption of the world."[42] In other words, what for Aristotle is πλεονεξία may appear in Mark's account of the life of Jesus.[43] For example, according to Mark 7:21–22, vices include fornication (πορνεῖαι), theft (κλοπαί), murder (φόνοι), adultery (μοιχεῖαι), greed (πλεονεξίαι), wickedness (πονηρίαι), treachery (δόλος), senseless violence (ἀσέλγεια), an evil eye (ὀφθαλμὸς πονηρός), blasphemy (βλασφημία), pride (ὑπερηφανία), and stupidity (ἀφροσύνη).[44] Several of the vices listed in 7:21–22 appear in character portraits in later narrative episodes. For example, murder, treachery, blasphemy, and senseless violence foreshadow elements in the passion scene (14:11, 18–21, 31, 42, 47, 50, 64–65; 15:19–20, 24, 32, 37–38).

Some vices in Mark carry an air of similarity to Aristotle's vices including stupidity (ἀφροσύνη), ill-temperedness (ὀργιλότης), lack of self-control (ἀκρασία), and injustice (ἀδικία).[45] Another analogy may be found in Aristotle's account of cowardice (δειλία), which leads one to "be overcome by fear" (ἐκπλήττονται ὑπὸ φόβων).[46] In his *Life of Nicias*, Plutarch claims to write "for the comprehension of character and way of life" (*Nic.* 1.4–5; ἀλλὰ τὴν πρὸς κατανόησιν ἤθους καὶ τρόπου). His central character, Nicias, while possessing many admirable traits (he is lauded as the best citizen of Athens; *Nic.* 2.1), also indulges in cowardice (*Nic.* 2.5; 4.3; 7.3; 8.2; cf. *Comp. Nic. Cras.* 1.2).[47] Nicias's cowardice leads him to commit the disgraceful act of "voting himself out of office" (*Nic.* 8.2).[48] Similarly, the themes of fear and cowardice seem to play a significant role in sections of Mark's narrative (5:15, 33; 9:32; 11:32; 16:8).

Illustrations of the pitfalls of certain vices also appear throughout Josephus's *Antiquities*. In the case of Daniel, Josephus emphasizes his courage, temperance, and justice to "an audience of both Jews and non-Jews."[49] For this reason, Daniel's virtues are set in contrast to his enemies, who possess "envy" (φθόνου) and "jealousy" (βασκανία;

---

[42] De Boer, "Paul and Jewish Apocalyptic Eschatology," 175–6.
[43] As Alasdair MacIntyre demonstrates, one's definition for vice also changes depending on one's embedded narrative: "*Pleonexia*, a vice in the Aristotelian scheme, is now the driving force of modern productive work" (*After Virtue*, 192). The negative connotation for πλεονεξία is present in New Testament usage (cf. Mark 7:22; Rom 1:29; 1 Thess 2:5). God's will and the arrival of God's kingdom determines the virtues necessary for and vices opposed to achieving the outcome of God's way (1:2–3).
[44] In the broader Markan landscape, the concepts of unbelief (6:6; 9:24) and fear (5:15, 33; 11:32; 16:8) also play an integral role in shaping the self (cf. 4:13–20).
[45] Vice lists, of course, were common in the Greco-Roman world. For an exhaustive list, see John T. Fitzgerald, "Virtue/Vice Lists," in *ABD* 6.857.
[46] *Vir.* 3.1–8; 1250a20; as Morton Smith notes, the only occurrence of this word δειλία in the New Testament is in 2 Tim 1:7 ("De Superstitione [Moralia 164E–171F]," in *Plutarch's Theological Writings and Early Christian Literature*, ed. Hans Dieter Betz, SCHNT 3 [Leiden: Brill, 1975], 30).
[47] Initially, Plutarch says that Nicias is able to hide his cowardice (2.5); however, this vice catches up with him later in the story. The people will later criticize his cowardice (7.3; 8.2).
[48] As J. J. Mulhern points out, Plutarch's account of Dion has a similar negative assessment based on his possession of ἀφροσύνη, among other vices (cf. *Comp. Dion. Brut.* 4.7; "Kakia in Aristotle," in *Kakos: Badness and Anti-Value in Classical Antiquity*, ed. Ineke Sluiter and Ralph M. Rosen, MS 307 [Boston: Brill, 2008], 234 n. 4).
[49] Feldman, *Josephus's Interpretation of the Bible*, 656.

Ant. 10.250, 256). God's judgment of Nebuchadnezzar (cf. Dan 4:28–33) is based on his "impious acts" (ἠσέβησε; *Ant.* 10.242), and Darius's men devise a "wicked scheme" (κακουργίαν) against Daniel "out of envy" (*Ant.* 10.254–256). In another example, Josephus retells the story of Nabal the Cynic (cf. 1 Sam 25:2–43), who had an "evil way of life" (*Ant.* 7.296). Nabal stands in contrast with not only David and David's men but also with his good (ἀγαθῆς) and temperate (σώφρονος) wife. In the end, after Nabal's untimely death, Josephus provides an aphoristic summary not found in the Hebrew Bible: "The wicked are smitten by God, who does not overlook any person's deeds, but gives to the good in the same way, and upon the wicked he inflicts hasty punishment" (7.307–308). Josephus, in a manner similar to Plutarch, has "moralized" the story of Nabal the Cynic.[50]

The moral categories of envy, impiety, or wickedness are implicit in many Markan vignettes, and God's judgment is enacted in Mark as a moral consequence for specific attitudes and habits (e.g., 9:42–50; 12:1–12).[51] Satan, as a character in Mark, intends to thwart God's plans (1:13; 3:19b–30; 4:15; 8:33); the Pharisees and scribes likewise devise schemes to trap Jesus and, eventually, to have him killed. The disciples' lust for greatness (μεγάς) leads Jesus to condemn abusive leadership in the harshest of terms (9:42–50; 10:42–43). Possessions (χρῆμα) hinder one's ability to enter God's kingdom (10:23; cf. 6:8–9) as does a lack of spiritual perception (4:12–13; 8:17–18). Mark's Gospel offers moral cues in the presentation of Satan, the Pharisees and scribes, Herod, Pilate, Judas, and the disciples. In the conduct of these figures, the traits embedded in Mark's vice lists (7:21–23; 10:19–21) are illustrated. Pilate's reason for turning over Jesus is motivated out of vanity (15:6–15; cf. 7:22), as is Herod's motive for beheading John (6:19–20).

In Mark, vices may be defined as moral dispositions that engender practices in opposition to the virtues mentioned in Chapter 4 (faith, love, and humility). The distinction between dispositions and practices was common in popular philosophy. Zeno distinguished between dispositions (διαθέσεις) and propensities (εὐκαταφορίας), such as enviousness (φθονερία), from "activities in respect of the vices" (κατὰ κακίας ἐνεργείας), such as acts of injustice (ἀδίκευσιν).[52] In an analogous manner, this section contends that Mark condemns certain dispositions, such as misanthropy, greed, and pride, which lead to a set of morally corrupt practices, including the neglect of those in need or taking advantage of the poor.

---

[50] See Attridge, *Interpretation of Biblical History*, 165–76.

[51] Consider Herod in 6:14–29, the sons of Zebedee in 10:35–45, or Judas in 14:1–11, 43–53.

[52] Stobaeus, *Extracts, Sayings, and Advice* 2.7.5–6 (Greek text and translation from *Arius Didymus: Epitome of Stoic Ethics*, ed. Arthur J. Pomeroy, TTGRS 14 [Atlanta, GA: Society of Biblical Literature, 1999]). The Stoic account of human actions is, of course, more complex than presented here. As Brad Inwood notes, Stoic ethics consist of such things as impulses, appropriate actions, reservations, and a core concern for consistency (*Ethics and Human Action*, 111–26). These examples serve as an analogy: I do not suggest Mark's Gospel interacts with Stoic philosophy. Vice, for instance, is curable for the Stoics, as Inwood explains, by way of "redoubled efforts at moral improvement" (ibid., 169). Mark's account depicts nothing of this nature. Stoics, according to Christoph Jedan, account for the bad done by people by way of "corrupting influence outside the original design" (*Stoic Virtues: Chrysippus and the Religious Character of Stoic Ethics*, CSAP [New York: Continuum International, 2009], 99). Mark's Gospel assigns evil to outside forces as well as to the human heart.

Additionally, the second evangelist presents the reader with a sharp either/or divide. One is either on the side of God or Satan (Mark 9:38–41), there is either good or evil to do (3:4), and moral absolutisms abound (7:3, 19; 10:11–12; 11:16). Seeds of faith may thrive only in good (καλός) soil. Otherwise, their future growth is bleak: threated by Satan (4:4, 15), trouble or persecution (θλίψεως ἢ διωγμοῦ; 4:5, 17), worry, the deceitfulness of wealth, and lust for other things (4:7, 18–19; μέριμναι τοῦ αἰῶνος καὶ ἡ ἀπάτη τοῦ πλούτου καὶ αἱ περὶ τὰ λοιπὰ ἐπιθυμίαι). In this way, Mark leaves little room for the moral nuances one finds in Zeno's account of propensities. The virtues of faith, love, and humility, and their accompanying practices of healing, demonic exorcism, and prayer, all have their antitheses. The virtue of faith is often opposed to fear (5:33–34; 16:8); the virtue of loving God meets opposition in the temptation to worship the self (Mark 7:1–15; cf. 12:31) or one's possessions (6:6b–13; 14:3–9); humility is opposed to pride and the lust for power (9:33–37; 10:35–45). Indulgence in such vices are dangerous in that they may lead one to take advantage of the most vulnerable members of God's family (9:42–50; 12:38–44) or even to kill God's children (6:14–29; 12:1–12; 15:6–15).

Mark's First Vice List (Mark 7:1–23)

Let us now take a closer look at Mark's first vice list (7:21–23). Vice lists are a rhetorical feature common to the literature of early Christianity (e.g., Gal 5:19–21; Rom 1:29–31; 1 Tim 1:9–11) and Judaism (e.g., Philo, *Sacrifices* 32; T. Ash. 2:5; 1QS 4:9–13):

> And he said, "That which comes out of the human, *that* profanes the human. For from within, out of human hearts that is, comes evil desires [οἱ διαλογισμοὶ]: fornication [πορνεῖαι], theft [κλοπαί], murder [φόνοι], adultery [μοιχεῖαι], greed [πλεονεξίαι], wickedness [πονηρίαι], treachery [δόλος], senseless violence [ἀσέλγεια],[53] an evil eye [ὀφθαλμὸς πονηρός], blasphemy [βλασφημία], pride [ὑπερηφανία], and stupidity [ἀφροσύνη]. All these evil things come out from within and profane the human." (Italics added)

Matthew's list (15:19–20), shorter than Mark's, includes murder, adultery, fornication, theft, and blasphemy. Matthew adds false witness (ψευδομαρτυρίαι)—a term of significance in the passion narrative (Mark 14:56–57; cf. 10:19). These types of lists were common, especially among Stoic philosophers, as recorded in Diogenes Laertius:

> Likewise of vices [κακιῶν], some are primary while others are subordinate, such as stupidity [ἀφροσύνην], cowardice [δειλίαν], injustice [ἀδικίαν], and recklessness [ἀκολασίαν] are considered primary, while lack of self-control [ἀκρασίαν], dimwittedness [βραδύνοιαν], and ill-advisedness [κακοβουλίαν] are subordinate. They consider the vices to be forms of ignorance and the virtues [ἀρεταὶ] to be forms of knowledge.[54]

---

[53] For my translation of "senseless violence," see n. 57 below.
[54] *Lives* 7.93. Zeno's list offers other examples, including "inappropriate" (παρὰ τὸ καθῆκον) actions, such as "neglecting our parents, ignoring our brothers, being out of sympathy with our friends,

If one were to compile a résumé for the disciples in Mark, it would arguably include several of the vices documented in Diogenes Laertius. The vice list recorded by Mark begins with Jesus's question in 7:18, "Do you also lack understanding [ἀσύνετοί]?" The disciples are not the only ones who meet criteria for Mark's vices: Herod is engaged in some kind of πορνεῖαι with his brother's wife (6:14–29); a rich man demonstrates inability to enter God's kingdom when asked to give up his wealth (10:17–31); Judas betrays Jesus for money (14:10–11); and, perhaps most central to the narrative, Jesus, the son of God, is killed (12:7–8; 15:33–41).⁵⁵ Thus, Mark's vice list provides the reader with cues for the morally deviant character and character traits throughout the narrative. While each term contained therein could receive a study of its own to determine its correlative moral meaning within Mark, I will limit myself to Mark's use of pride (ὑπερηφανία) and greed (πλεονεξίαι) to be discussed in detail below.⁵⁶

Another aspect of this list worth noting is the repetition of the word ἄνθρωπος (twelve times in vv. 1–23).⁵⁷ Mark's vice list and its immediate literary context is anthropocentric. God's kingdom arrives in a world totally disarrayed and confronts both Satan and the human heart (7:21). The moral life is apocalyptic: time is up

---

overlooking [the interests of] our fatherland and such things" (*Lives* 7.108; trans. Brad Inwood and Lloyd P. Gerson, *The Stoics Reader: Selected Writings and Testimonia* [Indianapolis, IN: Hackett, 2008], 119).

⁵⁵ The death of Jesus raises important theological questions: Was Jesus killed (12:7–8)? Or did Jesus give his own life at the request of God (14:32–42)? What is the role of God in Jesus's death (15:34)? Helen Bond suggests that Jesus is given the choice to die, evidenced by the passion predictions (8:31–32; 9:30–32; 10:32–33). In the Gethsemane prayer especially, the reader sees that Jesus surrenders his own will to God's (14:36; "A Fitting End?," 437). Bond's account highlights the virtue of Jesus's self-sacrificial attitude: "Jesus' choice to submit to the will of the Father, even though he has done nothing deserving death, is the ultimate expression of what it means to be a 'slave of all'" (ibid., 438). My account highlights the opposite: Jesus's death also gives the reader information regarding vice in Mark. Jesus is subjected to violence (14:46, 65; 15:15, 17, 19), which Mark condemns (7:21–22). In Mark 14:41, Jesus is "delivered into the hands of sinners" (ἰδοὺ παραδίδοται ὁ υἱὸς τοῦ ἀνθρώπου εἰς τὰς χεῖρας τῶν ἁμαρτωλῶν). To understand the role of God in Jesus's death, one might compare Mark's use of παραδίδωμι (1:14; 3:19; 9:31, 10:33; 13:9, 11–12; 14:10, 11, 18, 21, 41–42, 44; 15:1, 10, 15) to Paul's (Rom 4:25a; Gal 1:4; 2:20). On the similarities between Mark and Paul's use of παραδίδωμι in regard to Jesus's death, see Cilliers Breytenbach, "Narrating the Death of Jesus in Mark: Utterances of the Main Character, Jesus," *ZNW* 105 (2014): 153–68, esp. 155–59. While Breytenbach concludes negatively that Mark does not draw from the Pauline tradition, his comment about the tradition's use of the passive voice is worth repeating: "The focus of the passives [in Mark's use of παραδίδωμι] ... cannot be on God as actor" (ibid., 157). My case here is that Jesus's death is less about virtue and more about evil (principally manifest in Rome's execution of Jesus).

⁵⁶ The length of this chapter precludes detailed dissection of each of the terms found in Mark 7:21–22. One could consider the use of "senseless violence" (ἀσέλγεια) in Mark 7:21, which various translations render as "lewdness" (NIV) "lasciviousness" (KJV), "sensuality" (ESV), "licentiousness" (NRSV), or "unrestrained immorality" (CEB). The term ἀσέλγεια may also mean "wanton violence" (*LSJ*, s.v.). In the New Testament, ἀσέλγεια often appears in vice lists (Rom 13:13; 2 Cor 12:21; Gal 5:19; Eph 4:19; 1 Pet 4:3) without detailed context to discern its meaning. In *Life of Gaius Marius*, Plutarch describes the activity of the Bardyae as follows: "The people were most distressed, however, by the wanton licence [ἀσέλγεια] of the Bardyaei, as they were called, who butchered fathers of families in their houses" (44.10 [Perrin, LCL]; see also Plutarch, *Marius* 16.5 and *Life of Pelopidas* 26.3 for similar imagery of violence). If Mark's Jesus condemns violence in the narrative in 7:21, then one could examine the later episodic appearances of violence in the passion (14:46, 65; 15:15, 17, 19).

⁵⁷ Since the word ἄνθρωπος appears fifty-six times in Mark, this small section would account for a little over 21 percent of the total appearances of the term in Mark.

(1:14–15) and the hour is at hand (13:32–37; 14:41), which demands *immediate* (εὐθὺς) change. One aspect of this apocalyptic dimension is that, much like the virtues discussed in Chapter 4, vices are not deed-oriented (Leander Keck's "deciding self"). Rather, the attitudes of one's heart indicate to whom one belongs (Keck's "accountable self"). Take the case of the rich man, for example: he lived a flawless, deed-oriented life (10:17–31). If he were measured by the standards of the deciding self, the rich man would exceed expectations: "All these [commandments] I have kept from childhood" (10:20). Jesus's inquiry about the rich man's attachment to his wealth suggests that the man's heart belongs to someone or something else (10:21). For "those who have wealth" (οἱ τὰ χρήματα ἔχοντες), the moral task of accountability is apparently more difficult. As in Chapter 4 on virtues, vices in Mark concern a lack of accountability to God. As in Jesus's words to the rich man, "you lack one thing." In effect, the rich man must first divest from his wealth to gain entrance into God's kingdom. In terms of vice, the rich man appears guilty of greed (πλεονεξίαι), an image we will return to later in this chapter. For now, let us examine the vice of pride (ὑπερηφανία).

Pride

Not uncommon in Second Temple Judaism (Ps 138:6; Prov 8:13; Tob 4:13; Sir 10:18; Philo, *Virt.* 30.163) and early Christianity (Jas 4:6; 1 Pet 5:5–6), pride is regularly condemned as an attitude of the heart in contention with God. As in the unsettling words in the book of Judith, "see their pride, send your wrath on their heads" (Jdt 9:9). Of his many damnable characteristics, Antiochus IV, according to 1 and 2 Maccabees, was a man of insufferable pride (1 Macc 1:21, 24; 2 Macc 5:21; 9:7). Philo refers to pride as "a vice of the soul," because it elevates one to the status of God (*Virt.* 33.172).[58] This same appraisal of pride, especially as an affront to God, may be found in Mark 7:1–23.

Moral Impurity in Second Temple Judaism

Scholars have long acknowledged the preoccupation with purity rituals in Mark 7:1–23. For some, such as Heikki Räisänen, Jesus's words in 7:15 are "a radical if implicit attack on important parts of the Torah."[59] However, it would seem that Jesus is not concerned with biblical laws here (Lev 15:5, 11; Exod 20:17–19), but, rather, with a tradition of handwashing that developed in the Second Temple period.[60] According

---

[58] Philo employs both the terms ὑπερηφανία and ἀλαζονεία for pride, the former in a quotation of Num 15:30. Later on in this section (*Virt.* 33.173), Philo describes an arrogant man in more detail: "The arrogant man is always filled with the spirit of unreason, holding himself, as Pindar says, to be neither man nor demigod, but wholly divine, and claiming to overstep the limits of human nature" (Colson, LCL). Pride, according to Philo, directly challenges God.

[59] Heikki Räisänen, "Jesus and the Food Laws: Reflections on Mark 7:15," *JSNT* 16 (1982): 79–100, here 82.

[60] The relationship of handwashing and eating was more developed by the rabbinic period (*m. Yad.* 1:1–2; 3:1–2; *m. Zab* 5:12). Roger P. Booth notes that certain hand- and body-washing traditions, with no exact parallel to Mark 7:1–23, developed during the Second Temple period, as in Let. Aris. 305–306, in which the translators of the Hebrew Bible washed their hands before prayer (*Jesus and the Laws of Purity: Tradition History and Legal History in Mark 7*, JSNTSup 13 [Sheffield: JSOT Press, 1986], 155–86; cf. 1QS 5:13–14; Josephus, *War* 2.129). Booth suggests instead, by analogy,

to Jonathan Klawans and Christine E. Hayes, the difference between ritual and moral impurity in Second Temple Judaism is undervalued in scholarship.[6] Texts traditionally connected with the former, they argue, may display concerns for the latter (cf. Jub. 22:16; Let. Aris. 129–151; 3 Macc 3:10; Josephus, *Ag. Ap.* 2.209–210; Sib. Or. 3.496–500; Acts 10:28). Following Klawans and Hayes, it seems plausible that Jesus's dispute with the Pharisees in Mark 7:1–23 illustrates a debate over the differences between ritual and moral purity: by placing ritual concerns above moral ones, some have abandoned the commandment of God. In short, Jesus indicts them on moral, and not ritual, grounds.[62]

Two texts that take seriously issues of moral impurity in Second Temple Judaism are worth quoting at length here. In Jubilees, a second-century BCE work acutely concerned with purity, the following judgment is made concerning gentiles:

> Separate from the nations, and do not eat with them. Do not act as they do, and do not become their companion, for their actions are something that is impure, and all their ways are defiled and something abominable and detestable. They offer their sacrifices to the dead, and they worship demons. They eat in tombs, and everything they do is empty and worthless. (22:16–17)[63]

---

that the practices of the *haberim*, a group of Jews who undertook voluntary purity obligations, may have been the subject of Jesus's discussion (ibid., 192–203). For more on the *haberim*, see the discussion in Hyam Maccoby, *Ritual and Morality: The Ritual Purity System and Its Place in Judaism* (New York: Cambridge University Press, 1999), 209–13.

[61] Jonathan Klawans, *Impurity and Sin in Ancient Judaism* (New York: Oxford University Press, 2000), 3–20; Christine E. Hayes, *Gentile Impurities and Jewish Identities: Intermarriage and Conversion from the Bible to the Talmud* (New York: Oxford University Press, 2002). The dominant position in the field, according to Klawans and Hayes, focuses on ritual impurity and, specifically, the ritually impure status of gentiles, to which Klawans retorts, "No biblical text considers Gentiles to be ritually impure" (Klawans, *Impurity and Sin*, 291). Hayes adds a third, moral, category to two other modes of impurity in ancient and early Judaism (ritual and genealogical). Hayes's distinction between ritual and moral impurity, in this regard, is helpful:

> It bears emphasizing that moral impurity differs significantly from ritual impurity. Moral impurity is not communicable to others, nor is it cleansed by rituals of lustration and sacrifice. For example, an adulteress does not defile other persons by contact, nor does she bear a ritual defilement that can be removed by ablutions. The conflation of these distinct modes of impurity is a commonplace of much scholarly literature. (*Gentile Impurities*, 23)

One concrete example offered by Hayes is the policy of social *amixa* in some sources as evidence not of ritual but of moral concerns (Jub. 22:16; Let. Aris. 129–151; 3 Macc. 3:10; Josephus, *Ag. Ap.* 2.209–210; Sib. Or. 3.496–500; Acts 10:28).

[62] I agree with Eyal Regev here: "The tradition does not, however, imply that Jesus rejected the observation of ritual purity; it indicates, rather, that Jesus ranked moral purity as more important than ritual purity" ("Moral Impurity and the Temple in Early Christianity in Light of Ancient Greek Practice and Qumranic Ideology," *HTR* 97 [2004]: 383–411, here 387). Similarly, Thomas Kazen notes that the issues of ritual and moral purity need not exclude each other: "Mk 7:15 has often been interpreted as Jesus advocating ethical purity instead of ritual. However, if a relative interpretation represents an answer of the historical Jesus to a question about hand-washing, it would rather imply a way of establishing priorities" (*Jesus and Purity Halakhah: Was Jesus Indifferent to Impurity?*, rev. ed., CBNTS 38 [Winona Lake, IN: Eisenbrauns, 2010], 88).

[63] Trans. Klawans, *Impurity and Sin*, 47.

As Klawans observes, "the concern here is not that Gentile persons are ritually defiling, but that Gentile behavior is morally abominable."[64] The moral tradition in Jubilees of banning all "interethnic sexual unions" (cf. Jub. 30:7–13) demonstrates one trend in the Second Temple period to moralize issues of purity.[65] For Mark, as in Jubilees, moral purity is the priority. Similarly, Jubilees's attitude toward gentile taboos may also exist, by way of a paradigmatic foil, in Mark (5:1–20). The Gerasene demonic lives among the tombs: perhaps more than any other character in Mark, he is associated with ritual impurity. As in Mark 7:1–23, the crowd's reaction in Mark 5:1–20 stems from a community's ostracism toward this "unclean" gentile (vv. 14–17). Ritual purity must not replace God's moral demands, such as hospitality toward a stranger, treatment of his illness, or honoring one's parents.

A second example of moral impurity comes from the difficult-to-date Testament of Levi, which contains, according to Klawans, the "clearest articulation of the idea of moral defilement":[66]

> You will teach the Lord's commandments for your own greedy advantage [πλεονεξία]. You will profane married women and pollute the virgins of Jerusalem, and you will be united with prostitutes and adulteresses. You will take the daughters of Gentiles as wives and purify them with a form of unlawful purification; and your sexual union [μεῖξις] will be like Sodom and Gomorrah in ungodliness [ἀσεβείᾳ]. And you will be filled with pride [φυσιωθήσεσθε] because of the priesthood, being exalted over other people; and not only this, but you also will be exalted over [φυσιούμενοι] the commandments of God, and you will mock the holy things and, while cracking jokes, will despise them. (T. Levi 14:6–7; author translation)

Concerns for purity in T. Levi 14:6–7 revolve around the issue of Israelites marrying gentiles (cf. Ezra 9:1–12). For the author of the Testament of Levi, intermingling with gentiles is much more than a ritual concern: "You will be like Sodom and Gomorrah in ungodliness." The author of Levi charges those who intermarry as exalting themselves over the commandments of God, not because of ritual defilement per se but on account of moral defilement. Pride, exalting themselves over and against others, and greed, teaching God's commandments for advantage (πλεονεξίᾳ), condemn them. A similar moral indictment may appear in Mark 7:20, "That which comes out of the human [is] that which profanes the human." According to Jub. 22 and T. Levi 14:6–7, moral infractions derive not only from intermingling with gentiles and appropriating their immoral way of life, but also from disregarding the commandments of God, the latter of which amounts to an offense of pride. For Mark's Jesus, the moral attitude toward impurity, found within Second Temple Judaism, is retained. While some Pharisees

---

[64] Ibid., 48.
[65] Hayes, *Gentile Impurities*, 68. Cana Werman lists at least two other trends in response to intermarriage ("*Jubilees* 30: Building a Paradigm for the Ban on Intermarriage," *HTR* 90 [1997]: 1–22). First, one may marry a gentile if he or she abandons idolatry and observes the commandments of God (Josephus, *Ant.* 20.139–146). Second, Werman finds "retention of the ancient tolerance of intermarriage, even in the absence of conversion" ("*Jubilees* 30," 2).
[66] Klawans, *Impurity and Sin*, 57.

and scribes exalt themselves "over the commandments of God" (T. Levi 14:6), Jesus is not concerned with the "deciding self," its performance of specific human actions (e.g., not washing one's hands or marrying a gentile), but with the broader, moral contamination of humanity: "the accountable self." One recalls the lament of Ezra that Adam's totalizing transgression is caused because he is "burdened with an evil heart" (4 Ezra 3:21; cf. Mark 7:21).[67] By this reading, Jesus in Mark 7 condemns his interlocutors for their pride, attempting to play the role of God, thus usurping the authority that belongs to God alone.

Returning to the passage in question, the scene opens with a group of Pharisees and scribes from Jerusalem observing that the disciples eat with unwashed hands (7:1–2). Mark provides the editorial aside that "all Jews" practice handwashing before eating meals (7:3–4). According to E. P. Sanders, this hyperbolic aside favors a gentile Christian audience, unfamiliar with Jewish laws and practices when, in reality, "the Pharisees themselves probably did not regard it as obligatory to wash their hands before every meal."[68] Regardless, the foundation for the ensuing confrontation is set: "Why do your disciples not live according to the tradition of the elders?" (7:5). By inquiring about the disciple's way of life, this group of Pharisees and scribes begin their critique on a moral footing. It is not only that the disciples do not wash their hands; they are accused, generally, of not living a particular way. At this point, Jesus cites their hypocrisy as the main offense. In the tradition of Corban, some had found a way around God's command to honor one's father and mother (cf. Deut 5:16; Exod 20:12), surely a moral consideration. They appear, in other words, to be acting duplicitously. In addition to this, in the second half of the passage (vv. 14–23), Jesus turns to the crowd to offer an overtly moral explanation of his exchange (vv. 1–13). While the confrontation begins with concerns over ritual impurity, Mark's Jesus utilizes traditions about moral impurity within Second Temple Judaism in his reply.[69]

Furthermore, as Klawans correctly observes, Jesus turns away from ritual defilement to the "morally defiling effect that sin can have on individual sinners."[70] Jesus's discourse still concerns defilement (κοινόω), but instead of focusing on things "outside" (ἔξωθεν), ritual matters, Jesus's parable refers to the "inside" (ἔσωθεν), moral matters: a juxtaposition characteristic of Jesus's parables (7:17; cf. 4:11–12). Who is at fault for replacing human tradition with God's law? According to Mark's presentation, Jesus's interlocutors, some Pharisees and scribes from Jerusalem, are guilty of such (7:1), but the problem's scope, eventually, extends to all of humanity (7:21). The moral

---

[67] Trans. B. M. Metzger, "The Fourth Book of Ezra," in *OTP* 1.529. As Brand puts it, "in this manner the author of 4 Ezra describes the particularly cruel predicament of the human: while the law does not effectively combat the evil inclination from Ezra's human perspective, it does make the hapless human a full moral agent in the eyes of God" (*Evil within and Without*, 133).

[68] E. P. Sanders, *Jewish Law from Jesus to the Mishnah: Five Studies* (Minneapolis, MN: Fortress Press, 2016), 54.

[69] The overlap of ritual and moral concerns is closely related in the doctrine of the *yetzer ha 'ra*, or evil inclination. Rosen-Zvi argues that this traditional rabbinic doctrine may be nascent in early Judaism and Christianity, as a "demonic desire," especially as evidence in 4 Ezra's "evil heart" and Qumran (*Demonic Desires*, 44–86).

[70] Klawans, *Impurity and Sin*, 150.

purity tradition is expanded to a broader, more universal horizon.[71] Mark's vice list is embedded in this literary and historical context: any attempt to relativize God's moral order is a symptom of an evil and disobedient heart.

In summary, the vice list in Mark 7:21-23 further exposes the chasm between humanity and God. Jesus condemns the attitude of a group of scribes because they have replaced God's law with human tradition. This moral attitude toward purity issues may also be found within Second Temple Judaism (such as Jub. 22 and T. Levi 14), including Jesus's condemnation of all humanity (Wis 15:10-11; 1QHa 5:32; 7:34; 11:14, 22; 14:37). For Mark, some users of the ritual purity system had circumvented the moral change required by God: a judgment rendered already in some Jewish traditions (Isa 66:1-4; 2 Chron 36:14; 1 Esd 1:49; 1QpHab 8:8-13; 12:7-10). Furthermore, in the case of Mark 7, it is pride, the elevation of self above God's moral demands, that leads to Jesus's discourse on the origin of evil. To be clear, the elevation of human tradition, in and of itself, is not the crime: it is evacuating God's role in rendering moral judgment.[72] Mark's condemnation of pride may also be seen in other character depictions throughout his Gospel: Herod's motivation for beheading John (6:26), James's and John's request for power (10:35-45), Pilate's desire to satisfy the crowd (15:15), or the chief priests' jealousy (15:10). Set in terms of accountability, the self belongs entirely to God. In these cases, pride evacuates divine accountability and places the self in the role of God. If destruction of the self is in bounds for Mark's moral world (8:34-38; 9:42-50; 10:31, 45; 14:36; 15:16-41), then worship of the self would classify as immoral.

Greed in Mark 10:17-31

Mark's second list of vices appears in Jesus's dialogue with the rich man in 10:19-21:

> You know the commandments: Do not murder [μὴ φονεύσῃς]; do not commit adultery [μὴ μοιχεύσῃς]; do not steal [μὴ κλέψῃς]; do not bear false witness [μὴ ψευδομαρτυρήσῃς]; do not defraud [μὴ ἀποστερήσῃς]; honor your mother and father. ... You lack one thing; go sell as much as you have and give to the poor and you will have treasure in heaven, then come follow me.

In the story of the rich man, the list of immoral practices derives from the Pentateuch. As in Exod 20:13-16 and Deut 5:16-20 LXX, murder (οὐ φονεύσεις), adultery (οὐ μοιχεύσεις), theft (οὐ κλέψεις), and bearing false witness (οὐ ψευδομαρτυρήσεις) are all condemned; conversely, honoring one's parents is praised. In addition to these vices, Mark's list contains one curious addition: the imperative "do not defraud" (μὴ

---

[71] This is no innovation in Mark's Gospel. Second Temple Jews frequently place a universal scope on the human condition (cf. Wis 15:10-11; 1QHa 5:32; 7:34; 11:14, 22; 14:37; 1 Cor 15:47-49; Rom 3:19).

[72] A similar attitude toward temple practices exists in the Qumran corpus (e.g., 1QpHab 8:8-13; 12:7-10). It is worth clarifying that criticism of temple practices is not the same as total rejection of them. See Eyal Regev, *The Temple in Early Christianity: Experiencing the Sacred* (New Haven, CT: Yale University Press, 2019), 96-126.

ἀποστερήσῃς) appears.[73] Matthew (19:16-30) and Luke (18:18-30) follow Mark's version for the most part but appear to correct Mark toward the LXX, which makes no mention of defrauding.[74] In the New Testament, the verb ἀποστερέω may refer to cheating someone out of his money (1 Cor 6:7-8; Jas 5:4) or to be deprived from something, such as intercourse (1 Cor 7:5) or the truth (1 Tim 6:5). In Aristotle, the term carries a similar valence of deprivation (e.g., *EN* 4.3.35; 1125a20) but may also refer to extortion (e.g., *EN* 8.9.3; 1160a5). In Plutarch's *Life of Aemilius Paulus*, the avaricious conduct (φιλαργυρίαν) of Perseus is contrasted to the good fortune (τύχην ἀγαθὴν) of Aemilius (12.3). In one episode, Perseus defrauds a group of Cretans out of a priceless gold plate formerly belonging to Alexander the Great for virtually nothing in exchange (*Aem.* 23.11; cf. 13.3; 26.8). Similar to Perseus's offense, Mark's notion of defrauding seems to carry this nuance of cheating someone out of their money.

On Mark's use of the term "defraud," Morna Hooker declared that "no satisfactory explanation of this has ever been given."[75] Joachim Gnilka offers the interesting suggestion that the final command not found in the Decalogue derives from a "moral code" (*Sittenkodex*), an interpretative strand of Hellenistic Judaism. His evidence for this reading, typical for most modern commentators, is Sir 4:1: "My child, do not cheat the poor [μὴ ἀποστερήσῃς] of their living, and do not keep needy eyes waiting (NRSV)."[76] Marcus suggests that Mark may paraphrase the tenth commandment, citing certain rabbinic sources that forbid "not only craving for others' possessions but also usurping them."[77] This interpretation seems plausible, if framed in a manner similar to Gnilka's: a strand of Jewish moral tradition is preserved by Mark, deriving from the Decalogue.[78]

---

[73] NA[28] lists Sir 4:1 as a possible intertext in the marginalia: Τέκνον, τὴν ζωὴν τοῦ πτωχοῦ μὴ ἀποστερήσῃς. Defrauding the poor appears to be the chief offense of the scribes in Mark 12:38-40.

[74] According to Metzger, the appearance of "do not defraud" is omitted by Matthew, Luke, and "many copyists" of Mark because it "may have seemed inappropriate" (*Textual Commentary*, 105; Adela Collins agrees [*Mark*, 474]). One would expect Luke, with a characteristic interest in the poor (4:18; 6:20; 7:22; 14:13, 21; 16:19-31), to have retained this prohibition, but Luke's text does not.

[75] Morna Hooker, *The Gospel According to Mark*, BNTC (London: A & C Black, 1991), 241.

[76] Gnilka, *Markus*, 2.86-7.

[77] Marcus, *Mark 8-16*, 2.721. Marcus cites *Mekilta* Baḥodesh 8; *Mekilta R. Šim. Yitro* 17. In a similar move, Metzger cites evidence from Exod 20:17 and Deut 24:14 (*Textual Commentary*, 89). The phrase "do not withhold the wages of the poor" (οὐκ ἀπαδικήσεις μισθὸν πένητος: in Deut 24:14) approximates the context of Mark's μὴ ἀποστερήσῃς. Before Marcus, William Lane suggested that the defrauding command is an "application of the eighth and ninth commandments" (*Mark*, 366). Collins adds Mal 3:5 and Philo, *Spec. Laws* 4.7.30-38 (*Mark*, 478). In each of the cases listed—Deut 24:14, Mal 3:5, and Philo, *Special Laws* 4.7.30-38—there is an economic application of the Decalogue that appears to resonate with the verbal addition in Mark 10:19.

[78] It seems likely that a stream of Jewish moral tradition either paraphrased or conflated portions of the Decalogue. So *Mekilta* Baḥodesh 8: "How does one know from Scripture that the person who covets will eventually steal? As it says in Scripture, 'They covet fields, and seize them' (Mic. 2:2). ... This tells us that all of [the commandments] effect each other" (W. David Nelson, trans., *Mekhilta de-Rabbi Shimon bar Yoḥai* [Philadelphia: Jewish Publication Society, 2006], 251-2). France briefly references Pliny's letter to Trajan, *Ep.* 10.96.7 (*Gospel of Mark*, 402). In this letter, Pliny lists the moral vices of early Christians as theft (*furta*), robbery (*latrocinia*), adultery (*adulteria*), "no breach of trust" (*ne fidem fallerent*), and "to refuse a deposit when called upon" (*ne depositum appellati abnegarent*). While the connection remains vague, Pliny's economic application may corroborate the evidence in rabbinic interpretations of Deut 24:14 and Mal 3:5.

Michael Peppard has drawn attention to Mark's Jesus's peculiar command in 10:19.[79] Peppard argues that the unexpected imperative in Mark condemns the practice in antiquity of attaining wealth by defrauding the poor (cf. Jas 5:1–5).[80] For this reason, Jesus's embedded command on this issue may be "the main point of the encounter."[81] Peppard's reading is justified, in part, by evidence from Philo (*Virt.* 15.88) and Josephus (*Ant.* 4.285–288), who condemn, based on such passages such as Deut 24:14–15, the practice of defrauding a poor person of his wages. In short, Jesus's prohibition may be tailored for a person of significant wealth.[82] Other episodes in Mark adopt similar moral attitudes toward the poor (12:38–40, 41–44; 14:1–11).[83] If this is the case, it is possible that, following certain taxation practices by wealthy land owners, this particular rich man has not been accountable to his more vulnerable neighbors.[84] Even without a precise economic analogue, the man's greed seems to prevent him from acting with generosity (10:22).

Economic considerations aside, we may say with more confidence that the rich man's quest for eternal life (10:17) is reframed by Mark's Jesus around theology and morals. Rather than focus on the latter half of his question about obtaining eternal life, Jesus is interested in his use of the adjective "good" (ἀγαθός). The only other use of ἀγαθός in Mark is moral in nature: Jesus's question to those gathered in the synagogue about doing good on the Sabbath (3:4). Here, Mark's morally loaded term is applied theologically: God alone is good.[85] The self is not accountable to the Decalogue in and of itself, as the rich man seems to assume, but also to the God of the Decalogue. One could paraphrase that the rich man's approach to Jesus is set in terms of the deciding self: What must I do? Jesus responds in terms of the accountable self: To whom do

---

[79] Michael Peppard, "Torah for the Man Who Has Everything: 'Do Not Defraud' in Mark 10:19," *JBL* 134 (2015): 595–604.

[80] Peppard's economic analysis of the first century depends largely on Ekkehard W. Stegemann and Wolfgang Stegemann, *The Jesus Movement: A Social History of Its First Century*, trans. O. C. Dean Jr. (Minneapolis, MN: Fortress Press, 1999); and Richard Horsley, *Jesus and the Powers: Conflict, Covenant, and the Hope of the Poor* (Minneapolis, MN: Fortress Press, 2010). Some of Peppard's best primary evidence for the late antique Christian use of ἀποστερέω derives from John Chrysostom's *De Lazaro* sermon (PG 48, 488). Chrysostom defines ἀποστερέω as "when we take and keep what belongs to others" (trans. Peppard, "Do Not Defraud," 601).

[81] Peppard, "Do Not Defraud," 604.

[82] So Stegemann and Stegemann, "The narrative on the meaning of wealth shows that forgoing possessions was the demand of *the rich* that led to the failure of their discipleship (Mark 10:17ff)" (*Jesus Movement*, 201).

[83] In Moore's reading, "the woman is read as epitomizing instead the oppressed peasantry mercilessly bled dry by the indigenous, Rome-allied elites" (*Empire and Apocalypse*, 41).

[84] So Horsley, "This episode thus presents a negative example of a man who has gained wealth by defrauding others" (*Jesus and the Powers*, 142). The evidence is speculative. Stegemann and Stegemann conclude, "Therefore, the indebtedness of small farmers and expropriation of their land are the hallmarks of this Roman epoch" (*Jesus Movement*, 112; cited by Peppard, "Do Not Defraud," 600); they rely on the secondary source of S. Applebaum, "Economic Life in Palestine," in *The Jewish People in the First Century*, ed. S. Safrai and M. Stern (Philadelphia: Fortress Press, 1976), 2.631–700. Applebaum appears to extrapolate his evidence primarily from Josephus and from the later rabbinic period (ibid., 643–6).

[85] The phrase εἰ μὴ εἷς ὁ θεός appears in Mark 2:7. In that verse, it is God alone who can forgive sins—here, ironically, placed on the lips of Jesus's critics. In the case of 10:18, another overtly theological statement about God appears: God alone is good.

I belong? In his discourse *On Special Laws*, Philo expounds upon the need for moral purity in offering gifts to God:

> But do you suppose that God may be bribed ... the everlasting spring of wisdom and righteousness and all virtue, who turns away from the gifts of the unjust. And is not the one who would offer a portion [to God] out of treachery or greed or denial or fraudulence [ἀπεστέρησε] the most abominable of all things, as if, in giving, partnering with him in wickedness and greed? (*Spec. Laws*, 1.51.277–278; author translation)

In this passage, Philo expounds on the practice of offering sacrifices on the altar (cf. Exod 27–30). His thesis, essentially, is that the gift itself matters less in comparison with the moral status or "pure rational spirit" of the giver (καθαρώτατον τοῦ θύοντος πνεῦμα λογικόν; *Spec. Laws* 1.51.277). One may offer money to God, but, if obtained dishonestly, the giver, according to Philo, insults "the power of God" to detect the motivations of one's heart (*Spec. Laws* 1.51.279). Even worse, the giver tacitly co-opts God in his misdeed. Philo condemns fraudulence, among other unethical practices of obtaining wealth, as "the most abominable of all things" (πάντων ἀναισχυντότατος). The moral action itself pales in comparison to one's accountability. The deciding self may complete the right moral task, such as giving generously at the altar, but it is the accountable self with whom God is concerned. Philo, like Mark, asks instead: What kind of person commits fraudulence? Certainly not one who belongs to "the everlasting spring of wisdom and righteousness and all virtue" (*Spec. Laws* 1.51.277–278).

In Mark 10:17–31, not only do material possessions appear to be a central concern but also, following Philo, how one obtains their possessions. This would explain, in part, Mark's odd insertion of "do not defraud" in this vice list. Kee picks up on these tones in Mark 10 when he writes, "Commitment to following Jesus must have a radical priority over devotion to one's possessions."[86] To go a step beyond Kee, the moral responsibility outlined in this pericope is more than simply prioritizing one's commitments; it is directed toward the insidious vice of greed and the origin of one's wealth. This passage also illustrates moral accountability to neighbor: the rich man is not just giving away his possessions; he is returning his wealth to the ones he defrauded. "Leaving everything," as Peter declares to have done (10:28), is a task more difficult for those who benefit from the poverty of others. In this case, the rich man may have robbed his neighbor to pay God. In Mark, God's way (1:2–3) is more than a set of tasks one ought to do, more than the rich man's rules to keep. It involves a moral commitment to God alone and accountability to God's family, including the poor.

Images of Greed: The Character of Judas

It is also worth mentioning how greed, as a vice, plays an important role in Mark's depiction of certain characters. From among the characteristics of greed evidenced

---

[86] Kee, *Community*, 154.

by the rich man (10:17-31), the scribes (12:38-40), and the soldiers (15:20, 24), I will briefly examine Judas.

The early traditions of Judas are overwhelmingly negative (Matt 27:1-10; Acts 1:18), often portraying him as a strategic pawn in Satan's hands (Luke 22:3; John 13:2). Mark's account of evil, however, is mixed: Mark portrays Judas as a character of vice, subject to the human pitfalls of greed. On Mark 14:10-11, Ched Myers observes, "Mark does not invoke a theory of 'satanic inspiration' to explore [Judas's change of loyalties] ... the transaction is stated matter of factly in monetary terms."[87] As previously mentioned, vices, like virtues, appear in character portraits rendered by ancient biographies. Recall again Josephus's account of Nabal the Cynic (cf. 1 Sam 25:2-43), who had an "evil way of life" (*Ant.* 7.296). In the case of Mark's Gospel, Judas receives negative character descriptions (3:19; 6:3; 14:10, 43), as the one who eventually betrayed God's son. In 14:11 the reader receives an explicit motive for Judas's decision: "They promised to give him money." This motive is further emphasized when compared to the interpolated tale of lavish generosity (14:3-9). In between the plot to kill Jesus (vv. 1-2, 10-11), a woman approaches Jesus to pour out a "genuine [or "trustworthy"; πιστικός], expensive, jar of nard ointment." The woman acts out of self-giving generosity; Judas acts out of greed. In the words of James Edwards, "the bracketing of the woman's devotion by the betrayal plot creates an acid contrast between her faith and Judas's treachery."[88] Similar to the characterization of the rich man in Mark 10, a desire for money seems to be the source of Judas's downfall—a feature Matthew (26:14-16) and John (12:4-5) explicate.

In summary, greed plays a significant role in the vice list found in Mark 10:17-31 and in the character portrayals of the inquiring rich man and Judas. Accountability to God entails not only divesting oneself from earthly wealth (10:22) but also divesting from the immoral methods for obtaining one's wealth. The task of giving away money poses a substantial challenge to the wealthy who are able to maintain their wealth at the expense of others. In this connection, Jesus's reply to Peter that those who have left everything will receive recompense in this time (10:30) is worth considering (removed by Matthew; cf. Matt 19:29). Yet again it seems that possessions, in and of themselves, play a less significant role compared to one's attachment to them. The desire for wealth and its subsequent retention competes with God for ownership of the self. Indeed, a desire for money is the downfall of one of Mark's central antagonists, Judas (14:10-11). In antiquity, the collection of wealth, in some cases, may have had impact on the fair treatment of one's less advantaged neighbors. Commonly denounced in both prophetic literature (Mic 2:2; Mal 3:5) and in Greco-Roman philosophy (Xenophon, *Mem.* 1.2.12; 2.1.4; Diogenes Laertius, *Lives* 7.19),[89] the rich man's possibly deleterious acquisition of wealth may be in view in Mark 10. Greed also has consequences for one's

---

[87] Myers, *Binding*, 360.
[88] Edwards, "Markan Sandwiches," 209.
[89] Richard Hicks makes the interesting case that Mark 10:17-22 is illuminated by the specific intertext of Mal 3. While his suggestion is difficult to prove with certainty, the context of Mal 3 and the prophetic denouncement of defrauding the poor presents compelling parallels to Mark 10 such as Malachi's use of way (3:1) and the theme of repentance ("Markan Discipleship according to Malachi: The Significance of μὴ ἀποστερήσῃς in the Story of the Rich Man [Mark 10:17-22]," *JBL* 132 [2013]: 179-99).

neighbor. If the rich man's acquisition of wealth came at the expense of his neighbor's impoverishment—an action Mark overtly condemns later (12:38-40)—he is living contrary to the virtues of God's kingdom. In the case of Judas, his greed sets off a chain of events that result in the death of Jesus.

5.4 Punitive Consequences in Mark

Integral to Mark's moral scheme is the subject of punitive consequences. Those who claim to probe Mark's Gospel with an ethical interest, by and large, overlook Mark's presentation of consequences for immoral activity.[90] In so doing, interpreters have sidelined another question for Mark's moral life: What are the consequences for immoral action? Framed in terms of accountability, Mark describes penalties for those who do not belong to God. In Jesus's exorcism of the unclean spirits especially, Mark introduces the reader to language of destruction (1:24; ἦλθες ἀπολέσαι ἡμᾶς) and torture (5:7; μή με βασανίσῃς), a grim fate awaiting God's enemies. Only nascent in Mark, concepts of eternal punishment are expounded more thoroughly by Matthew (10:15, 28; 11:22; 12:42; 13:20; 18:6-9; 22:13; 24:51; 25:31-46) and Luke (9:54; 10:12, 14; 11:31-32; 12:2, 4-5, 47-48; 13:5, 28; 14:24; 16:19-31; 18:8; 20:47). Though the topic appears infrequently, the reality that "the kingdom of God has come near" (1:14) requires an equally coercive consequence: God "will come" to set things right (12:9: 13:35; cf. Isa 66:15-16; 1 En. 21:1-10; Apoc. Abr. 31.2-4).

Keck's language for judgment as a divine sanction proves helpful for the analysis to follow. In Keck's short essay on biblical ethics, he defines God's wrath in Col 3:6 as a moral sanction because "it motivates a change in behavior by threatening punishment."[91] Similarly, one may ask of Mark, how does the accountable self avoid habits of vice? Especially when the temptations to indulge in greed (10:17-31; 14:1-11), pride (7:1-15; 15:15), or violence (14:47, 65; 15:13-14, 19) lurk around every corner? In another example, Keck offers the system of honor and shame as an analogy for moral sanctions:

> When a sanction is already in place, it needs only to be brought to bear. This is particularly evident in sanctions that appeal to honor and shame, or to a sense of group identity. Thus Jesus warrants the demand to love the enemy by referring to what is required to be a child of the heavenly Father who sends rain on just and unjust alike, but then he reinforces it with a sanction based on the group's sense of special identity, "If you greet only your brothers and sisters, what more are you doing than others? Do not even the Gentiles do the same?" (Matt 5:47).[92]

---

[90] This is especially true, as Alan F. Segal notes, among American mainline churches: "In most of our permissive society, a vision of hell would probably be greeted with disbelief by most Americans and even by derisive laughter by some" (*Life After Death: A History of the Afterlife in the Religions of the West* [New York: Doubleday, 2004], 10-11).

[91] Keck, "Rethinking," 13.

[92] Ibid., 14.

The following section explores the role of punitive consequences as a reinforcement of the "group's sense of special identity" within Mark's most vivid judgment scene.

Mark 9:42–50

Of the available places in Mark that concern moral sanctions (1:24; 3:29–30; 4:4, 6–7, 15, 18–19; 5:7; 8:35–38; 9:42–50; 12:9, 40; 13:14–19, 35–36; 14:21), Mark 9:42–50 is the principal judgment text in Mark. Previously discussed in detail in Chapter 3, God enacts judgment in Mark's moral world, while Jesus serves as a proxy for God's judgment (3:27; 9:19; 11:12–14, 15–19). Recall, for example, the aorist and perfect passives of βάλλω in Mark 9:42, 45, and 47. When read as divine passives, God becomes the actor who throws violators into Gehenna (Isa 66:24; 4 Ezra 7.35–44; Sib. Or. 2.283–296). God presumes the role of judge over the world, but, the nature of what, or whom, God judges requires further consideration.

Ian Henderson has rightly argued that efforts to reconstruct the "behind-the-text possibilities" of Mark 9:42–50 only dramatize "the problem of following the argument" in its proper form and context.[93] Instead, Henderson opts for a rhetorical approach that places the sayings of Jesus within its larger narrative context, namely as a conversation between "insiders" in a private setting (9:33).[94] Mark 9:33 begins with a location change to Capernaum, a signal for a new scene in Mark (8:22, 27; 9:2; 10:1) and in the intimate space of a home (2:1; 3:19b; 5:19; 7:24; 8:26). If we consider the narrative sequence, the disciples' initial argument over greatness (μεῖζον; 9:34; cf. 10:43) prompts the teaching that follows. In stark contrast to their request, Jesus summons a child, the subject of his later discourses (9:42; 10:13–16), to explain the posture of servitude that his kingdom requires. Jesus, once more, directs the reader beyond himself to God: "Whoever accepts me accepts not me but the one who sent me [τὸν ἀποστείλαντά με]." According to Jesus's teaching, children exemplify the kingdom of God in a way that the disciples' request for greatest cannot (9:36–37; 10:13–16). The presence of children in vv. 36–37 also informs the interpretation of ἕνα τῶν μικρῶν τούτων in 9:42.[95] Children, paradigmatic characters for the accountable self in Mark, require God's protection.

The story of the unnamed exorcist appears next in the narrative sequence (9:38–41), revealing pertinent information about the boundaries of God's family in Mark with an emphasis on inclusion (9:39). The unnamed exorcist joins the ranks of the disciples by casting out demons in Jesus's name. The closing line of this pericope makes an emphatic reference to not losing (lit., "destroying") one's reward (ὅτι οὐ μὴ ἀπολέσῃ τὸν μισθὸν αὐτοῦ). The term μισθὸς can appear in eschatological reward/punishment texts, and in combination with ἀπόλλυμι, Jesus's saying anticipates the pericope to follow (9:42–50).[96] Importantly, the unnamed exorcist's rectitude is not

---

[93] Henderson, "Salted with Fire," 50.
[94] The larger narrative context is often overlooked as in Donahue and Harrington, *Mark*, 290; Best, *Disciples*, 40–2.
[95] See, e.g., A. Y. Collins, *Mark*, 450.
[96] See Luke 6:23–26; Col 3:23–25; Rev 11:18; 4 Ezra 7:83; 2 Bar. 54:16.

simply deed-oriented (i.e., the act of giving a cup of water) but status-oriented: he recognizes the nature of those within God's community as "belonging to Christ [ὅτι χριστοῦ ἐστε]."

Within this narrative framework of kingdom membership, the reader encounters the grisliest words of Jesus in Mark.[97] Most modern commentaries on Mark 9:42–50 conclude that Jesus's statement refers to individual ethical responsibility of some kind,[98] potentially related to sexual sin,[99] or carelessly causing one to stumble.[100] Other commentators have suggested that Jesus envisions ecclesial responsibility (i.e., the body of Christ)[101] or cutting out family and friends that cause one to go astray (cf. Mark 3:31–35).[102] One reader posits that 9:42–50 exhorts Mark's community to withstand torture.[103] Still others have seen the shadow of Judas behind Jesus's words.[104] In virtually all interpretations, Jesus's words are hyperbolic.[105] Because the content of Jesus's teaching within the narrative sequence refines community boundaries (9:33–41), then the ecclesial or familial interpretation is more appropriate, such as one finds in Origen's interpretation of Matt 18:

> And it is possible to use these words to refer to our family members [οἰκειοτάτων], who are also our members [μελῶν]. They have been considered our members because of the close bond of family, whether it is hereditary or out of the habitual intimacy among friends [ἔκ τινος συνηθείας φιλικῆς], so to speak. We are not to spare even these if they are damaging [βλαπτόντων] our soul. For let us cut off from ourselves, as a hand or a foot or an eye, father or mother wishing us to do the things opposed to godly activity [θεοσεβείᾳ].[106]

---

[97] The reception of Jesus's words here have a long and gruesome history, beginning with Matthew (5:27–30; 18:6–9; 19:12). Eusebius's alleged report of Origen's self-mutilation, for example, is connected with Matt 19:12, a text that closely resembles Matt 5:27–30 (E.H. 6.8; Comm. Matt. 15.3 [GCS 40, 354]; on the history of Matt 19:12 and self-castration, see Daniel F. Caner, "The Practice and Prohibition of Self-Castration in Early Christianity," VC 51 [1997]: 396–415). The literal reading has also received minor attention. For example, J. Duncan M. Derrett provides detail about punitive amputation practices in antiquity, including both Jewish (Deut 25:11–12; Josephus, Life 34.170–173; 35.177; War 2.642–644) and Greco-Roman sources (Studies in the New Testament, Volume 1: Glimpses of the Legal and Social Presuppositions of the Authors [Leiden: Brill, 1977], 4–27). In other words, Jesus's gory exhortation could have literal application in certain settings (Deut 14:1; Zech 13:6; cf. Mark 5:5).
[98] Via: "unethical acts" (Ethics of Mark's Gospel, 81–3); Mann: "sacrificial attitudes" (Mark, 382); Douglas Hare: "shocking sinners into taking drastic steps to avoid practices that are hateful to God" (Mark [Louisville, KY: Westminster John Knox Press, 1996], 117); France: "the demands of discipleship" (Gospel of Mark, 380).
[99] Deming, "Mark 9.42–10.12," 130–41; A. Y. Collins, Mark, 450–3; Allison, Jesus of Nazareth, 178–82.
[100] Best, Gospel as Story, 89; Cranfield, Saint Mark, 314.
[101] Donahue and Harrington, Mark, 287; Koester, "Mark 9:43–47," 151–3.
[102] Theophylactus, St. Mark, 80.
[103] Bas van Iersel, Reading Mark, trans. W.H. Bisscheroux (Edinburgh: T&T Clark, 1989), 135–6. Cranfield also notes a context of persecution (Saint Mark, 316).
[104] Philip Carrington picks up on the "would be better language" (cf. 14:21; According to Mark: A Running Commentary on the Oldest Gospel [New York: Cambridge University Press, 1960], 206).
[105] See Marcus, Mark 8–16, 2.690.
[106] Author's translation. Origen, Comm. Matt. 13.25; GCS 40, 247.

Following Origen, Mark 9:42–50 concerns community boundaries and the punitive consequence of hell (γέεννα).

The term γέεννα appears only here in Mark (vv. 43, 45, 47). Elsewhere in the New Testament, it appears in Jas 3:6, Matt 10:28, and Luke 12:5. In addition to the Markan parallels, Matthew employs the term twice more (23:15, 33; cf. 5:29, 30; 18:9). In the Hebrew Bible, γέεννα becomes associated with a morbid burial site (Jer 7:31–32; 19:2, 6) and a place of idol worship (Jer 32:35; 2 Chr 28:3; 33:6),[107] recalling the imagery of burning bodies in Isa 66:24 (cf. Mark 9:48). Mark tends to clarify certain customs for its audience (cf. 7:3–4, 11; 13:14), which may be why γέεννα is described in such detail. In other words, Mark tells its audience that γέεννα, wherever it is or whatever happens there, ought to be feared.[108]

Finally, the leading offense in 9:42–50 is "causing one of these little ones who believes in me to stumble [σκανδαλίσῃ]." The verb, σκανδαλίζω, commonly rendered as "stumble" (NIV, NRSV, NASB) or "cause to sin" (ESV, NLT), can carry a connotation of enticement.[109] As in the Testament of Solomon, a demon casts (ἐμβάλλω) "dissensions among people" and delights "in causing them to stumble" (σκανδαλίζων; 18:16). In other words, those who entice, or better, scandalize, God's children, have appropriated a characteristic of the demonic (Mark 4:4, 15). This type of condemnation against oppressive, demonic leadership is not uncommon in apocalyptic literature (1 En. 21:1–10; 54:6; 55:4). The Apocalypse of Abraham, for example, criticizes a certain oppressive group, who has not only "burned the Temple with fire" but also killed and robbed the people of God (27.1–7):

> And I will burn with fire those who mocked them and ruled over them in this age and I will deliver those who have covered me with mockery over to the scorn of the coming age. Because I have prepared them to be food for the fire of Hades, and to be ceaseless soaring in the air of the underworld regions of the uttermost depths … to be the contents of a wormy belly. (*Apoc. Abr.* 31.2–4)[110]

In a similar manner, Mark provides a vividly horrid sanction for those who take advantage of the most vulnerable members of God's family. According to Mark 9:33–50, the boundaries of God's family include little children and those who stand opposed to Satan. These boundaries may mean, if we follow Origen's reading, severing ties with

---

[107] Duane F. Watson, "Gehenna," in *ABD* 2.926–8.

[108] Consider the image of worms from Isa 66:24 removed by Matthew and Luke. Regardless of one's knowledge of Jewish prophetic literature, worms depict a gruesome death in the ancient world (Acts 12:23; 2 Macc 9:9; for a more exhaustive treatment, see Thomas Africa, "Worms and the Death of Kings: A Cautionary Note on Disease and History," *Classical Antiquity* 1 [1982]: 1–17). Worms are also a common motif in comparative eschatological judgment texts (Jdt 16:17; Sir 7:17). As in 3 Bar. 16:4, "And you will see the torture of the impious, wailing and groans and lamentations and the eternal worm" (trans. Gaylord, in *OTP*; cf. Apoc. Abr. 31.3). For the influence of Isa 66 on later apocalyptic texts, see Reiser, *Jesus and Judgment*, 27.

[109] While a common interpretation is "falling away" (Mark 4:17; 14:27; cf. Did. 16.5; *Herm.* 22.3; 38.10), epitomized by Peter in Mark (14:66–72), the term also appears in the LXX in the context of idolatry (Judg 2:3, 8:27; Ps 105:36; Wis 14:11; Hos 3:17), malicious trapping (Josh 23:13; Ps 139:6; Jdt 5:1, 20; 1 Macc 5:4), and sexual temptation (Sir 9:5; 16:7).

[110] Trans. Rubinkiewicz, in *OTP* 1.681–705.

blood relatives. The sanction of eternal destruction awaits those who align themselves with God's enemies. In this way, fighting for positions of power or "greatness," as the disciples do, is a characteristic of tyrants (10:42) and not of God's children. In Mark, it is characters such as Herod who exploit daughters and indulge in violence in front of "Galilee's finest" (πρώτοις τῆς Γαλιλαίας; 6:21), or the unclean spirits who violently harm children (9:22). God's punitive sanction awaits those who take advantage of these little ones.

5.5 Conclusion: Evil's Role in the Moral Landscape of Mark

This chapter began by outlining Mark's account of evil in the figure of Satan. Those who oppose God have aligned themselves with the evil one (3:23–26; 9:40), appropriating his attitude of misanthropy and his practice of harming the innocent (3:4; 5:5; 9:18; 12:1–12; 14:1–2; 15:14). Similar to Mark's theological account of virtue and the practices of the kingdom of God, Mark also contains an antithetical account of evil, embodied by those who seek to harm and to destroy. This chapter has considered, by way of example, pride and greed as major vices in Mark. These vices have corresponding practices that Mark condemns. For example, the practice of defrauding is denounced in Mark 10:19, and later, it is denounced in the narrative presentation of the scribes who "devour widows' houses" (12:40). The vice of greed prevents the rich man from following Jesus (10:22). For the vice of pride, consider Herod's motivations for beheading John. Not only is Herod accompanied by "his great ones" (τοῖς μεγιστᾶσιν), executives, and the best of the best (τοῖς πρώτοις), but it also is "because of his guests" (6:26) that he is unable to refuse Herodias's daughter's request. Likewise, Pilate decides to release Barabbas because he wishes to satisfy the crowd (15:15); and the chief priests, in this same pericope, act "out of envy" (διὰ φθόνον). In yet another example, James and John request to sit at the right and left of Jesus (10:35–45), closely mirroring the wrongheaded desires of the gentile rulers and their "great ones" (οἱ μεγάλοι).

Once more, these examples of greed and pride may be contrasted with the minor characters in Mark in whom virtues of God's kingdom may be found.[111] The Markan intercalation in 14:1–11 highlights the greed of Judas and the implied arrogance of the chief priests and scribes (vv. 1–2, 10–11) as well as the humility and generosity of an anonymous woman (vv. 3–9). In her study of minor characters, Elizabeth Struthers

---

[111] On what makes a minor character minor in the context of the nineteenth-century novel, Alex Woloch refers to a "strange significance":

> The strange significance of minor characters, in other words, resides largely in the way that the character disappears, and in the tension or relief that results from this vanishing. These feelings are often solicited by the narrative, and it is the disappearance of the minor character … that, finally, is integrated into his or her interesting speech or memorable gesture. We feel interest and outrage, painful concern or amused consent at what happens to minor characters: not simply their faith within the story … but also in the narrative discourse itself. (*The One vs. The Many: Minor Characters and the Space of the Protagonist in the Novel* [Princeton, NJ: Princeton University Press, 2004], 38)

Malbon connects the exemplary woman in 14:3-9 with the widow in 12:41-44. Both women, Malbon contends, contrast with the characters presented alongside them. In the case of the generous woman, the story "is itself framed by two stories of evil men. ... The contrast with Judas is especially marked: an unnamed woman gives up money for Jesus; a named man, even 'one of the twelve', gives up Jesus for money."[112] Taken together, Mark offers the example of marginal characters for exemplary action in God's kingdom in contrast with character antitypes. In this way, Mark's account of evil is a tapestry woven with both the threads of external, demonic forces as well as internal, anthropological desires to disobey God.

Finally, Mark's Gospel unequivocally condemns evil in its presentation of judgment. As Chapter 3 notes, God is the judge, who reserves the right to act in defense of God's "little ones" (9:42). There are severe and irreversible consequences for those who violate God's moral order. As Keck reminds us, moral sanctions frame the circumstances under which the moral agent acts. To this end, lack of attention to little "details" (τα μικρά) invites severe consequences (8:38; 9:42-50; 12:9; 13:14-19). These punitive sanctions function to override "the coercive capacities of other sanctions, like the threat of prosecution or persecution."[113] In other words, the evil and chaotic realities of the world, including promises of political power, threats of persecution, or even demonic mischief, may coerce one to actions motivated out of misanthropy, pride, or greed. Even worse, the internal vice of jealousy or external, demonic manipulation may lead one to commit murder (3:6; 12:4-8). For this reason, the moral warrant that "the kingdom of God has come near" (1:14) requires an equally coercive sanction that God "will come" to judge (12:9; 13:35). For Mark in particular, God's judgment is employed at key narrative junctures in defense of the story's marginal characters (e.g., 9:42-50;[114] 12:1-12, 38-40[115]). As was established in Chapter 4, God's preference for these "little ones" reflects a moral mandate. These minor characters exhibit the qualities of God's kingdom, especially as they are contrasted within the narrative to greed (10:13-31; 12:38-44; 14:1-11), pride (7:1-30; 10:35-52), and the agenda of the demonic to harm the innocent (1:26; 5:1-20; 9:14-29).

---

[112] Malbon, "The Major Importance of Minor Characters," 77. In the case of the poor widow, she "is both opposite of the religious leaders of ch. 12 ... and the model for the disciples ... of ch. 13" (ibid., 78).
[113] Keck, "Rethinking," 13.
[114] One cannot say the same for Matthew, who understands the sayings of Jesus in Mark 9:42-50 to apply to sexual ethics (Matt 5:27-30). Among Matthew's judgment material (cf. 10:15, 28; 11:22; 12:42; 13:20; 18:6-9; 22:13; 24:51; 25:31-46), Matt 18:1-9 and 25:31-46 appear closer to Mark's use of judgment in 9:42-50.
[115] Jesus's condemnation of the scribes (12:28, 38) in direct connection with the treatment of the widow at the treasury (12:41-44) is somewhat lost in Matthew's redaction (23:1-36).

Conclusion

This study began by identifying the long-standing trend in Markan scholarship to neglect the moral dimensions of Mark's Gospel. Historically, Mark has been viewed as providing virtually no description of, or mandate for, the moral life of first-century Christians. Instead, the Markan motifs of Christology and discipleship remained front and center in Markan studies. This trend in scholarship has started to shift. As a unique literary production, many understand Mark to offer a theological account of Jesus different from the one found in Matthew, Luke, and John. The renewed trend in scholarship to view the Gospels as biographies has also produced interest in the moral tenor of Mark. Furthermore, Mark's ambivalent or, according to some, downright negative portrait of the Roman Empire has placed Mark at the storm center for postcolonial studies of the New Testament. While studies of this kind are ripe for moral consideration, surprisingly few have concentrated on Mark's moral life in their investigations. When studies of Mark's ethics have appeared, with the exception of Dan O. Via's *The Ethics of Mark's Gospel in the Middle of Time* (1985), they are typically partial or incomplete. In light of this problem, this project has attempted to offer a more thorough account of the moral life in Mark.

By placing Mark within the general category of biography, Chapter 2 claimed that describing the moral life is a necessary objective for many biographical productions in antiquity. Furthermore, evidence from Philo and Josephus demonstrates that the separation of theology from morality, or theology from history, is both unnecessary and misleading. Philo's Moses answers to God, as does Josephus's Saul and Mark's Jesus. Contrary to the verdict of Rudolf Bultmann, the Gospel of Mark's theology need not exclude it from the moral world of ancient biographies. With that said, however, Mark's form and content still resist some classic features of biographies. In many cases, Mark's central figure is quite difficult to imitate, evidenced chiefly by his disciples. Chapter 2 proposed "genre bending" as a solution to this problem, consonant with Mark's moral paradigm.

The third chapter attempted to expound on the kind of genre bending Mark intends by way of its presentation of God. Often lurking in the shadows, God is the moral impetus for all of Jesus's activity in Mark. For this reason, Leander Keck's use of accountability to describe Pauline ethics proves useful for Markan interpretation. Similar to Paul, Mark presents a moral life of accountability to God. Jesus, and those who follow him, must answer to God. Contrary to accounts of ethics that focus on the moral agent's actions, Mark's moral life is framed in terms of belonging: allegiance to an authority to whom the moral self must render an account. The example of God's role in the prologue (Mark 1:1-15) demonstrates the theocentrically moral nature of Mark's Gospel. Three correlative images of God—as parent, authority, and judge—showcase the moral agent's accountability.

In Chapter 4, I outlined specific implications of Mark's moral life for the moral agent. If one belongs to God, then for what is such a person accountable? Mark's Gospel presents a set of virtues, epitomized by love, faith, and humility, as well as accompanying practices, such as loving one's neighbor, exorcizing the demonic, and prayer. Once more, these virtues and practices are not commanded by God as a specific "must" or "ought to"; rather, they serve as evidence of one's status of belonging to God's new family. Those portrayed with faith do not muster up measurable quantities of faith because it is "the right thing to do." These marginal figures display faith out of complete desperation, and by their faith, they are recognized as God's children. Moreover, accountability in Mark also extends to one's neighbor. Not only are parents accountable for their children (5:21-43; 9:14-29) but also friends for one another (2:1-12), neighbors for those who may harm themselves (5:1-20), foreigners (7:24-30), strangers (9:38-41), and those with little means to support themselves (10:13-16; 12:41-44; 14:3-9). Without such accountability, Mark's moral world foretells complete chaos (13:12-13). This characteristic of Mark's moral life often inverts insiders and outsiders (3:31-35), expanding God's family beyond blood relations to a new community. This community is marked by the virtues of faith, love, and humility, and the practices of caring for those in need. My selection of virtues and practices may be expanded upon. For example, the counterpart to Jesus's imperative "believe" is repent (Mark 1:15). What does repentance look like as a virtuous practice within Mark's Gospel? Does Jesus himself illustrate repentance (7:24-30)?

Finally, Chapter 5 contended that Mark's depiction of the moral life also illustrates a competing moral force, driven by Satan. Mark's Gospel is set to the beat of apocalyptic urgency (1:14-15): Satan and his unclean spirits are actively destroying the world. This portrait of evil, I argue, may be best illustrated by those who live contrary to the mores of God's kingdom. One witnesses such antitypes in Judas, Herod, and even, at times, in Jesus's own disciples. Mark's account of evil is accompanied by descriptions of certain vices, such as pride and greed, as well as certain practices, such as taking advantage of the poor and murder. The final culmination of Mark's account of evil is depicted in the eternal sanction of hell (1:24; 3:29; 5:7; 9:42-50; 12:9), couched as a form of radical protection of God's children.

As a story, Mark was, and remains, instructive for the moral life. Especially when compared to Jewish and Greco-Roman biographies in antiquity, Mark's cast of characters illustrates both ideals and pitfalls, virtues and vices for moral living. The central character, Jesus, offers readers imitable characteristics in his own obedience to God (14:32-42), love for others (10:21; 12:28-34), and even in his servitude unto death (10:45); however, the evidence is also mixed, complicating studies that propose an *imitatio Christi* ethic for Mark. Jesus's teaching lacks clarity in places (4:12-13; 8:14-21; 9:10; 10:24; 10:35-45), and his actions are often obtuse (6:45-52; 11:12-14). Moreover, the forces of evil are strong, impeding the human capacity to follow after

Jesus (8:31–33). In concession to this problem, I have framed the moral life in terms of accountability to the God of Jesus and to those who are included among God's children ("all nations" in 11:17; 13:10). Mark's God reclaims the world from misanthropic evil found both within the human heart and without, in demonic, unclean spirits. Finally, Markan soteriology illustrates that the stakes for such a victory are high (12:6; 15:33–41). In perhaps the most significance instance of genre bending, the central character in Mark's biography dies *for the many* (10:45). Still, prescribing an ethic of imitation here is perilous. Giving up claims to power, even life itself, is something Jesus's own followers are not ready to do (9:33–37; 10:35–45) and those with claims to power actively oppose (6:14–29; 12:12, 38–40; 14:1–2). Those in Mark who appear better situated to understand the meaning of Jesus's death are those who act in behalf of others (ἀντὶ πολλῶν).

In conclusion, we return to the fundamental questions with which this study began: Does Mark's Gospel contain discernable ethics? If so, how would one describe the so-called ethics of Mark? Martin Dibelius's frustration with Mark 5:1–20 and its perceived lack of constructive ethical content is worth repeating:

> The indifference of the narrator to the harm which had been done, and to the wish of the people that Jesus should leave their district, shows the narrator is only interested in the greatness of the actual miracle, not in the benefit to the sufferer and other help for the people.[1]

While certain strands of ethical inquiry, centered on an agent's individual actions, are rather scarce in Mark, what we do find, instead, is a narrative world of agents accountable to God. To what, or to whom, these agents owe an account runs contrary to Dibelius's verdict upon "the indifference of the narrator." This study has contended that Mark's moral emphasis is not so much on "doing" as it is on belonging to God. For that reason, according to Mark, it is not those in positions of power who gain entrance into God's kingdom, but it is the "sufferer" and the ones in greatest need to whom God's kingdom belongs.

---

[1] Dibelius, *From Tradition*, 101.

Bibliography

Achtemeier, Paul J. *Mark*. PC. Philadelphia: Fortress Press, 1975.
Achtemeier, Paul J. "Miracles and the Historical Jesus: Mark 9:14–29." *CBQ* 37 (1975): 424–51.
Achtemeier, Paul J. "'He Taught Them Many Things': Reflections on Marcan Christology." *CBQ* 42 (1980): 465–81.
Ådna, Jostein. "The Encounter of Jesus with the Gerasene Demoniac." Pages 279–302 in *Authenticating the Activities of Jesus*. Edited by Bruce Chilton and Craig A. Evans. NTTS 28. Boston: Brill, 1999.
Africa, Thomas. "Worms and the Death of Kings: A Cautionary Note on Disease and History." *Classical Antiquity* 1 (1982): 1–17.
Aichele, George. "Jesus' Uncanny 'Family Scene.'" *JSNT* 74 (1999): 29–49.
Aletti, Jean-Noël. *Jésus, une vie à raconter: Essai sur le genre littéraire des évangiles de Matthieu, de Marc et de Luc*. Bruxelles: Lessius, 2016.
Alexander, Loveday. "What Is a Gospel?" Pages 13–33 in *The Cambridge Companion to the Gospels*. Edited by Stephen C. Barton. Cambridge: Cambridge University Press, 2006.
Alexander, Philip S. "Demonology of the Dead Sea Scrolls." Pages 331–53 in vol. 2 of *The Dead Sea Scrolls after Fifty Years: A Comprehensive Assessment*. Edited by Peter W. Flintand and James C. Vanderkam. Boston: Brill, 1999.
Allison, Dale C. "Mark 12.28–31 and the Decalogue." Pages 270–8 in *The Gospels and the Scriptures of Israel*. Edited by Craig A. Evans and W. Richard Stegner. JSNTSup 104. Sheffield: Sheffield Academic Press, 1994.
Allison, Dale C. *Jesus of Nazareth: Millenarian Prophet*. Minneapolis, MN: Fortress Press, 1998.
Allison, Dale C. *Testament of Abraham*. CEJL. New York: Walter de Gruyter, 2003.
Allison, Dale C. "Structure, Biographical Impulse, and the *Imitatio Christi*." Pages 135–55 in *Studies in Matthew: Interpretation Past and Present*. Grand Rapids, MI: Baker Academic, 2005.
Anderson, Graham. *Philostratus, Biography and Belles Lettres in the Third Century A.D.* Dover: Croom Helm, 1986.
Anderson, Hugh. *The Gospel of Mark*. NCBC. London: Marshall, Morgan & Scott, 1976.
Andrews, Mary E. "Peirasmos: A Study in Form Criticism." *ATR* 24 (1942): 229–44.
Angert-Quilter, Theresa, and Lynne Wall. "The 'Spirit Wife' at Endor." *JSOT* 92 (2001): 55–72.
Anna, Julia. *The Morality of Happiness*. New York: Oxford University Press, 1995.
Annen, Franz. *Heil für die Heiden: Zur Bedeutung und Geschichte der Tradition vom besessenen Gerasener (Mk 5,1–20 parr.)*. FTS 20. Frankfurt am Main: Knecht, 1976.
Anscombe, G. E. M. "Modern Moral Philosophy." *Philosophy* 33 (1958): 1–19.
Applebaum, S. "Economic Life in Palestine." Pages 631–400 in vol. 2 of *The Jewish People in the First Century*. Edited by S. Safrai and M. Stern. Philadelphia: Fortress Press, 1976.

Aquinas, Thomas. *Catena Aurea: Commentary on the Four Gospels Collected out of the Works of the Fathers*. 4 vols. Edited by John Henry Newman. Oxford: John Henry Parker, 1842.

Aquinas, Thomas. *Summa Theologica: First Complete American Edition in Three Volumes*. 3 vols. Translated by the Fathers of the English Dominican Province. New York: Benziger Brothers, 1947.

Aristotle. *Politics*. Translated by H. Rackham. LCL 264. Cambridge, MA: Harvard University Press, 1932.

Aristotle. *Nicomachean Ethics*. Translated by H. Rackham. LCL 73. Cambridge, MA: Harvard University Press, 1926.

Attridge, Harold. "Genre Bending in the Fourth Gospel?" *JBL* 121 (2002): 3–21.

Attridge, Harold. *The Interpretation of Biblical History in the Antiquitates Judaicae of Flavius Josephus*. Harvard Dissertations in Religion 7. Missoula, MT: Scholars Press, 1976.

Aune, David E. "Greco-Roman Biography." Pages 107–26 in *Greco-Roman Literature and the New Testament: Selected Forms and Genres*. Edited by David E. Aune. SBLSBS 21. Atlanta, GA: Scholars Press, 1988.

Aune, David E. "Genre Theory and the Genre-Function of Mark and Matthew." Pages 145–75 in *Mark and Matthew I, Comparative Readings: Understanding the Earliest Gospels in their First-Century Settings*. Edited by Eve-Marie Becker and Anders Runesson. WUNT 271. Tübingen: Mohr Siebeck, 2011.

Aune, David E. *The New Testament in Its Literary Environment*. Philadelphia: Westminster Press, 1987.

Aune, David E. "The Problem of Genre of the Gospels: A Critique of C. H. Talbert's *What Is a Gospel?*" Pages 9–60 in *Gospel Perspectives II: Studies of History and Tradition in the Four Gospels*. Edited by R. T. France and D. Wenham. Sheffield: JSOT Press, 1981.

Aus, Roger David. *My Name Is "Legion": Palestinian Judaic Traditions in Mark 5:1–20 and Other Gospel Texts*. SJ. Lanham, MD: University Press of America, 2003.

Azoulay, Vincent. *Xénophon et les grâces du pouvoir: de la charis au charisme*. HAM 77. Paris: Publications de la Sorbonne, 2004.

Barth, Karl. *Church Dogmatics, Volume II: The Doctrine of God, Part 2*. Translated by G. W. Bromiley, J. C. Campbell, Iain Wilson, J. Strathearn McNab, Harold Knight, and R. A. Stewart. Edited by G. W. Bromiley and T. F. Torrance. Edinburgh: T&T Clark, 1957.

Barth, Karl. *The Epistle to the Romans*. Translated by Edwyn C. Hoskyns. New York: Oxford University Press, 1968.

Barth, Karl. *Prayer*. 50th anniversary ed. Edited by Don E. Saliers. Translated by Sara F. Terrien. Louisville, KY: Westminster John Knox Press, 2002.

Bartlett, David L. "Exorcism Stories in the Gospel of Mark." PhD diss. New Haven, CT: Yale University, 1972.

Basil of Caesarea. *Ascetical Works*. Translated by Sister M. Monica Wagner. FC 9. Washington, DC: Catholic University of America Press, 1962.

Bauckham, Richard. "For Whom Were the Gospels Written?" Pages 9–48 in *The Gospels for All Christians: Rethinking the Gospel Audiences*. Edited by Richard Bauckham. Grand Rapids, MI: Eerdmans, 1998.

Baur, Ferdinand Christian. *Apollonius von Tyana und Christus: Ein Beitrag zur Religionsgeschichte derersten Jahrhunderte nach Christus*. Leipzig: Fues, 1876; repr., Hildesheim: G. Olms, 1966.

Beasley-Murray, G. R. *Jesus and the Kingdom of God*. Grand Rapids, MI: Eerdmans, 1986.

Beavis, Mary Ann. "Women as Models of Faith in Mark." *BTB* 18 (1988): 3–9.
Beavis, Mary Ann. *Mark's Audience: The Literary and Social Setting of Mark 4:11–12*. JSNTSup33. Sheffield: Sheffield Academic Press, 1989.
Becker, Eve-Marie. *Das Markus-Evangelium im Rahmen antiker Historiographie*. WUNT 194. Tübingen: Mohr Siebeck, 2006.
Becker, Eve-Marie. *The Birth of Christian History: Memory and Time from Mark to Luke-Acts*. AYBRL. New Haven, CT: Yale University Press, 2017.
Benovitz, Moshe. *KOL NIDRE: Studies in the Development of Rabbinic Votive Institutions*. BJS 315. Atlanta, GA: Scholars Press, 1998.
Best, Ernest. *Disciples and Discipleship: Studies in the Gospel of Mark*. Edinburgh: T&T Clark, 1986.
Best, Ernest. "Discipleship in Mark: Mark 8.22–10.52." *SJT* 23 (1970): 323–37.
Best, Ernest. *Following Jesus: Discipleship in the Gospel of Mark*. JSNTSup 4. Sheffield: JSOT Press, 1981.
Best, Ernest. *Mark: The Gospel as Story*. SNTW. Edinburgh: T&T Clark, 1983.
Best, Ernest. *The Temptation and the Passion: The Markan Soteriology*. SNTSMS 2. Cambridge: Cambridge University Press, 1965.
Bettiolo, Paolo, Alda G. Kossova, Claudio Leonardi, Enrico Norelli, and Lorenzo Perrone, eds. *Ascensio Isaiae Textus*. CCSA 7. Trunhout: Brepols, 1995.
Bilde, Per. "Josephus and Jewish Apocalypticism." Pages 151–69 in *Collected Studies on Philo and Josephus*. Edited by Eve-Marie Becker, Morten Hørning Jensen, and Jacob Mortensen. SANt 7. Göttingen: Vandenhoeck & Ruprecht, 2016.
Billault, Alain. *L'Univers de Philostrate*. CL 252. Bruxelles: Latomus, 2000.
Birch, Bruce C., and Larry L. Rasmussen. *The Bible and Ethics in the Christian Life*. Minneapolis, MN: Augsburg Publishing House, 1976.
Bird, Michael F. *The Gospel of the Lord: How the Early Church Wrote the Story of Jesus*. Grand Rapids, MI: Eerdmans, 2014.
Black, C. Clifton. "Does Suffering Possess Educational Value in Mark's Gospel?" Pages 3–17 in *Character Ethics and the New Testament: Moral Dimensions of Scripture*. Edited by Robert L. Brawley. Louisville, KY: Westminster John Knox Press, 2007.
Black, C. Clifton. *Mark*. ANTC. Nashville, TN: Abingdon Press, 2011.
Black, C. Clifton. "Mark as Historian of God's Kingdom." *CBQ* 71 (2009): 64–83.
Black, C. Clifton. *The Disciples according to Mark: Markan Redaction in Current Debate*. 2nd ed. Grand Rapids, MI: Eerdmans, 2012.
Blount, Brian K. *Then the Whisper Put on Flesh: New Testament Ethics in an African American Context*. Nashville, TN: Abingdon Press, 2001.
Blount, Brian K. "Jesus as Teacher: Boundary Breaking in Mark's Gospel and Today's Church." *Interpretation* 70 (2016): 184–93.
Boer, Martinus C. de. "Paul and Jewish Apocalyptic Eschatology." Pages 169–90 in *Apocalyptic and the New Testament: Essays in Honor of J. Louis Martyn*. Edited by Joel Marcus and Marion L. Soards. JSNTSup 24. Sheffield: JSOT Press, 1989.
Bond, Helen K. "A Fitting End? Self-Denial and a Slave's Death in Mark's Life of Jesus." *NTS* 65 (2019): 425–42.
Booth, Roger P. *Jesus and the Laws of Purity: Tradition History and Legal History in Mark 7*. JSNTSup 13. Sheffield: JSOT Press, 1986.
Boring, M. Eugene. "Markan Christology: God Language for Jesus?" *NTS* 45 (1999): 451–71.

Boring, M. Eugene. *Mark: A Commentary*. NTL. Louisville, KY: Westminster John Knox Press, 2006.

Boring, M. Eugene. *I & II Thessalonians: A Commentary*. NTL. Louisville, KY: Westminster John Knox Press, 2015.

Boswell, James. *The Life of Samuel Johnson, LL, D, Comprehending an Account of his Studies and Numerous Works in Chronological Order; A Series of His Epistolary Correspondence and Conversations with Many Eminent Persons and Various Original Pieces of His Composition Never Before Published: The Whole Exhibiting a View of Literature and Literary Men in Great-Britain, for Near Half a Century during which He Flourished*. London: Henry Baldwin for Charles Duly, 1791.

Botner, Max. "The Role of Transcriptional Probability in the Text-Critical Debate on Mark1:1." *CBQ* 77 (2015): 467–80.

Böttrich, Christfried. "Jesus und der Feigenbaum: Mk 11:12–14, 20–25 in der Diskussion." *NovT* 39 (1997): 328–59.

Bousset, Wilhelm. "Die Textüberlieferung der Apophthegmata Patrum." Pages 102–16 in *Festgabe von Fachgenossen und Freunden A. von Harnack zum siebzigsten Geburtstagdargebracht*. Tübingen: J. C. B. Mohr, 1921.

Bowersock, G. W. *Greek Sophists in the Roman Empire*. Oxford: Clarendon Press, 1969.

Bowler, Kate. *Blessed: A History of the American Prosperity Gospel*. New York: Oxford University Press, 2013.

Box, G. H., and J. I. Landsman. *The Apocalypse of Abraham: Edited with a Translation from the Slavonic Text and Notes*. New York: Macmillan, 1918.

Brand, Miryam T. *Evil within and Without: The Source of Sin and Its Nature as Portrayed in Second Temple Literature*. JAJSup 9. Göttingen: Vandenhoeck & Ruprecht, 2013.

Brawley, Robert L. "Generating Ethics from God's Character in Mark." Pages 57–74 in *Character Ethics and the New Testament: Moral Dimensions of Scripture*. Edited by Robert L. Brawley. Louisville, KY: Westminster John Knox Press, 2007.

Brennema, Cornelius. "The Character of Pilate in the Gospel of John." Pages 240–54 in *Characters and Characterization in the Gospel of John*. Edited by Christopher W. Skinner. LNTS 461. London: Bloomsbury/T&T Clark, 2013.

Brennema, Cornelis. *Mimesis in the Johannine Literature: A Study in Johannine Ethics*. LNTS 498. New York: T&T Clark, 2018.

Breytenbach, Cilliers. "Current Research on the Gospel according to Mark: A Report on Monographs Published from 2000–2009." Pages 13–32 in *Mark and Matthew I, Comparative Readings: Understanding the Earliest Gospels in their First-Century Settings*. Edited by Eve-Marie Becker and Anders Runesson. WUNT 271. Tübingen: Mohr Siebeck, 2011.

Breytenbach, Cilliers. "Narrating the Death of Jesus in Mark: Utterances of the Main Character, Jesus." *ZNW* 105 (2014): 153–68.

Broadhead, Erwin K. *Naming Jesus: Titular Christology in the Gospel of Mark*. JSNTSup 175. Sheffield: Sheffield Academic Press, 1999.

Brooke, George J. "Isaiah 40:3 and the Wilderness Community." Pages 117–32 in *New Qumran Text and Studies: Proceedings of the first Meeting of the International Organization for Qumran Studies, Paris, 1992*. Edited by George J. Brooke and Florentino Garcia Martinez. STDJ 15. Leiden: Brill, 1994.

Bultmann, Rudolf. *Jesus and the Word*. Translated by Louise P. Smith and Erminie H. Lantero. New York: Scribner's Sons, 1958.

Bultmann, Rudolf. *The History of the Synoptic Tradition*. Translated by J. Marsh. New York: Harper & Row, 1963.

Bultmann, Rudolf. *Die Geschichte der synoptischen Tradition*. 10th ed. FRLANT 29. Gottingen: Vandenhoeck & Ruprecht, 1995.

Burdon, Christopher. "'To the Other Side': Construction of Evil and Fear of Liberation in Mark 5.1-20." *JSNT* (2004): 149-67.

Burridge, Richard. "Ethics and Genre: The Narrative Setting of Moral Language in the NewTestament." Pages 383-96 in *Moral Language in the New Testament, Vol. II: The Interrelatedness of Language and Ethics in Early Christian Writings*. Edited by Ruben Zimmerman and Jan G. van der Watt. WUNT 2.296. Tübingen: Mohr Siebeck, 2010.

Burridge, Richard. "Gospel: Genre." Pages 335-42 in *Dictionary of Jesus and the Gospels*. 2nd ed. Edited by Joel B. Green, Jeannine K. Brown, and Nicholas Perrin. Downers Grove, IL: InterVarsity Press Academic, 2013.

Burridge, Richard. *Imitating Jesus: An Inclusive Approach to New Testament Ethics*. Grand Rapids, MI: Eerdmans, 2007.

Burridge, Richard. *What Are the Gospels? A Comparison with Graeco-Roman Biographies*. 2nd ed. Grand Rapids, MI: Eerdmans, 2004.

Buxton, Richard Fernando. "Xenophon on Leadership: Commanders as Friends." Pages 323-37 in *The Cambridge Companion to Xenophon*. Edited by Michael A. Flowers. Cambridge: Cambridge University Press, 2017.

Cadbury, Henry J. *The Perils of Modernizing Jesus*. New York, Macmillan, 1937.

Cahill, Lisa Sowle. "Christian Character, Biblical Community, and Human Values." Pages 3-17 in *Character and Scripture: Moral Formation, Community, and Biblical Interpretation*. Edited by William P. Brown. Grand Rapids, MI: Eerdmans, 2002.

Calvin, John. *Commentary on a Harmony of the Evangelists: Matthew, Mark, and Luke*. 3 vols. Translated by William Pringle. Grand Rapids, MI: Eerdmans, 1949; repr., Grand Rapids, MI: Baker, 1989.

Camery-Hoggatt, Jerry. *Irony in Mark's Gospel: Text and Subtext*. SNTSMS 72. New York: Cambridge University Press, 1992.

Cancik, Hubert. "Die Gattung Evangelium: Markus im Rahmen der antikenHistoriographie." Pages 85-113 in *Markus-Philologie: Historische, literaturgeschichtliche undstilistische Untersuchungen zum zweiten Evangelium*. Edited by H. Cancik. WUNT 33.Tübingen: J. C. B. Mohr, 1984.

Caner, Daniel F. "The Practice and Prohibition of Self-Castration in Early Christianity." *VC* 51 (1997): 396-415.

Card, Michael. *Mark: The Gospel of Passion*. BIS. Downers Grove, IL: InterVarsity Press, 2012.

Carlson, Reed. "Provocateurs, Examiners, and Fools: Divine Opponents to the Aqedah in Early Judaism." *CBQ* 83 (2021): 373-89.

Carrington, Philip. *According to Mark: A Running Commentary on the Oldest Gospel*. New York: Cambridge University Press, 1960.

Carroll, John T. *Jesus and the Gospels: An Introduction*. Louisville, KY: Westminster John Knox Press, 2016.

Carter, Warren. "Cross-Gendered Romans and Mark's Jesus: Legion Enters the Pigs (Mark5:1-20)." *JBL* 134 (2015): 139-55.

Case, Shirley Jackson. *The Social Origins of Christianity*. Chicago: University of Chicago Press, 1923.

Charlesworth, James H., ed. *The Dead Sea Scrolls, Hebrew Aramaic, and Greek Texts with English Translations: Volume 1, Rule of the Community and Related Documents*. PTSDSSP. Louisville, KY: Westminster John Knox Press, 1994.

Charlesworth, James H. "*Intertextuality: Isaiah 40.3* and the Serek Ha-Yahad." Pages 197–224 in *The Quest for Context and Meaning: Studies in Biblical Intertextuality in Honor of James A. Sanders*. Edited by Craig A. Evans and Shemaryahu Talmon. Leiden: Brill, 1997.

Cicero. *Tusculan Disputations*. Translated by J. E. King. LCL 141. Cambridge, MA: Harvard University Press, 1927.

Clark, Gillian. *Women in the Ancient World*. Oxford: Oxford University Press, 1989.

Cocksworth, Ashley. *Karl Barth on Prayer*. New York: Bloomsbury/T&T Clark, 2015.

Coles, Robert. *Simone Weil: A Modern Pilgrimage*. Woodstock: Skylight Paths, 2001.

Collins, Adela Yarbro. *Is Mark's Gospel a Life of Jesus?: The Question of Genre*. PMLT. Milwaukee, WI: Marquette University Press, 1990.

Collins, Adela Yarbro. "Genre and the Gospels." *JR* 75 (1995): 239–46.

Collins, Adela Yarbro. *Mark: A Commentary*. Hermeneia. Minneapolis, MN: Fortress Press, 2007.

Collins, Adela Yarbro. "Apocalypse Now: The State of Apocalyptic Studies Near the End of the First Decade of the Twenty-First Century." *HTR* 104 (2011): 447–57.

Collins, John J. *Apocalyptic Imagination: An Introduction to the Jewish Matrix of Christianity*. New York: Crossroad, 1984.

Collins, John J. *Between Athens and Jerusalem: Jewish Identity in the Hellenistic Diaspora*. Grand Rapids, MI: Eerdmans, 2000.

Collins, Raymond F. *Christian Morality: Biblical Foundations*. Notre Dame, IN: University of Notre Dame Press, 1986.

Collman, Ryan D. "Beware of the Dogs! The Phallic Epithet in Phil 3:2." *NTS* 67 (2021): 105–20.

Connolly, Michele A. *Disorderly Women and the Order of God: An Australian Feminist Reading of the Gospel of Mark*. TTCBS. New York: Bloomsbury T&T Clark, 2018.

Conzelmann, Hans. *An Outline of the Theology of the New Testament*. Translated by John Bowden. New York: Harper & Row, 1969.

Cook, Michael L. *Mark's Treatment of the Jewish Leaders*. Leiden: Brill 1978.

Cook, Michael L. *Christology as Narrative Quest*. Collegeville, MN: Liturgical Press, 1997.

Corbett, Edward P. J. "The Theory and Practice of Imitation in Classical Rhetoric." *College Composition and Communication* 22 (1971): 243–51.

Cordovana, O. D. "Between History and Myth: Septimius Severus and Leptis Magna." *GR* 59 (2012): 56–75.

Cotter, Wendy. "Mark's Hero of the Twelfth-Year Miracles: The Healing of the Woman with the Hemorrhage and the Raising of Jairus's Daughter (Mark 5.21–43)." Pages 54–79 in *A Feminist Companion to Mark*. Edited by Amy-Jill Levin. Sheffield: Sheffield Academic Press, 2001.

Cotter, Wendy. *The Christ of the Miracle Stories: Portrait through Encounter*. Grand Rapids, MI: Baker Academic, 2010.

Cox, Patricia. *Biography in Late Antiquity: A Quest for the Holy Man*. TCH 5. Berkeley: University of California Press, 1983.

Cox, Patricia. "Origen and the Witch of Endor: Toward an Iconoclast Typology." *ATR* 66 (1984): 137–47.

Cranfield, C. E. B. *The Gospel According to Saint Mark: An Introduction and Commentary*. CGTC. Cambridge: Cambridge University Press, 1959.

Crawford, Cory. "On the Exegetical Function of the Abraham/Ravens Tradition in Jubilees 11." *HTR* 97 (2004): 91–7.

Cribiore, Raffaella. *Gymnastics of the Mind: Greek Education in the Hellenistic and Roman Egypt*. Princeton, NJ: Princeton University Press, 2001.
Cullmann, Oscar. *Christ and Time: The Primitive Christian Concept of Time and History*. Translated by Floyd V. Filson. Philadelphia: Westminster Press, 1950.
Cullmann, Oscar. *The Christology of the New Testament*. Translated by Shirley C. Guthrie and Charles A. M. Hall. Rev. ed. Philadelphia: Westminster Press, 1963.
D'Angelo, Mary Rose. "Abba and 'Father': Imperial Theology and the Jesus Tradition." *JBL* 111 (1992): 611–30.
Danove, Paul L. *The Rhetoric of the Characterization of God, Jesus, and Jesus' Disciples in the Gospel of Mark*. JSNTSup 290. New York: T&T Clark, 2005.
Daube, David. "Responsibilities of Master and Disciples in the Gospels." *NTS* 19 (1972-3): 1–15.
Davidsen, Ole. *The Narrative Jesus: A Semiotic Reading of Mark's Gospel*. Aarhus: Aarhus University Press, 1993.
Davies, J. P. *Paul among the Apocalypses? An Evaluation of "Apocalyptic Paul" in the Context of Jewish Christian Apocalyptic Literature*. New York: Bloomsbury/T&T Clark, 2016.
Davies, W. D., and Dale C. Allison. *A Critical and Exegetical Commentary on the Gospel According to Saint Matthew*. 3 vols. ICC. New York: T&T Clark, 1988–97.
Deming, Will. "Mark 9.42–10.12; Mathew 5.27–32, and *B. Nid.* 13b: A First Century Discussion of Male Sexuality." *NTS* 36 (1990): 130–41.
Derrett, J. Duncan M. "ΚΟΡΒΑΝ, Ο ΕΣΤΙΝ ΔΩΡΟΝ." *NTS* 16 (1969–70): 364–8.
Derrett, J. Duncan M. *Studies in the New Testament, Volume 1: Glimpses of the Legal and Social Presuppositions of the Authors*. Leiden: Brill, 1977.
Derrett, J. Duncan M. "Contributions to the Study of the Gerasene Demoniac." *JSNT* 3 (1979): 2–17.
Derrett, J. Duncan M. "Spirit-Possession and the Gerasene Demoniac." *Man* 14 (1979): 286–93.
Dewar, Lindsay. *An Outline of New Testament Ethics*. Philadelphia: Westminster Press, 1949.
Dibelius, Martin. *From Tradition to Gospel*. Translated by Bertram L. Woolf. London: James Clarke, 1971.
Dihle, Albrecht. *Studien zur griechischen Biographie*. Göttingen: Vandenhoeck & Ruprecht, 1956.
Dihle, Albrecht. "Die Evangelien und die biographische Tradition der Antike." *ZTK* 80 (1983): 33–49.
Dihle, Albrecht. "The Gospels and Greek Biography." Pages 361–86 in *The Gospel and the Gospels*. Edited by Peter Stuhlmacher. Grand Rapids, MI: Eerdmans, 1990.
Dinkler, Michal Beth. "Suffering, Misunderstanding, and Suffering Misunderstanding: The Markan Misunderstanding Motif as a Form of Jesus' Suffering." *JSNT* 38 (2016): 316–38.
Diogenes Laertius. "*Lives* 7.84–131." Pages 113–24 in *The Stoics Reader: Selected Writings and Testimonia*. Translated by Brad Inwood and Lloyd P. Gerson. Indianapolis, IN: Hackett, 2008.
Dixon, Suzanne. *The Roman Family*. Baltimore, MD: Johns Hopkins University Press, 1992.
Dobschütz, Ernst von. *Vom Auslegen insonderheit des Neuen Testaments*. HU 18. Halle: M. Niemeyer, 1922.
Dobschütz, Ernst von. "Zur Erzählerkunst des Markus." *ZNW* 27 (1928): 193–8.

Dodd, C. H. "The Framework of the Gospel Narrative." *ExpTim* 43 (1931–2): 396–400.
Dodd, C. H. *The Apostolic Preaching*. New York: Harper, 1935.
Dodd, C. H. *According to the Scriptures: The Sub-Structure of New Testament Theology*. London: Nisbet, 1952.
Dodd, C. H. *The Parables of the Kingdom*. New York: Scribner's Sons, 1958.
Doergens, H. "Apollonius von Tyana in Parallele zu Christus dem Herren." *Theologie und Glaube* 25 (1933): 292–304.
Döhler, Marietheres, ed. *Acta Petri: Text Übersetzung und Kommentar zu den Actus Vercellenses*. TUGAL 171. Boston: de Gruyter, 2018.
Donahue, John. *Are You the Christ? The Trial Narrative in the Gospel of Mark*. SBLDS 10. Missoula, MT: Society of Biblical Literature, 1973.
Donahue, John. "A Neglected Factor in the Theology of Mark." *JBL* 101 (1982): 562–94.
Donahue, John. *The Theology and Setting of Discipleship in the Gospel of Mark*. Milwaukee, WI: Marquette University Press, 1983.
Donahue, John. *The Gospel in Parable: Metaphor, Narrative, and Theology in the Synoptic Gospels*. Philadelphia: Fortress Press, 1988.
Donahue, John, and Daniel J. Harrington. *The Gospel of Mark*. SPS. Collegeville, PA: Liturgical Press, 2002.
Dorion, Louis-André. "Xenophon and Greek Philosophy." Pages 37–56 in *The Cambridge Companion to Xenophon*. Edited by Michael A. Flowers. Cambridge: Cambridge University Press, 2017.
Dormandy, Richard. "The Expulsion of Legion: A Political Reading of Mark 5:1–20." *ExpTim* 111 (2000): 335–7.
Dowd, Sharyn Echols. *Prayer, Power, and the Problem of Suffering: Mark 11:22–25 in the Context of Markan Theology*. SBLDS 105. Atlanta, GA: Scholars Press, 1988.
Dowd, Sharyn Echols, and Elizabeth S. Malbon. "The Significance of Jesus' Death in Mark: Narrative Context and Authorial Audience." *JBL* 125 (2006): 271–97.
Downing, F. G. "A Genre for Q and Socio-Cultural Context for Q: Comparing Sets of Similarities with Sets of Differences." *JSNT* 55 (1994): 3–26.
Draper, Jonathan A. "'You Shall Not Give What is Holy to the Dogs' (*Didache* 9.5): The Attitude of the *Didache* to the Gentiles." Pages 242–58 in *Attitudes to Gentiles in Ancient Judaism and Early Christianity*. Edited by David C. Sim and James S. McLaren. LNTS 499. New York: Bloomsbury/T&T Clark, 2013.
Duff, Tim. *Plutarch's Lives: Exploring Virtue and Vice*. Oxford: Clarendon Press, 1999.
Duling, Dennis C. "Kinship, Genealogy, and Fictive Kinship in the Mediterranean Cultureand in the Matthean Gospel." Pages 195–219 in *Exploring Biblical Kinship: Festschrift in Honor of John J. Pilch*. Edited by Joan C. Campbell and Patrick J. Hartin. CBQMS 55. Washington, DC: Catholic Biblical Association of America, 2016.
Dunn, James. *Jesus Remembered: Christianity in the Making*. Grand Rapids, MI: Eerdmans, 2003.
Dupont, Anthony. "The Prayer Theme in Augustine's *Sermons ad Populum* at the Time of the Pelagian Controversy: A Pastoral Treatment of a Focal Point of his Doctrine of Grace." *ZAC* 14 (2010): 379–408.
Eck, Ernest van. "Mission, Identity, and Ethics in Mark: Jesus, the Patron for Outsiders." Pages 101–32 in *Sensitivity Towards Outsiders: Exploring the Dynamic Relationship between Mission and Ethics in the New Testament and Early Christianity*. Edited by Jacobus Kok, Tobias Nicklas, Dieter T. Roth, and Christopher M. Hays. WUNT 2.364. Tübingen: Mohr Siebeck, 2014.

Eckstein, Arthur M. *Moral Vision in the Histories of Polybius*. HCS 6. Berkeley: University of California Press, 1995.

Edwards, James R. "Markan Sandwiches: The Significance of Interpolations in Markan Narratives." *NovT* 31 (1989): 193–216.

Edwards, Richard A. "A New Approach to the Gospel of Mark." *LQ* 22 (1970): 333–5.

Egger, Wilhelm. *Frohbotschaft und Lehre: Die Sammelberichte des Wirkens Jesu im Markusevangelium*. FTS 19. Frankfurt: Josef Knecht, 1976.

Ehrman, Bart D., ed. *The Apostolic Fathers*. 2 vols. LCL. Cambridge, MA: Harvard University Press, 2003.

Elder, Nicholas. "Of Porcine and Polluted Spirits: Reading the Gerasene Demoniac (Mark 5:1–20) with the Book of Watchers (1 Enoch 1–36)." *CBQ* 78 (2016): 430–46.

Elmer, Ian J. "Fishing the Other Side: The Gentile Mission in Mark's Gospel." Pages 154–72 in *Attitudes to Gentiles in Ancient Judaism and Early Christianity*. Edited by David C. Sim and James S. McLaren. LNTS 499. New York: Bloomsbury/T&T Clark, 2013.

Emadi, Samuel. "Intertextuality in New Testament Scholarship: Significance, Criteria, and Intertextual Reading." *CBR* 14 (2015): 8–23.

Epictetus. *Discourses, Books 1–2*. Translated by W. A. Oldfather. LCL 131. Cambridge, MA: Harvard University Press, 2014.

Feldman, Louis H. *Josephus's Interpretation of the Bible*. Berkeley: University of California Press, 1998.

Feldman, Louis H. *Flavius Josephus: Translation and Commentary, Volume 3: Judean Antiquities 1–4*. Edited by Steve Mason. Boston: Brill, 2000.

Feldman, Louis H. *Philo's Portrayal of Moses in the Context of Ancient Judaism*. CJA 15. Notre Dame, IN: University of Notre Dame Press, 2007.

Fiorenza, Elizabeth Schlüsser *In Memory of Her: A Feminist Theological Reconstruction of Christian Origins*. New York: Crossroad, 1994.

Fleddermann, Harry. "The Discipleship Discourse (Mark 9:33–50)." *CBQ* 43 (1981): 57–75.

Flew, R. Newton. *Jesus and His Way: A Study of the Ethics of the New Testament*. London: Epworth Press, 1963.

Flowers, Michael A. "Introduction." Pages 1–12 in *The Cambridge Companion to Xenophon*. Edited by Michael A. Flowers. Cambridge: Cambridge University Press, 2017.

Fonrobert, Charlotte. "The Woman with a Blood-Flow (Mark 5.24–34) Revisited: Menstrual Laws and Jewish Culture in Christian Feminist Hermeneutics." Pages 121–40 in *Early Christian Interpretations of the Scriptures of Israel: Investigations and Proposals*. Edited by Craig A. Evans and James A. Sanders. JSNTSup 148. Sheffield: Sheffield Academic Press, 1997.

Foster, Paul. "Why Did Matthew Get the Shema Wrong? A Study of Matthew 22:37." *JBL* 122 (2003): 309–33.

Fornara, Charles W. *The Nature of History in Ancient Greece and Rome*. Berkeley: University of California Press, 1983.

Fortenbaugh, William W. "Biography and the Aristotelian Peripatos." Pages 45–78 in *Die griechische Biographie in hellenistischer Zeit: Akten des internationalen Kongresses vom 26–29. Juli 2006 Würzburg*. Edited by Michael Erler and Stefan Schorn. BzA 245. New York: Walter de Gruyter, 2007.

Fowler, Robert M. *Let the Reader Understand*. Minneapolis, MN: Fortress Press, 1991.

France, R. T. *The Gospel of Mark: A Commentary on the Greek Text*. NIGNTC. Grand Rapids, MI: Eerdmans, 2002.

Frazier, Françoise. *Histoire et Morales dans les Vies parallèles de Plutarque*. 2nd ed. CEASG 152. Paris: Les Belles Lettres, 2016.

Fredriksen, Paula. *Paul: The Pagan's Apostle*. New Haven, CT: Yale University Press, 2017.

Freyne, Seán. "Early Christian Imagination and the Gospels." Pages 2–12 in *The Earliest Gospels: The Origins and Transmission of the Earliest Christian Gospels, the Contributions of the Chester Beatty Gospel Codex P⁴⁵*. Edited by Charles Horton. JSNTSup 258. New York: T&T Clark, 2004.

Freyne, Seán. "Mark's Gospel and Ancient Biography." Pages 63–75 in *The Limits of Ancient Biography*. Edited by Brian McGing and Judith Mossman. Swansea: Classical Press of Wales, 2006.

Freyne, Seán. "In Search of Identity: Narrativity, Discipleship, and Moral Agency." Pages 67–85 in *Moral Language in the New Testament, Vol. II: The Interrelatedness of Language and Ethics in Early Christian Writings*. Edited by Ruben Zimmerman and Jan G. van derWatt. WUNT 2.296. Tübingen: Mohr Siebeck, 2010.

Frickenschmidt, Dirk. *Evangelium als Biographie: Die vier Evangelien im Rahmen antiker Erzählkunst*. TANZ 22. Tübingen: Francke, 1997.

Fuller, R. H. *The Mission and Achievement of Jesus: An Examination of the Presuppositions of New Testament Theology*. SBT 12. London: SCM Press, 1954.

Furnish, Victor Paul. *The Love Command in the New Testament*. Nashville, TN: Abingdon Press, 1972.

Gager, John. *Moses in Greco-Roman Paganism*. Nashville, TN: Abingdon Press, 1972.

Gager, John. *Kingdom and Community: The Social World of Early Christianity*. Englewood Cliffs, NJ: Prentice-Hall, 1975.

Galen. *Quod optimus medicus sit quoque philosophus*. Pages 53–63 in vol. 1 of *Claudii Galeni Opera Omnia*. Edited by K. G. Kühn. Leipzig: Knobloch, 1821.

Galen. *De placitis Hippocratis et Platonis*. Pages 720–805 in vol. 5 of *Claudii Galeni Opera Omnia*. Edited by K. G. Kühn. Leipzig: Knobloch, 1823.

Garrett, Susan R. *The Temptations of Jesus in Mark's Gospel*. Grand Rapids, MI: Eerdmans, 1998.

Garroway, Joshua. "The Invasion of a Mustard Seed: A Reading of Mark 5.1–20." *JSNT* 32 (2009): 57–75.

Gaventa, Beverly R. "Reading Romans 13 with Simone Weil: Toward a More Generous Hermeneutic." *JBL* 136 (2017): 7–22.

Gentili, Bruno, and Giovanni Cerri. *History and Biography in Ancient Thought*. LSCP 20. Amsterdam: J. C. Gieben, 1988.

Gerhardsson, Birger. *The Testing of God's Son (Matt 4:1–11 & Par): An Analysis of Early Christian Midrash*. CBNTS 2. Lund: Gleerup, 1966.

Gibson, Jeffrey B. "Jesus' Wilderness Temptation according to Mark." *JSNT* 53 (1994): 3–34.

Gibson, Jeffrey B. *The Temptations of Jesus in Early Christianity*. JSNTSup 112. Sheffield: Sheffield Academic Press, 1995.

Gnilka, Joachim. *Das Evangelium nach Markus*. 2 vols. EKK 2. Zürich: Benziger; Neukirchen-Vluyn: Neukirchener Verlag, 1978–9.

Goarzin, Moël. "Presenting a Practical Way of Life through Biographical Discourse: The Examples of Gregory of Nyssa and Marinus." Pages 115–29 in *Tradition and Transformation: Dissent and Consent in the Mediterranean: Proceedings of the 3rd CEMS International Graduate Conference*. Kiel: Solivagus-Verlag, 2016.

Goodacre, Mark. *The Case against Q: Studies in Markan Priority and the Synoptic Problem*. Harrisburg, PA: Trinity Press International, 2002.

Goodenough, Erwin R. "Philo's Exposition of the Law and His De Vita Mosis." *HTR* 26 (1933): 109–25.
Gosnell, Peter W. *The Ethical Vision of the Bible: Learning Good From Knowing God*. Downers Grove, IL: InterVarsity Press Academic, 2014.
Goulder, Michael D. "Those Outside (Mk 4:10–12)." *NovT* 33 (1991): 289–302.
Gray, Vivienne J. *Xenophon's Mirror of Princes: Reading the Reflections*. Oxford: Oxford University Press, 2011.
Guelich, Robert A. "'The Beginning of the Gospel': Mark 1:1–15." *BR* 27 (1982): 5–15.
Gundry, Judith M. "Children in the Gospel of Mark, with Special Attention to Jesus' Blessing of the Children (Mark 10:13-16) and the Purpose of Mark." Pages 143–76 in *The Child in the Bible*. Edited by Marcia J. Bunge, Terence E. Fretheim, and Beverly R. Gaventa. Grand Rapids, MI: Eerdmans, 2008.
Gundry, Robert H. *Mark: A Commentary on His Apology for the Cross*. Grand Rapids, MI: Eerdmans, 1993.
Gundry, Robert H. *The Old Is Better: New Testament Essays in Support of Traditional Interpretations*. WUNT 178. Tübingen: Mohr Siebeck, 2005.
Gushee, David P., and Glen H. Stassen. *Kingdom Ethics: Following Jesus in Contemporary Context*. 2nd ed. Grand Rapids, MI: Eerdmans, 2016.
Gustafson, James M. *Christ and the Moral Life*. Chicago: University of Chicago Press, 1968.
Guthrie, Donald. *New Testament Theology*. Downers Grove, IL: InterVarsity Press, 1981.
Haber, Susan. "A Woman's Touch: Feminist Encounters with the Hemorrhaging Woman in Mark 5.24–34." *JSNT* 26, no. 2 (2003): 171–92.
Hadas, Moses, and Morton Smith. *Heroes and Gods: Spiritual Biographies in Antiquity*. RP 13. New York: Harper & Row, 1965.
Hadas-Lebel, Mireille. *Philo of Alexandria A Thinker in the Jewish Diaspora*. Translated by Robyn Fréchet. SPA 7. Boston: Brill, 2012.
Hägg, Thomas. *The Art of Biography in Antiquity*. New York: Cambridge University Press, 2012.
Hamerton-Kelly, Robert G. *The Gospel and the Sacred: Poetics of Violence in Mark*. Minneapolis, MN: Fortress Press, 1994.
Hamori, Esther J. *Women's Divination in Biblical Literature: Prophecy, Necromancy, and Other Arts of Knowledge*. AYBRL. New Haven, CT: Yale University Press, 2015.
Hanson, James S. *The Endangered Promises: Conflict in Mark*. SBLDS 171. Atlanta, GA: Society of Biblical Literature, 2000.
Hare, Douglas R. A. *The Son of Man Tradition*. Minneapolis, MN: Fortress Press, 1990.
Hare, Douglas R. A. *Mark*. Louisville, KY: Westminster John Knox Press, 1996.
Harnack, Adolf von. *Sokrates und die alte Kirche*. Berlin: G. Schade, 1900.
Harrill, J. Albert. "Paul and the Slave Self." Pages 51–69 in *Religion and the Self in Antiquity*. Edited by David Brakke, Michael L. Satlow, and Steven Weitzman. Bloomington: Indiana University Press, 2005.
Harrington, Daniel J., and James F. Keenan. *Jesus and Virtue Ethics: Building Bridges between New Testament Studies and Moral Theology*. Chicago: Sheed & Ward, 2002.
Hart, J. H. A. "Corban." *JQR* 19 (1907): 615–50.
Hatina, Thomas. *In Search of a Context: The Function of Scripture in Mark's Narrative*. JSNTSup232. New York: Sheffield Academic Press, 2002.

Hauerwas, Stanley. *A Community of Character: Toward a Constructive Social Ethic*. Notre Dame, IN: University of Notre Dame Press, 1981.

Hauw, Andreas. *The Function of Exorcism Stories in Mark's Gospel*. Eugene, OR: Wipf and Stock, 2019.

Hayes, Christine E. *Gentile Impurities and Jewish Identities: Intermarriage and Conversion from the Bible to the Talmud*. New York: Oxford University Press, 2002.

Hays, Richard B. *The Moral Vision of the New Testament: Community, Cross, New Creation: A Contemporary Introduction to New Testament Ethics*. San Francisco: HarperSanFrancisco, 1996.

Hedrick, Charles W. "The Role of 'Summary Statements' in the Composition of Mark: A Dialog with Karl Schmidt and Norman Perrin." *NovT* 26 (1984): 289–311.

Hellerman, Joseph H. *The Ancient Church as Family*. Minneapolis, MN: Fortress Press, 2001.

Henderson, Ian. "'Salted with Fire' (Mark 9:42–50): Style, Oracles and (Socio)Rhetorical Gospel Criticism." *JSNT* 80 (2000): 44–65.

Henderson, Suzanne Watts. *Christology and Discipleship in the Gospel of Mark*. New York: Cambridge University Press, 2006.

Hengel, Martin. *The Charismatic Leader and His Followers*. Translated by James Greig. New York: Crossroad, 1981.

Hengel, Martin. *Studies in the Gospel of Mark*. Philadelphia: Fortress Press, 1985.

Hengel, Martin, and R. Hengel. "Die Heilungen Jesu und medizinische Denken." Pages 338–74 in *Der Wunderbegriff im Neuen Testament*. Edited by A. Suhl. Darmstadt: Wissenschaftliche Buchgesellschaft, 1959.

Heron, Alasdair. "The Two Pseudo-Athanasian Dialogues against the Anomoeans." *JTR* 24 (1973): 101–22.

Hicks, Richard. "Markan Discipleship according to Malachi: The Significance of μὴἀποστερήσῃς in the Story of the Rich Man (Mark 10:17–22)." *JBL* 132 (2013): 179–99.

Hidalgo, Esteban. "A Redaction-Critical Study on Philo's *On the Life of Moses*, Book One." Pages 277–300 in *Biographies and Jesus: What Does It Mean for the Gospels to Be Biographies?* Edited by Craig S. Keener and Edward T. Wright. Lexington, KY: Emeth Press, 2016.

Higgins, A. J. B. *Jesus and the Son of Man*. London: Lutterworth Press, 1964.

Hill, Andrew E. *Malachi: A New Translation with Introduction and Commentary*. AB 25D. New York: Doubleday, 1998.

Hodge, Caroline Johnson. *If Sons, Then Heirs: A Study of Kinship and Ethnicity in the Letters of Paul*. New York: Oxford University Press, 2007.

Hoffman, Paul, and Volker Eid. *Jesus von Nazareth und eine christliche Moral*. QD 66. Freiburg: Herder, 1975.

Hooker, Morna. *The Son of Man in Mark: A Study of the Background of the Term "Son of Man" and Its Use in St. Mark's Gospel*. Montreal: McGill University Press, 1967.

Hooker, Morna. *The Message of Mark*. London: Epworth Press, 1983.

Hooker, Morna. *The Gospel According to Mark*. BNTC. London: A & C Black, 1991.

Horrell, David G. "Whither Social-Scientific Approaches to the New Testament? Reflectionson Contested Methodologies and the Future." Pages 6–20 in *After the First Urban Christians: The Social-Scientific Study of Pauline Christianity Twenty-Five Years Later*. Edited by Todd D. Still and David G. Horrell. New York: Continuum, 2009.

Horsley, Richard. *Jesus and the Powers: Conflict, Covenant, and the Hope of the Poor*. Minneapolis, MN: Fortress Press, 2010.

Horsley, Richard. *Sociology and the Jesus Movement*. New York: Crossroad, 1989.
Horstmann, Maria. *Studien zur markinischen Christologie. Mk 8,27–9,13 als Zugang zum Christusbild des zweiten Evangeliums*. NA 6. Münster: Verlag Aschendorff, 1969.
Houlden, J. L. *Ethics and the New Testament*. Harmondsworth: Penguin, 1973.
Hultgren, Arland. *The Parables of Jesus: A Commentary*. Grand Rapids, MI: Eerdmans, 2000.
Hurtado, Larry. *God in New Testament Theology*. LBT. Nashville, TN: Abingdon Press, 2010.
Hurtado, Larry. "The Place of Jesus in Earliest Christian Prayer." Pages 35–56 in *Early Christian Prayer and Identity Formation*. Edited by Reidar Hvalvik and Karl Olav Sandnes. WUNT 336. Tübingen: Mohr Siebeck, 2014.
Husbands, Mark Anthony. "Barth's Ethics of Prayer: A Study in Moral Ontology and Action." PhD diss. Toronto: University of St. Michael's College, 2005.
Iersel, Bas van. *Reading Mark*. Translated by W. H. Bisscheroux. Edinburgh: T&T Clark, 1989.
Inwood, Brad. *Ethics and Human Action in Early Stoicism*. New York: Oxford University Press, 1985.
Iverson, Kelly R. *Gentiles in the Gospel of Mark: "Even the Dogs Under the Table Eat the Children's Crumbs."* LNTS 339. New York: T&T Clark, 2007.
Jacob of Sarug. *Jacob of Sarug's Homilies on Jesus' Temptation*. Edited and translated by Adam Carter McCollum. TCLA 38. Piscataway, NJ: Gorgias Press, 2014.
Jacoby, D. Hermann. *Neutestamentliche Ethik*. Königsberg: Thomas & Oppermann, 1899.
James, William. *The Will to Believe and Other Essays in Popular Philosophy*. Edited by Frederick H. Burkhardt, F. Bowers, and I. Skrupskelis. Cambridge, MA: Harvard University Press, 1979.
Jedan, Christoph. *Stoic Virtues: Chrysippus and the Religious Character of Stoic Ethics*. CSAP. New York: Continuum International, 2009.
Jeremias, Joachim. *Jesus' Promise to the Nations: The Franz Delitzsch Lectures for 1953*. Translated by S. H. Hooke. SBT 24. London: SCM Press, 1958.
Jeremias, Joachim. *The Problem of the Historical Jesus*. Philadelphia: Fortress Press, 1964.
Jeremias, Joachim. *The Prayers of Jesus*. London: S.C.M. Press, 1967.
Jeremias, Joachim. *Neutestamentliche Theologie. Erster Teil Die Verkündigung Jesu*. Gütersloh: Gütersloher Verlagshaus, 1971.
Jeremias, Joachim. *Parables of Jesus*. 2nd ed. New York: Charles Scribner's Sons, 1972.
Johnson, David M. "Aristippus at the Crossroads: The Politics of Pleasure in Xenophon's *Memorabilia*." *Polis* 26 (2009): 204–22.
Johnson, Luke Timothy. "The Jesus of the Gospels and Philosophy." Pages 63–83 in *Jesus and Philosophy: New Essays*. Edited by P. K. Moser. Cambridge: Cambridge University Press, 2009.
Johnson, Nathan C. "Anger Issues: Mark 1.41 in Ephrem the Syrian, the Old Latin Gospels and Codex Bezae." *NTS* 63 (2017): 183–202.
Johnson, Sherman E. *A Commentary on the Gospel According to St. Mark*. BNTC. 2nd ed. London: A & C Black, 1972.
Jones, Christopher P. "Introduction." Pages 1–30 in *Apollonius of Tyana, Volume I: Life of Apollonius of Tyana, Books 1–4*. LCL 16. Cambridge, MA: Harvard University Press, 2005.
Jonge, Marinus de. *The Testaments of the Twelve Patriarchs: A Critical Edition of the Greek Text*. PVTG 1.2. Leiden: Brill, 1978.

Jordan, David. "Two Papyri with Formulae for Divination." Pages 25–36 in *Magic and Ritual in the Ancient World*. Edited by Paul Mirecki and Marvin Meyer. RGRW 141. Boston: Brill, 2002.

Jouanna, Jacques. *Greek Medicine from Hippocrates to Galen*. Translation by Neil Allies. Edited by Philip van der Eijk. SAM 40. Boston: Brill, 2012.

Juel, Donald H. *A Master of Surprise: Mark Interpreted*. Minneapolis, MN: Fortress Press, 1994.

Kähler, Martin. *Der sogenannte historische Jesus und der geschichtliche, biblische Christus*. Leipzig: Deichert, 1892; repr., Berlin: Berlin University Press, 2013.

Käsemann, Ernst. *New Testament Questions of Today*. Translated by W. J. Montague. London: SCM Press, 1969.

Kazen, Thomas. *Jesus and Purity Halakhah: Was Jesus Indifferent to Impurity?* Rev. ed. CBNTS 38. Winona Lake, IN: Eisenbrauns, 2010.

Keck, Leander. "The Introduction to Mark's Gospel." *NTS* 12 (1956–66): 352–70.

Keck, Leander. "The Accountable Self." Pages 1–13 in *Theology and Ethics in Paul and His Interpreters: Essays in Honor of Victor Paul Furnish*. Edited by Eugene H. Lovering Jr. and Jerry L. Sumney. Nashville, TN: Abingdon Press, 1996.

Keck, Leander. "Rethinking 'New Testament Ethics.'" *JBL* 115 (1996): 3–16.

Keck, Leander. *Who Is Jesus? History in the Perfect Tense*. Minneapolis, MN: Fortress Press, 2001.

Kee, Howard Clark. "Aretalogy and Gospel." *JBL* 92 (1972): 402–22.

Kee, Howard Clark. *Community of the New Age: Studies in Mark's Gospel*. Philadelphia: Westminster Press, 1977.

Keener, Craig S., and Edward T. Wright, eds. *Biographies and Jesus: What Does It Mean for the Gospels to Be Biographies?* Lexington, KY: Emeth Press, 2016.

Keerankeri, George. *The Love Commandment in Mark: An Exegetico-Theological Study of Mk 12,28–34*. Analecta Biblica 150. Roma: Editrice Pontificio Istituto Biblico, 2003.

Kelber, Werner H. "Mark 14:32–42: Gethsemane: Passion Christology and Discipleship Failure." *ZNW* 63 (1972): 166–87.

Kelber, Werner H. *The Kingdom in Mark: A New Place and a New Time*. Philadelphia: Fortress Press, 1974.

Kelber, Werner H. *Mark's Story of Jesus*. Philadelphia: Fortress Press, 1979.

Kelhoffer, James A. "'How Soon a Book' Revisited: EUANGELION as a Reference to 'Gospel' Materials in the First Half of the Second Century." *ZNW* 95 (2004): 1–34.

Kellenbach, Katharina von. *Anti-Judaism in Feminist Religious Writings*. AARCC 1. Atlanta, GA: Scholars Press, 1994.

Kelly, Henry A. "The Devil in the Desert." *CBQ* 26 (1964): 190–220.

Kemezis, Adam M. *Greek Narratives of the Roman Empire under the Severans: Cassius Dio, Philostratus and Herodian*. GCRM. New York: Cambridge University Press, 2014.

Kennedy, George A. *Classical Rhetoric and Its Christian and Secular Tradition from Ancient to Modern Times*. Chapel Hill: University of North Carolina Press, 1980.

Kennedy, George A. *A New History of Classic Rhetoric*. Princeton, NJ: Princeton University Press,1994.

Kermode, Frank. *The Genesis of Secrecy: On the Interpretation of Narrative*. Cambridge, MA: Harvard University Press, 1979.

Kierkegaard, Søren. *Works of Love*. Translated by Howard and Edna Hong. New York: Harper Perennial, 2009.

Kingsbury, Jack D. *The Christology of Mark's Gospel*. Philadelphia: Fortress Press, 1983.

Kirk, J. R. Daniel. "Time for Figs, Temple Destruction, and Houses of Prayer in Mark 11:12–25." *CBQ* 74 (2012): 510–28.

Klawans, Jonathan. *Impurity and Sin in Ancient Judaism*. New York: Oxford University Press, 2000.

Klutz, Todd E. *Rewriting the Testament of Solomon: Tradition, Conflict and Identity in a Late Antique Pseudepigraphon*. LSTS 53. New York: T&T Clark, 2005.

Knigge, Heinz-Dieter. "The Meaning of Mark: The Exegesis of the Second Gospel." *Interpretation* 22 (1968): 53–70.

Koester, Helmut. "Mark 9:43–47 and Quintilian 8.3.75." *HTR* 71 (1978): 151–3.

Kofsky, Aryeh. *Eusebius of Caesarea Against Paganism*. JCPS 3. Boston: Brill, 2000.

Korn, Joachim H. ΠΕΙΡΑΣΜΟΣ: *die Versuchung des Gläubigen in der griechischen Bibel*. BWANT 72. Stuttgart: Kohlhammer, 1937.

Koskenniemi, Erkki. *Apollonius von Tyana in der neutestamentlichen Exegese: Forschungsbericht und Weiterführung der Diskussion*. WUNT 2.61. Tübingen: J. C. B. Mohr, 1994.

Koskenniemi, Erkki. "Apollonius of Tyana: A Typical ΘΕΙΟΣ ΑΝΗΡ?" *JBL* 117 (1998): 455–67.

Koskenniemi, Erkki. "The Function of the Miracle Stories in Philostratus' *Vita Apollonii Tyanensis*." Pages 70–83 in *Wonders Never Cease: The Purpose of Narrating Miracle Stories in the New Testament and Its Religious Environment*. Edited by M. Labahn and B. J. LietaertPeerbolte. LNTS 288. New York: T&T Clark, 2006.

Koskenniemi, Erkki. "The Philostratean Apollonius as a Teacher." Pages 321–34 in *Theios Sophistes: Essays on Flavius Philostratus' Vita Apollonii*. Edited by K. Demoen and D. Praet. MS 305. Boston: Brill, 2009.

Kotansky, Roy. "An Early Christian Gold Lamella for Headache." Pages 37–46 in *Magic and Ritual in the Ancient World*. Edited by Paul Mirecki and Marvin Meyer. RGRW 141. Boston: Brill, 2002.

Kümmel, Werner G. *Promise and Fulfilment: The Eschatological Message of Jesus*. Translated by Dorothea M. Barton. SBT 23. London: SCM Press, 1957.

Kurke, Leslie. *Aesopic Conversations: Popular Tradition, Cultural Dialogue, and the Invention of Greek Prose*. Princeton, NJ: Princeton University Press, 2011.

Ladd, George E. *A Theology of the New Testament*. Grand Rapids, MI: Eerdmans, 1974.

LaFosse, Mona Tokarek. "Women, Children, and House Churches." Pages 385–405 in *The Early Christian World*. 2nd ed. Edited by Philip F. Esler. New York: Routledge, 2017.

Lamb, William R. S., ed. and trans. *The Catena in Marcum: A Byzantine Anthology of Early Commentary on Mark*. Boston: Brill, 2012.

Lampe, Kurt. *The Birth of Hedonism: The Cyrenaic Philosophers and Pleasure as a Way of Life*. Princeton, NJ: Princeton University Press, 2015.

Lane, William L. *The Gospel According to Mark: The English Text with Introduction, Exposition and Notes*. Grand Rapids, MI: Eerdmans, 1974.

Lanigan, R. "From Enthymeme to Abduction: The Classical Law of Logic and thePostmodern Rule of Rhetoric." Pages 49–70 in *Recovering Pragmatism's Voice: TheClassical Tradition, Rorty, and the Philosophy of Communication*. Edited by L. Langsdorf and Andrew R. Smith. Albany: SUNY Press, 1995.

Larsen, Matthew D. C. "Accidental Publication, Unfinished Texts and the Traditional Goalsof New Testament Textual Criticism." *JSNT* 39 (2017): 362–87.

Layton, Richard. *Didymus the Blind and His Circle in Late-Antique Alexandria: Virtue and Narrative in Biblical Scholarship*. Urbana: University of Illinois Press, 2004.

Leander, Hans. *Discourses of Empire: The Gospel of Mark from a Postcolonial Perspective*. SS 71. Atlanta, GA: Society of Biblical Literature, 2013.
Leo, Friedrich. *Die griechisch-römische Biographie nach ihrer literarischen Form*. Leipzig: Teubner, 1901.
Licona, Michael R. *Why Are There Differences in the Gospels? What We Can Learn from Ancient Biography*. Oxford: Oxford University Press, 2017.
Liew, Tat-siong Benny. *Politics of Parousia: Reading Mark Inter(con)textuality*. BIS 42. Boston: Brill, 1999.
Lightfoot, John. *Horae Hebraicae et Talmudicae: Hebrew and Talmudic Exercitations upon the Gospels, the Acts, Some Chapters of St. Paul's Epistle to the Romans, and the First Epistle to the Corinthians*. 4 vols. Oxford: Oxford University Press, 1859.
Lindsay, Dennis R. *Josephus and Faith: Πίστις and Πιστεύειν as Faith Terminology in the Writings of Flavius Josephus and in the New Testament*. AGAJU 19. New York: Brill, 1993.
Loader, William. *Jesus' Attitude towards the Law: A Study of the Gospels*. WUNT 2.97. Tübingen: Mohr Siebeck, 1997.
Lohfink, Gerhard. *Jesus and Community: The Social Dimensions of Christian Faith*. Translated by John P. Galvin. Philadelphia: Fortress Press, 1984.
Lohse, Eduard. *Theological Ethics of the New Testament*. Translated by Eugene Boring. Minneapolis, MN: Fortress Press, 1991.
Löhr, Hermut. "The Decalogue in the New Testament Apocrypha: A Preliminary Overview and Some Examples." Pages 57–71 in *The Decalogue and its Cultural Influence*. Edited by Dominik Markl. HBM 58. Sheffield: Sheffield Phoenix Press, 2013.
Lu, Houliang. *Xenophon's Theory of Moral Education*. Newcastle: Cambridge Scholars, 2015.
Lucian. *Volume I: Phalaris. Hippias or The Bath. Dionysus. Heracles. Amber or The Swans. The Fly. Nigrinus. Demonax. The Hall. My Native Land. Octogenarians. A True Story. Slander. The Consonants at Law. The Carousal (Symposium) or The Lapiths*. Translated by A. M. Harmon. LCL 14. Cambridge, MA: Harvard University Press, 1913.
Lundbom, Jack R. *Jeremiah 1–20: A New Translation with Introduction and Commentary*. AB 21A. New York: Doubleday, 1999.
Luther, Martin. *Luther's Works: Volume 12, Selected Psalms I*. Edited by Jaroslav Pelikan. Saint Louis, MO: Concordia, 1955.
Lyons, William John. "On the Life and Death of Joseph of Arimathea." *JSHJ* 2 (2004): 29–53.
Macaskill, Grant. "Apocalypse and the Gospel of Mark." Pages 53–78 in *The Jewish Apocalyptic Tradition and the Shaping of New Testament Thought*. Edited by Benjamin E. Reynolds and Loren T. Stuckenbruck. Minneapolis, MN: Fortress Press, 2017.
Maccoby, Hyam. *Ritual and Morality: The Ritual Purity System and Its Place in Judaism*. New York: Cambridge University Press, 1999.
MacDonald, Dennis R. *My Turn: A Critique of Critics of "Mimesis Criticism."* OPIAC 53. Claremont, CA: Institute for Antiquity and Christianity, 2009.
MacDonald, Dennis R. *The Homeric Epics and the Gospel of Mark*. New Haven, CT: Yale University Press, 2000.
MacIntyre, Alasdair. *After Virtue: A Study in Moral Theory*. 3rd ed. Notre Dame, IN: University of Notre Dame Press, 2007.
Mack, Burton. *Myth of Innocence: Mark and Christian Origins*. Philadelphia: Fortress Press, 1988.

Macleod, M. D. *Xenophon: Apology and Memorabilia I: With Introduction, Translation, and Commentary*. Oxford: Oxbow Books, 2008.
Madigan, Kevin. "Ancient and High Medieval Interpretations of Jesus in Gethsemane: Some Reflections on Tradition and Continuity in Christian Thought." *HTR* 88 (1995): 157–73.
Maimonides. "Eight Chapters." Pages 59–104 in *Ethical Writings of Maimonides*. Translated by Raymond L. Weiss and Charles E. Butterworth. New York: New York University Press, 1975.
Malbon, Elizabeth Struthers. "Fallible Followers: Women and Men in the Gospel of Mark." *Semeia* 23 (1983): 29–48.
Malbon, Elizabeth Struthers. *Narrative Space and Mythic Meaning in Mark*. BS 13. Sheffield: JSOT Press, 1991.
Malbon, Elizabeth Struthers. "The Major Importance of Minor Characters in Mark." Pages 58–86 in *The New Literary Criticism and the New Testament*. Edited by Elizabeth Struthers Malbon and Edgar V. McKnight. JSNTSup 109. Sheffield: Sheffield Academic Press, 1994.
Malbon, Elizabeth Struthers. *Mark's Jesus: Characterization as Narrative Christology*. Waco, TX: Baylor University Press, 2009.
Malherbe, Abraham. "Exhortation in First Thessalonians." *NovT* 25 (1983): 238–56.
Malherbe, Abraham. *Moral Exhortations: A Greco-Roman Sourcebook*. Philadelphia: Westminster Press, 1986.
Malherbe, Abraham. *Paul and the Thessalonians: The Philosophic Tradition of Pastoral Care*. Philadelphia: Fortress Press, 1987.
Malina, Bruce J. "Rhetorical Criticism and Social-Scientific Criticism: Why Won't Romanticism Leave Us Alone?" Pages 5–21 in *The Social World of the New Testament: Insights and Models*. Edited by Jerome H. Neyrey and Eric C. Stewart. Peabody, MA: Hendrickson, 2008.
Malina, Bruce J. *The New Testament World: Insights from Cultural Anthropology*. 3rd rev. ed. Louisville, KY: Westminster John Knox Press, 2001.
Mann, C. S. *Mark: A New Translation with Introduction and Commentary*. Garden City, NY: Doubleday, 1986.
Manson, T. W. "The Life of Jesus: Some Tendencies in Present-Day Research." Pages 211–21 in *The Background of the New Testament and Its Eschatology: In Honour of C. H. Dodd*. Edited by W. D Davies and D. Daube. Cambridge: Cambridge University Press, 1956.
Manson, T. W. *The Teachings of Jesus: Studies in Its Form and Content*. 2nd rev. ed. Cambridge: Cambridge University Press, 1967.
Marcus, Joel. *Mark 1–8: A New Translation with Introduction and Commentary*. AB 27. New York: Doubleday, 1999.
Marcus, Joel. *Mark 8–16: A New Translation with Introduction and Commentary*. AB 27A. New Haven, CT: Yale University Press, 2009.
Marcus, Joel. "Mark 4:10–12 and Marcan Epistemology." *JBL* 103 (1984): 560–3.
Marcus, Joel. *The Way of the Lord: Christological Exegesis of the Old Testament in the Gospel of Mark*. Louisville, KY: Westminster John Knox Press, 1992.
Marshall, Christopher D. *Faith as a Theme in Mark's Narrative*. New York: Cambridge University Press, 1989.
Marshall, I. Howard. *New Testament Theology: Many Witnesses, One Gospel*. Downers Grove, IL: InterVarsity Press, 2004.
Marshall, L. H. *The Challenge of New Testament Ethics*. London: Macmillan, 1946.

Martin, Dale. *The Corinthian Body*. New Haven, CT: Yale University Press, 1995.
Martin, Ralph P. *Mark: Evangelist and Theologian*. Exeter: Paternoster Press, 1972.
Martínez, Florentino García, and Eibert J. C. Tigchelaar, eds. *The Dead Sea Scrolls Study Edition: Volume One, 1Q1–4Q273*. Grand Rapids, MI: Eerdmans, 1997
Marxsen, Willi. *Mark the Evangelist: Studies on the Redaction History of the Gospel*. Translated by James Boyce. Nashville, TN: Abingdon Press, 1969.
Marxsen, Willi. *New Testament Foundations for Christian Ethics*. Translated by O. C. Dean Jr. Minneapolis, MN: Fortress Press, 1993.
Mason, Steve. "Introduction to the *Judean Antiquities*." Pages xiii–xxxvi in Feldman, Louis H. *Flavius Josephus: Translation and Commentary, Volume 3: Judean Antiquities 1–4*. Edited by Steve Mason. Boston: Brill, 2000.
Mason, Steve. *Josephus and the New Testament*. 2nd ed. Peabody, MA: Hendrickson, 2003.
Mason, Steve. "'Should Any Wish to Enquire Further' (*Ant.* 1.25): The Aim and Audience of Josephus's *Judean Antiquities/Life*." Pages 64–103 in *Understanding Josephus: Seven Perspectives*. Edited by Steve Mason. JSPSup 32. Sheffield: Sheffield Academic Press, 1998.
Matera, Frank. *The Legacies of Jesus and Paul: New Testament Ethics*. Louisville, KY: Westminster John Knox Press, 1996.
Matheson, George. *Landmarks of New Testament Morality*. London: James Nisbet, 1888.
Mathews, Shailer. *The Social Teaching of Jesus: An Essay in Christian Sociology*. New York: Macmillan, 1897.
McInerney, Joseph J. *The Greatness of Humility: St. Augustine on Moral Excellence*. Eugene, OR: Pickwick, 2016.
McAdon, Brad. *Rhetorical Mimesis and the Mitigation of Early Christian Conflicts: Examining the Influence That Greco-Roman Mimesis May Have in the Composition of Matthew, Luke, and Acts*. Eugene, OR: Pickwick, 2018.
McDonald, J. Ian H. *The Crucible of Christian Morality*. New York: Routledge, 1998.
McGing, B. C. "Philo's Adaption of the Bible in his 'Life of Moses.'" Pages 117–40 in *The Limits of Ancient Biography*. Edited by B. C. McGing and J. Mossman. Swansea: Classical Press of Wales, 2006.
McKeon, Richard. "Literary Criticism and the Concept of Imitation in Antiquity." Pages 147–57 in *Critics and Criticism: Ancient and Modern*. Edited by R. S. Crane. Chicago: University of Chicago Press, 1968.
McQuilkin, Robertson, and Paul Copan. *An Introduction to Biblical Ethics: Walking in the Way of Wisdom*. 3rd ed. Downers Grove, IL: InterVarsity Press Academic, 2014.
McWhirter, Jocelyn. "Messianic Exegesis in Mark 1:2–3." Pages 158–78 in *"What Does the Scripture Say?" Studies in the Function of Scripture in Early Judaism and Christianity, Volume 1: The Synoptic Gospels*. Edited by Craig Evans and H. Daniel Zacharias. LNTS 469. New York: T&T Clark, 2012.
Meeks, Wayne. *Origins of Christian Morality: The First Two Centuries*. New Haven, CT: Yale University Press, 1993.
Meeks, Wayne. "The Ethics of the Fourth Evangelist." Pages 317–26 in *Exploring the Gospel of John: In Honor of D. Moody Smith*. Edited by R. Alan Culpepper and C. Clifton Black. Louisville, KY: Westminster John Knox Press, 1996.
Meeks, Wayne. *The First Urban Christians: The Social World of the Apostle Paul*. New Haven, CT: Yale University Press, 1983.
Meeks, Wayne. *The Moral World of the First Christians*. Philadelphia: Westminster Press, 1986.

Mennen, Inge. "The Image of an Emperor in Trouble: Legitimation and Representation of Power by Caracalla." Pages 253-67 in *The Impacts of Imperial Rome on Religions, Rituals and Religious Life in the Roman Empire*. Edited by L. De Blois, P. Funke, and J. Hahn. Impact of Empire 5. Boston: Brill, 2006.

Mercedes, Anna. *Power For: Feminism and Christ's Self-Giving*. New York: T&T Clark, 2011.

Metzger, Bruce M. *A Textual Commentary on the Greek New Testament*. 2nd ed. Stuttgart: German Bible Society, 1994.

Meye, Robert P. *Jesus and the Twelve: Discipleship and Revelation in Mark's Gospel*. Grand Rapids, MI: Eerdmans, 1968.

Migliore, Daniel L. "Commanding Grace: Karl Barth's Theological Ethics." Pages 1-25 in *Commanding Grace: Karl Barth's Theological Ethics*. Edited by Daniel L. Migliore. Grand Rapids, MI: Eerdmans, 2010.

Migliore, Daniel L. "Freedom to Pray: Karl Barth's Theology of Prayer." Pages 95-113 in *Prayer*. 50th anniversary ed. Edited by Don E. Saliers. Translated by Sara F. Terrien. Louisville, KY: Westminster John Knox Press, 2002.

Miles, Graeme. "Reforming the Eyes: Interpreters and Interpretation in the Vita Apollonii." Pages 129-60 in *Theios Sophistes: Essays on Flavius Philostratus' Vita Apollonii*. Edited by K. Demoen and D. Praet, MS 305. Boston: Brill, 2009.

Miles, Margaret R. "Achieving the Christian Body: Visual Incentives to Imitations of Christ in the Christian West." Pages 1-23 in *Interpreting Christian Art: Reflections on Christian Art*. Edited by Heidi J. Hornik and Mikeal C. Parsons. Macon, GA: Mercer University Press, 2004.

Miller, Susan. *Women in Mark's Gospel*. JSNTSup 259. New York: T&T Clark, 2004.

Mitchell, Joan L. *Beyond Fear and Silence: A Feminist-Literary Approach to the Gospel of Mark*. New York: Continuum, 2001.

Moloney, Francis J. "The Vocation of the Disciples in the Gospel of Mark." *Salesianum* 43 (1981): 487-516.

Momigliano, Andrew. *The Development of Greek Biography*. Cambridge, MA: Harvard University Press, 1971.

Momigliano, Andrew. *The Development of Greek Biography*. Exp. ed. Cambridge, MA: Harvard University Press, 1993.

Moore, Stephen D. *Empire and Apocalypse: Postcolonialism and the New Testament*. BMW 12. Sheffield: Sheffield Academic Press, 2006.

Moore, Stephen D. "Mark and Empire: 'Zealot' and 'Postcolonial' Readings." Pages 206-23 in *The Postcolonial Biblical Reader*. Edited by R. S. Sugirtharajah. Malden, MA: Blackwell, 2006.

Morgan, Teresa. *Roman Faith and Christian Faith: Pistis and Fides in the Early Roman Empire and Early Churches*. Oxford: Oxford University Press, 2015.

Morris, Leon. *New Testament Theology*. Grand Rapids, MI: Zondervan, 1986.

Morrison, Donald R. "Xenophon's Socrates as Teacher." Pages 195-227 in *Xenophon*. Edited by V. J. Gray. Oxford: Oxford University Press, 2010.

Morrison, Gregg S. *The Turning Point in the Gospel of Mark: A Study in Markan Christology*. Eugene, OR: Pickwick, 2014.

Moses, Robert Ewusie. *Practices of Power: Revisiting the Principalities and Powers in the Pauline Letters*. ES. Minneapolis, MN: Fortress Press, 2014.

Moss, Candida R. "The Man with the Flow of Power: Porous Bodies in Mark 5:25-34." *JBL* 129 (2010): 507-19.

Moyise, Steve. "Deuteronomy in Mark's Gospel." Pages 27–41 in *Deuteronomy in the New Testament*. Edited by Maarten J. J. Menken and Steve Moyise. LNTS 358. New York: T&T Clark, 2008.

Mulhern, J. J. "*Kakia* in Aristotle." Pages 233–54 in *Kakos: Badness and Anti-Value in Classical Antiquity*. Edited by Ineke Sluiter and Ralph M. Rosen. MS 307. Boston: Brill, 2008.

Müller, Ulrich B. "Die christologische Absicht des Markusevangeliums und die Verklärungsgeschichte." *ZNW* 64 (1973): 159–93.

Munro, Winsome. "Women Disciples in Mark?" *CBQ* 44 (1982): 225–41.

Myers, Ched. *Binding the Strong Man: A Political Reading of Mark's Story of Jesus*. 20th anniversary ed. Maryknoll, NY: Orbis Books, 2008.

Myles, Robert J. "The Fetish for a Subversive Jesus." *JSHJ* 14 (2016): 52–70.

Najman, Hindy. *Seconding Sinai: The Development of Mosaic Discourse in Second Temple Judaism*. SJSJ 77. Boston: Brill, 2003.

Naluparayil, Jacob Chacko. *The Identity of Jesus in Mark: An Essay on Narrative Christology*. SBFA 49. Jerusalem: Franciscan Printing Press, 2000.

Nathan, Geoffrey S. *The Family in Late Antiquity: The Rise of Christianity and the Endurance of Tradition*. New York: Routledge, 2000.

Neirynck, Frans, ed. *The Minor Agreements of Matthew and Luke against Mark, with a Cumulative List*. BETL 37. Leuven: Leuven University, 1974.

Niehoff, Maren R. *Philo of Alexandria: An Intellectual Biography*. AYBRL. New Haven, CT: Yale University Press, 2018.

Nietzsche, Friedrich. *On the Advantage and Disadvantage of History for Life*. Translated by Peter Preuss. Cambridge: Hackett, 1980.

Nelson, W. David, trans. *Mekhilta de-Rabbi Shimon bar Yoḥai*. Philadelphia: Jewish Publication Society, 2006.

Nineham, Dennis E. *The Gospel of Saint Mark*. Philadelphia: Westminster Press, 1963.

Neufeld, Dietmar. *Mockery and Secretism in the Social World of Mark's Gospel*. LNTS 503. New York: Bloomsbury T&T Clark, 2014.

O'Brien, Peter T. "Prayer in Luke-Acts." *TynBul* 24 (1973): 111–27.

O'Connor, M. John-Patrick. "The Devil Will Flee: James 4:7, the Jesus Tradition, and the Testaments of the Twelve Patriarchs." *JBL* 138 (2019): 883–97.

O'Connor, M. John-Patrick. "Void of Ethics No More." *CBR* (forthcoming).

O'Donovan, Oliver. "Prayer and Morality in the Sermon on the Mount." *SEC* 22 (2000): 21–33.

Origen. "De engastrimutho." Pages 44–74 in *La maga di Endor: Origene, Eustazio, Gregorio di Nissa*. Edited by Manlio Simonetti. Florence: Nardini, Centro Internazionale del Libro, 1989.

Overbeck, Franz. "Über die Anfänge der patristischen Literatur." *Historische Zeitschrift* 12 (1882): 417–72.

Oyen, Geert van. *Demons and the Devil in Ancient and Medieval Christianity*. VCSup 108. Boston: Brill, 2011.

Pagels, Elaine. "The Social History of Satan, the "Intimate Enemy": A Preliminary Sketch." *HTR* 84 (1991): 105–28.

Pagels, Elaine. "The Social History of Satan, Part II: Satan in the New Testament Gospels." *JAAR* 62 (1994): 17–58.

Painter, John. "When Is a House Not a Home? Disciples and Family in Mark 3.13–35." *NTS* 45 (1999): 498–513.

Palu, Ma'afu. *Jesus and Time: An Interpretation of Mark 1.15*. LNTS 463. New York: T&T Clark, 2012.

Paulus, H. E. G. *Das Leben Jesu als Grundlage einer reinen Geschichte des Urchristentums I*. Heidelberg: C. F. Winter, 1828.

Penner, Ken M. "Philo's Eschatology, Personal and Cosmic." *JSJ* 50 (2019): 383–402.

Penny, Douglas L., and Michael O. Wise. "By the Power of Beelzebub: An Aramaic Incantation Formula from Qumran (4Q560)." *JBL* 113 (1994): 627–50.

Peppard, Michael. "Torah for the Man Who Has Everything: 'Do Not Defraud' in Mark 10:19." *JBL* 134 (2015): 595–604.

Pero, Cheryl. *Liberation from Empire: Demonic Possession and Exorcism in the Gospel of Mark*. Studies in Biblical Literature 150. New York: Peter Lang, 2013.

Perrin, Bernadotte. "Introduction." Pages xi–xix in *Lives, Volume 1: Theseus and Romulus. Lycurgus and Numa. Solon and Publicola*. LCL 46. Cambridge, MA: Harvard University Press, 1914.

Perrin, Norman. "The Wredestrasse Becomes the Hauptstrasse: Reflections on the Reprinting of the Dodd Festschrift." *JR* 46 (1966): 296–300.

Perrin, Norman. "The Creative Use of the Son of Man Traditions by Mark." *USQR* 23 (1968): 357–65.

Perrin, Norman. *What Is Redaction Criticism?* Philadelphia: Fortress Press, 1969.

Perrin, Norman. "The Literary *Gattung* 'Gospel'—Some Observations." *ExpTim* 82 (1970): 4–7.

Perrin, Norman. "The Christology of Mark: A Study in Methodology." *JR* 51 (1971): 173–87.

Perrin, Norman. "Towards an Interpretation of the Gospel of Mark." Pages 1–78 in *Christology and a Modern Pilgrimage: A Discussion with Norman Perrin*. Edited by Hans Dieter Betz. Claremont, CA: New Testament Colloquium, 1971.

Perrin, Norman. *Jesus and the Language of the Kingdom: Symbol and Metaphor in New Testament Interpretation*. Philadelphia: Fortress Press, 1976.

Perrin, Norman, and Dennis C. Duling. *The New Testament: An Introduction*. 2nd ed. New York: Harcourt Brace Jovanovich, 1982.

Pesch, Rudolf. *Naherwartungen: Tradition und Redaktion in Mk 13*. Düsseldorf: Patmos-Verlag, 1968.

Pesch, Rudolf. *Der Besessene von Gerasa: Entstehung und Überlieferung einer Wundergeschichte*. SB 56. Stuttgart: Verlag, 1972.

Petersen, Norman. "Can One Speak of a Gospel Genre?" *Neot* 28 (1994): 137–58.

Petitfils, James M. "A Tale of Two Moseses: Philo's *On the Life of Moses* and Josephus's *Jewish Antiquities* 2–4 in Light of the Roman Discourse of Exemplarity." Pages 153–64 in *Reading and Teaching Ancient Fiction: Jewish, Christian, and Greco-Roman Narratives*. Edited by Sara R. Johnson, Rubén R. Dupertuis, and Christine Shea. WGRWSup 11. Atlanta, GA: SBL Press, 2018.

Petzke, Gerd. *Die Traditionen über Apollonius von Tyana und Das Neue Testament*. SCHNT 1. Leiden: Brill, 1970.

Philo. Translated by F. H. Colson and G. H. Whitaker. 12 vols. LCL. Cambridge, MA: Harvard University Press, 1929–53.

Philostratus. *Apollonius of Tyana, Volume III: Letters of Apollonius. Ancient Testimonia. Eusebius's Reply to Hierocles*. Edited and translated by Christopher P. Jones. LCL 458. Cambridge, MA: Harvard University Press, 2006.

Philostratus. *Life of Apollonius of Tyana*. Edited and translated by Christopher P. Jones. 2 vols. LCL 16–17. Cambridge, MA: Harvard University Press, 2006.

Pincoff, Edmund. "Quandary Ethics." *Mind* 80 (1971): 552–71.
Pitts, Andrew. "The Origins of Greek Mimesis and the Gospel of Mark: Genre as a Potential Constraint in Assessing Markan Imitation." Pages 107–36 in *Ancient Education and Early Christianity*. Edited by Matthew Ryan Hauge and Andrew W. Pitts. LNTS 533. New York: Bloomsbury T&T Clark, 2016.
Pliny the Younger. *Letters and Panegyricus. Volume 1: Letters, Books I–VI*. Translated by Betty Radice. 2 vols. LCL 55. Cambridge, MA: Harvard University Press, 1969.
Plutarch. *Lives, Volume III: Pericles and Fabius Maximus. Nicias and Crassus*. Translated by Bernadotte Perrin. LCL 65. Cambridge, MA: Harvard University Press, 1916.
Plutarch. *Lives, Volume VI: Dion and Brutus. Timoleon and Aemilius Paulus*. Translated by Bernadotte Perrin. LCL 98. Cambridge, MA: Harvard University Press, 1918.
Plutarch. *Lives, Volume VII: Demosthenes and Cicero. Alexander and Caesar*. Translated by Bernadotte Perrin. LCL 99. Cambridge, MA: Harvard University Press, 1919.
Plutarch. *Lives, Volume IX: Demetrius and Anthony. Pyrrhus and Caius Marius*. Translated by Bernadotte Perrin. LCL 101. Cambridge, MA: Harvard University Press, 1920.
Plutarch. *Moralia, Volume VII: On Love of Wealth. On Compliancy. On Envy and Hate. On Praising Oneself Inoffensively. On the Delays of the Divine Vengeance. On Fate. On the Sign of Socrates. On Exile. Consolation to His Wife*. Translated by Phillip H. De Lacy and Benedict Einarson. LCL 405. Cambridge, MA: Harvard University Press, 1959.
Pomeroy, Arthur J., ed. *Arius Didymus: Epitome of Stoic Ethics*. TTGRS 14. Atlanta, GA: Society of Biblical Literature, 1999.
Quesnell, Quentin. *The Mind of Mark: Interpretation and Method through the Exegesis of Mark 6,52*. Analecta biblica 38. Rome: Pontifical Biblical Institute, 1969.
Quintilian. *The Orator's Education, Volume 1: Books 1–2*. Translated by Donald A. Russell. LCL 124. Cambridge, MA: Harvard University Press, 2002
Räisänen, Heikki. "Jesus and the Food Laws: Reflections on Mark 7:15." *JSNT* 16 (1982): 79–100.
Regev, Eyal. "Moral Impurity and the Temple in Early Christianity in Light of Ancient Greek Practice and Qumranic Ideology." *HTR* 97 (2004): 383–411.
Regev, Eyal. *The Temple in Early Christianity: Experiencing the Sacred*. New Haven, CT: Yale University Press, 2019.
Renan, Ernest. *Life of Jesus*. Complete ed. New York: Brentano's, 1863.
Reis, Pamela Tamarkin. "Eating the Blood: Saul and the Witch of Endor." *JSOT* 73 (1997): 3–23.
Reiser, Marius. *Jesus and Judgment: The Eschatological Proclamation in Its Jewish Context*. Translated by Linda M. Maloney. Minneapolis, MN: Fortress Press, 1998.
Rhoads, David. "Review of *Binding the Strong Man* by Ched Myers." *CBQ* 53 (1991): 336–8.
Rhoads, David, Joanna Dewey, and Donald Michie. *Mark as Story: An Introduction to the Narrative of a Gospel*. 3rd ed. Philadelphia: Fortress Press, 2012.
Riches, John K. *Conflicting Mythologies: Identity Formation in the Gospels of Mark and Matthew*. SNTW. Edinburgh: T&T Clark, 2000.
Rietz, Henry W. Morisada. "Interpreting Traditions: The Qumran Community and the Gospels." *Perspectives in Religious Studies* 37 (2010): 391–406.
Rohrbaugh, Richard L. "The Social Location of the Markan Audience." Pages 143–62 in *The Social World of the New Testament: Insights and Models*. Edited by Jerome H. Neyrey and Eric C. Stewart. Peabody, MA: Hendrickson, 2008.
Rowland, Christopher. *The Open Heaven: A Study of Apocalyptic in Judaism and Early Christianity*. New York: Crossroad, 1982.

Rindge, Matthew S. "Reconfiguring the Akedah and Recasting God: Lament and Divine Abandonment in Mark." *JBL* 131 (2012): 755-74.
Robbins, Vernon K. *Jesus the Teacher: A Socio-Rhetorical Interpretation of Mark*. Minneapolis, MN: Fortress Press, 1992.
Robinson, James M. *The Problem of History in Mark*. SBT. London: SCM Press, 1962.
Robinson, James M., ed. *The Nag Hammadi Library in English*. 4th rev. ed. New York: Brill, 1996.
Robinson, James M., and Helmut Koester. *Trajectories through Early Christianity*. Philadelphia: Fortress Press, 1971.
Rosen-Zvi, Ishay. *Demonic Desires: Yetzer Hara and the Problem of Evil in Late Antiquity*. Divinations. Philadelphia: University of Pennsylvania Press, 2011.
Rosler, Andrés. *Political Authority and Obligation in Aristotle*. Oxford: Clarendon Press, 2005.
Rubenson, Samuel. "Philosophy and Simplicity: The Problem of Classical Education in Early Christian Biography." Pages 110-39 in *Greek Biography and Panegyric in Late Antiquity*. Edited by Thomas Hägg and Philip Rousseau. Berkeley: University of California Press, 2000.
Rubinkiewicz, Ryszard. *L'Apocalypse D'Abraham en vieux slave: Introduction, texte critique, traduction et commentaire*. Lublin: Société des Lettres et des Sciences de l'Université Catholique de Lublin, 1987.
Russell, Bertrand. *Why I Am Not a Christian and Other Essays on Religion and Other Subjects*. Edited by Paul Edwards. New York: Simon and Schuster, 1957.
Russell, D. A. "De Imitatione." Pages 1-16 in *Creative Imitation and Latin Literature*. Edited by David West and Tony Woodman. Cambridge: Cambridge University Press, 1979.
Russell, D. A. "On Reading Plutarch's *Lives*." Pages 75-94 in *Essays on Plutarch's Lives*. Edited by Barbara Scardigli. Oxford: Clarendon Press, 1995.
Saldarini, Anthony J. *Pharisees, Scribes and Sadducees in Palestinian Society: A Sociological Approach*. Wilmington, DE: Michael Glazier, 1988.
Samuel, Simon. *A Postcolonial Reading of Mark's Story of Jesus*. London: T&T Clark, 2007.
Sanders, E. P. *Jewish Law from Jesus to the Mishnah: Five Studies*. Minneapolis, MN: Fortress Press, 2016.
Sanders, Jack T. *Ethics in the New Testament: Change and Development*. Philadelphia: Fortress Press 1975.
Sanders, Jack T. "The Criterion of Coherence and the Randomness of Charisma: Poring through Some Aporias in the Jesus Tradition." *NTS* 44 (1998): 1-25.
Sandmel, Samuel. "Parallelomania." *JBL* 81 (1962): 1-13.
Santos, Narry F. *Slave of All: The Paradox of Authority and Servanthood in the Gospel of Mark*. JSNTSup 237. Sheffield: Sheffield Academic Press, 2003.
Schnackenburg, Rudolf. *The Moral Teaching of the New Testament*. London: Burns & Oats, 1964.
Schmid, C. F. *Biblical Theology of the New Testament*. Translated by G. H. Venables. CFTL 27. Edinburgh: T&T Clark, 1877.
Schmidt, Karl Ludwig. *Der Rahmen der Geschichte Jesu: literarkritische Untersuchungen zur ältesten Jesusüberlieferung*. Berlin: Trowitzsch, 1919; repr., Darmstadt: Wissenschaftliche Buchgesellschaft, 1969.
Schneider, Gerhard. "Imitatio Dei als Motiv der 'Ethik Jesu.'" Pages 71-33 in *Neues Testament und Ethik für Rudolf Schnackenburg*. Edited by Helmut Merklein. Freiburg: Herder, 1989.

Schneider, Gottfried. "Pater familias." Pages 595–8 in vol. 10 of *Brill's New Pauly: Encyclopaedia of the Ancient World*. Edited by Hubert Cancik and Helmuth Schneider. Boston: Brill, 2007.

Schnelle, Udo. *Theology of the New Testament*. Translated by M. Eugene Boring. Grand Rapids, MI: Eerdmans, 2009.

Schrage, Wolfgang. *Ethik des Neuen Testaments*. Göttingen: Vandenhoeck & Ruprecht, 1982.

Schrage, Wolfgang. *The Ethics of the New Testament*. Translated by David E. Green. Philadelphia: Fortress Press, 1988.

Schreiber, Johannes. "Die Christologie des Markusevangeliums–Beobachtungen zurTheologie und Komposition des zweiten Evangeliums." *ZTK* 58 (1961): 154–83.

Schuller, Eileen M., and Carol A. Newsom. *The Hodayot (Thanksgiving Psalms): A Study Edition of 1QHa*. EJL 36. Atlanta, GA: Society of Biblical Literature, 2012.

Schulz, Siegfried. *Neutestamentliche Ethik*. ZGZB. Zürich: Theologischer Verlag, 1987.

Schulze, W. A. "Der Heilige und die wilden Tiere. Zur Exegese von Mc 1,13b." *ZNW* 46 (1955): 280–3.

Schweitzer, Albert. *The Mystery of the Kingdom of God: The Secret of Jesus' Messiahship and Passion*. Translated by Walter Lowrie. Buffalo: Prometheus Books, 1985.

Schweitzer, Albert. *The Quest of the Historical Jesus*. Edited by John Bowden. Translated by W. Montgomery, J. R. Coates, Susan Cupitt, and John Bowden. First complete ed. Minneapolis, MN: Fortress Press, 2001.

Schweizer, Eduard. *The Good News According to Mark*. Translated by Donald H. Madvig. Richmond: John Knox Press, 1970.

Schweizer, Eduard. "Towards a Christology of Mark?" Pages 29–42 in *God's Christ and His People: Studies in Honour of Nils Alstrup Dahl*. Edited by Jacob Jervell and Wayne A. Meeks. Oslo: Universitetsforlaget, 1977.

Schwiebert, Jonathan. "Jesus's Question to Pilate in Mark 15:2." *JBL* 136 (2017): 937–47.

Segal, Alan F. *Life after Death: A History of the Afterlife in the Religions of the West*. New York: Doubleday, 2004.

Selvidge, Marla J. *Woman, Cult, and Miracle Recital: A Redactional Critical Investigation on Mark 5:24–34*. Lewisburg, PA: Bucknell University Press, 1990.

Seneca. *Epistles, Volume 1: Epistles 1–65*. Translated by Richard M. Gummere. LCL 75. Cambridge, MA: Harvard University Press, 1917.

Shäfer, Peter. *Judeophobia: Attitudes toward the Jews in the Ancient World*. Cambridge, MA: Harvard University Press, 1997.

Shiner, Whitney T. *Follow Me! Disciples in Markan Rhetoric*. SBLDS 145. Atlanta, GA: Scholars Press, 1995.

Shively, Elizabeth E. *Apocalyptic Imagination in the Gospel of Mark: The Literary and Theological Role of Mark 3:22–30*. BZNW 189. Boston: de Gruyter, 2012.

Skinner, Christopher W. "Ethics and the Gospel of John: Toward an Emerging New Consensus?" *CBR* 18 (2020): 280–304.

Skinner, Christopher W. "Telling the Story: The Appearance and Impact of *Mark as Story*." Pages 1–18 in *Mark as Story: Retrospect and Prospect*. Edited by Kelly R. Iverson and Christopher W. Skinner. SBLRBS 65. Atlanta, GA: Society of Biblical Literature, 2011.

Smelik, K. A. D. "The Witch of Endor: 1 Samuel 28 in Rabbinic and Christian Exegesis till 800 A.D." *VC* 33 (1977): 160–79.

Smith, Morton. "De Superstitione (Moralia 164E–171F)." Pages 1–35 in *Plutarch's Theological Writings and Early Christian Literature*. Edited by Hans Dieter Betz. SCHNT 3. Leiden: Brill, 1975.

Smith, Julien C. H. "The Epistle of Barnabas and the Two Ways of Teaching Authority." *VC* 68 (2014): 465–97.
Smith, Justin M. *Why Bios? On the Relationship between Gospel Genre and Implied Audience*. LNTS 518. New York: Bloomsbury/T&T Clark, 2015.
Snodgrass, Klyne R. "Streams of Tradition Emerging from Isaiah 40:1–5 and Their Adaptation in the New Testament." *JSNT* 8 (1980): 24–45.
Söding, Thomas. *Glaube bei Markus: Glaube an das Evangelium, Gebetsglaube und Wunderglaube im Kontext der markinischen Basileiatheologie und Christologie*. SBB 12. Stuttgart: Katholisches Bibelwerk, 1985.
Spencer, F. Scott. *Dancing Girls, Loose Ladies, and Women of the Cloth: The Women in Jesus' Life*. New York: Continuum, 2004.
Spicq, Ceslas. *Théologie Morale du Nouveau Testament*. 2 vols. Paris: Librairie Lecoffre, 1965.
Stadter, Philip A. *Plutarch and His Roman Readers*. Oxford: Oxford University Press, 2015.
Stanton, Graham N. *Jesus of Nazareth in New Testament Preaching*. SNTSMS 27. New York: Cambridge University Press, 1974.
Stegemann, Ekkehard W., and Wolfgang Stegemann. *The Jesus Movement: A Social History of Its First Century*. Translated by O. C. Dean Jr. Minneapolis, MN: Fortress Press, 1999.
Stein, Robert H. "The Proper Methodology for Ascertaining a Markan Redaction History." *NovT* 13 (1971): 181–98.
Sterling, Gregory E. *Historiography and Self-Definition: Josephus, Luke-Acts, and Apologetic Historiography*. NovTSup 64. New York: Brill, 1992.
Sterling, Gregory E. "Jesus as Exorcist: An Analysis of Matthew 17:14–20; Mark 9:14–29; Luke 9:37–43a." *CBQ* 55 (1993): 467–93.
Stowers, Stanley K. "Jesus the Teacher and Stoic Ethics in the Gospel of Matthew." Pages 59–75 in *Stoicism in Early Christianity*. Edited by T. Rasimus, T. Engberg-Pedersen, and I. Dunderberg. Grand Rapids, MI: Baker Academic, 2010.
Strecker, George. *Theology of the New Testament*. Translated by M. Eugene Boring. Louisville, KY: Westminster John Knox Press, 2000.
Stuckenbruck, Loren T. *The Myth of Rebellious Angels: Studies in Second Temple Judaism and New Testament Texts*. Grand Rapids, MI: Eerdmans, 2017.
Swain, Simon. "Biography and Biographic in the Literature of the Roman Empire." Pages 1–17 in *Portraits: Biographical Representation in the Greek and Latin Literature of the Roman Empire*. Edited by Mark J. Edwards and Simon Swain. New York: Oxford University Press, 1997.
Swartley, Willard M. *Covenant of Peace: The Missing Peace in New Testament Theology and Ethics*. Grand Rapids, MI: Eerdmans, 2006.
Sweat, Laura C. *The Theological Role of Paradox in the Gospel of Mark*. LNTS 492. New York: Bloomsbury, 2013.
Talbert, Charles. *What Is a Gospel? The Genre of Canonical Gospels*. Philadelphia: Fortress Press, 1977.
Talbert, Charles. "Once Again: Gospel Genre." *Semeia* 43 (1988): 53–73.
Tamiolaki, Melina. "Virtue and Leadership in Xenophon: Idea Leaders or Losers?" Pages 563–89 in *Xenophon: Ethical Principles and Historical Enquiry*. Edited by Fiona Hobden and Christopher Tuplin. Boston: Brill, 2012.

Tannehill, Robert C. "The Disciples in Mark: The Function of a Narrative Role." *JR* 57 (1977): 386–405.
Taylor, Vincent. *The Gospel According to St. Mark*. 2nd ed. London: Macmillan, 1966.
Telford, William R. *The Barren Temple and the Withered Tree: A Redaction-Critical Analysis of the Cursing of the Fig-Tree Pericope in Mark's Gospel and Its Relation to the Cleansing of the Temple Tradition*. JSNTSup 1. Sheffield: JSOT Press, 1980.
Telford, William R. *The Theology of the Gospel of Mark*. New York: Cambridge University Press, 1999.
Theissen, Gerd. *The Miracle Stories of the Early Christian Tradition*. Translated by Francis McDonagh. Edited by John Riches. Philadelphia: Fortress Press, 1983.
Theissen, Gerd. *Social Reality and the Early Christians: Theology, Ethics, and the World of the New Testament*. Translated by Margaret Kohl. Minneapolis, MN: Fortress Press, 1992.
Theissen, Gerd, and Annette Merz. *The Historical Jesus: A Comprehensive Guide*. Translated by John Bowden. Minneapolis, MN: Fortress Press, 1998.
Theophylactus. *The Explanation by Blessed Theophylact of the Holy Gospel According to St. Mark*. Translated by Christopher Stade. House Springs, MO: Chrysostom Press, 1993.
Thiessen, Matthew. *Contesting Conversion: Genealogy, Circumcision, and Identity in Ancient Judaism and Christianity*. New York: Oxford University Press, 2011.
Thiessen, Matthew. *Paul and the Gentile Problem*. New York: Oxford University Press, 2016.
Thiessen, Matthew. "Gentiles as Impure Animals in the Writings of Early Christ Followers." Pages 19–32 in *Perceiving the Other in Ancient Judaism and Early Christianity*. Edited by Michael Bar-Asher Siegal, Wolfgang Grünstäudl, and Matthew Thiessen. WUNT 394. Tübingen: Mohr Siebeck, 2017.
Thorsteinsson, Runar M. *Jesus as Philosopher: The Moral Sage in the Synoptic Gospels*. Oxford: Oxford University Press, 2018.
Thorsteinsson, Runar M. *Roman Christianity and Roman Stoicism: A Comparative Study of Ancient Morality*. Oxford: Oxford University Press, 2010
Tiede, David. *The Charismatic Figure as Miracle Worker*. SBLDS 1. Missoula, MT: Society of Biblical Literature, 1972.
Tolbert, Mary Ann. *Sowing the Gospel: Mark's World in Literary-Historical Perspective*. Minneapolis, MN: Fortress Press, 1989.
Trozzo, Lindsey M. *Exploring Johannine Ethics: A Rhetorical Approach to Moral Efficacy in the Fourth Gospel Narrative*. WUNT 2.449. Tübingen: Mohr Siebeck, 2017.
Trummer, Peter. *Die blutende Frau: Wunderheilung im Neuen Testament*. Freiburg: Herder, 1991.
Twelftree, Graham H. *Jesus the Exorcist: A Contribution to the Study of the Historical Jesus*. WUNT 2.54. Tübingen: J. C. B. Mohr, 1993.
Twelftree, Graham H. *In the Name of Jesus: Exorcism among Early Christians*. Grand Rapid, MI: Baker Academic, 2007.
Urbano, Arthur P. *The Philosophical Life: Biography and the Crafting of Intellectual Identity in Late Antiquity*. PMS 21. Washington, DC: Catholic University of America Press, 2013.
Van Uytfanghe, Marc. "La Vie d'Apollonius de Tyane et le discours Hagiographie." Pages 335–74 in *Theios Sophistes: Essays on Flavius Philostratus' Vita Apollonii*. Edited by K. Demoen and D. Praet. MS 305. Boston: Brill, 2009.

VanderKam, James C. "The Demons in the *Book of Jubilees*." Pages 339–64 in *Demons: The Demonology of Israelite-Jewish and Early Christian Literature in Context of Their Environment*. Edited by Armin Lange, Hermann Lichtenberger, and K. F. Diethard Römheld. Tübingen: Mohr Siebeck, 2003.
Verhey, Allen. *Remembering Jesus: Christian Community, Scripture, and the Moral Life*. Grand Rapids, MI: Eerdmans, 2002.
Verhey, Allen. *The Great Reversal: Ethics and the New Testament*. Grand Rapids, MI: Eerdmans, 1984.
Via, Dan O. *The Ethics of Mark's Gospel. In the Middle of Time*. Philadelphia: Fortress Press, 1985.
Vielhauer, Philipp. "Erwägungen zur Christologie des Markusevangeliums." Pages 155–69 in *Zeit und Geschichte: Dankesgabe an Rudolf Bultmann zum 80. Geburtstag*. Edited by Erich Dinkler. Tübingen: Mohr, 1964.
Vines, Michael E. *The Problem of Markan Genre: The Gospel of Mark and the Jewish Novel*. Academia Biblica 3. Atlanta, GA: Society of Biblical Literature, 2002.
Vinson, Richard B., and B. Diane Lipsett. "Mark." Pages 4–10 in *Oxford Encyclopedia of theBible and Ethics*. 2 vols Edited by Robert L. Brawley. New York: Oxford University Press, 2015.
Voorwinde, Stephen. *Jesus' Emotions in the Gospels*. New York: T&T Clark, 2011.
Votaw, Clyde Weber. "The Gospels and Contemporary Biographies." *AJT* 19 (1915): 45–73.
Votaw, Clyde Weber. "The Gospels and Contemporary Biographies—Concluded." *AJT* 19 (1915): 217–49.
Wahlen, Clinton. *Jesus and the Impurity of Spirits in the Synoptic Gospels*. WUNT 2.185. Tübingen: Mohr Siebeck, 2004.
Walsh, P. G. *Livy: His Historical Methods and Aims*. Cambridge: Cambridge University Press, 1961.
Wansbrough, Henry. "Mark III.21—Was Jesus Out of His Mind?" *NTS* 18 (1972): 233–5.
Wardman, Alan. *Plutarch's Lives*. Berkeley: University of California Press, 1974.
Warren, James. "Plato." Pages 28–41 in *The Cambridge History of Moral Philosophy*. Edited by Sacha Golob and Jens Timmermann. New York: Cambridge University Press, 2017.
Wassermann, Tommy. "The 'Son of God' Was in the Beginning (Mark 1:1)." *JTS* 62 (2011): 20–50.
Watson, David F. *Honor among Christians: The Cultural Key to the Messianic Secret*. Minneapolis, MN: Fortress Press, 2010.
Watson, David F. "The Life of Aesop and the Gospel of Mark: Two Ancient Approaches to Elite Values." *JBL* 129 (2010): 699–716.
Watson, Francis. *Paul and the Hermeneutics of Faith*. 2nd ed. London: Bloomsbury T&T Clark, 2016.
Watson, Francis. "Social Function of Mark's Secrecy Motif." *JSNT* 24 (1985): 49–69.
Watts, Joel L. *Mimetic Criticism and the Gospel of Mark: An Introduction and Commentary*. Eugene, OR: Wipf and Stock, 2013.
Watts, Rikki. *Isaiah's New Exodus and Mark*. WUNT 2.88. Tübingen: Mohr Siebeck, 1997.
Weeden, Theodore J. *Mark: Traditions in Conflict*. Philadelphia: Fortress Press, 1971.
Weil, Simone. *Simone Weil: An Anthology*. Edited by Siân Miles. New York: Penguin Books, 2005.
Weiss, Johannes. *Das älteste Evangelium: Ein Beitrag zum Verständnis des Markus-Evangeliums und der ältesten evangelischen Überlieferung*. Göttingen: Vanderhoeck & Ruprecht, 1903.
Weiss, Johannes. *Jesus von Nazareth, Mythus oder Geschichte?* Tübingen: Mohr, 1910.

Wenham, David. "The Meaning of Mark 3:21." *NTS* 21 (1975): 295–300.
Werman, Cana. "*Jubilees* 30: Building a Paradigm for the Ban on Intermarriage." *HTR* 90 (1997): 1–22.
Whitmarsh, Tim. *The Second Sophist*. GR 35. Oxford: Oxford University Press, 2005.
Williams, James G. *Gospel against Parable: Mark's Language of Mystery*. BLS 12. Sheffield: JSOT Press, 1985.
Williams, Joel F. *Other Followers of Jesus: Minor Characters as Major Figures in Mark's Gospel*. JSNTSup 102. Sheffield: JSOT Press, 1994.
Wills, Lawrence. *The Quest of the Historical Gospels: Mark, John, and the Origins of the Gospel Genre*. New York: Routledge, 1997.
Winn, Adam. "The Markan Secrecy Motif and Roman Political Ideology." *JBL* 133 (2014): 583–601.
Winter, Paul. *On the Trail of Jesus*. Berlin: de Gruyter, 1961.
Woloch, Alex. *The One vs. The Many: Minor Characters and the Space of the Protagonist in the Novel*. Princeton, NJ: Princeton University Press, 2004.
Wrede, William. *The Messianic Secret*. Translated by J. C. G. Greig. Cambridge: J. Clarke, 1971.
Wright, N. T. *The New Testament and the People of God*. London: SPCK, 1992.
Wright, W. C. "Introduction." Pages ix–xli in *Lives of the Sophists, Eunapius: Lives of Philosophers*. LCL 134. Cambridge, MA: Harvard University Press, 1921.
Zurawski, Jason M. "Mosaic *Paideia*: The Law of Moses within Philo of Alexandria's Modelof Jewish Education." *JSJ* 48 (2017): 480–505.

Index of Ancient Sources

HEBREW BIBLE

Genesis
1:2 LXX	53 n.73
1:24 LXX	53 n.79
1:25 LXX	53 n.79
1:30 LXX	53 n.79
2:19 LXX	53 n.79
2:20 LXX	53 n.79
3:1 LXX	53 n.79
3:14 LXX	53 n.79
6:4	52, 71
6:19 LXX	53 n.79
12:17	96
15:6 LXX	74 n.19
15:17	87 n.96
18:22–33	61
22	54, 82
22:1–2	54 n.87
22:17	15
39	54

Exodus
19:9	74
20:12	62, 129
20:13–16 LXX	130
20:17–19	126
20:22	48
23	48
23:20	47–8, 48 n.44
23:20–33	48
27–30	133

Leviticus
1:2	62
1:3	62
1:10	62
11:7	97
14:1–20	65
15	76, 76 n.33
15:5	125
15:11	125
19:18	92

Numbers
5:2	97
7:3	62
9:7	97
24:2 LXX	53 n.73

Deuteronomy
5:16	62, 129
5:16–20 LXX	130
5:32–33	51 n.65
6:4	79–80
6:4–5	81
6:5	80
8:2	54 n.87
11:28	51 n.65
14:8	97
24:14–15	132

Judges
3:10 LXX	53 n.73

1 Samuel
15:22	81 n.63
16	118
16:1–23	96 n.139
16:14	118
19:20 LXX	53 n.73
25:2–43	123, 134
28	34 n.112
28:3–24	34
28:9	35
28:16–20	34 n.111
28:24–25	35

1 Kings
8:27–30	66
18:12 LXX	53 n.73

19:19–21	59 n.119	61:1 LXX	53 n.73
21:1–18	54	63:11 LXX	53 n.73
		66:1–4	130
2 Chronicles		66:15–16	135
28:3	138	66:24	69, 136, 138
33:1–9	54		
33:6	138	**Jeremiah**	
36:14	130	5:21	87
		7:5 LXX	104
Ezra		7:11	104
9:1–12	128	7:11 LXX	104
		7:13–15 LXX	104
Job		7:31–32	138
1:6–12	52 n.68	19:2	138
20:28	67 n.160	19:6	138
		32:35	138
Psalms			
2:7	82, 82 n.69	**Lamentations**	
10:6 LXX	107	2:1	67 n.160
50:13 LXX	53 n.73		
115:4 LXX	107	**Ezekiel**	
138:6	126	7:12	56 n.100
		9:1	56 n.100
Proverbs		11:24 LXX	53 n.73
8:13	126		
		Daniel	
Isaiah		4:28–33	123
1:11–17	81 n.63	5:12	53 n.75
6:9	87, 88 n.101	6:3	53 n.75
13:9	68	7:22	56 n.100
13:21 LXX	53 n.79		
29:13	44 n.20, 63	**Hosea**	
40:3	47, 47 n.35, 48–50, 104	6:6	81 n.63
40:19	48 n.43	**Obadiah**	
40:28	48 n.43	8	68
42:1	82, 82 n.70		
43:7	48 n.43	**Micah**	
44:2 LXX	82	2:2	134
45:7	48 n.43	5:10	68
45:9	48 n.43	7:6	59
46:8 LXX	57		
51:17	107	**Zephaniah**	
51:22	107	1:18	67 n.160
56	104	2:13	68
56:4 LXX	104		
56:7	44 n.20, 81 n.63	**Zechariah**	
56:7 LXX	104	13:3	59

Index of Ancient Sources

Malachi

3	48
3:1	44 n.20, 47, 47 n.35, 48
3:5	134
3:17 LXX	48
3:18 LXX	48
4:1 LXX	48
4:3 LXX	48
4:5 LXX	48

NEW TESTAMENT

Matthew

3:2	56 n.95
3:3	47
3:14–15	56 n.95
4:1	50 n.57, 53 n.77
4:11	55
4:17	56 n.95
4:23	56 n.95
5:2–7:27	3
5:29	138
5:30	138
5:47	135
6:12–13	102
7:7–11	61
8:18–22	120
8:26	120
8:28–34	97
9:9	120
10:5–42	3
10:15	67 n.162, 111, 135
10:21	59
10:28	67 n.162, 111, 135, 138
11:10	47
11:22	67 n.162, 111, 135
12:22–29	52
12:22–32	115
12:42	67 n.162, 111, 135
12:46–50	115
13:13	13, 88 n.101
13:20	67 n.162, 111, 135
13:51	120
14:31	120
14:33	120
15:16	120
15:19–20	124
15:24	101
16:8	120
16:12	120
16:17	44 n.12, 85
17:14–20	75
17:16	75, 75 n.29
17:20	75 n.30, 120
18	137
18:4	84 n.84
18:6–9	67 n.162, 111, 135
18:9	138
19:16–30	131
19:18–26	77
19:21	82
19:29	134
19:29–30	62 n.136
21:6	120
21:19	104
22:13	67 n.162, 111, 135
22:35	80
22:37	80
23:2–39	3
23:9	62
23:12	84 n.84
23:15	138
23:33	138
24:4–25:46	3
24:51	67 n.162, 111, 135
25:31–46	67 n.162, 111, 135
26:6–13	120
26:14–16	134
26:19	120
26:39	106
27:1–10	134
28:7	120
28:16–20	120

Mark

1:1	6, 13, 44 n.13, 44 n.15, 47, 47 n.32, 54, 61, 86, 106
1:1–2	72
1:1–8	66
1:1–13	39
1:1–15	42, 46, 142
1:2	44 n.20, 47, 47 n.36, 48
1:2–3	42, 47, 50–1, 51 n.62, 65, 87, 104, 133

1:3–4	50	1:40	89, 92, 94
1:3	44 n.16, 48–9	1:40–45	92, 94
1:4	66	1:41	91–2
1:4–8	47	1:44	83
1:4–11	48	1:45	86, 93, 101
1:7	52, 55, 106, 117	2:1	58, 93, 136
1:8	44 n.20, 53	2:1–2	93
1:9–11	49	2:1–12	65–6, 69, 73, 79, 94,
1:9–13	47		108, 142
1:10	44, 44 n.20, 53	2:2	86, 101, 115
1:11	42, 54, 61, 82, 113	2:5	58, 62–3, 70, 70
1:12	44 n.20, 53		n.178, 71, 74,
1:12–13	42, 50, 52, 55, 70		78–9
	n.178, 111, 113–14	2:6	64 n.146
1:13	50 n.57, 52–54, 53	2:7	43, 43 n.9, 44 n.13,
	n.79, 64, 106, 123		53 n.72, 61, 81
1:14	55, 135, 140	2:8	53
1:14–15	2, 2 n.6, 40, 42, 44	2:10	42, 64
	n.13, 47, 50, 55, 55	2:11	99
	n.94, 56 n.95, 56	2:12	44, 44 n.13, 115
	n.99, 57, 60, 86, 93,	2:13	93
	126, 142	2:13–17	65
1:15	44 n.14, 45, 53, 56,	2:14	120
	57 n.109, 66–7,	2:16	64 n.146
	72, 74, 88, 90, 104,	2:17	94
	118, 142	2:18–28	65
1:16–20	7, 13, 39, 45, 60, 76,	2:19	66
	108, 120	2:20	51
1:17	85	2:22	85
1:19–20	59	2:25	66
1:20	58, 85, 108	2:27	42
1:21–28	53, 55, 64, 69, 73,	2:28	49
	94, 113	3:1–6	65
1:21b–22	93	3:4	42–3, 43 n.7, 111,
1:22	64–5		119, 124, 132, 139
1:23	55, 97	3:6	85, 119, 140
1:23–27	99	3:7–12	93
1:24	44 n.13, 44 n.15, 65,	3:11	44 n.13, 44 n.15, 53,
	65 n.149, 67, 85, 99,		55, 67, 83, 97
	113, 117, 135–6, 142	3:11–12	93
1:26	52, 115, 121, 140	3:13	92
1:26–27	97	3:13–19	60
1:27	64	3:14	99, 121
1:30	58, 108	3:14–15	55 n.89, 113
1:32	55	3:15	45, 53, 55, 64, 94
1:32–34	93–4	3:16	58, 121
1:34	53, 55, 63, 83, 93	3:17	106
1:35	50, 103	3:19	55, 115, 134, 136
1:39	53, 55, 93–4	3:19b–30	43 n.6, 52, 65–6, 123

3:19b–35	58, 66 n.156, 113–15, 117	4:24–25	67 n.164
		4:25	67 n.164
3:20–27	42	4:26	44 nn.13–14
3:20–34	112	4:29	67 n.164
3:21	62, 115	4:30	44 nn.13–14
3:21–35	89	4:30–32	58, 88
3:22	52, 54, 64 n.146, 115	4:33	86, 101
3:22–23	53	4:35–41	87
3:23	52, 66, 112	4:38	64 n.144, 85, 87
3:23–26	139	4:40	70
3:24	66	4:40–41	120
3:24–27	66	4:41	42, 83
3:25	115	5:1	100
3:26	52	5:1–13	52, 97
3:27	47, 66 n.155, 106, 115–17, 136	5:1–20	13, 39, 50, 90–2, 94, 97, 100 n. 157, 101, 108, 113, 128, 140, 142–3
3:28–29	42, 67 n.164		
3:29	44 n.20, 53, 142		
3:29–30	136	5:2	54, 97
3:30	42, 52, 97	5:3	117
3:31–33	115	5:4	52
3:31–35	13, 39, 66, 76, 90, 108, 137, 142	5:5	115, 119, 121, 139
		5:6	100
3:32	72	5:7	44 n.13, 44 n.15, 53, 67, 117, 135–6, 142
3:33	58		
3:35	2 n.6, 42, 44 n.13, 61, 63, 72, 85	5:8	97
		5:13	52, 54, 97–8
4:1	89, 93	5:14–17	128
4:1–2	93	5:15	99, 108, 119, 122
4:1–12	88 n.101	5:15–16	97
4:3–9	86 n.95, 90	5:16	99
4:4	51, 87, 124, 136, 138	5:17	22, 98
4:5	124	5:18	97–8
4:6	104	5:19	44, 44 n.17, 49, 51, 58, 99–100, 136
4:6–7	136		
4:7	124	5:20	100
4:11	44 nn.13–14, 57, 72, 88	5:21	92–3
		5:21–24a	78
4:11–12	83, 88 n.101, 129	5:21–43	50, 73, 76–7, 79, 92, 100, 108, 119, 141
4:12	39, 108		
4:12–13	123, 142	5:23	69, 76
4:13	22, 39, 83	5:24–34	76
4:15	51–2, 55 n.92, 66 n.155, 87, 123–4, 136, 138	5:25	76, 77 n.33
		5:26	77 n.34
		5:28	89
4:15–20	86, 101	5:29	77, 101
4:17	124	5:30	64, 78 n.46, 105
4:18–19	124, 136	5:31	83, 115, 120
4:22	88 n.101	5:33	76, 119, 122

5:33–34	124	7:1	64 n.146, 129
5:34	35, 58, 62–3, 70, 74, 76, 78	7:1–2	129
		7:1–13	129
5:34–35	76	7:1–15	101, 124, 135
5:35	64 n.144, 78	7:1–23	62, 91, 108–9, 125–8
5:35–43	78	7:1–30	140
5:36	57, 76, 78–9, 86, 101, 108, 119	7:3	124
		7:3–4	47 n.36, 129, 138
5:37	106, 121	7:5	22, 64 n.146, 129
5:38–40	78	7:6	44 n.20, 47 n.36
5:39	78	7:7–8	63
5:41	22, 78 n.44, 106	7:7–9	62
5:41–42	78	7:8	42, 81, 101
5:42	76	7:8–9	44 n.13, 62 n.139
5:43	83	7:10–13	59
6:1–6	58, 60, 74, 77	7:11	106, 138
6:2	64	7:13	44 n.13, 101
6:3	58, 87, 134	7:14–23	129
6:5	64	7:15	126
6:6	73, 74, 93	7:17	129
6:6b–13	94, 120–1, 124	7:18	120, 125
6:7	45, 54–5, 64, 94, 97, 113	7:19	39, 42, 47 n.36, 124
		7:20	128
6:7–12	60 n.124	7:21	64, 101, 112, 125, 129
6:8–9	123		
6:11	67 n.164	7:21–22	122
6:11–12	93	7:21–23	63, 123–4, 130
6:12–13	93	7:22	113, 123
6:13	45, 53–5, 93–5	7:24	58, 100, 136
6:14–29	119, 124–5, 143	7:24–26	22
6:17	117	7:24–30	13, 50, 52, 76, 77 n.38, 90, 92, 94, 100, 100 n.157, 101, 105, 107–8, 113, 115, 142
6:18	58		
6:19–20	113, 123		
6:20	119		
6:21	139	7:25	55, 97, 100
6:26	130, 139	7:26–27	69
6:30	55 n.91, 93–4	7:27	100, 108
6:30–33	93	7:29	35
6:30–44	101	7:30	99, 100
6:31–32	50	7:31	100
6:34	92, 94	7:31–37	92
6:45–52	142	7:34	78 n.44, 106
6:46	103	8	11
6:50	87, 119–20	8–10	12
6:52	83, 120	8:2	91–2
6:53–56	93–4	8:11	52–3, 106
6:55–56	93	8:14	83
6:56	92	8:14–21	142
7	63, 129–30	8:17	39, 73 n.15, 90

8:17–18	120, 123		106–7, 115, 120–1,
8:18	87		139
8:21	39, 83, 89, 120	9:19	73, 76, 136
8:22	136	9:20	52, 97, 120
8:22–26	87, 92	9:21–24	75
8:22–10:52	3 n.10, 8, 8 n.53,	9:22	85, 96, 115, 119, 139
	9, 11, 51	9:23	57, 74, 106
8:26	58, 99, 136	9:24	42, 70, 73, 75, 78–
8:27	4, 51, 136		9, 108
8:27–33	52 n.67, 111	9:25	54, 76, 97
8:27–10:45	8, 12 n.75	9:26	76, 78
8:28	66	9:27	78
8:29	85	9:28	75
8:30	83	9:29	70, 103
8:31	9, 51, 64 n.146	9:30	83
8:31–32b	83	9:30–32	9, 33
8:31–33	22, 119, 143	9:31	55
8:32	91	9:32	120, 122
8:33	42, 43 n.10, 44 n.13,	9:33	69, 136
	52, 55 n.92, 70, 85,	9:33–34	51
	90, 106, 108, 117,	9:33–37	84, 88, 124, 143
	119, 121, 123	9:33–41	137
8:33–34	70	9:33–50	138
8:34	70, 85	9:34	83, 120, 136
8:34–35	98, 107	9:35–37	69
8:34–37	83	9:36	69, 69 n.177, 88, 91
8:34–38	72, 85–7, 91, 108,	9:36–37	136
	118, 130	9:37–50	68
8:35	67, 85–6	9:37	88
8:35–38	42, 67, 136	9:38	64 n.144, 120
8:36–37	58	9:38–41	90, 95, 107, 111, 113,
8:38	44, 58, 60, 67 n.164		117, 124, 136, 142
	111, 140	9:39	64, 136
9:1	44 nn.13–14, 64,	9:40	139
	72	9:41	67, 85
9:2	106, 121, 136	9:42	57–8, 69, 70 n.178,
9:6–7	86		74, 136, 140
9:7	61, 82	9:42–50	32, 67, 67 n.161, 68
9:9	83		n.172, 68–70, 72, 88,
9:9–10	86		99, 113, 118, 123–4,
9:10	39, 142		130, 136–8, 140, 142
9:11	64 n.146	9:42–47	87
9:14	64 n.146	9:43	68–9, 138
9:14–29	47 n.33, 75–6, 78–9,	9:43–49	67 n.164
	94, 100, 108, 113,	9:45	69, 136, 138
	119, 140, 142	9:47	44 nn.13–14, 67,
9:17	52, 64 n.144, 69, 76		69, 69 n.173, 72,
9:18	22, 47 n.33, 55 n.91,		136, 138
	70, 75–6, 83, 97,	9:48	138

180 *Index of Ancient Sources*

9:50	104	10:42	139
10	8 n.53, 12, 133–4	10:42–43	123
10:1	93, 136	10:43	136
10:1–12	58	10:43–45	83
10:2	52–3, 106	10:44	92
10:9	44 n.13, 81	10:45	91, 118, 130, 142–3
10:11	104		
10:11–12	39, 124	10:46	51
10:13	83	10:46–52	39, 79, 87, 92, 94
10:13–16	58, 69, 73, 84, 88, 94, 107, 120, 136, 142	10:47	89
		10:47–48	92
10:13–31	140		
10:14	13	**Mark (cont.)**	
10:14–15	44 nn.13–14, 72, 88	10:51	64 n.144. 92
10:16	91	10:52	35, 51, 70, 74, 78, 87, 108
10:17	51, 64 n.144, 132		
10:17–18	43	11:2–4	120
10:17–31	88, 125–6, 130, 133–5	11:3	49
		11:9	44 n.16, 49
10:18	44 n.13, 45, 81	11:11–25	66, 82 n.69, 103
10:19	59, 124, 132, 139	11:12–14	136, 142
10:19–21	123, 130	11:13	103
10:20	64 n.144, 126	11:14	39, 104
10:21	82–3, 126, 142	11:15–16	104
10:22	132, 134, 139	11:15–19	104, 136
10:23	123	11:16	39, 104, 124
10:23–25	44 nn.13–14	11:17	44 n.20, 50, 59, 82 n.69, 90, 101, 103–4, 143
10:24	58, 62, 83, 142		
10:25	67 n.164		
10:26–27	119, 121	11:18	64 n.146, 85
10:27	40, 42, 44 n.13, 106	11:20	103–4
10:28	60, 121, 133	11:20–21	104
10:28–31	58, 62	11:20–25	13
10:29	86, 98	11:21	121
10:29–30	72, 76, 108	11:22	44 n.13, 70, 74–5, 78, 82 n.69, 104
10:30	56, 62–3, 87, 104, 134		
		11:22–25	103–5
10:31	67 n.164, 118, 130	11:23	57
10:32	51, 120	11:23–24	74
10:32–34	9, 83	11:24–25	104
10:33	55, 64 n.146	11:25	44, 58, 60–1, 71, 74, 105
10:35	64 n.144, 91		
10:35–45	22, 39, 90, 107, 120, 124, 130, 139, 142–3	11:27	64 n.146
		11:27–33	42, 66, 82 n.69, 113
10:35–52	140	11:28–29	64
10:36	92	11:30	42, 114
10:38	51, 83	11:31	44 n.20, 74
10:38–39	106	11:32	122
10:39	107	11:33	64

12:1–12	67 n.164, 87, 113, 123–4, 139–40	13:1–37	39
		13:3	121
12:4–8	140	13:4	67 n.164
12:6	51, 55, 58, 60, 82, 82 n.69, 143	13:5	87
		13:7–9	59
12:7–8	125	13:9	87
12:8	44 n.17	13:10	50, 86, 90, 101, 143
12:9	44, 44 n.17, 51, 67, 72, 85, 135–6, 140, 142	13:11	44 n.20, 106
		13:12	58–9, 107
		13:12–13a	60
12:11	44 n.16, 49	13:12–13	142
12:12	119, 143	13:13	67 n.164
12:13–17	66	13:14	59, 138
12:14	42, 44 n.13, 47, 51, 51 n.62, 64 n.144, 72, 87	13:14–19	67, 136, 140
		13:17	59
		13:19	43, 44 n.13, 87
12:15	52–3, 106	13:20	44, 67 n.164
12:15b	51 n.64	13:21	57
12:17	42, 44 n.13, 51, 52, 82 n.69	13:22	59
		13:23	87
12:19	64 n.144	13:24	87
12:24	44 n.13, 64, 82 n.69	13:24–27	67 n.164
12:24–27	58	13:26	64
12:26–27	44 n.13	13:31	86
12:28	64 n.146	13:32	44, 44 n.17, 58, 60–1, 67, 106
12:28–31	80, 82–3, 82 n.69		
12:28–34	50, 80, 81 n.59, 82–3, 91, 142	13:32–37	126
		13:33	56, 87, 106
12:29	44 n.16, 49	13:34–35	106
12:29–30	44 n.13	13:35	44, 44 n.17, 106, 135, 140
12:30	44 n.16, 49		
12:30–31	73	13:35–36	136
12:31	91, 99, 124	13:36	106
12:32	64 n.144, 64 n.146, 81 n.65	13:37	106
		13:41	106
12:33	81, 91, 104	14–16	8, 83
12:34	44 nn.13–14, 72, 82, 89, 108	14:1	64 n.146
		14:1–2	134, 139, 143
12:35	64 n.146	14:1–11	50, 84 n.80, 132, 135, 139–40
12:36	44 n.16, 44 n.20, 49		
12:38	64 n.146	14:3	73 n.16
12:38–40	132, 134–5, 140, 143	14:3–9	124, 134, 139, 142
12:38–44	124, 140	14:4–5	120
12:40	67 n.164, 103, 107–9, 136, 139	14:9	86
		14:10	55, 134
12:41–44	50, 73, 132, 142	14:10–11	119, 125, 134, 139
13	8, 8 n.51, 19, 59	14:11	55, 122, 134
13:1	64 n.144	14:14	64 n.144
13:1–2	82 n.69	14:18	55

14:18–21	122	15:19	135
14:21	55, 67 n.164, 136	15:19–20	122
14:25	44 nn.13–14	15:20	134
14:27	51, 86–7	15:21–32	39
14:27–31	90	15:22	106
14:29	87, 121	15:24	122, 134
14:31	122	15:25–32	86
14:32	103	15:31	64 n.146
14:32–42	84 n.80, 103, 105–8, 142	15:31–32	79 n.49
		15:32	57, 122
14:32–43	52 n.67	15:33–41	22, 125, 143
14:33	105, 111, 119, 121	15:34	44 n.13, 51, 55, 78 n.44, 103, 106
14:34	106		
14:35	103, 105	15:37–38	122
14:35–36	106	15:38	44
14:36	40, 43 n.10, 44, 51, 58, 60–1, 87, 92, 105–6, 118, 130	15:39	39, 44 n.13, 44 n.15, 84 n.80, 89, 108
		15:40	58
14:37	106, 121	15:40–41	50, 78 n.39
14:37–38	106	15:43	44 nn.13–14, 88 n.100
14:38	103, 106–7		
14:39	103, 105	16:1	58, 122
14:41	126	16:8	13, 40, 83, 87, 99, 120, 124
14:41–42	55		
14:42	122	16:17–18	116
14:43	64 n.146, 134		
14:43–52	86	**Luke**	
14:44	55	1:6	44 n.12
14:47	122, 135	1:10	103
14:50	90, 120, 122	1:13	103
14:53	64 n.146	1:50	80 n.57
14:53–65	87	1:54	80 n.57
14:56–57	124	1:58	80 n.57
14:61	44 n.20	1:72	80 n.57
14:62	64, 67 n.164	1:78	80 n.57
14:63–72	86	2:47	115
14:64	53 n.72	3:4	47
14:64–65	122	3:18	55 n.93
14:65	135	3:21	103
14:66–72	86, 119–20	3:22	53
14:68	121	4:1	50 n.57, 53 n.77
14:70–71	121	4:13	55
15:1	64 n.146, 117	5:5	120
15:6–15	86, 113, 123–4	5:11	120
15:10	130	6:20–49	3
15:13–14	135	7:21	65
15:14	139	7:27	47
15:15	130, 135, 139	7:29–30	120
15:16–41	118, 130	7:43	120

8:2	65	19:11–27	3
8:19–21	115	20:47	67 n.162, 111, 135
8:26–39	97	21:6	59
9:15	120	22:3	119, 134
9:18	103	22:31	52 n.68
9:35	82 n.70	22:42	106
9:37–43a	75	24:45	120
9:40	75		
9:41	75 n.29	**John**	
9:43	77 n.34	12:4–5	134
9:45	120	12:27	106
9:54	67 n.162, 135	13:2	119, 134
10:2–37	3		
10:12	67 n.162	**Acts**	
10:12–14	111, 135	1:14	103, 120
10:14	67 n.162	1:18	134
10:25	80	2:1–4	103
10:27	80	2:42	120
10:28	80, 81 n.59	4:23–31	103
10:37	80 n.57	4:24	120
11:1	120	5:3	52 n.68
11:1–14	103	6:4	120
11:2–13	3	8:15–17	103
11:14–23	52, 115	9:2	49
11:29–52	3	9:40	78 n.44
11:31–32	67 n.162, 111	10:9	120
12:2	67 n.162, 111, 135	10:28	127
12:4–5	67 n.162, 111, 135	19:9	49
12:5	138	19:12	65
12:10	115	19:13–15	111 n.2
12:28	61	22:4	49
12:47–48	67 n.162, 111, 135		
		Romans	
12:56	56 n.101	1:18	42 n.4
13:5	67 n.162, 111, 135	1:29–31	124
13:16	52 n.68	2:2	42 n.4
13:28	67 n.162, 111, 135	4:17	42 n.4
14:24	67 n.162, 111, 135	9:22	42 n.4
14:36	85	2:1–11	41
16:19–31	67 n.162, 111, 135	3:5–6	41
18:1	102	3:19	41
18:1–8	103	5:5	80
18:8	67 n.162, 111, 135	7:14–25	86 n.90
18:9–14	103	8:15	106
18:18–30	131	8:26	102
18:20	82	8:38	65
18:22	82	8:39	80
18:29–30	62 n.136	14:1–9	41
18:30	56 n.101	14:10	90

15:9–12	90	3:5	80
16:20	52 n.68		

1 Corinthians

		1 Timothy	
1:10–11	90	1:9–11	124
1:20–31	42 n.4	6:5	131
3:9	42 n.4		
3:17	42 n.4	**James**	
4:1–5	41	3:6	138
5:5	52 n.68	4:6	126
5:13	42 n.4	4:7	52 n.68, 119
6:7–8	131	4:10	84 n.84
6:13	42 n.4	4:12	67 n.166
6:19	42 n.4	5:1–5	132
6:19b–20	86 n.90	5:4	131
7	86 n.90		
7:5	131	**1 Peter**	
9:5	58 n.114	1:11	56 n.100
10:10	67 n.166	2:8	84 n.84
10:14–22	41	5:5–6	126
12:18	86 n.90	5:8–9	119
13:2	104		
14:23	90	**1 John**	
15:18	67 n.166	3:7–10	111
		4:8	80

Galatians

		Jude	
2:11–21	90	21	80
4:4	56, 56 n.100		
4:6	106	**Revelation**	
5:19–21	124	2:13	52 n.68
5:22	103	12:14	56 n.101
		20:10	99

Ephesians

6:11	119
6:12	65

APOCRYPHA AND PSEUDEPIGRAPHA

Apocalypse of Abraham

Philippians

		13.7–14	54
2:8	84 n.84	14.6–7	46
4:12	84 n.84	20	52 n.68
		27.1–7	138
Colossians		31.1–4	68
2:15	73 n.13	31.2–4	135, 138

1 Thessalonians

		2 Baruch	
1:10	41, 42 n.4	6:3	53 n.75
5:2	67	21:4	53 n.75
		42:7	46 n.29
2 Thessalonians		48:2–3	89
2:10	67 n.166	70:6	59

Biblical Antiquities (LAB)
60:1–3   118

1 Enoch
1–6   52
6   52 n.68
6:1–8   66 n.154
8:1–4   116
9:1   118
9:6–9   118
10:7–9   118
12–16   118
15:8–16:2   118
21:1–10   68, 135, 138
21:10   68
32:6   118
41:8–9   46 n.29
41:9   68
42:1–3   121
53:1–6   68
54:6   68, 138
55:4   68, 138
67:8–9   68
99:5   59
100:1   59

1 Esdras
1:49   130

4 Ezra
3:21   129
7:35–44   69, 136

Joseph and Aseneth
11:11–13   63

Jubilees
5:1–8   52
10:18   66 n.154
11   87 n.96
11:4   121
11:4–9   116
11:10–23   87
17:15–18:12   54
17:17   54
19:8   54
22   128, 130
22:16   127
22:16–17   127
30:7–13   128
48:15   66 n.154

Judith
8:25–27   54 n.88
8:27   54 n.88
9:9   126

Letter of Aristeas
132   81 n.65
129–151   127
229   79 n.51
241–42   58

1 Maccabees
1:21   126
1:24   126

2 Maccabees
5:21   126
9:7   126

3 Maccabees
2:10   127

Martyrdom and Ascension of Isaiah
1:1–3:12   54 n.84
1:9–10   54
2:2   54
3:13–4:22   54 n.84
5:1–16   54, 54 n.84
6–11   54 n.84

Pseudo-Phocylides
8   63

Sibylline Oracles
2.283–296   69, 136
3.496–500   127

Sirach
4:1   131
10:18   126
38:24   64

Testament of Abraham
1:3   106
10:1–15   61
10:14   61 n.130

17:16	106	4:12	96
19:16	106	6:1–11	66
		6:4	96
Testament of Asher		6:8	66
2:5	124	6:9	65
3:1–4:5	51 n.59, 51 n.65	7:5–7	97
		9:2	97
Testament of Benjamin		12:2	97
3:3–4	116	17:5	65 n.149
5:2	53 n.79	18:6	65 n.149
6:1	54 n.86	18:16	138
Testament of Dan		**Tobit**	
5:1	52 n.68	4:13	126
5:3	79 n.51	6:18 AB	65 n.149
5:6	66 n.154		
6:1–11	66	**Wisdom of Solomon**	
		2.24	46 n.29
Testament of Issachar		15.10–11	130
5:2	79 n.51		
7:7	53 n.79, 54 n.86, 79 n.51	**DEAD SEA SCROLLS**	
		1QapGen	
Testament of Joseph		20	96, 118
2:7	54	20.16–18	96, 116
7:2–4	54	20.28–29	96
7:4	54 n.86		
		1QHa	
Testament of Levi		1:36	49
14	130	5:32	130
14:6	129	7:34	130
14:6–7	128	9:23–25	121
18:12	116	11:14	130
19:1	51 n.59	11:22	130
		12:32–33	53 n.74
Testament of Moses		14:37	130
10.1	68	15:23	61 n.135
		17:35–36	61
Testament of Naphtali		20:14–15	53 n.74
8:4	52 n.68, 53 n.79	21:34	53 n.74
Testament of Ruben		**1QM**	
5:6–7	52	1:1–15	61
		3:6	61
Testament of Solomon		3:9	61
1:2	96	13:1	61
1:5–7	95	13:10–12	116
1:7	96	13:11–12	52 n.68
2:9	117	14:7	49

15:4	61	PHILO	
1QpHab		*De Abrahamo*	
7:3–8	57 n.107, 61, 89	1.4	30
8:8–13	130	19.96–98	96
12:7–9	57 n.107, 130	37.208	31
		46.268–70	75
1QS		208	79 n.51
1:10	61		
1:18	52 n.68	*De cherubim*	
1:24	52 n.68	1.1	53 n.77
2:2	50		
3:10	50	*De decalogo*	
3:13	61	22.108–110	80, 94
3:13–4:8	51 n.65	22.110	91
3:13–4:26	51, 53 n.74	23.120	63
3:19–26	111	24.127–131	58
3:20–21	116	31.165–66	58
3:21–23	89		
4:1–11	121	*De fuga et inventione*	
4:9–13	124	34.188	77 n.33
6	59 n.116		
6:26	61	*De gigantibus*	
8:10	49	1–2	52
8:12b–14	49		
8:13	50	*De Josepho*	
8:18	49, 49 n.54	1.1	30
8:21	49, 49 n.54		
9:5	49 n.54	*De posteritate Caini*	
9:19	50	13.46–48	35 n.86
9:19–21	50	21.74	35 n.86
9:21	50		
10:21	50	*De sacrificiis Abelis et Caini*	
11:13	50	32	124
11:17	50		
		De specialibus legibus	
4Q560		1.51.277	133
1:4	95	1.51.277–78	133
		1.51.279	133
11QPsa		2.63	79 n.51
19:15–16	65, 97	4.147	31
11Q19		*De virtutibus*	
54:19–21	63	9.51	31, 79 n.51
		15.88	132
NAG HAMMADI		18.95	79 n.51, 80, 82
		30.163	126
Tripartite Tractate		33.172	126
90:10	89	33.175	31

Index of Ancient Sources — 187

51.95	79 n.51	*Legatio ad Gaium*	
		32.232	60 n.126
De vita Mosis			
1.3	30	*Legum allegoriae*	
1.6–7	30, 45	3.242	31
1.9	31		
1.9.48	30, 45	*Quod Deus sit immutabilis*	
1.14	45	14.69	80
1.17	45	34.156	80
1.18–24	31		
1.21	45	JOSEPHUS	
1.26	31		
1.28.158	30, 45, 107	*Against Apion*	
1.29–30	31	1.1	33
1.35	32	2.206	63 n.140
1.75	31	2.209–10	127
1.83	31 n.87	2.136	33, 45
1.146	31		
1.151	31	*Jewish Antiquities*	
1.152–153	31	1.7–8	32
1.154	31	1.14	33, 45
1.158	31	1.15–17	35
1.158–162	30	1.17	32
1.189	31	1.19	33, 45
1.279	31	1.22–24	33, 45
1.296–99	31	1.53	33
1.300–304	31	1.60–61	33
1.303	31 n.92	1.66	33
1.325	31	1.72	33
1.329	31	4.285–88	132
1.146	31–2	5.7.8	53 n.77
2.1	31 n.91	5.317	34 n.108
2.8–11	31	6.2.1	53 n.77
2.17	31	6.45	34
2.28–33	32	6.45–7.6	34, 34 n.106
2.36	32	6.160	34 n.108
2.53	32	6.168–69	95
2.66	31–2	6.296	33
2.81–103	31 n.88	6.327–43	34
2.108	31	6.331	35
2.135	31	6.338	35
2.171–73	31 n.93	6.339	35
2.183	31	6.340–42	21, 35
2.202	32	6.341	35
2.216	32	6.342	35
2.288–92	31	6.344–50	33
2.292	30	6.346	34
		6.347	34, 107

7.14.7	64		**APOSTOLIC FATHERS AND OTHER ANCIENT CHRISTIAN WRITINGS**
7.37–38	33		
7.296	123, 134		
7.307–8	123	**Acts of Peter**	
7.338	34 n.108	11	96, 118
8.2–5	118		
8.2.5	65 n.149	**Ambrose**	
9.282	33	*Expositio Evangelii secundum Lucam*	
10.242	123	5.42	105
10.250	122–3		
10.254–56	123	**Arnobius**	
10.256	122–3	*Against the Gentiles*	
13.318–19	33	1.52	26 n.59
18.4.1	59		
		Augustine	
Jewish War		*De civitate Dei*	
1.1–2	32	1.pr	34
2.8.2	59 n.116		
7.7	59	*De perfectione iustitiae hominis*	
		21.44	102
		Epistulae	
		130.9	102
RABBINIC WORKS			
Babylonian Talmud		**Clement of Alexandria**	
Me'ilah		*Quis dives salvetur*	
17b	95, 99 n.152	4.27–30	82
Pesah		**Clement of Rome**	
112b	99 n.152	*1 Clement*	
		35.5	51 n.65
Pirke Aboth			
5.4	54	**Didache**	
		5	51 n.65
Mishnah		5.1	51 n.65
Berakoth		6.1	51 n.65
1.1–4	81		
		Epistle of Barnabas	
Nedarim		4:1	56 n.101
48a	63	4:1–3	56
		4:9	56 n.101
Tamid		5	51 n.65
5.1	81	15:5	56 n.101
		18:1	57
Zabim			
5.1	76	**Epiphanius**	
		Panarion	
Genesis Rabbah		1.35.20	77 n.36
44.23	97		

Index of Ancient Sources

Eusebius
Against Hierocles
2.2	26 n.61, 27
43.3	26 n.61
44.2	26 n.61
44.3	26 n.61
48.2	26 n.61

Ecclesiastical History
7.18	77 n.36

Irenaeus
Adversus Haereses
3.11.8	48 n.42

Jerome
Commentary on Malachi
3.1	47 n.35, 48 n.38, 48 n.45

Commentary on Matthew
Lib. IV	105 n.182

Epistles
57.9	47 n.35, 48 n.38, 48 n.45

John Chrysostom
Homilies on Matthew
63	82 n.75

Justin Martyr
Dialogue with Trypho
93	80
106.3	23

Lactantius
Divine Institutes
5.2–3	26 n.61

On the Deaths of the Persecutors
16.4	26 n.61

Origen
Contra Celsum
2.25	105
3.55	58
6.41	26, 27 n.69

Commentary on John
6.41	97 n.143
10.2.5–9	56 n.99

Commentary on Matthew
10.19	77 n.37
11.9	62 n.139
13.25	137
16.29	103
90	105 n.186

Fragments on Luke
78	82

Pseudo-Athanasian Dialogue
Dialoghi contro i Macedoniani
28	105

Pseudo-Clementine Homilies
3.57	81 n.65
16.7	81 n.65

Shepherd of Hermas
Mandates
12.45, 4	119
12.47, 7	119
12.48, 2	119

Tertullian
Adversus Marcionem
5.8	80 n.55

De Ieiunio Adversus Psychicos
2	80 n.55

De Resurrectione Carnis
9	80 n.55

GREEK AND LATIN LITERATURE

Aristotle
De Virtutibus
5.1250b.22–23	31

Ethica Nicomachea
1.2.2	73
1.6.3	56 n.98
2.1.8	73 n.12, 108
1108a23	95

1124b25	84 n.85	2.156	58 n.114
1124b30	95		
1125a20	131	**Galen**	
1160a5	131	*De placitis Hippocratis et Platonis*	
		9.5.5	94

Historia Animalium
3.19   77 n.33

Quod optimus medicus sit quoque philosophus
1.56   94 n.127

Politics
1.5.3   59 n.117
5.9, 1315a24   64
6.2, 1318b40   64

Historia Augusta
Life of Septimius Severus
29.2   27

Cicero
Tusculanae Disputationes
5.4.10   24 n.44

Iamblichus
On the Pythagorean Life
17.71   58

Dio Cassius
Historia Romana
75.15.7   27
78.18.2   27
78.18.4   27

Justinian
Digest
50.16.195   58 n.114

Lucian
De Historia Conscribenda
59–63   16 n.6, 23 n.37

Diodorus
Bibliotheca historica
11.46.1   16 n.6
15.1.1   16 n.6

Demonax
1   20

Diogenes Laertius
Lives and Opinions of Eminent Philosophers

Lucretius
De Rerum Natura

2.6.48	23	3.9	61
2.8.66–83	24 n.48		
5.86–88	64 n.143	**Philostratus**	
7.19	134	*Life of Apollonius*	
7.93	39, 124	1.2	27–8, 30
7.108	39	1.2–3	27
7.109	58	1.2.3	28, 120
7.121	64	1.3	27–8, 27 n.69
7.125	64	1.15	28
10.10	61	1.16.3	28
10.143	59 n.116	1.16.4	28
		1.18	53 n.76
Epictetus		1.35	33 n.78
Dissertationes		1.37	98
3.22.45–49	60	2.41	28
		3.10	96
Gaius		3.17.2	28
Institutes			
1.127	58 n.114		

3.38	76 n.31, 95–6, 116, 118	**Plutarch**	
		Comparison of Lycurgus and Numa	
4.1.1	28, 120	1.2	37 n.132, 37 n.134
4.20	28, 95–6, 118	1.4	37 n.134
4.23	28	3.6	37 n.128
4.29	29		
4.31	28	*Comparison of Nicias and Crassus*	
4.35–38	28 n.72	1.2	122
4.36.1	28		
4.37.2	28	*Comparison of Pericles and Fabius Maximus*	
4.40	45		
4.45	78		37 n.136
4.47	28 n.71		
5.13	83	*Comparison of Solon and Publicola*	
5.14.2–3	29	1.1	37 n.136
5.14.3	29		
5.16.1	29	*Comparison of Theseus and Romulus*	
5.17	28, 83	1.4–5	37 n.134
5.21.1	28, 120		
5.31–39	29	*De laude ipsius*	
5.38.2	28	540d	84 n.85
6.3.2	28, 120		
6.18	28	*Life of Aemilius Paulus*	
7–8	28	12.3	131
8.21	28 n.72	13.3	131
8.29	27	23.11	131
		26.8	131
Lives of the Sophists			
481	27	*Life of Agesilaus*	
507	27	14.1	37 n.133
510	27 n.64		
570	27	*Life of Alexander*	
		1.2–3	20
Plato		8.4	20
Apology			
19e	24	*Life of Aristides*	
33a5–d9	24 n.47	2.1	37 n.136
		4.1	37 n.134
Phaedo		6.1–3	37 n.134
81b	65, 97 n.145		
		Life Brutus	
Protagoras		13.5	77 n.33
330b	31		
		Life of Cato the Elder (Marcus Cato)	
Pliny the Younger		6.1	37 n.133
Panegyricus		19.5	37 n.136
45.6	19 n.23	20.4	37 n.135
		20.8	37 n.135

Life of Cimon		2.2–3	37 n.136
2	20	2.3–4	45
		2.4	27
Life of Crassus		29.1–2	27 n.133
2.6	37 n.135		
		Life of Pompey	
Life of Demosthenes		1.3	37 n.132
1	20, 38	8	20
		8.6	36
Life of Dion			
10.1	37 n.135	*Life of Romulus*	
		28.3	37 n.133
Life of Fabius Maximus		29.7	37 n.128
3.6	37 n.132		
		Life of Solon	
Life of Lycurgus		6.2	37 n.132
1.3–4	37 n.128	27	20, 36
3.4	37 n.134, 64 n.141		
7.2	64 n.141	*Life of Timoleon*	
15.5	37 n.133	37	
27.3	37 n.132		
27.3–4	37 n.136	*On the Fortune of Alexander*	
		1.4	20
Life of Marius		1.6	75
17.5	74		
		Polybius	
Life of Nicias		*Histories*	
1.4	36	32	
1.4–5	122	1.17	32
1.5	36	10.21.2–8	16, 32
2.5	122	10.21.8	16
4.3	122		
7.3	122	**Quintilian**	
8.2	122	*Institutio Oratoria*	
29.4	36	1.1.36	21 n.28
Life of Numa		Seneca	
2.1	122	*De Vita Beata*	
2.7	64 n.141	15.7	40
3.5	37 n.132, 37 n.135		
15.1	37 n.135	*Epistles*	
15.6	35	6.5	21 n.28
20.8	37 n.132, 37 n.136		
		Strobaeus	
Life of Pericles		*Extract, Sayings, and Advice*	
1–2	20, 21 n.28, 36	2.7.5–6	123
1.1	36		
1.4	36	**Xenophon**	
2	20, 36 n.126	*Memorabilia*	

1	23	3.7.9	24
1.1–2	23	3.8.2–3	24
1.1.11	24 n.46	3.9.2	24
1.1.15	24 n.44	3.9.5	24
1.2.2	24	3.10.1–6	25
1.2.3	24–5	4.1	23
1.2.8	24	4.1.2	24
1.2.12	134	4.1.5	25
1.2.17–18	24 n.47	4.2.1	25, 108
1.2.19–28	24 n.47	4.2.8	25, 120
1.2.21–23	24	4.2.11	25
1.2.24	25	4.2.23	25
1.2.51	58	4.2.40	25
1.2.60	24, 119	4.3.2	23 n.36
1.2.64	24, 107	4.3.18	25
1.3–4.8	23	4.4.1	25
1.3.12	115	4.4.15–17	25
1.4.2	23, 23 n.36	4.4.20	25
1.5.1	24, 25 n.51	4.5.1	24–5
1.7.1–3	25	4.6.1–11	25
2.1	23–4, 119	4.6.12	25
2.1.1	24	4.7.6	24 n.46
2.1.1–10	24, 119	4.8.1–11	23
2.1.4	134	4.8.10	24, 25 n.54, 107
2.1.16–17	24, 120	4.8.11	23
2.2.14	25		
2.3	25	PAPYRI	
2.4–6	25		
2.4.1	23, 23 n.36	**Papyri Grecae Magicae**	
2.5.1	23–4	IV.154–285	65 n.149
2.5.4	24	IV.1017–19	99
2.6.22	24	IV.3039	99
2.6.39	24		
2.10.1	23 n.36	**Oxyrhynchus**	
3.1	23	VI.886	96 n.136
3.5.14	25		

Index of Modern Authors

Achtemeier, Paul J. 6
Alexander, Loveday 19 n.18
Anna, Julia 2 n.6, 15 n.3
Attridge, Harold 19 n.21, 34
Aune, David 17

Barth, Karl 43 n.8, 70, 102
Bartlett, David L. 121
Beasley-Murray, G. R. 57
Beavis, Mary Ann 90
Becker, Eve-Marie 17 n.13, 32 n.99
Best, Ernst 7, 7 nn.40–2, 53, 55 n.92
Black, C. Clifton 1 n.2, 4 n.15, 5, 7 nn.39, 42, 44, 8 nn.47, 50, 120 n.38
Blount, Brian 64
Boring, M. Eugene 17 n.15
Brawley, Robert L. 62
Broadhead, Edwin K. 9
Brooke, George J. 50
Bultmann, Rudolf 5, 38, 93, 141
Burridge, Richard 3 n.10, 19 n.22, 22 n.33, 27 n.68, 30 n.80, 30 n.86

Cahill, Lisa Sowle 2 n.5
Charlesworth, James 49–50
Collins, John 46
Cotter, Wendy 77–8
Cox, Patricia 18 n.16, 22 n.34, 23, 29 n.75, 34 nn.112–14
Cranfield, C. E. B. 53, 83
Cullmann, Oscar 56

Davies, J. P. 117–18
de Boer Martinus 112, 122
Dibelius Martin 5, 68, 93, 98, 143
Dihle, Albrecht 35
Donahue, John 3 n.10, 6–7, 11 n.71, 44–5, 89
Dowd, Sharyn E. 103
Duff, Tim 37–8

Edwards, James 134
Egger, William 93

Feldman, Louis 31, 32 nn.96–7, 33 nn.101–3, 34
Flowers, Michael 23
Frazier, Françoise 37
Freyne, Seán 19
Furnish, Victor Paul 10, 80–2, 91, 93

Garrett, Susan 54
Gnilka, Joachim 56, 131
Goarzin, Maël 16–17, 17 n.9
Goodacre, Mark 2 n.3
Guthrie, Donald 2 n.5, 3 n.10

Hägg, Thomas 16 nn.7–8, 19 n.19, 22 n.33, 23
Hayes, Christine 127
Hays, Richard 81
Henderson, Ian 69, 136
Henderson, S. W. 4, 10
Hengel, Martin 59–60
Hodge, Caroline J. 61
Hooker, Morna 131
Horsley, Richard 2 n.5
Horstmann, Maria 7–8
Houlden, J. L. 10, 12

Inwood, Brad 45
Iverson, Kelly 101

James, William 66
Jeremias, Joachim 100
Jouanna, Jacques 94

Käsemann, Ernst 12
Keck, Leander 1–2, 1 nn.1–2, 2 n.5, 11 n.70, 41–43, 57 n.111, 66–7, 71, 78–9, 91, 109, 135, 140–1

Kee, Howard Clark 7, 71, 91, 119, 126, 133, 135
Keerankeri, George 83
Kermode, Frank 86
Kingsbury, Jack D. 4 n.16, 9, 9 n.58
Klawans, Jonathan 127-9
Klutz, Todd E. 97
Koskenniemi, Erkki 28, 29 n.76

Leo, Friedrich 15-16, 35 n.120
Lohfink, Gerhard 62

MacIntyre, Alasdair 72
Malina, Bruce 58
Malbon, E. S. 9 n.56, 10, 58 n.112, 139-40
Malherbe, Abraham 2 n.7
Marxsen, Willi 5, 1
Marcus, Joel 51, 89-90, 131
Marshall, Christopher 73, 78-9
Mason, Steve 33, 35
Matheson, George 1 n.1
Meeks, Wayne 2 n.4, 42 n.5, 61
Meye, Robert P. 7
Miles, Graeme 28
Moloney, Francis J. 7-8
Moore, Stephen D. 98
Morgan, Teresa 74-5
Morrison, David 26
Myers, Ched 134

Oyen, Geert van 118

Peppard, Michael 132
Perrin, Norman 4 n.14, 5 nn.21-22, 6, 8, 8 n.52, 9

Räisänen, Heikki 126
Riches, John K. 112-13
Robinson, James M. 117
Robinson, James 48
Russell, Bertrand 98

Sanders, E. P. 129
Sanders, Jack T. 11-12
Schmidt, Karl L. 92-3
Schnelle, Udo 11-12
Schweizer, Eduard 5, 7 n.37, 8 n.53
Shiner, W. T. 12, 24 n.47, 28 n.70, 55, 59
Shively, Elizabeth 114, 118
Smith, Julien C. H. 57
Stanton, Graham 19
Strecker, Georg 10
Stuckenbruck, Loren 52
Sweat, Laura 83-4, 86-7

Taylor, Vincent 68
Telford, William 4, 12, 43
Tiede, David 20 n.24
Tolbert, Mary Ann 89

Verhey, Allen 4,
Via, Dan O. 3, 8 n.53, 13, 67 n.161, 72, 82, 84, 141
Vines, Michael E. 17 n.15
Voorwinde, Stephen 92

Watson, Francis 75
Weeden, Theodore 6, 9, 39
Weil, Simone 85
Wrede, William 4-5, 8 n.48, 9

www.ingramcontent.com/pod-product-compliance
Lightning Source LLC
Chambersburg PA
CBHW061829300426
44115CB00013B/2303